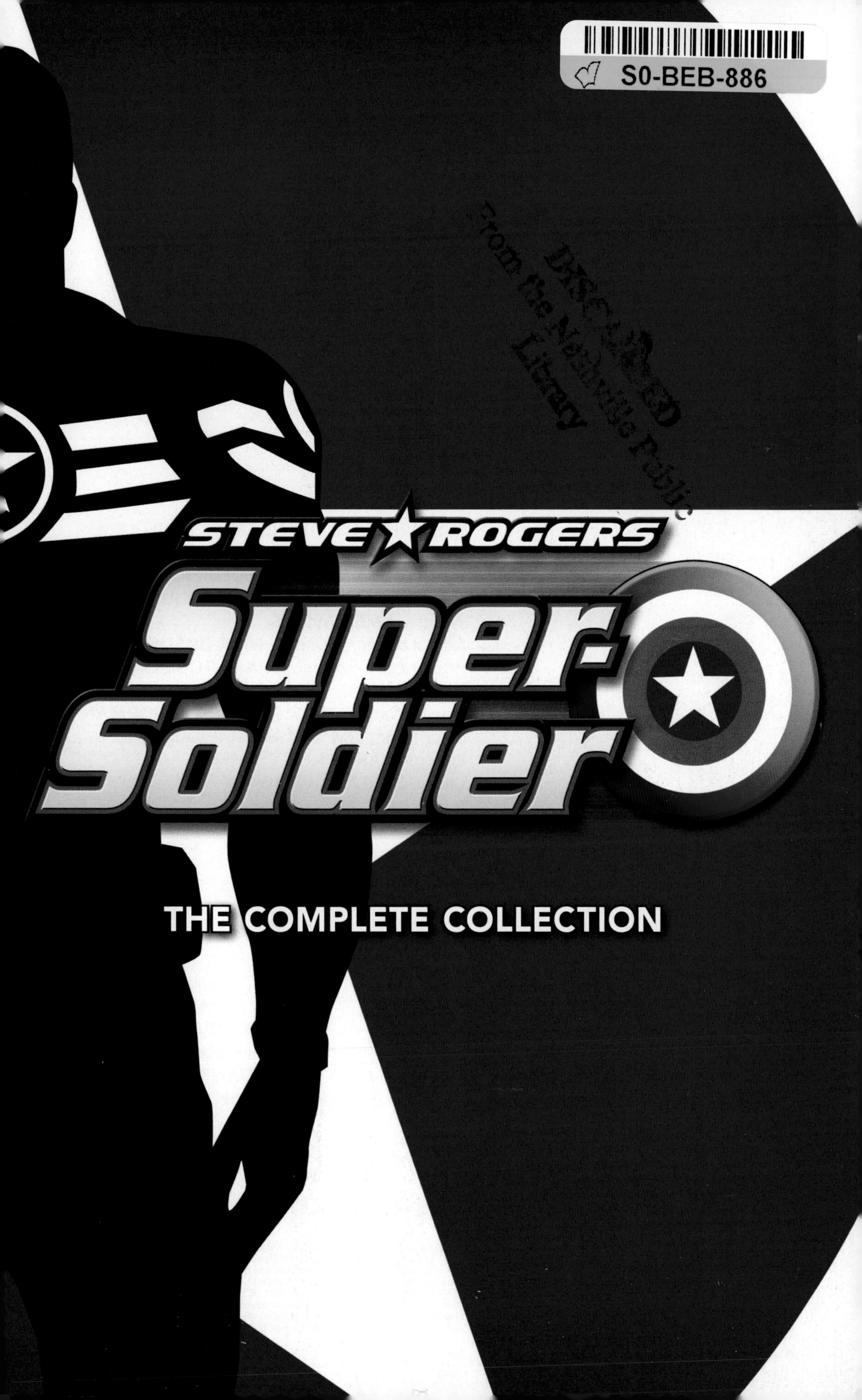
STEVE ROGERS
Super-Soldier
THE COMPLETE COLLECTION

STEVE ROGERS ★ Super-Soldier

STEVE ROGERS: SUPER-SOLDIER #1-4
Writer: **ED BRUBAKER**
Artist: **DALE EAGLESHAM**
Color Artist: **ANDY TROY**
Letterer: **VC'S JOE CARAMAGNA**
Cover Art: **CARLOS PACHECO, TIM TOWNSEND
    & FRANK D'ARMATA**

"ESCAPE FROM THE NEGATIVE ZONE"
UNCANNY X-MEN ANNUAL #3
STEVE ROGERS: SUPER-SOLDIER ANNUAL #1
NAMOR: THE FIRST MUTANT ANNUAL #1
Writer: **JAMES ASMUS**
Artist (*Uncanny X-Men*): **NICK BRADSHAW**
Artist (*Steve Rogers*): **IBRAIM ROBERSON**
Penciler (*Namor*): **MAX FIUMARA**
Inkers (*Namor*): **MAX FIUMARA & NORMAN LEE**
Color Artist: **JIM CHARALAMPIDIS**
Letterer: **JARED K. FLETCHER**
Cover Art: **BLACK FROG**

Front Cover Artist:
MARKO DJURDJEVIC
Front Cover Artists:
**CARLOS PACHECO,
TIM TOWNSEND &
FRANK D'ARMATA**

Collection Editor:
MARK D. BEAZLEY
Assistant Editor:
CAITLIN O'CONNELL
Associate Managing Editor:
KATERI WOODY
Associate Manager, Digital Assets
JOE HOCHSTEIN
Senior Editor, Special Projects:
JENNIFER GRÜNWALD
VP Production & Special Projects:
JEFF YOUNGQUIST
SVP Print, Sales & Marketing:
DAVID GABRIEL
Layout:
JEPH YORK
Book Designer:
RODOLFO MURAGUCHI

Editor in Chief: **AXEL ALONSO**
Chief Creative Officer: **JOE QUESADA**
Publisher: **DAN BUCKLEY**
Executive Producer: **ALAN FINE**

Assistant Editors:
**JAKE THOMAS
& JORDAN D. WHITE**
Associate Editors:
**DANIEL KETCHUM
& LAUREN SANKOVITCH**
Editors:
**TOM BREVOORT
& NICK LOWE**

Captain America created by **JOE SIMON** & **JACK KIRBY**

STEVE ROGERS: SUPER-SOLDIER — THE COMPLETE COLLECTION. Contains material originally published in magazine form as STEVE ROGERS: SUPER-SOLDIER #1-4 and ANNUAL #1, UNCANNY X-MEN ANNUAL #3, and NAMOR: THE FIRST MUTANT ANNUAL #1. First printing 2017. ISBN# 978-1-302-90873-7. Published by MARVEL WORLDWIDE, INC., a subsidiary of MARVEL ENTERTAINMENT, LLC. OFFICE OF PUBLICATION: 135 West 50th Street, New York, NY 10020. Copyright © 2017 MARVEL. No similarity between any of the names, characters, persons, and/or institutions in this magazine with those of any living or dead person or institution is intended, and any such similarity which may exist is purely coincidental. **Printed in the U.S.A.** DAN BUCKLEY, President, Marvel Entertainment; JOE QUESADA, Chief Creative Officer; TOM BREVOORT, SVP of Publishing; DAVID BOGART, SVP of Business Affairs & Operations, Publishing & Partnership; C.B. CEBULSKI, VP of Brand Management & Development, Asia; DAVID GABRIEL, SVP of Sales & Marketing, Publishing; JEFF YOUNGQUIST, VP of Production & Special Projects; DAN CARR, Executive Director of Publishing Technology; ALEX MORALES, Director of Publishing Operations; SUSAN CRESPI, Production Manager; STAN LEE, Chairman Emeritus. For information regarding advertising in Marvel Comics or on Marvel.com, please contact Vit DeBellis, Integrated Sales Manager, at vdebellis@marvel.com. For Marvel subscription inquiries, please call 888-511-5480. **Manufactured between 5/19/2017 and 6/20/2017** by LSC COMMUNICATIONS INC., SALEM, VA, USA.

10 9 8 7 6 5 4 3 2 1

IN THE DARK DAYS OF THE EARLY 1940s,
STEVE ROGERS,
A STRUGGLING YOUNG ARTIST FROM THE
LOWER EAST SIDE OF MANHATTAN,
FOUND HIMSELF HORRIFIED BY THE WAR RAGING OVERSEAS.
DESPERATE TO HELP, HE TRIED TO ENLIST WITH THE
U.S. ARMY
BUT HE WAS REJECTED AS UNFIT FOR SERVICE.

UNDETERRED, CONVINCED THIS WAS WHERE HE NEEDED TO BE,
HE WAS SELECTED TO PARTICIPATE IN
A COVERT MILITARY PROJECT CALLED
OPERATION: REBIRTH.
THERE, HE WAS CHOSEN BY SCIENTIST ABRAHAM ERSKINE
AS THE FIRST HUMAN TEST SUBJECT, AND OVERNIGHT WAS
TRANSFORMED INTO
**AMERICA'S FIRST SUPER-SOLDIER,
CAPTAIN AMERICA.**

NOW, DECADES LATER, STEVE ROGERS CARRIES ON THE
BATTLE FOR FREEDOM AND DEMOCRACY AS
**AMERICA'S TOP
LAW-ENFORCEMENT OPERATIVE
AND COMMANDER OF
THE MIGHTY AVENGERS.**

STEVE ROGERS:
SUPER-SOLDIER

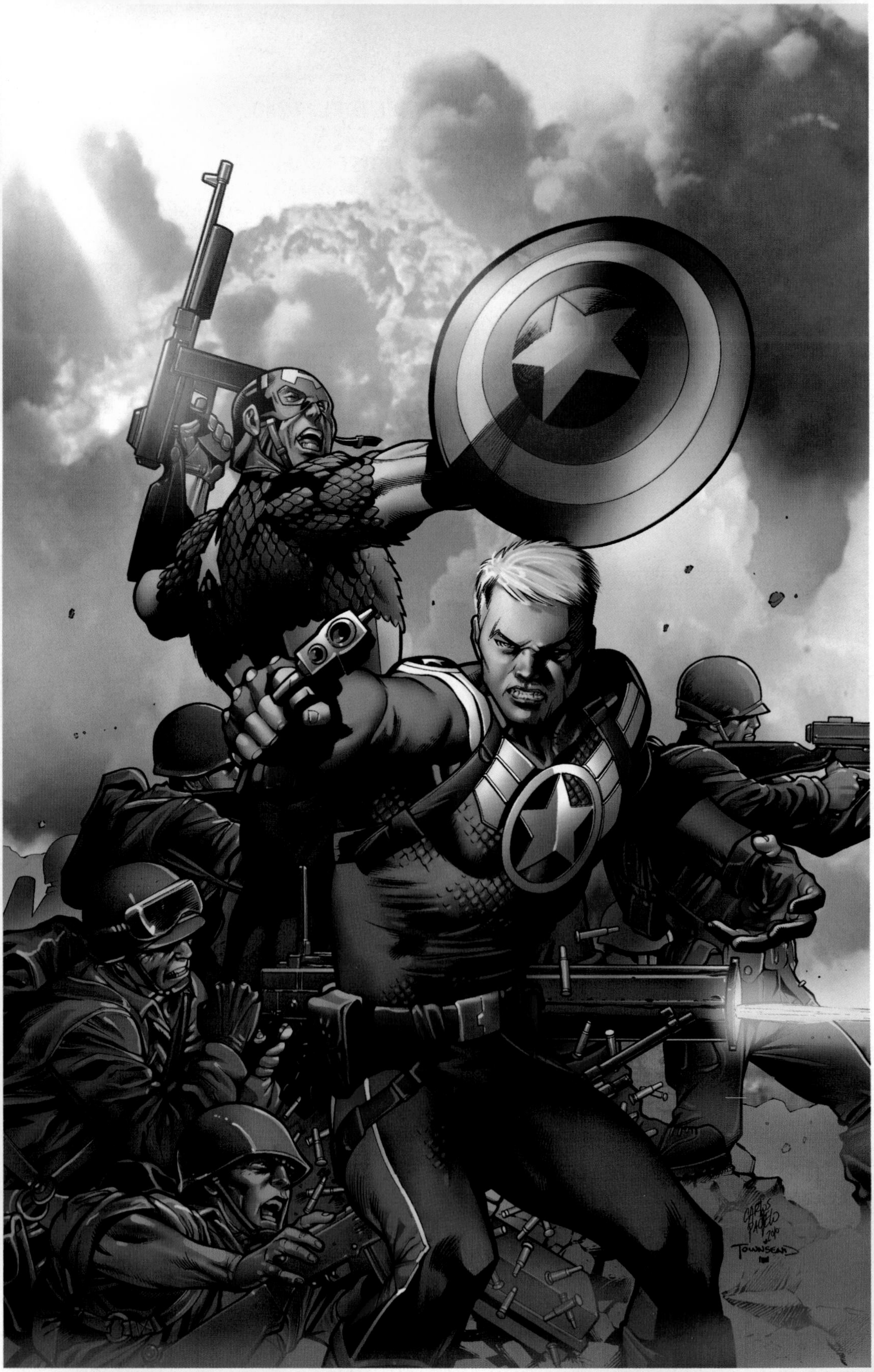
TOWNSEND

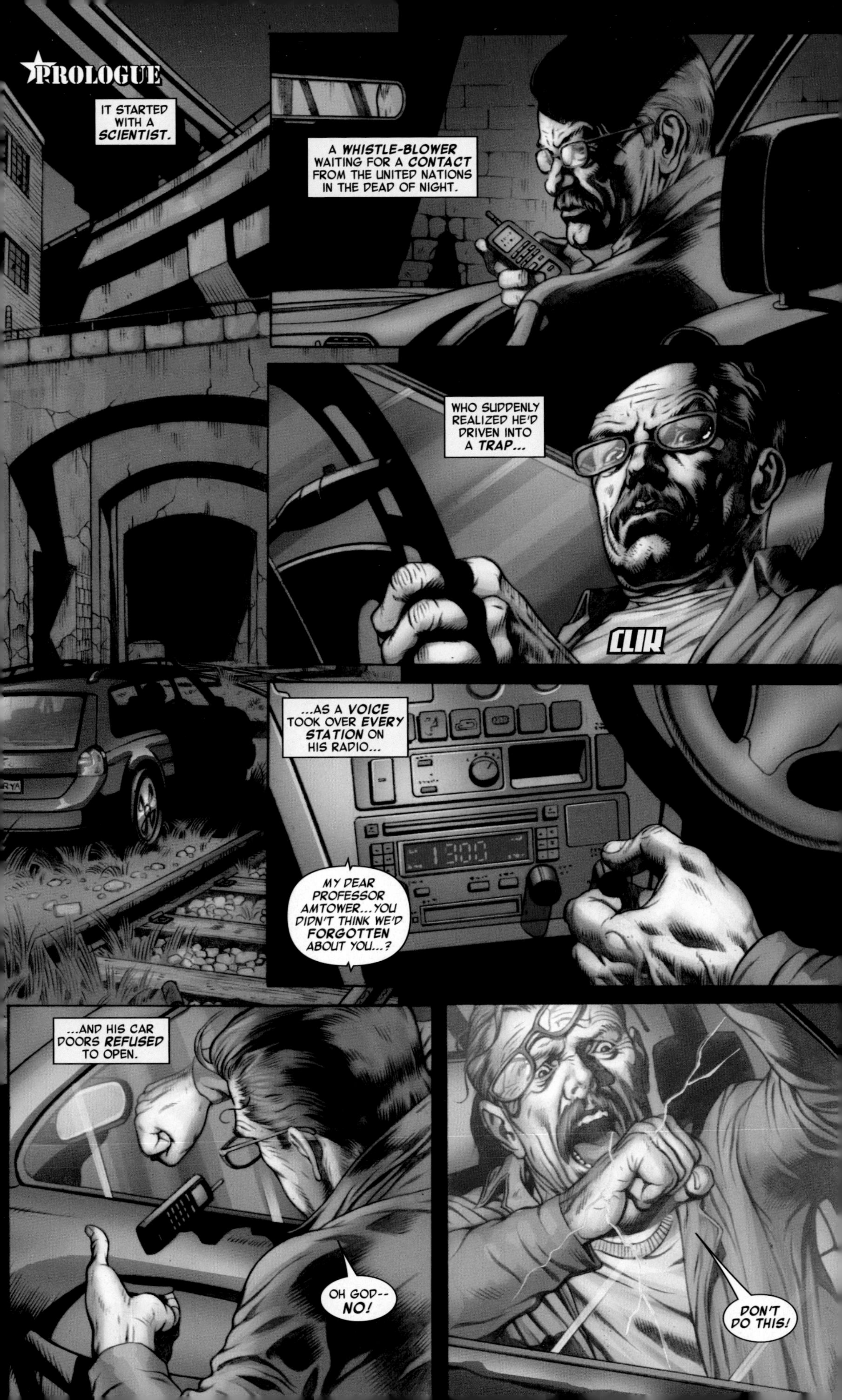
PROLOGUE
IT STARTED WITH A SCIENTIST.
A WHISTLE-BLOWER WAITING FOR A CONTACT FROM THE UNITED NATIONS IN THE DEAD OF NIGHT.
WHO SUDDENLY REALIZED HE'D DRIVEN INTO A TRAP...
CLIK
...AS A VOICE TOOK OVER EVERY STATION ON HIS RADIO...
MY DEAR PROFESSOR AMTOWER...YOU DIDN'T THINK WE'D FORGOTTEN ABOUT YOU...?
...AND HIS CAR DOORS REFUSED TO OPEN.
OH GOD-- NO!
DON'T DO THIS!

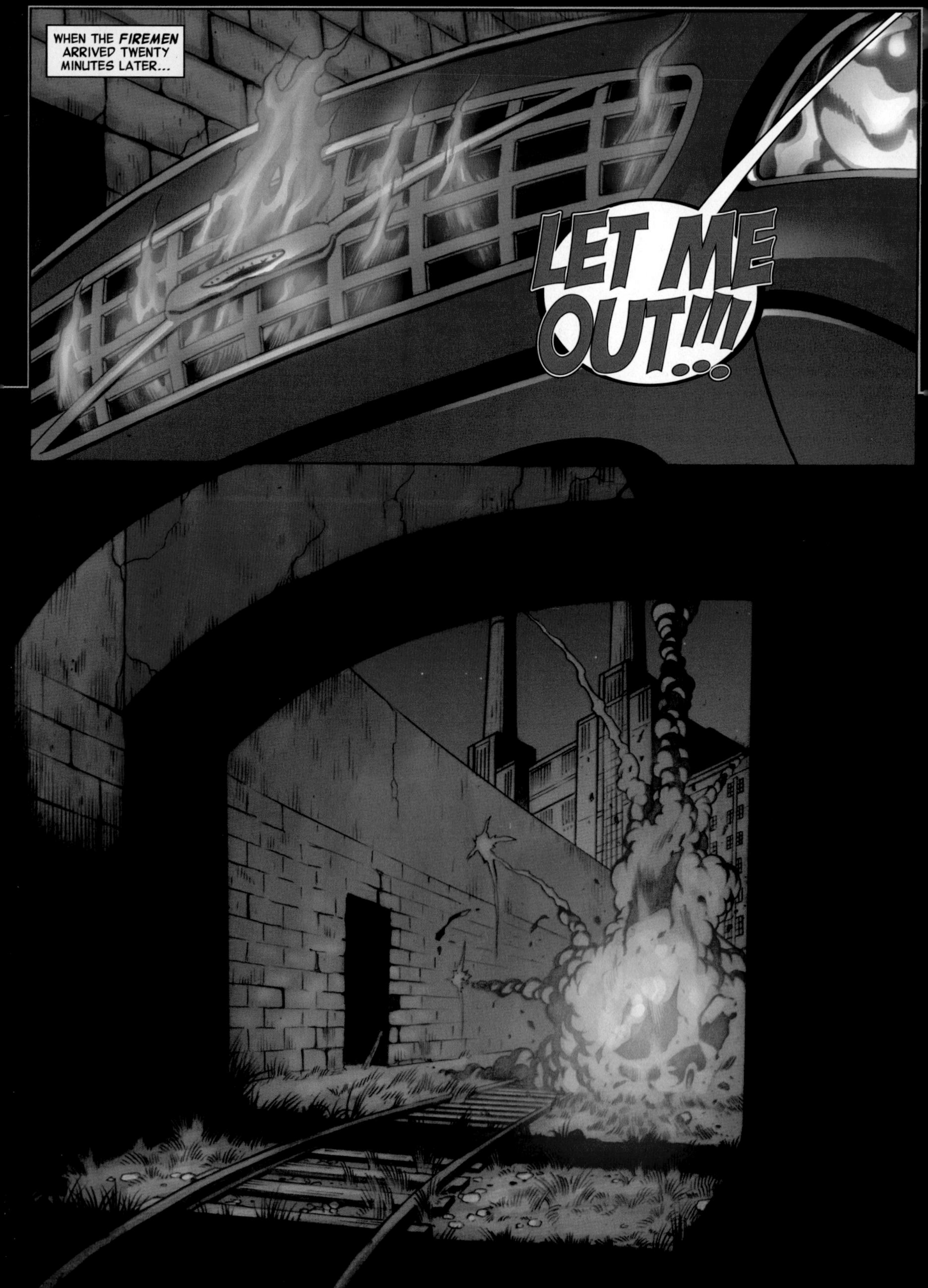
WHEN THE FIREMEN ARRIVED TWENTY MINUTES LATER...
LET ME OUT!!!
...THERE WASN'T MUCH OF HIM LEFT.

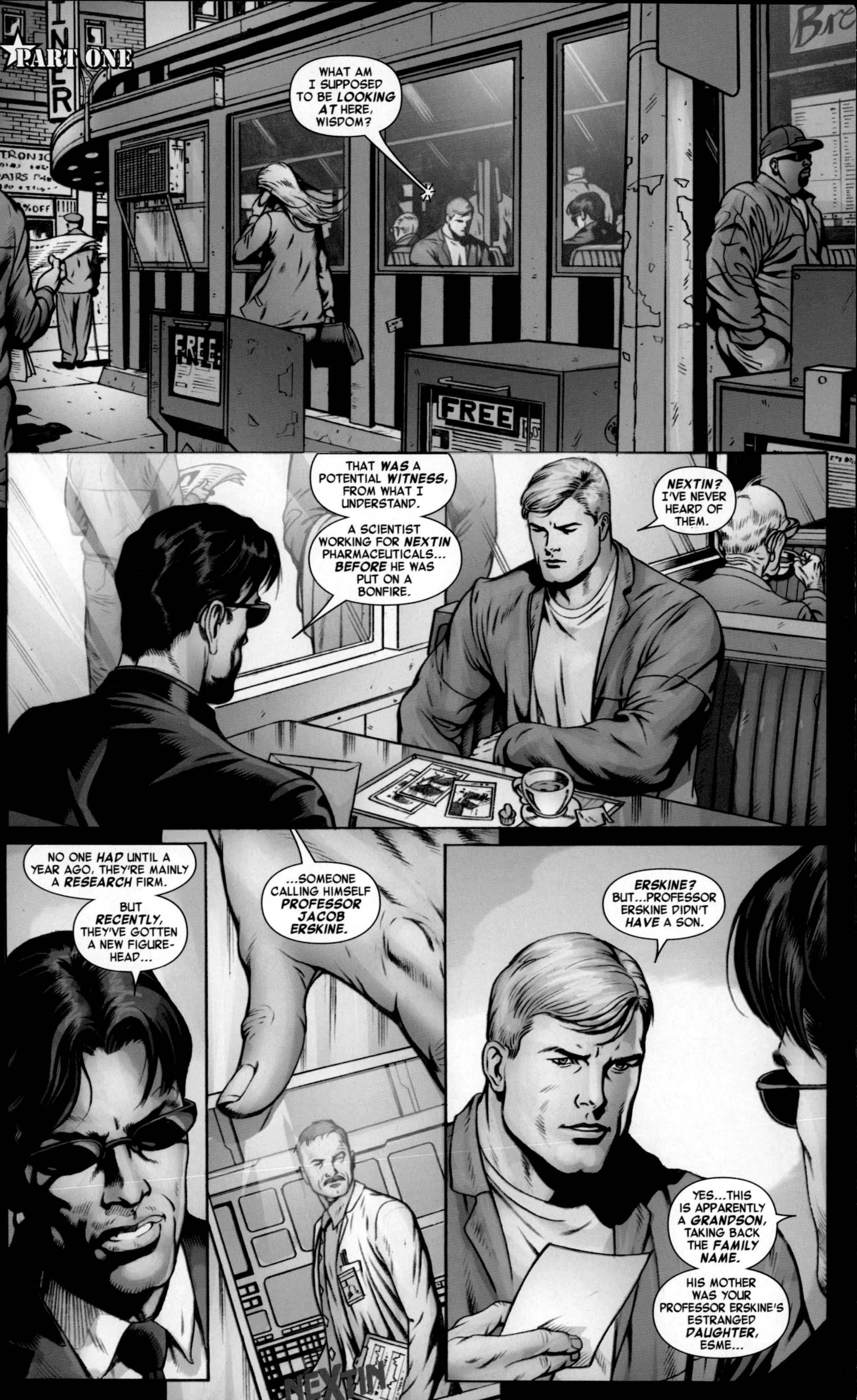
PART ONE
WHAT AM I SUPPOSED TO BE LOOKING AT HERE, WISDOM?
FREE
FREE
THAT WAS A POTENTIAL WITNESS, FROM WHAT I UNDERSTAND.
A SCIENTIST WORKING FOR NEXTIN PHARMACEUTICALS... BEFORE HE WAS PUT ON A BONFIRE.
NEXTIN? I'VE NEVER HEARD OF THEM.
NO ONE HAD UNTIL A YEAR AGO, THEY'RE MAINLY A RESEARCH FIRM.
BUT RECENTLY, THEY'VE GOTTEN A NEW FIGURE-HEAD...
...SOMEONE CALLING HIMSELF PROFESSOR JACOB ERSKINE.
NEXTIN
ERSKINE? BUT...PROFESSOR ERSKINE DIDN'T HAVE A SON.
YES...THIS IS APPARENTLY A GRANDSON, TAKING BACK THE FAMILY NAME.
HIS MOTHER WAS YOUR PROFESSOR ERSKINE'S ESTRANGED DAUGHTER, ESME...

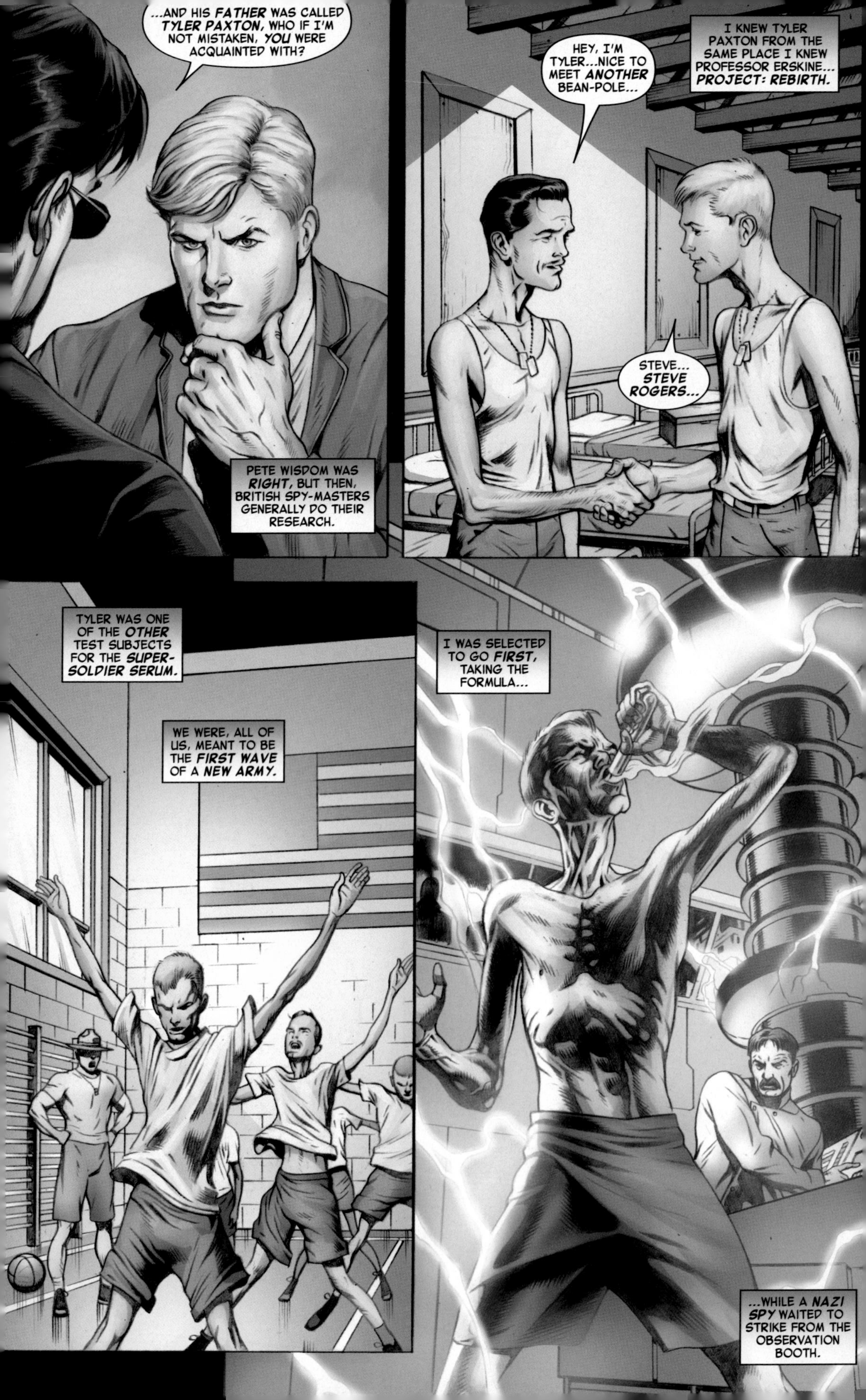
...AND HIS FATHER WAS CALLED TYLER PAXTON, WHO IF I'M NOT MISTAKEN, YOU WERE ACQUAINTED WITH?
PETE WISDOM WAS RIGHT, BUT THEN, BRITISH SPY-MASTERS GENERALLY DO THEIR RESEARCH.
I KNEW TYLER PAXTON FROM THE SAME PLACE I KNEW PROFESSOR ERSKINE... PROJECT: REBIRTH.
HEY, I'M TYLER...NICE TO MEET ANOTHER BEAN-POLE...
STEVE... STEVE ROGERS...
TYLER WAS ONE OF THE OTHER TEST SUBJECTS FOR THE SUPER-SOLDIER SERUM.
WE WERE, ALL OF US, MEANT TO BE THE FIRST WAVE OF A NEW ARMY.
I WAS SELECTED TO GO FIRST, TAKING THE FORMULA...
...WHILE A NAZI SPY WAITED TO STRIKE FROM THE OBSERVATION BOOTH.

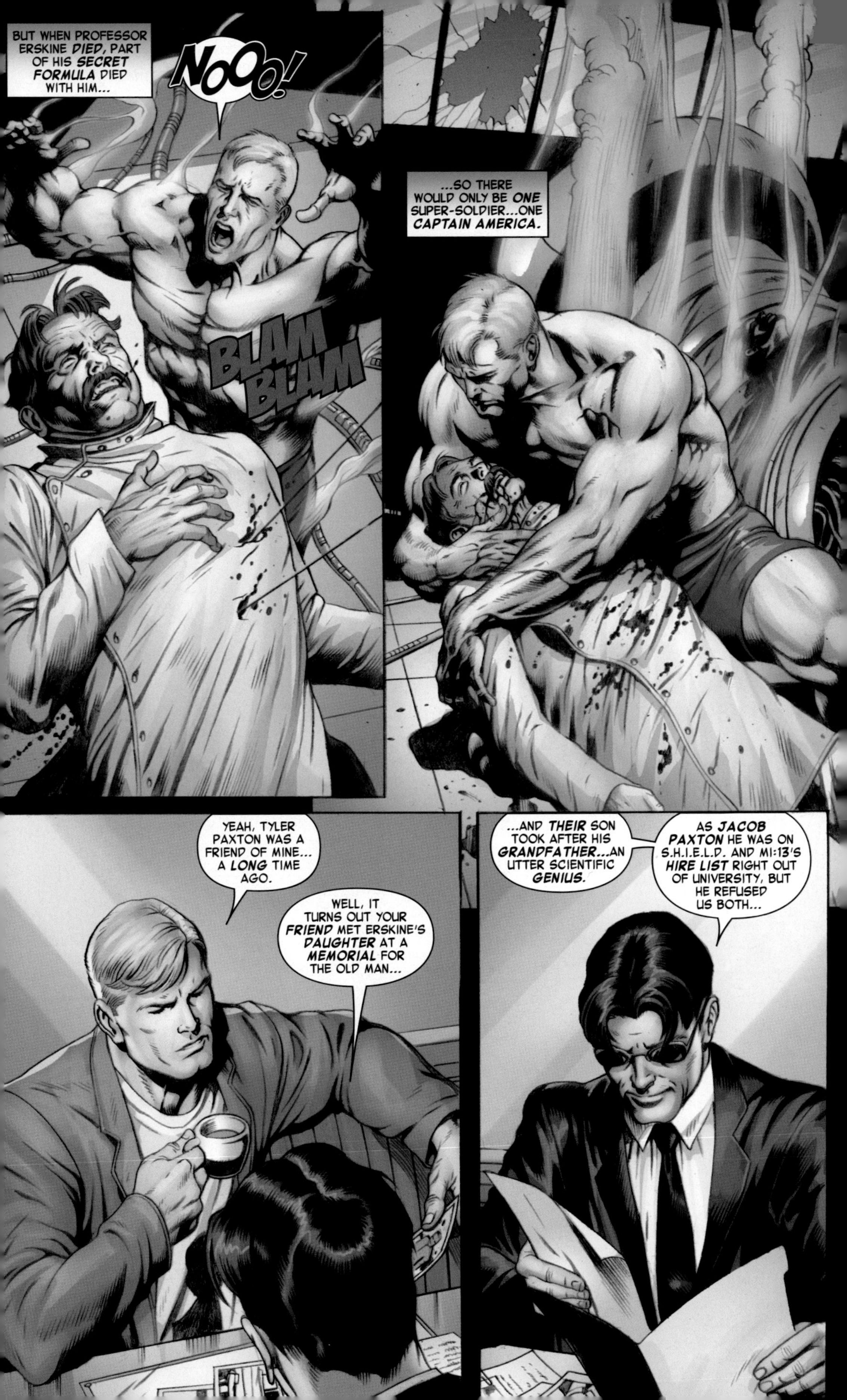
BUT WHEN PROFESSOR ERSKINE DIED, PART OF HIS SECRET FORMULA DIED WITH HIM...
NOOO!
BLAM BLAM
...SO THERE WOULD ONLY BE ONE SUPER-SOLDIER...ONE CAPTAIN AMERICA.
YEAH, TYLER PAXTON WAS A FRIEND OF MINE... A LONG TIME AGO.
WELL, IT TURNS OUT YOUR FRIEND MET ERSKINE'S DAUGHTER AT A MEMORIAL FOR THE OLD MAN...
...AND THEIR SON TOOK AFTER HIS GRANDFATHER...AN UTTER SCIENTIFIC GENIUS.
AS JACOB PAXTON HE WAS ON S.H.I.E.L.D. AND MI:13'S HIRE LIST RIGHT OUT OF UNIVERSITY, BUT HE REFUSED US BOTH...

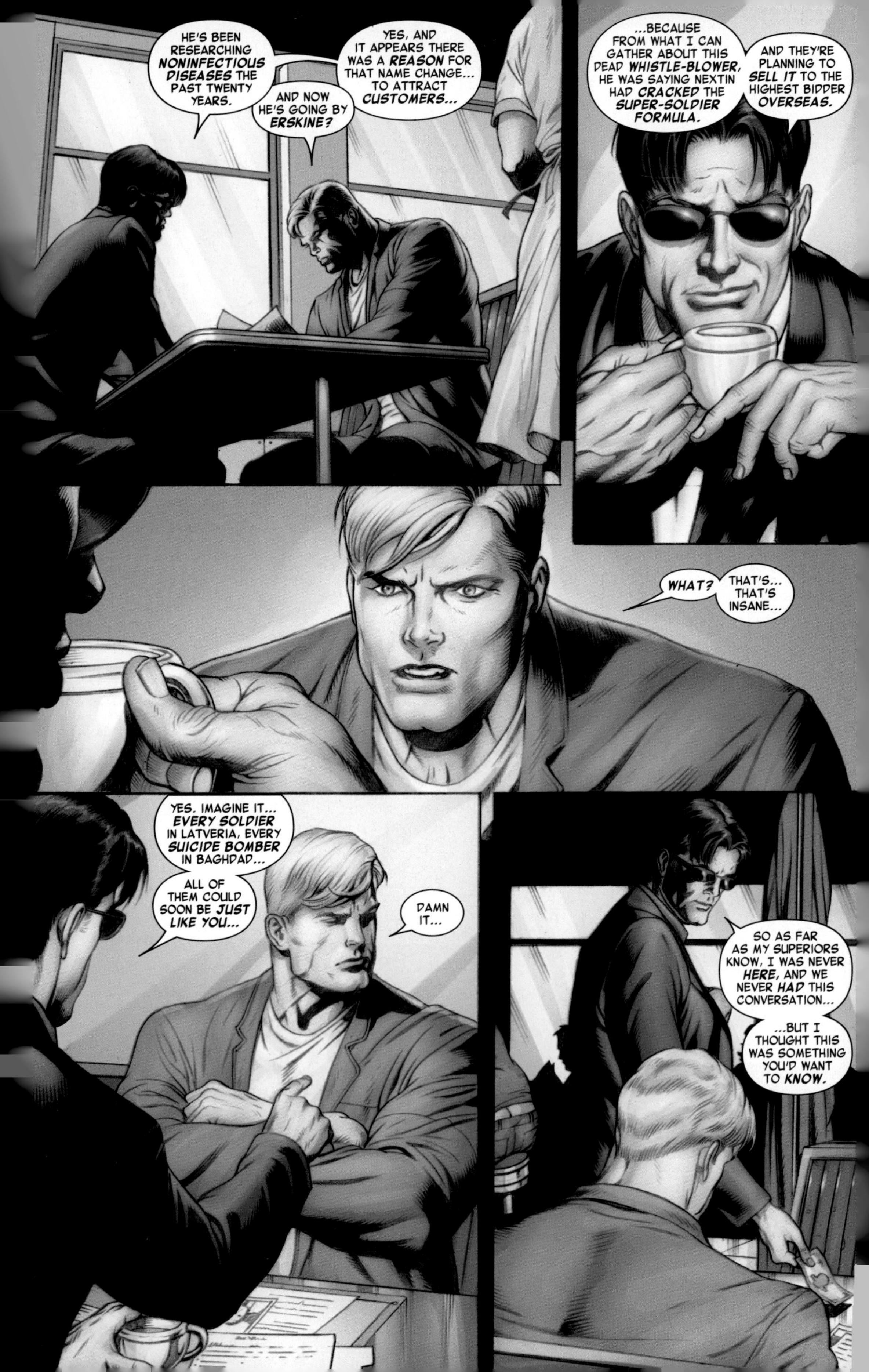
HE'S BEEN RESEARCHING NONINFECTIOUS DISEASES THE PAST TWENTY YEARS.
AND NOW HE'S GOING BY ERSKINE?
YES, AND IT APPEARS THERE WAS A REASON FOR THAT NAME CHANGE... TO ATTRACT CUSTOMERS...
...BECAUSE FROM WHAT I CAN GATHER ABOUT THIS DEAD WHISTLE-BLOWER, HE WAS SAYING NEXTIN HAD CRACKED THE SUPER-SOLDIER FORMULA.
AND THEY'RE PLANNING TO SELL IT TO THE HIGHEST BIDDER OVERSEAS.
WHAT?
THAT'S... THAT'S INSANE...
YES. IMAGINE IT... EVERY SOLDIER IN LATVERIA, EVERY SUICIDE BOMBER IN BAGHDAD...
ALL OF THEM COULD SOON BE JUST LIKE YOU...
DAMN IT...
SO AS FAR AS MY SUPERIORS KNOW, I WAS NEVER HERE, AND WE NEVER HAD THIS CONVERSATION...
...BUT I THOUGHT THIS WAS SOMETHING YOU'D WANT TO KNOW.

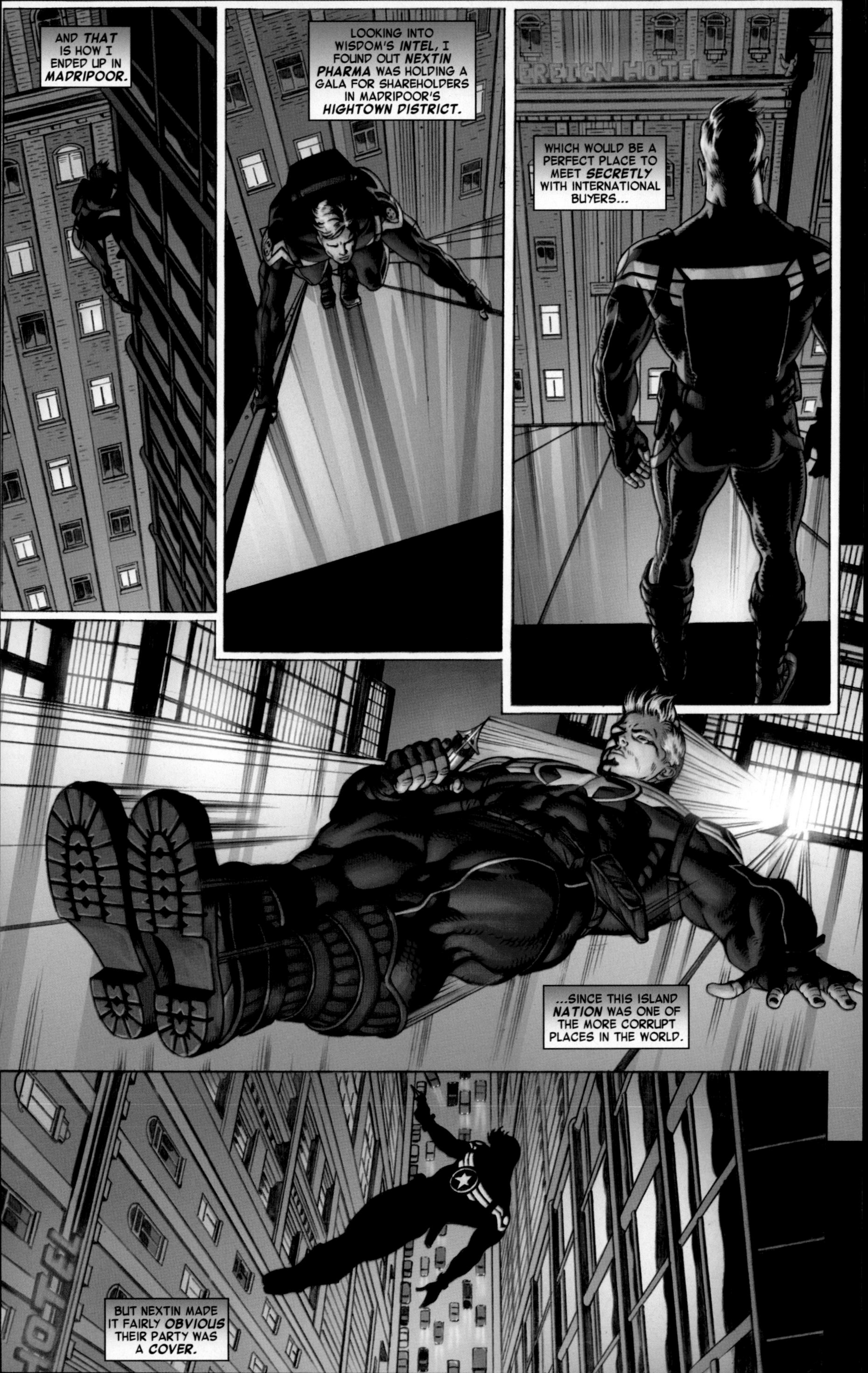
AND THAT IS HOW I ENDED UP IN MADRIPOOR.
LOOKING INTO WISDOM'S INTEL, I FOUND OUT NEXTIN PHARMA WAS HOLDING A GALA FOR SHAREHOLDERS IN MADRIPOOR'S HIGHTOWN DISTRICT.
EREIGN HOTEL
WHICH WOULD BE A PERFECT PLACE TO MEET SECRETLY WITH INTERNATIONAL BUYERS...
...SINCE THIS ISLAND NATION WAS ONE OF THE MORE CORRUPT PLACES IN THE WORLD.
HOTEL
BUT NEXTIN MADE IT FAIRLY OBVIOUS THEIR PARTY WAS A COVER.

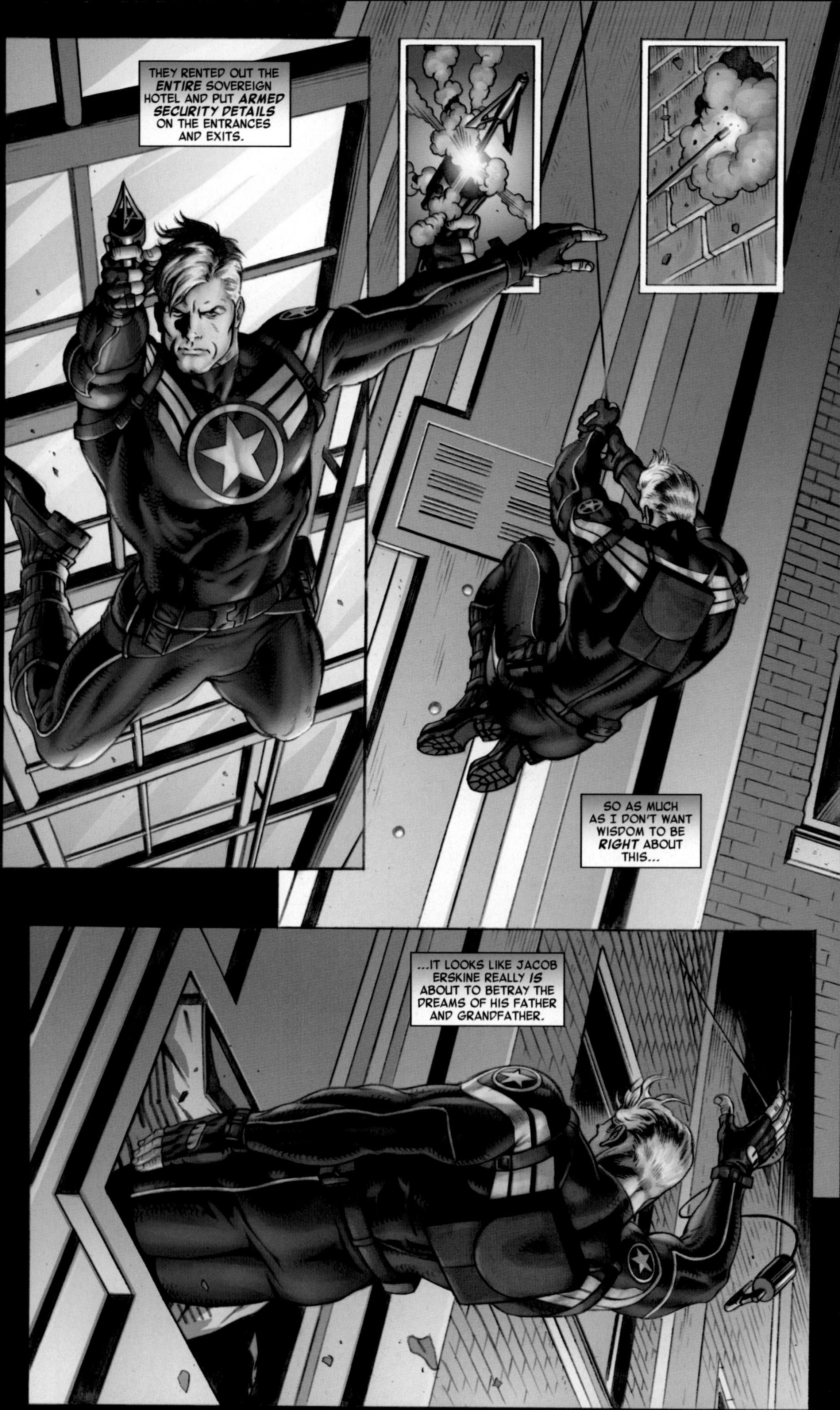
THEY RENTED OUT THE ENTIRE SOVEREIGN HOTEL AND PUT ARMED SECURITY DETAILS ON THE ENTRANCES AND EXITS.
SO AS MUCH AS I DON'T WANT WISDOM TO BE RIGHT ABOUT THIS...
...IT LOOKS LIKE JACOB ERSKINE REALLY IS ABOUT TO BETRAY THE DREAMS OF HIS FATHER AND GRANDFATHER.

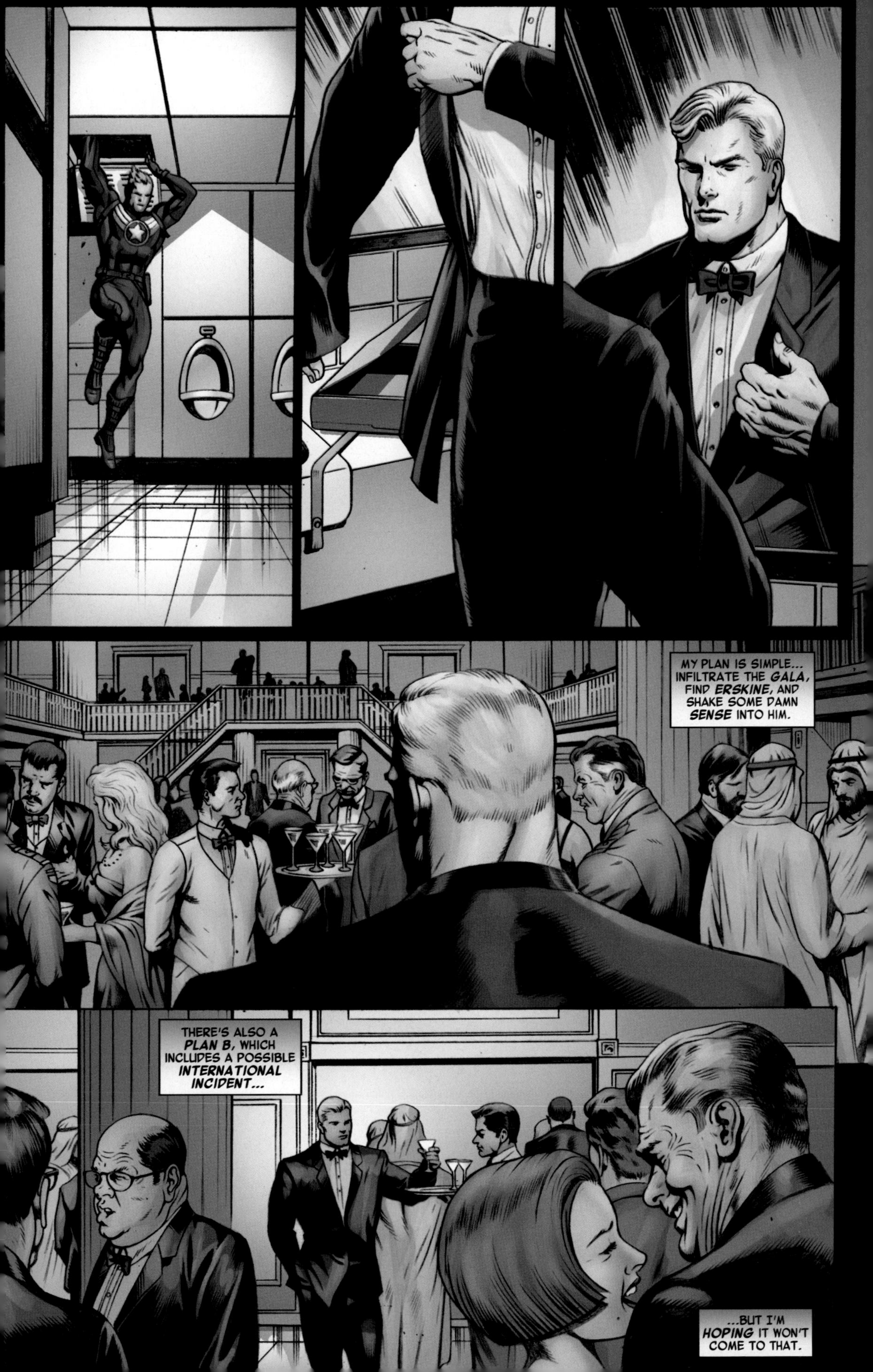
MY PLAN IS SIMPLE... INFILTRATE THE GALA, FIND ERSKINE, AND SHAKE SOME DAMN SENSE INTO HIM.
THERE'S ALSO A PLAN B, WHICH INCLUDES A POSSIBLE INTERNATIONAL INCIDENT...
...BUT I'M HOPING IT WON'T COME TO THAT.

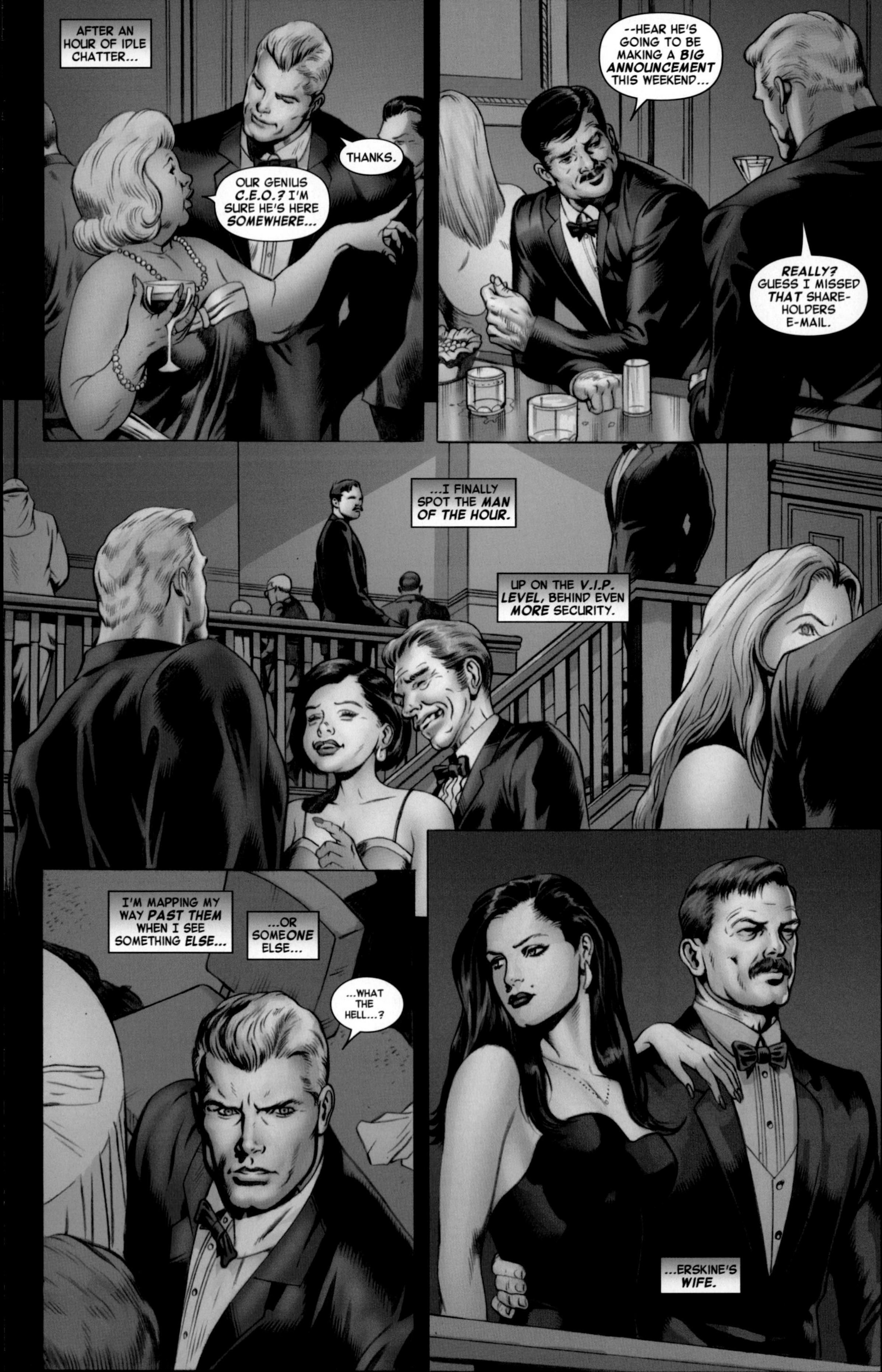
AFTER AN HOUR OF IDLE CHATTER...
OUR GENIUS C.E.O.? I'M SURE HE'S HERE SOMEWHERE...
THANKS.
--HEAR HE'S GOING TO BE MAKING A BIG ANNOUNCEMENT THIS WEEKEND...
REALLY? GUESS I MISSED THAT SHARE-HOLDERS E-MAIL.
...I FINALLY SPOT THE MAN OF THE HOUR.
UP ON THE V.I.P. LEVEL, BEHIND EVEN MORE SECURITY.
I'M MAPPING MY WAY PAST THEM WHEN I SEE SOMETHING ELSE...
...OR SOMEONE ELSE...
...WHAT THE HELL...?
...ERSKINE'S WIFE.

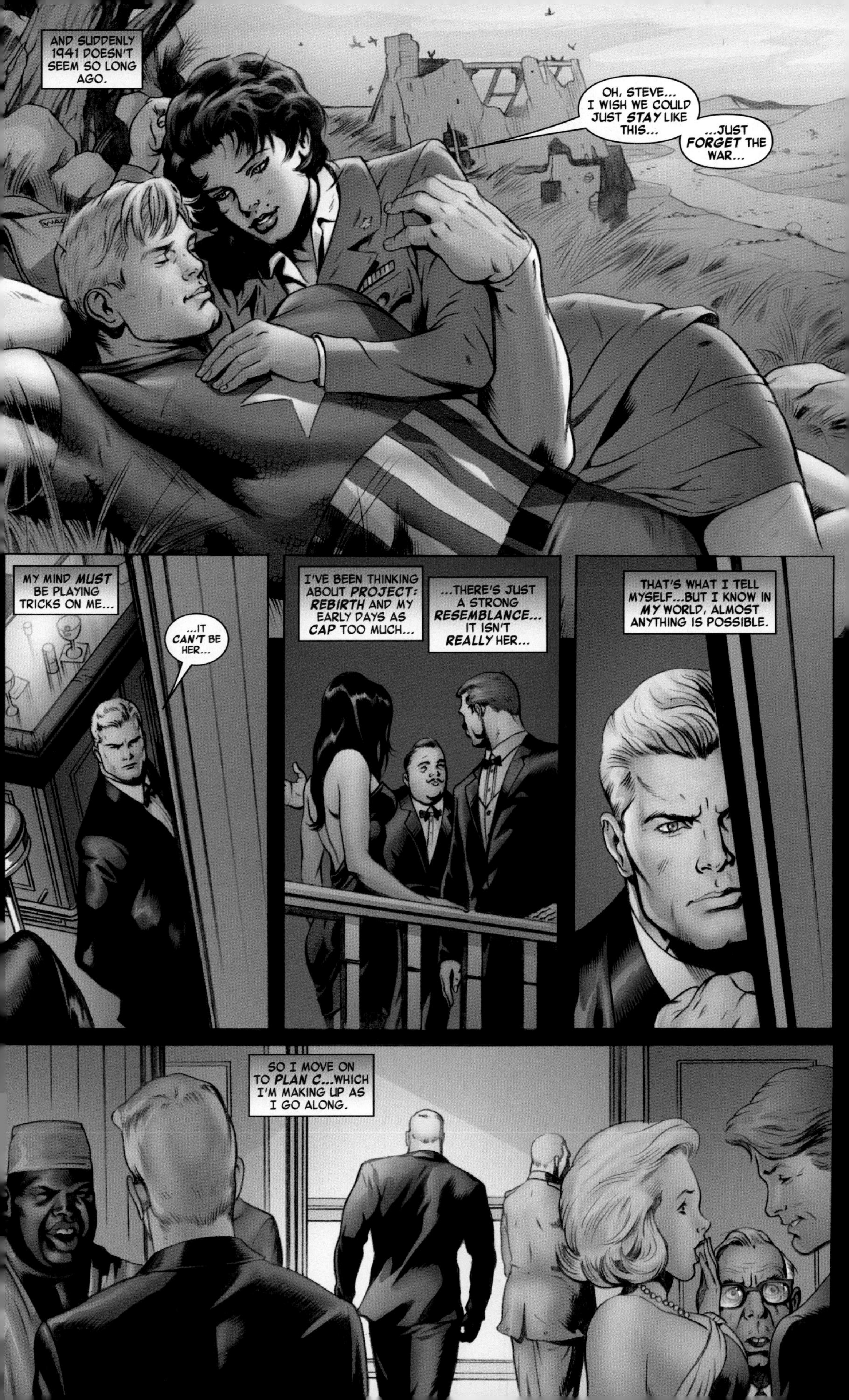
AND SUDDENLY 1941 DOESN'T SEEM SO LONG AGO.
OH, STEVE... I WISH WE COULD JUST STAY LIKE THIS...
...JUST FORGET THE WAR...
MY MIND MUST BE PLAYING TRICKS ON ME...
...IT CAN'T BE HER...
I'VE BEEN THINKING ABOUT PROJECT: REBIRTH AND MY EARLY DAYS AS CAP TOO MUCH...
...THERE'S JUST A STRONG RESEMBLANCE... IT ISN'T REALLY HER...
THAT'S WHAT I TELL MYSELF...BUT I KNOW IN MY WORLD, ALMOST ANYTHING IS POSSIBLE.
SO I MOVE ON TO PLAN C...WHICH I'M MAKING UP AS I GO ALONG.

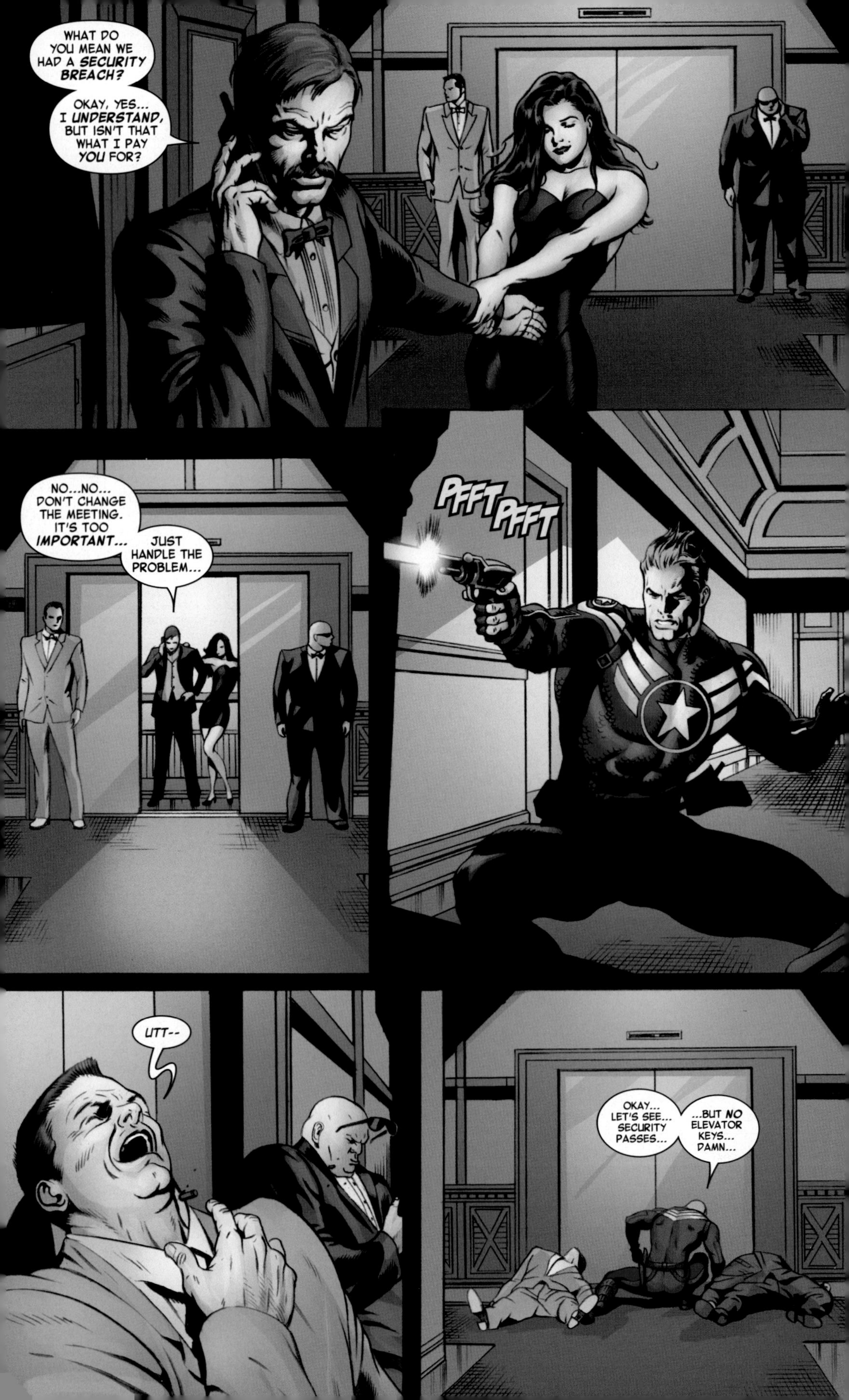
WHAT DO YOU MEAN WE HAD A SECURITY BREACH?
OKAY, YES... I UNDERSTAND, BUT ISN'T THAT WHAT I PAY YOU FOR?
NO...NO... DON'T CHANGE THE MEETING. IT'S TOO IMPORTANT...
JUST HANDLE THE PROBLEM...
PFFT PFFT
UTT--
OKAY... LET'S SEE... SECURITY PASSES...
...BUT NO ELEVATOR KEYS... DAMN...

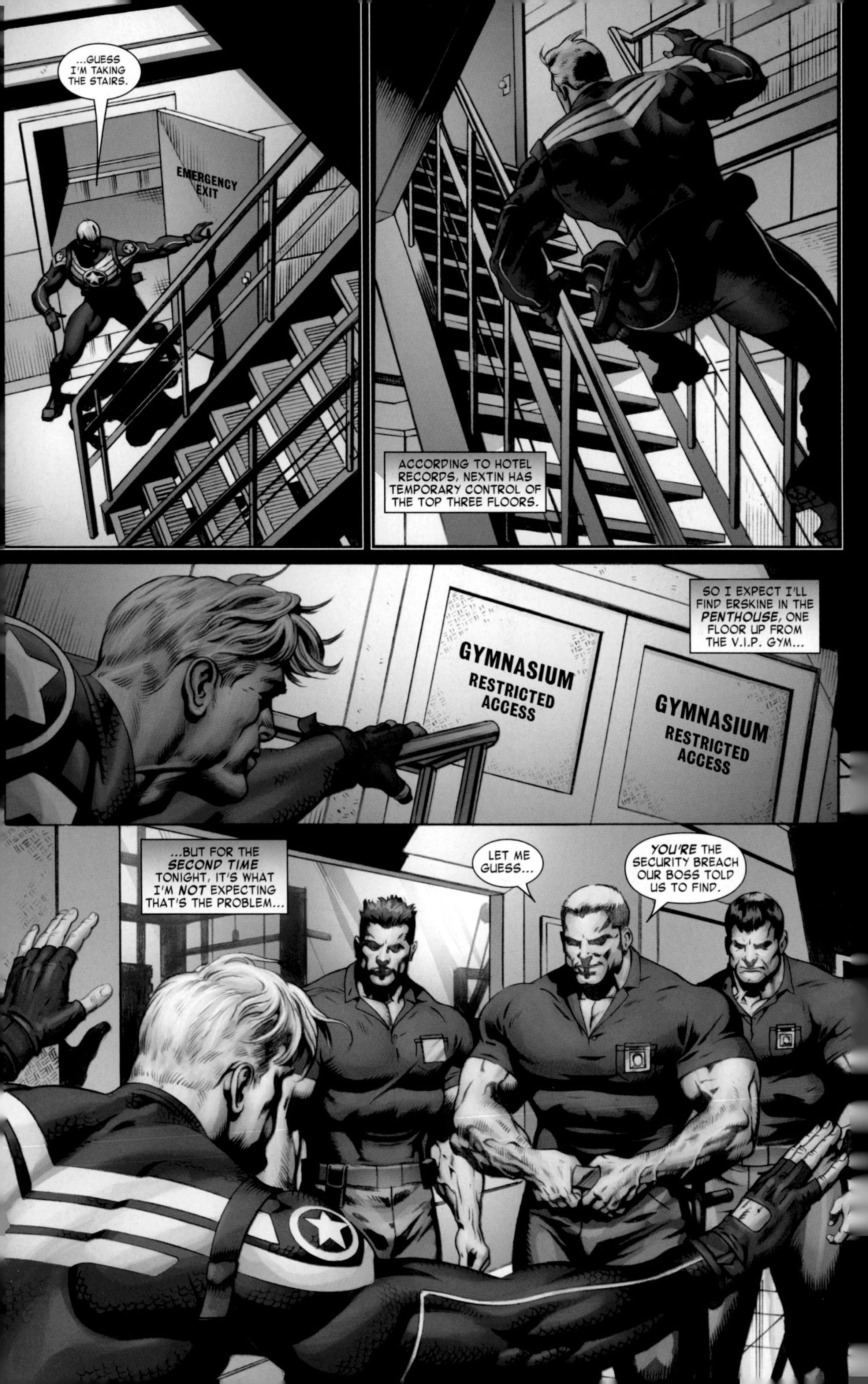
...GUESS I'M TAKING THE STAIRS.
EMERGENCY EXIT
ACCORDING TO HOTEL RECORDS, NEXTIN HAS TEMPORARY CONTROL OF THE TOP THREE FLOORS.
SO I EXPECT I'LL FIND ERSKINE IN THE PENTHOUSE, ONE FLOOR UP FROM THE V.I.P. GYM...
GYMNASIUM RESTRICTED ACCESS
GYMNASIUM RESTRICTED ACCESS
...BUT FOR THE SECOND TIME TONIGHT, IT'S WHAT I'M NOT EXPECTING THAT'S THE PROBLEM...
LET ME GUESS...
YOU'RE THE SECURITY BREACH OUR BOSS TOLD US TO FIND.

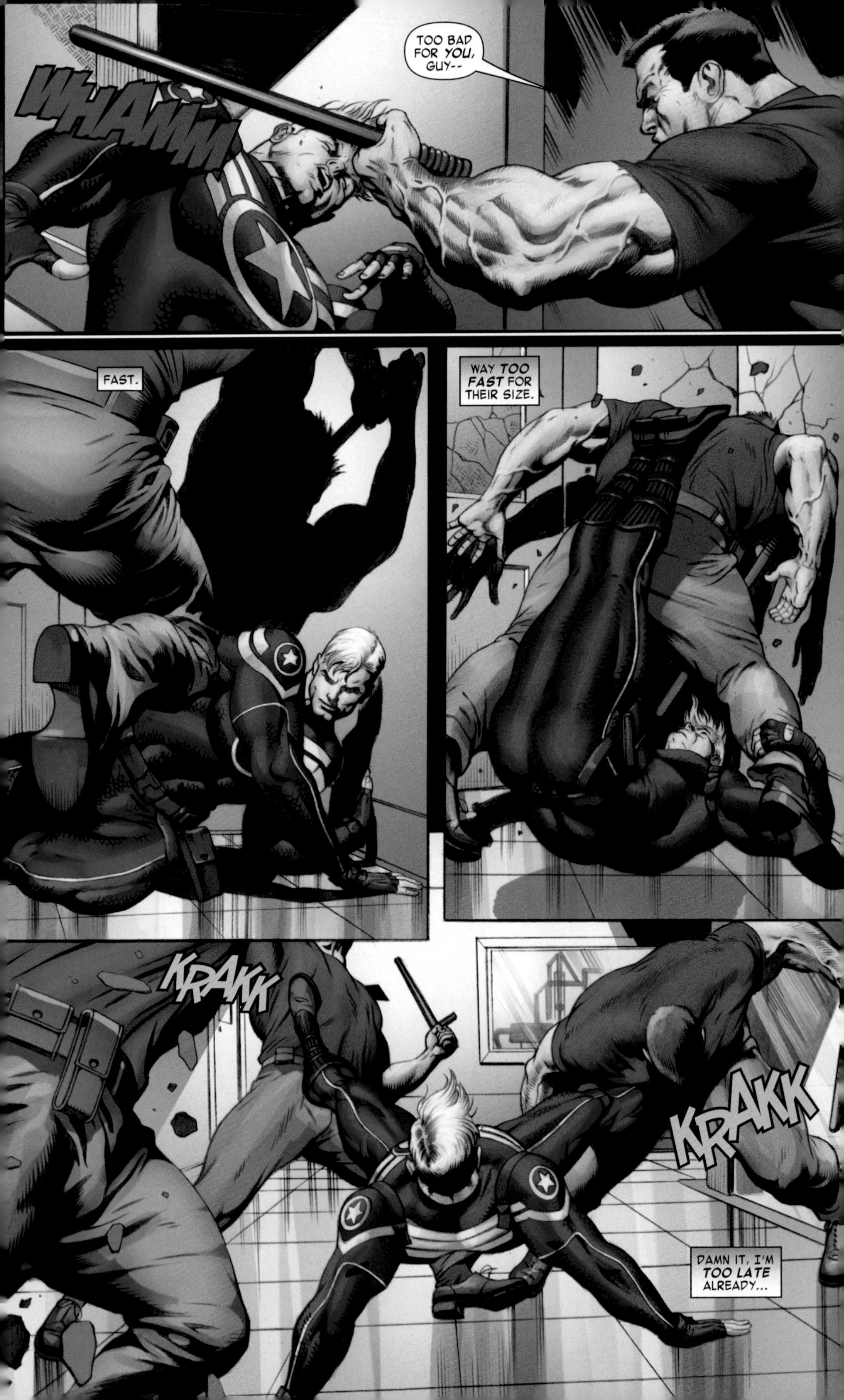
TOO BAD FOR YOU, GUY--
WHAMM
FAST.
WAY TOO FAST FOR THEIR SIZE.
KRAKK
KRAKK
DAMN IT, I'M TOO LATE ALREADY...

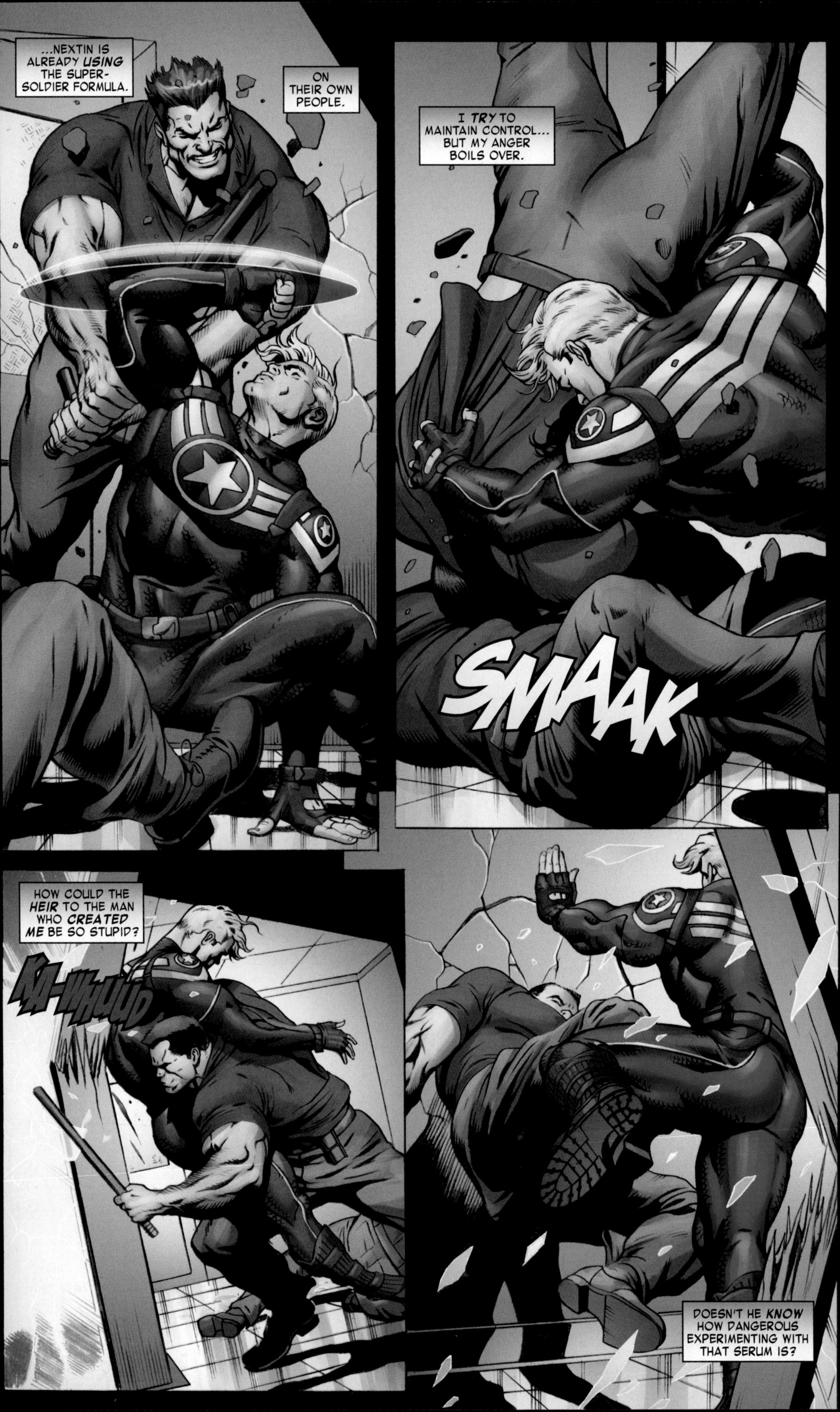
...NEXTIN IS ALREADY USING THE SUPER-SOLDIER FORMULA.
ON THEIR OWN PEOPLE.
I TRY TO MAINTAIN CONTROL... BUT MY ANGER BOILS OVER.
SMAAK
HOW COULD THE HEIR TO THE MAN WHO CREATED ME BE SO STUPID?
KA-WHUUD
DOESN'T HE KNOW HOW DANGEROUS EXPERIMENTING WITH THAT SERUM IS?

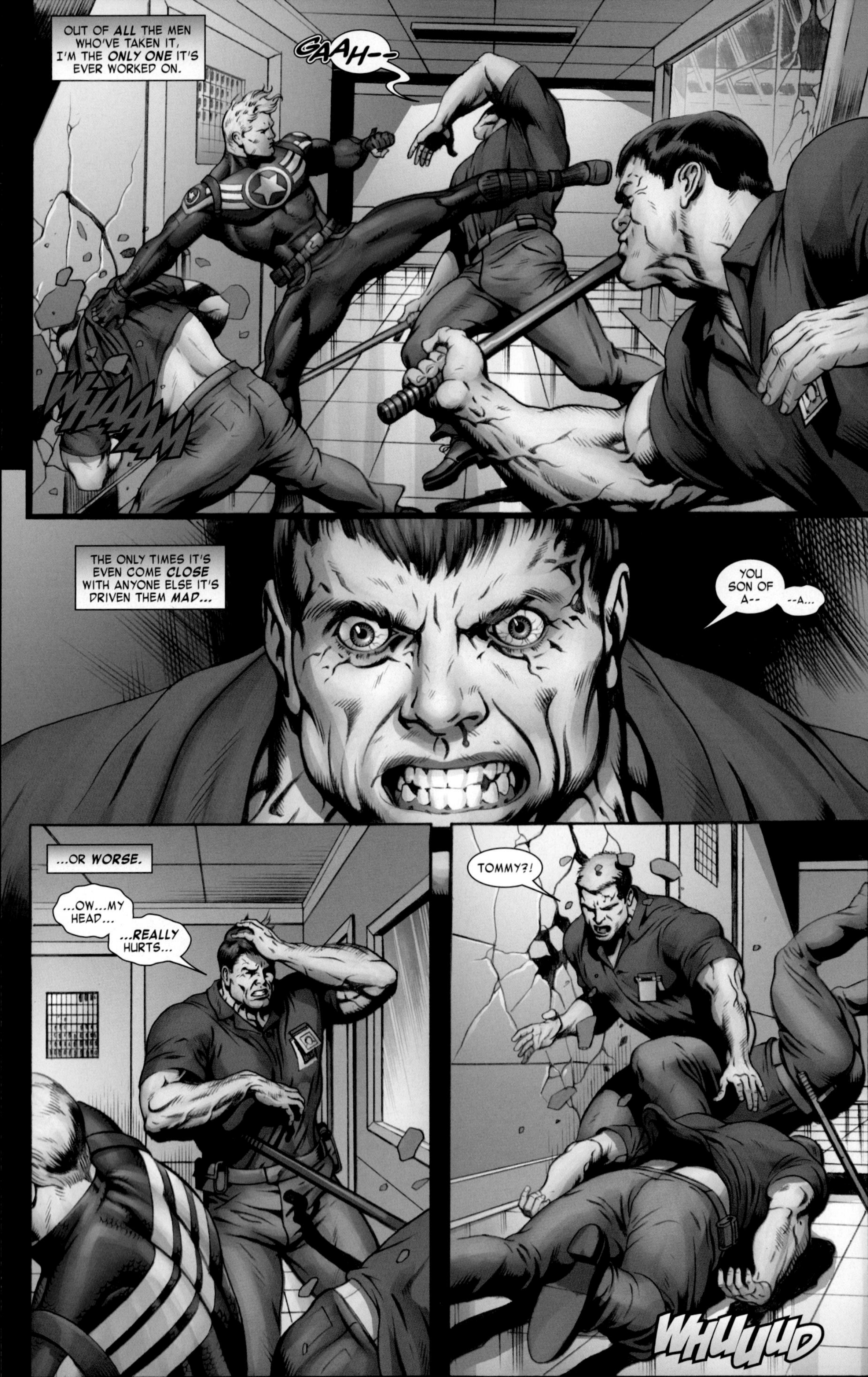
OUT OF ALL THE MEN WHO'VE TAKEN IT, I'M THE ONLY ONE IT'S EVER WORKED ON.
GAAH--
WHAAM
THE ONLY TIMES IT'S EVEN COME CLOSE WITH ANYONE ELSE IT'S DRIVEN THEM MAD...
YOU SON OF A--
--A...
...OR WORSE.
...OW...MY HEAD...
...REALLY HURTS...
TOMMY?!
WHUUUD

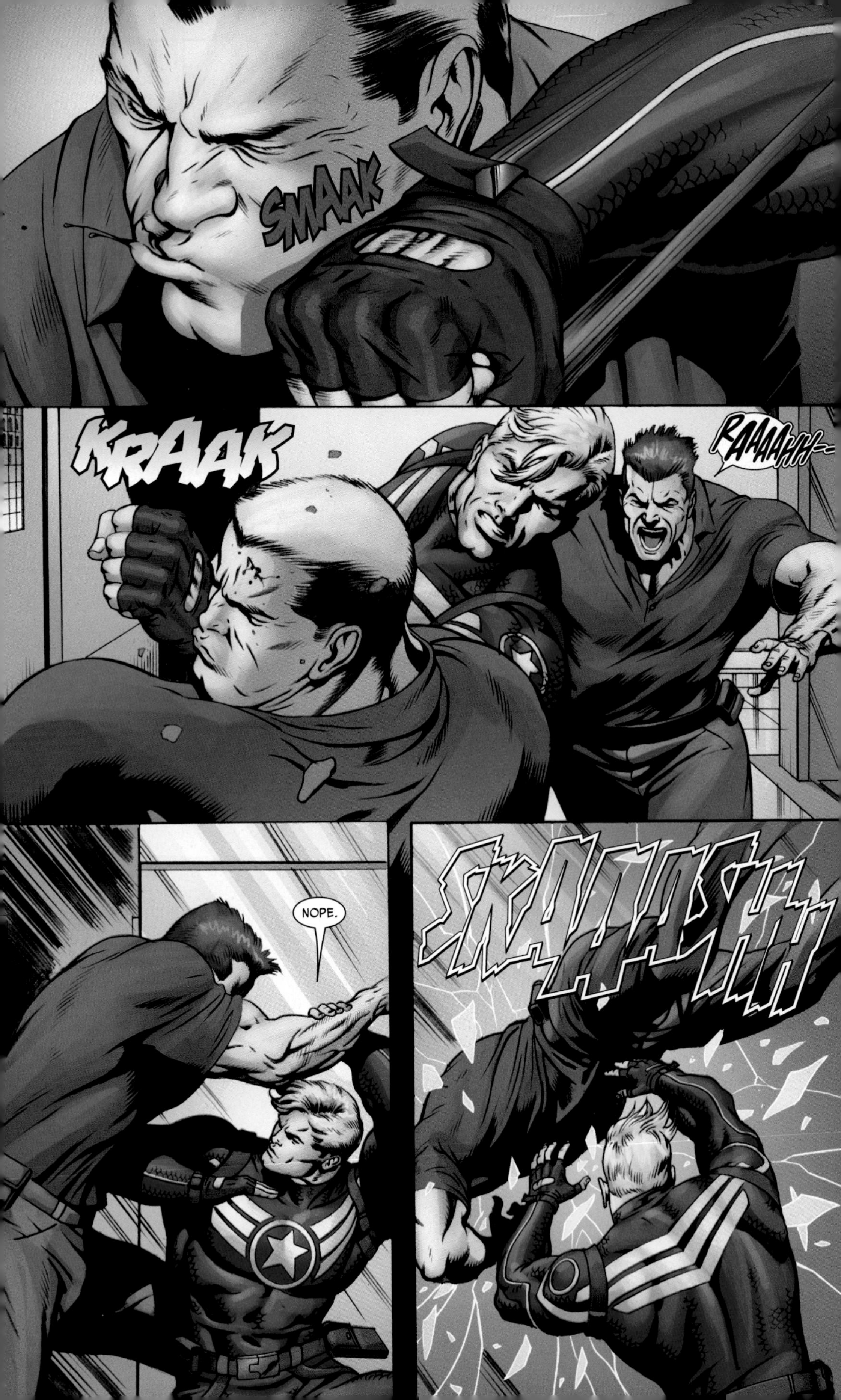
SMAAK
KRAAK
RAAAAHH--
NOPE.
SKRAASH

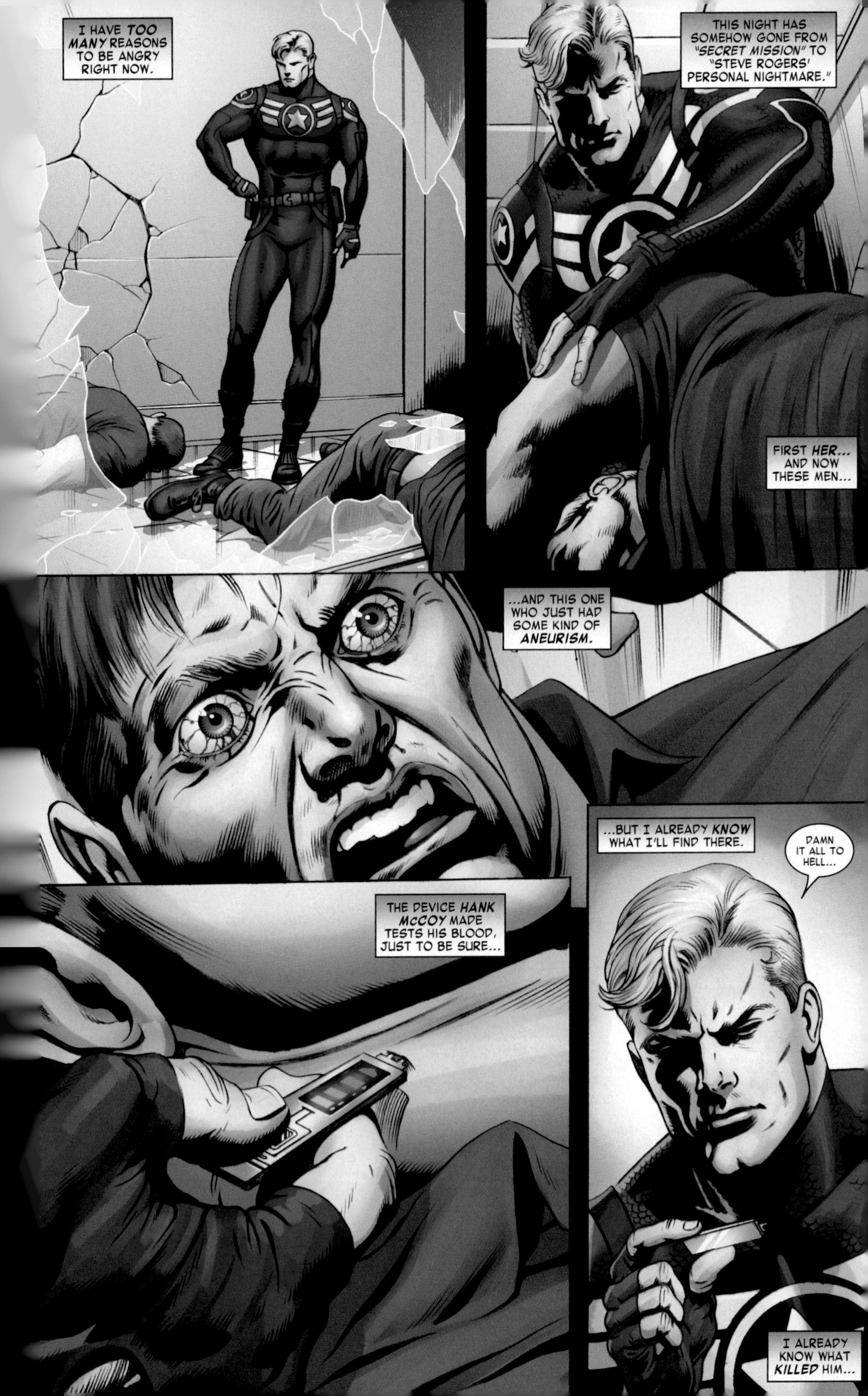
I HAVE TOO MANY REASONS TO BE ANGRY RIGHT NOW.
THIS NIGHT HAS SOMEHOW GONE FROM "SECRET MISSION" TO "STEVE ROGERS' PERSONAL NIGHTMARE."
FIRST HER... AND NOW THESE MEN...
...AND THIS ONE WHO JUST HAD SOME KIND OF ANEURISM.
THE DEVICE HANK McCOY MADE TESTS HIS BLOOD, JUST TO BE SURE...
...BUT I ALREADY KNOW WHAT I'LL FIND THERE.
DAMN IT ALL TO HELL...
I ALREADY KNOW WHAT KILLED HIM...

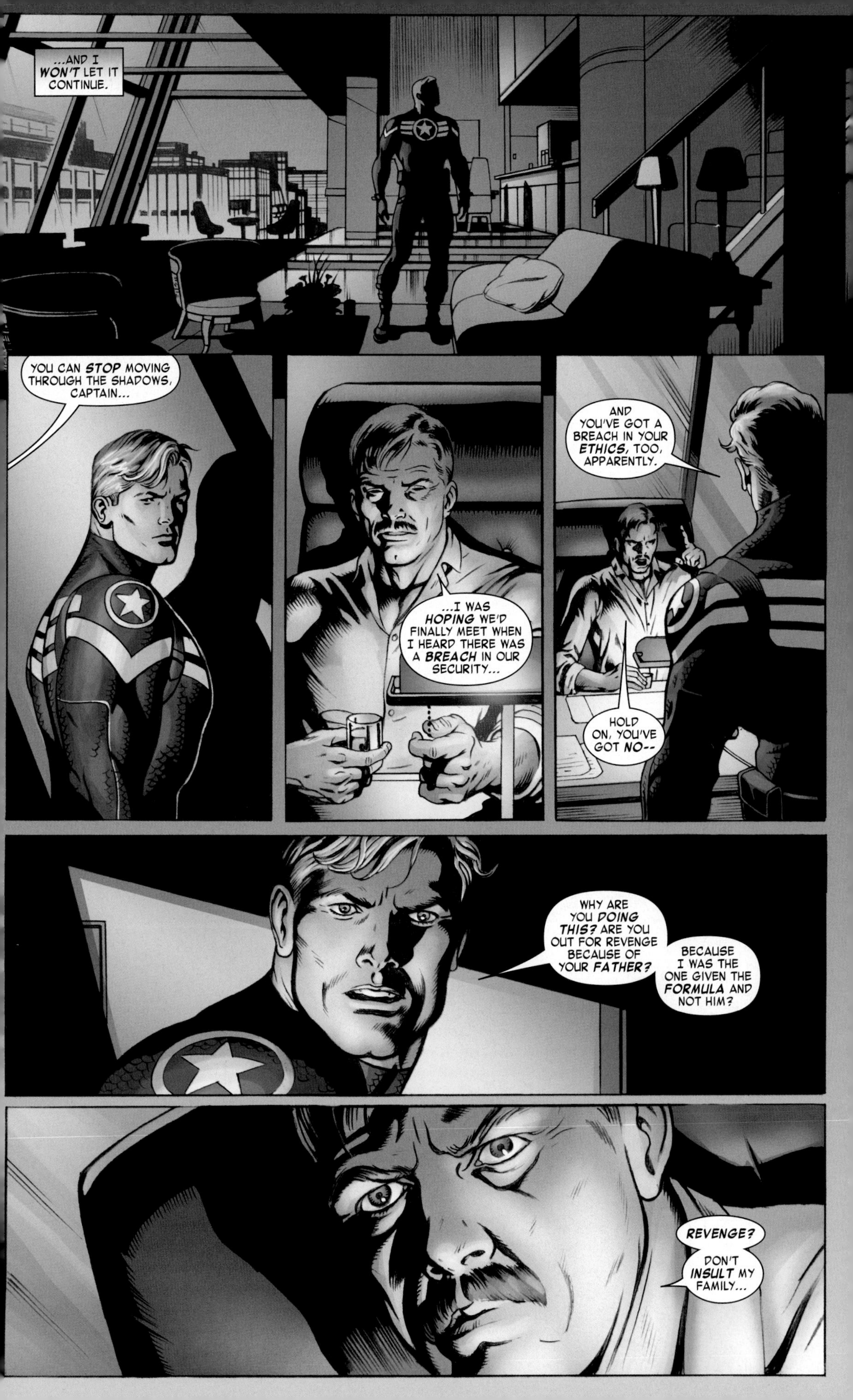
...AND I WON'T LET IT CONTINUE.
YOU CAN STOP MOVING THROUGH THE SHADOWS, CAPTAIN...
...I WAS HOPING WE'D FINALLY MEET WHEN I HEARD THERE WAS A BREACH IN OUR SECURITY...
AND YOU'VE GOT A BREACH IN YOUR ETHICS, TOO, APPARENTLY.
HOLD ON, YOU'VE GOT NO--
WHY ARE YOU DOING THIS? ARE YOU OUT FOR REVENGE BECAUSE OF YOUR FATHER?
BECAUSE I WAS THE ONE GIVEN THE FORMULA AND NOT HIM?
REVENGE?
DON'T INSULT MY FAMILY...

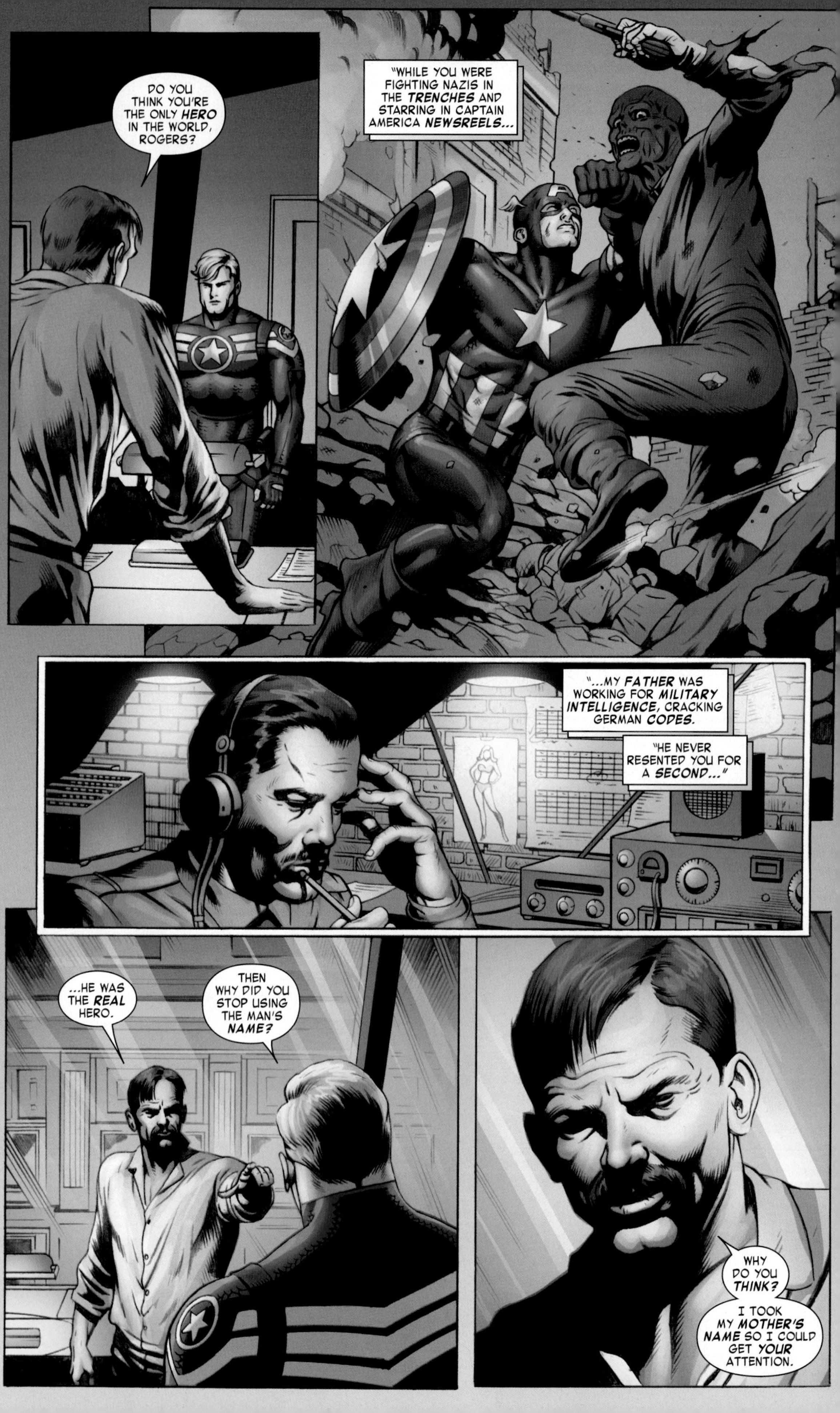
DO YOU THINK YOU'RE THE ONLY HERO IN THE WORLD, ROGERS?
"WHILE YOU WERE FIGHTING NAZIS IN THE TRENCHES AND STARRING IN CAPTAIN AMERICA NEWSREELS...
"...MY FATHER WAS WORKING FOR MILITARY INTELLIGENCE, CRACKING GERMAN CODES.
"HE NEVER RESENTED YOU FOR A SECOND..."
...HE WAS THE REAL HERO.
THEN WHY DID YOU STOP USING THE MAN'S NAME?
WHY DO YOU THINK?
I TOOK MY MOTHER'S NAME SO I COULD GET YOUR ATTENTION.

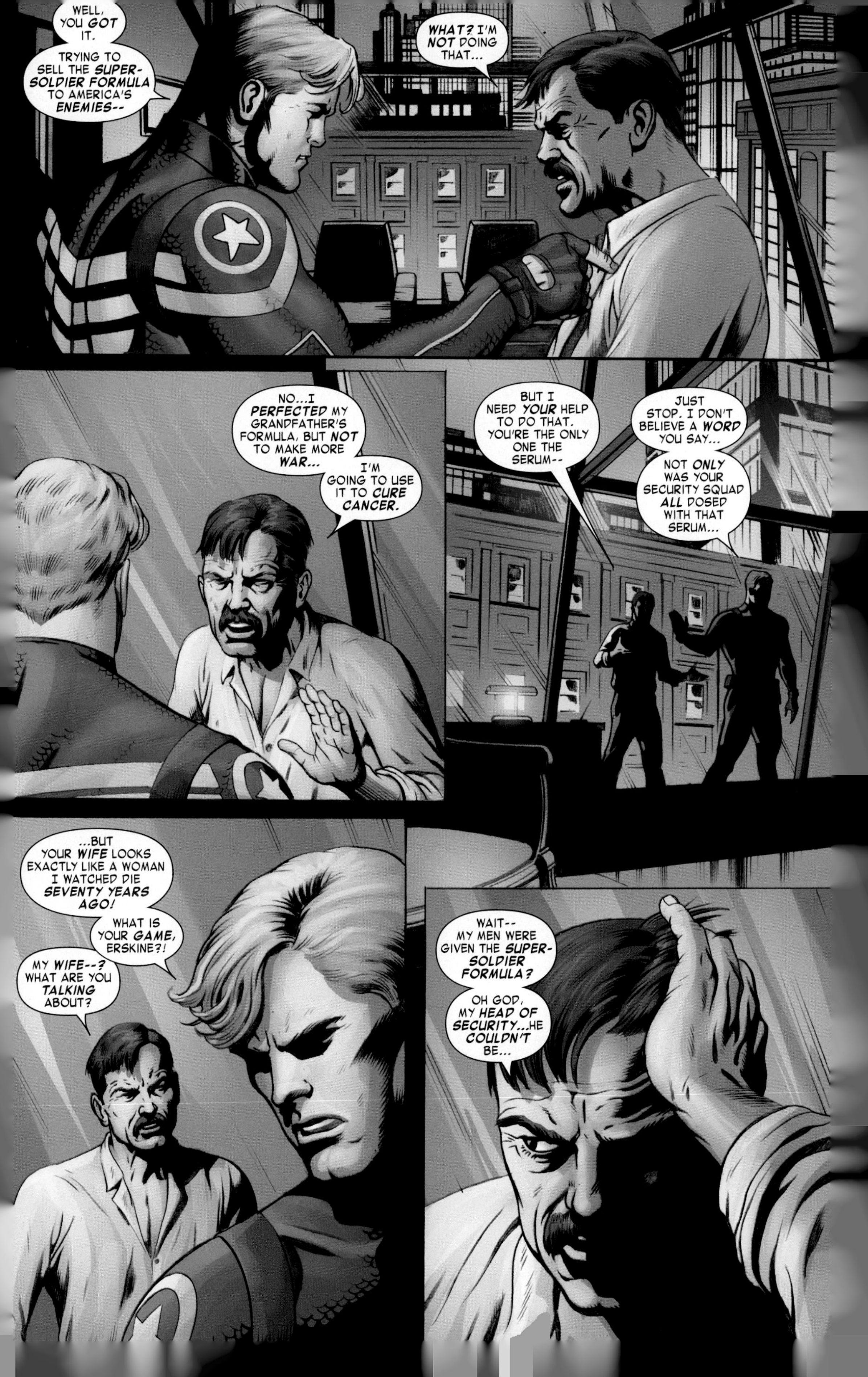
WELL, YOU GOT IT.
TRYING TO SELL THE SUPER-SOLDIER FORMULA TO AMERICA'S ENEMIES--
WHAT? I'M NOT DOING THAT...
NO...I PERFECTED MY GRANDFATHER'S FORMULA, BUT NOT TO MAKE MORE WAR...
I'M GOING TO USE IT TO CURE CANCER.
BUT I NEED YOUR HELP TO DO THAT. YOU'RE THE ONLY ONE THE SERUM--
JUST STOP. I DON'T BELIEVE A WORD YOU SAY...
NOT ONLY WAS YOUR SECURITY SQUAD ALL DOSED WITH THAT SERUM...
...BUT YOUR WIFE LOOKS EXACTLY LIKE A WOMAN I WATCHED DIE SEVENTY YEARS AGO!
WHAT IS YOUR GAME, ERSKINE?!
MY WIFE--? WHAT ARE YOU TALKING ABOUT?
WAIT-- MY MEN WERE GIVEN THE SUPER-SOLDIER FORMULA?
OH GOD, MY HEAD OF SECURITY...HE COULDN'T BE...

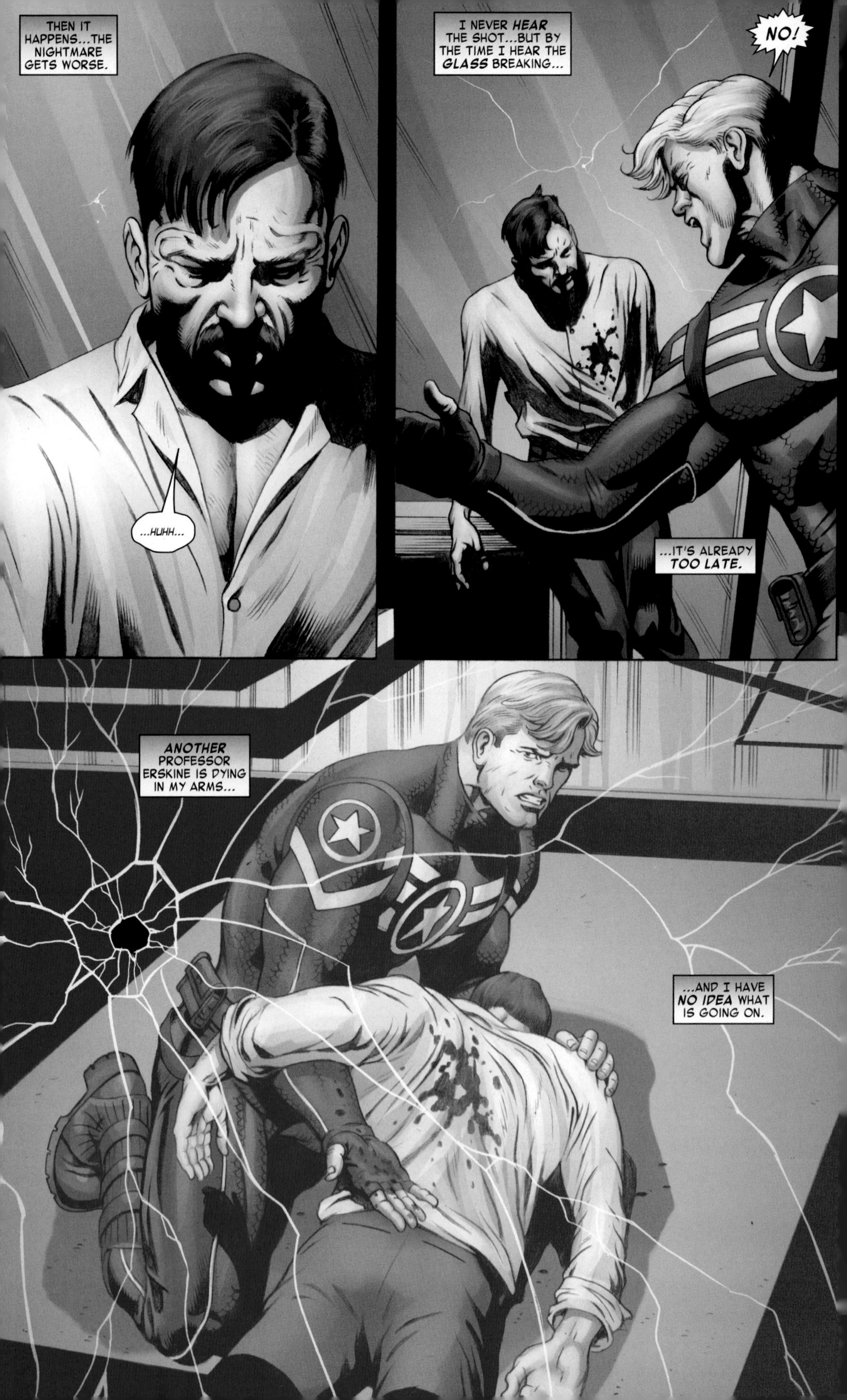
THEN IT HAPPENS...THE NIGHTMARE GETS WORSE.
...HUHH...
I NEVER HEAR THE SHOT...BUT BY THE TIME I HEAR THE GLASS BREAKING...
NO!
...IT'S ALREADY TOO LATE.
ANOTHER PROFESSOR ERSKINE IS DYING IN MY ARMS...
...AND I HAVE NO IDEA WHAT IS GOING ON.

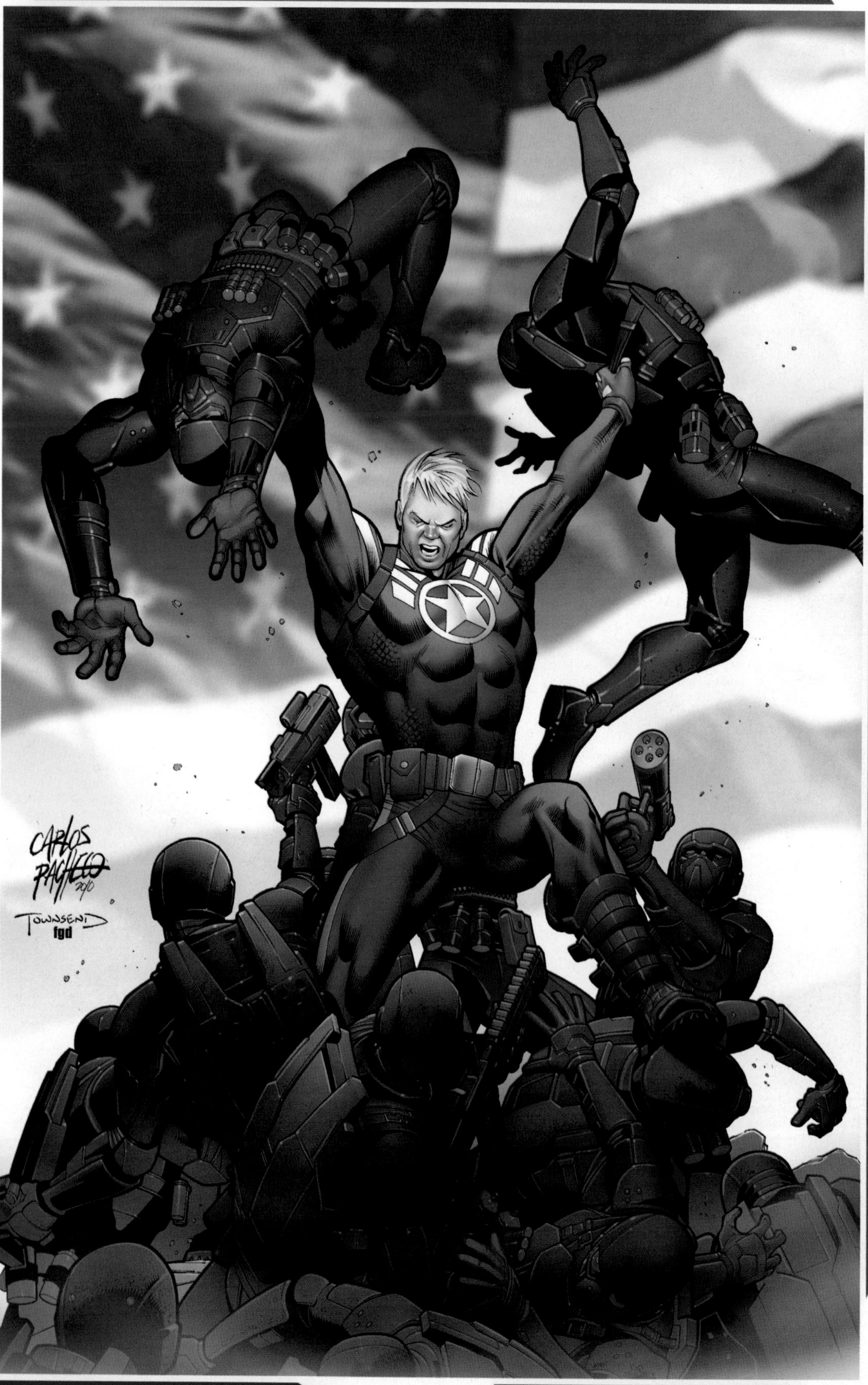
CARLOS PACHECO
TOWNSEND
fgd

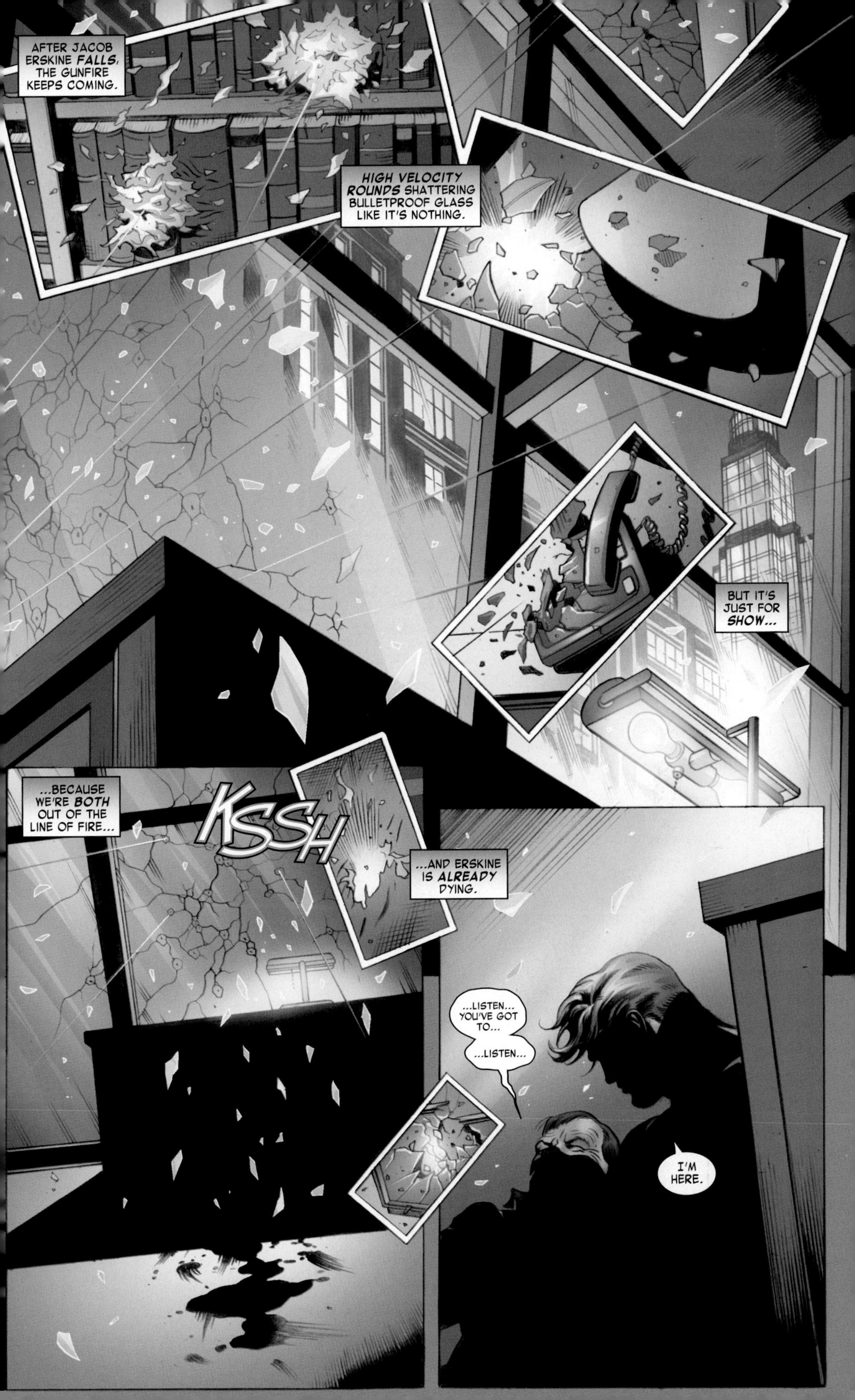
AFTER JACOB ERSKINE FALLS, THE GUNFIRE KEEPS COMING.
HIGH VELOCITY ROUNDS SHATTERING BULLETPROOF GLASS LIKE IT'S NOTHING.
BUT IT'S JUST FOR SHOW...
...BECAUSE WE'RE BOTH OUT OF THE LINE OF FIRE...
KSSH
...AND ERSKINE IS ALREADY DYING.
...LISTEN... YOU'VE GOT TO...
...LISTEN...
I'M HERE.

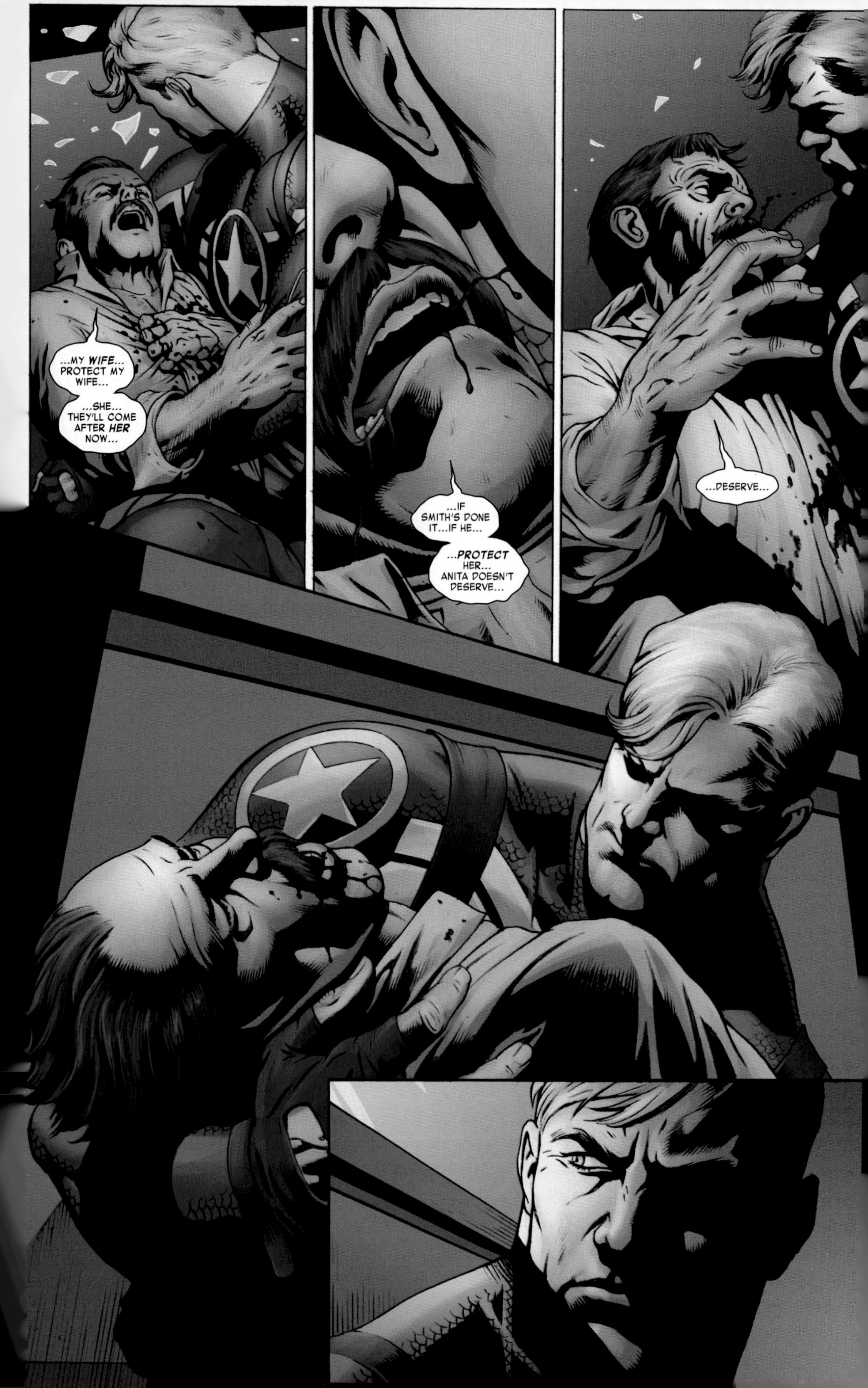
...MY WIFE... PROTECT MY WIFE...
...SHE... THEY'LL COME AFTER HER NOW...
...IF SMITH'S DONE IT...IF HE...
...PROTECT HER... ANITA DOESN'T DESERVE...
...DESERVE...

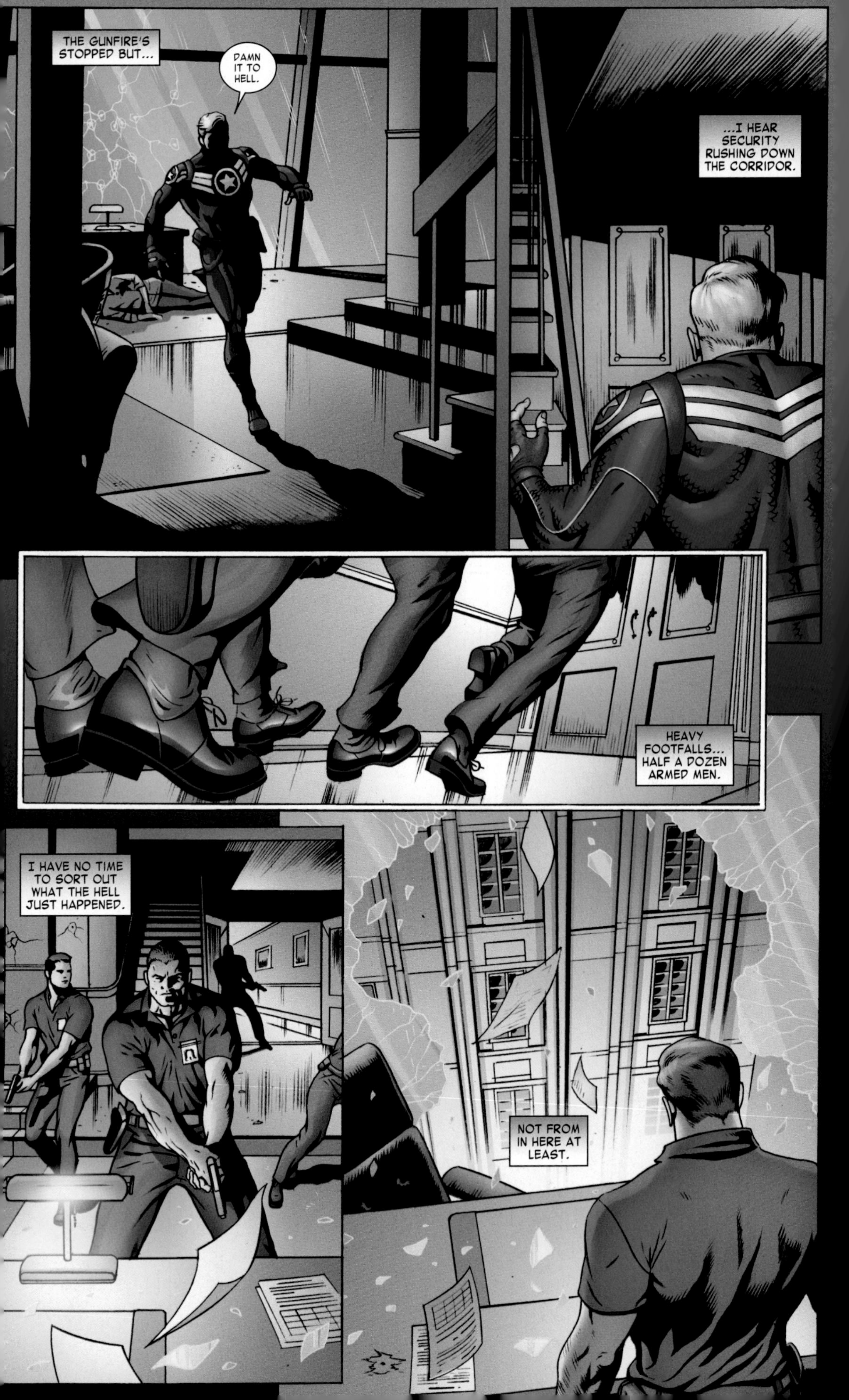
THE GUNFIRE'S STOPPED BUT...
DAMN IT TO HELL.
...I HEAR SECURITY RUSHING DOWN THE CORRIDOR.
HEAVY FOOTFALLS... HALF A DOZEN ARMED MEN.
I HAVE NO TIME TO SORT OUT WHAT THE HELL JUST HAPPENED.
NOT FROM IN HERE AT LEAST.

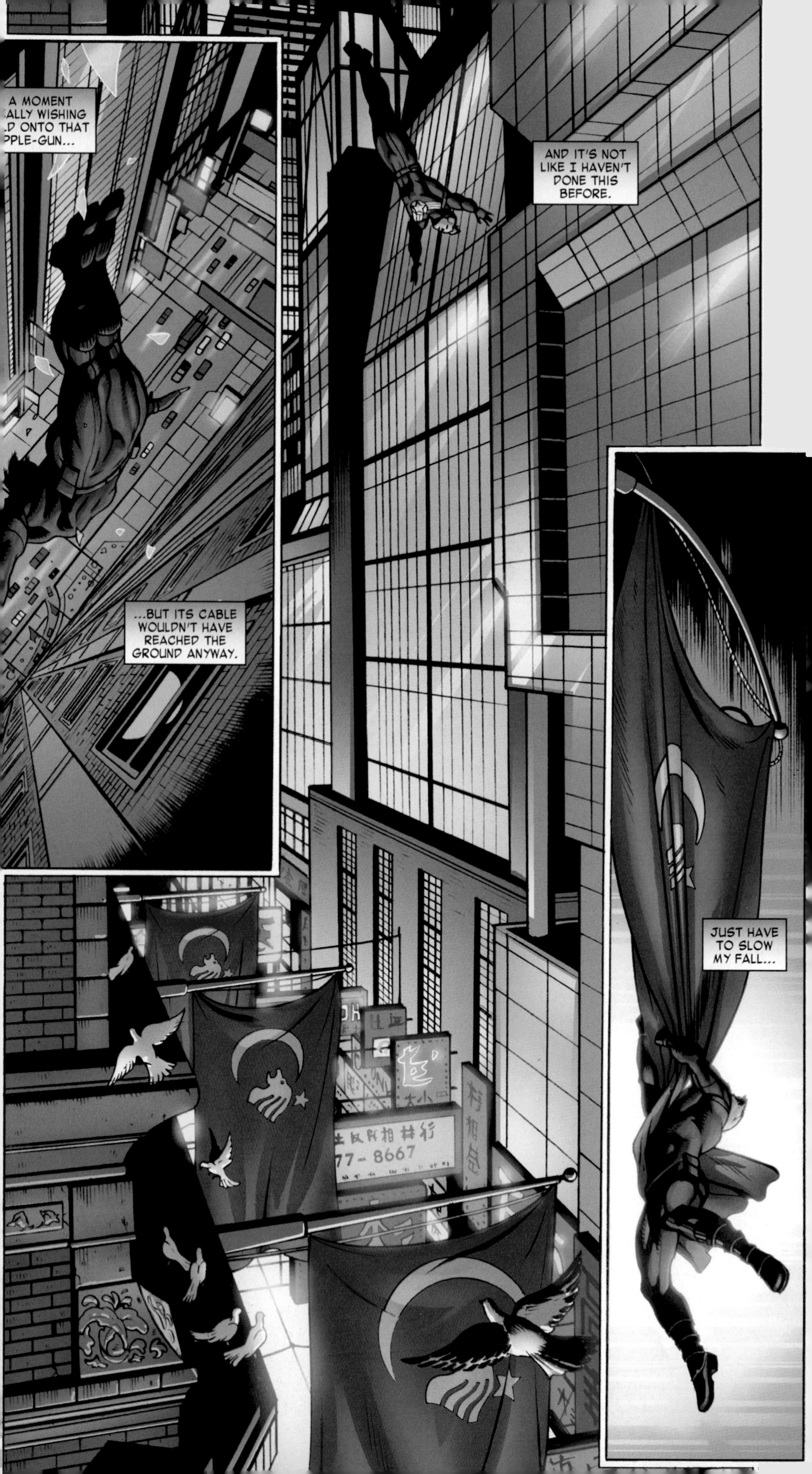
A MOMENT
ALLY WISHING
LD ONTO THAT
PPLE-GUN...
...BUT ITS CABLE WOULDN'T HAVE REACHED THE GROUND ANYWAY.
AND IT'S NOT LIKE I HAVEN'T DONE THIS BEFORE.
77-8667
JUST HAVE TO SLOW MY FALL...

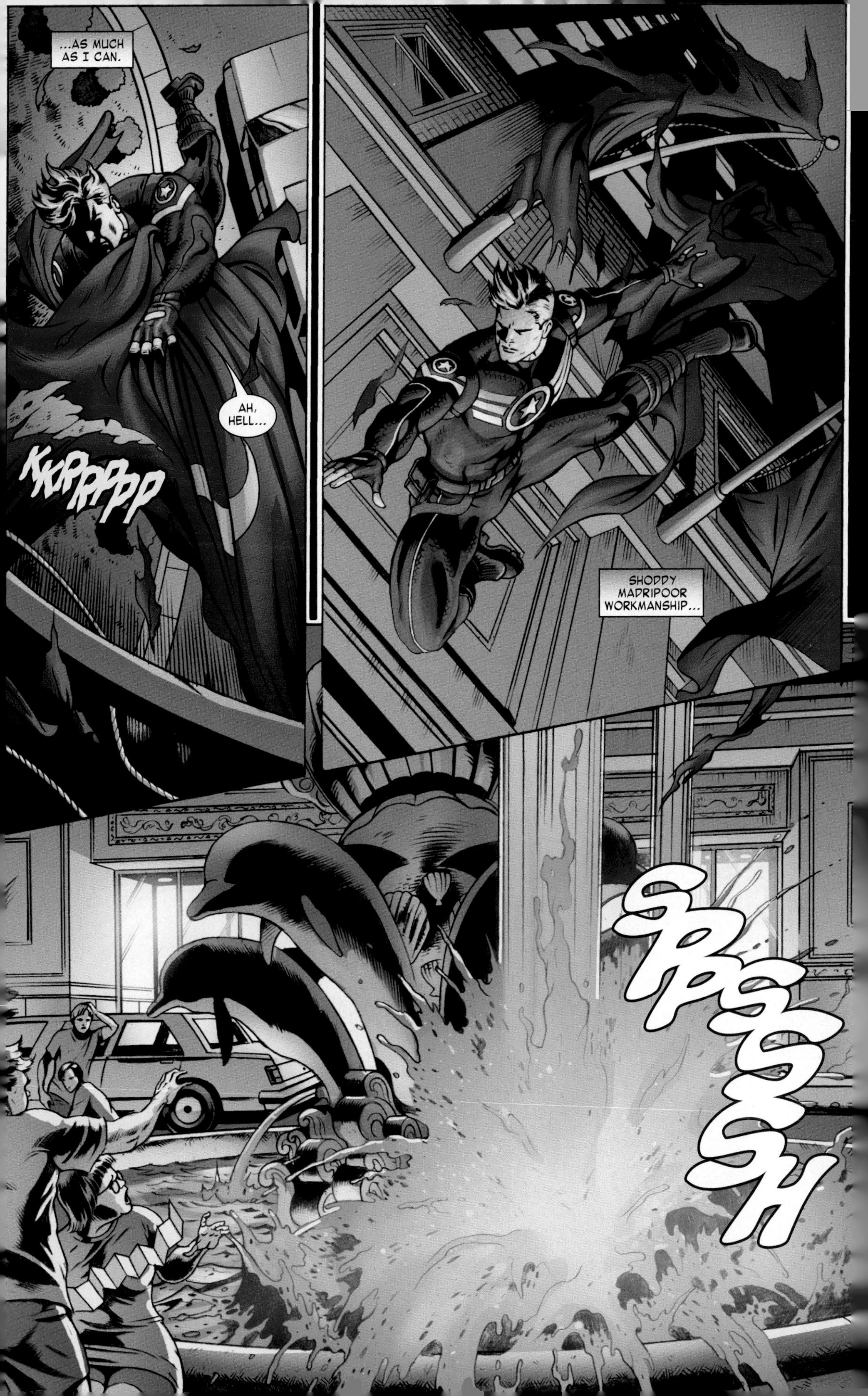
...AS MUCH AS I CAN.
AH, HELL...
KKRRPPP
SHODDY MADRIPOOR WORKMANSHIP...
SPPSSSH

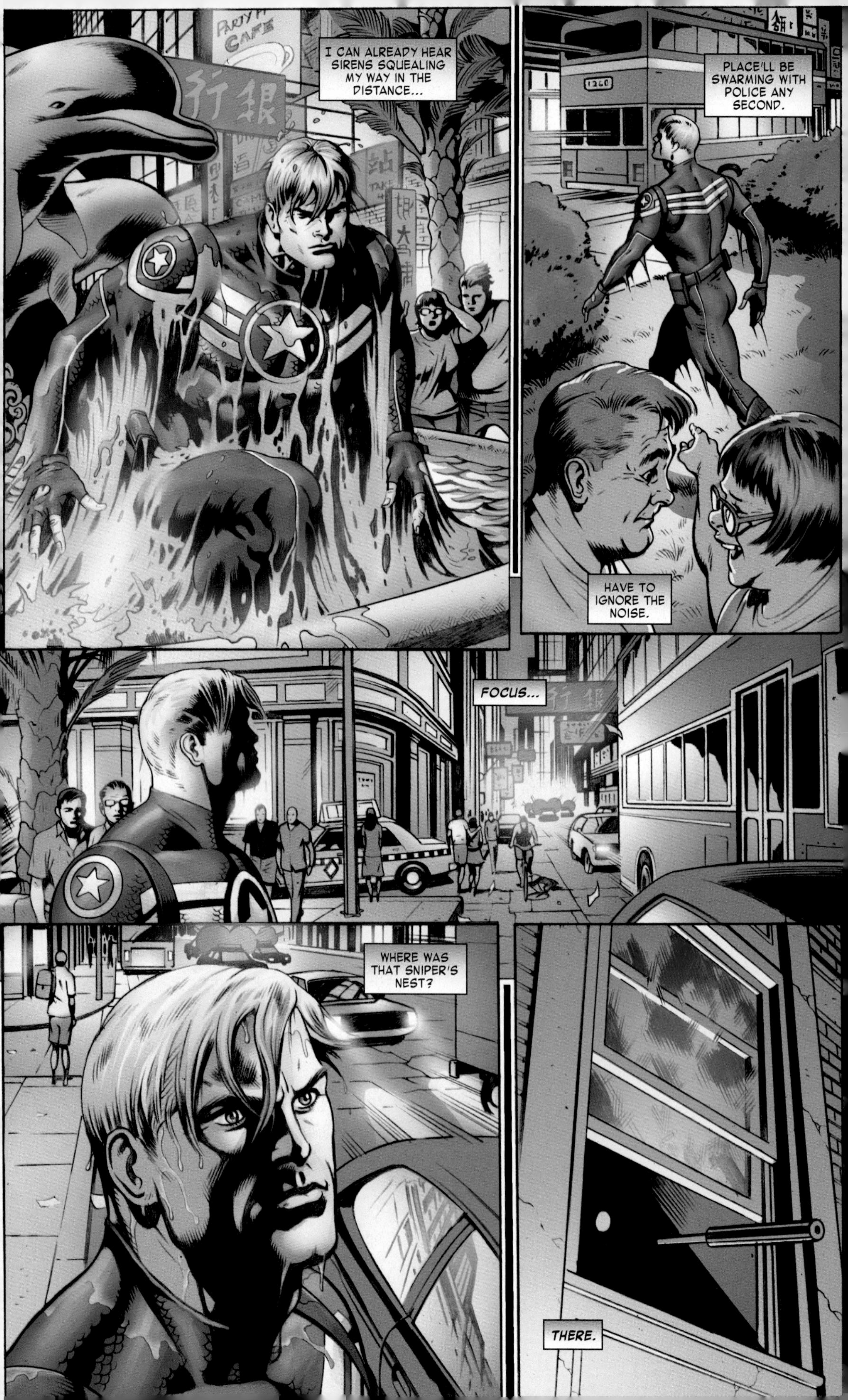

I CAN ALREADY HEAR SIRENS SQUEALING MY WAY IN THE DISTANCE...
PLACE'LL BE SWARMING WITH POLICE ANY SECOND.
HAVE TO IGNORE THE NOISE.
FOCUS...
WHERE WAS THAT SNIPER'S NEST?
THERE.

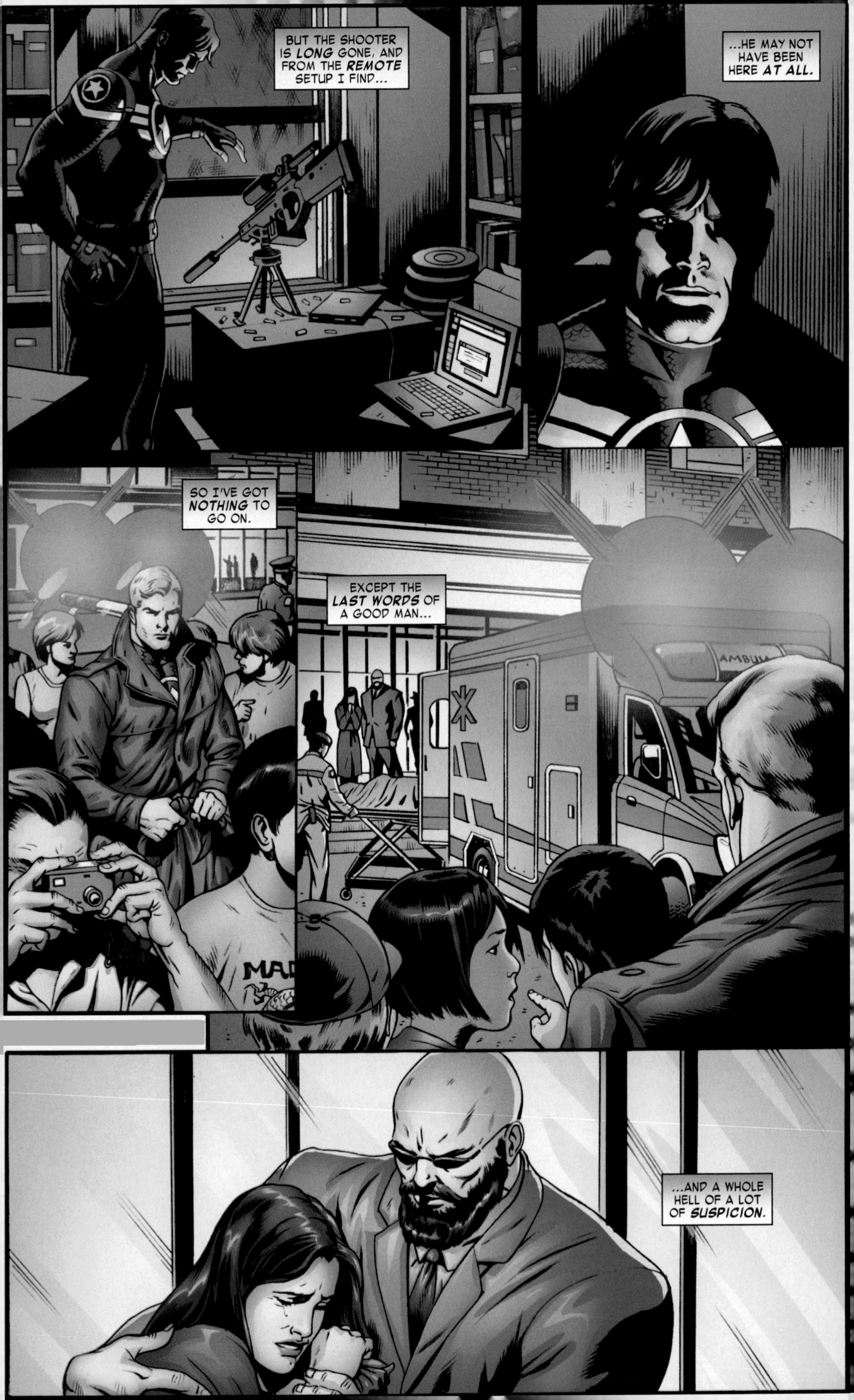

BUT THE SHOOTER IS LONG GONE, AND FROM THE REMOTE SETUP I FIND...
...HE MAY NOT HAVE BEEN HERE AT ALL.
SO I'VE GOT NOTHING TO GO ON.
EXCEPT THE LAST WORDS OF A GOOD MAN...
...AND A WHOLE HELL OF A LOT OF SUSPICION.

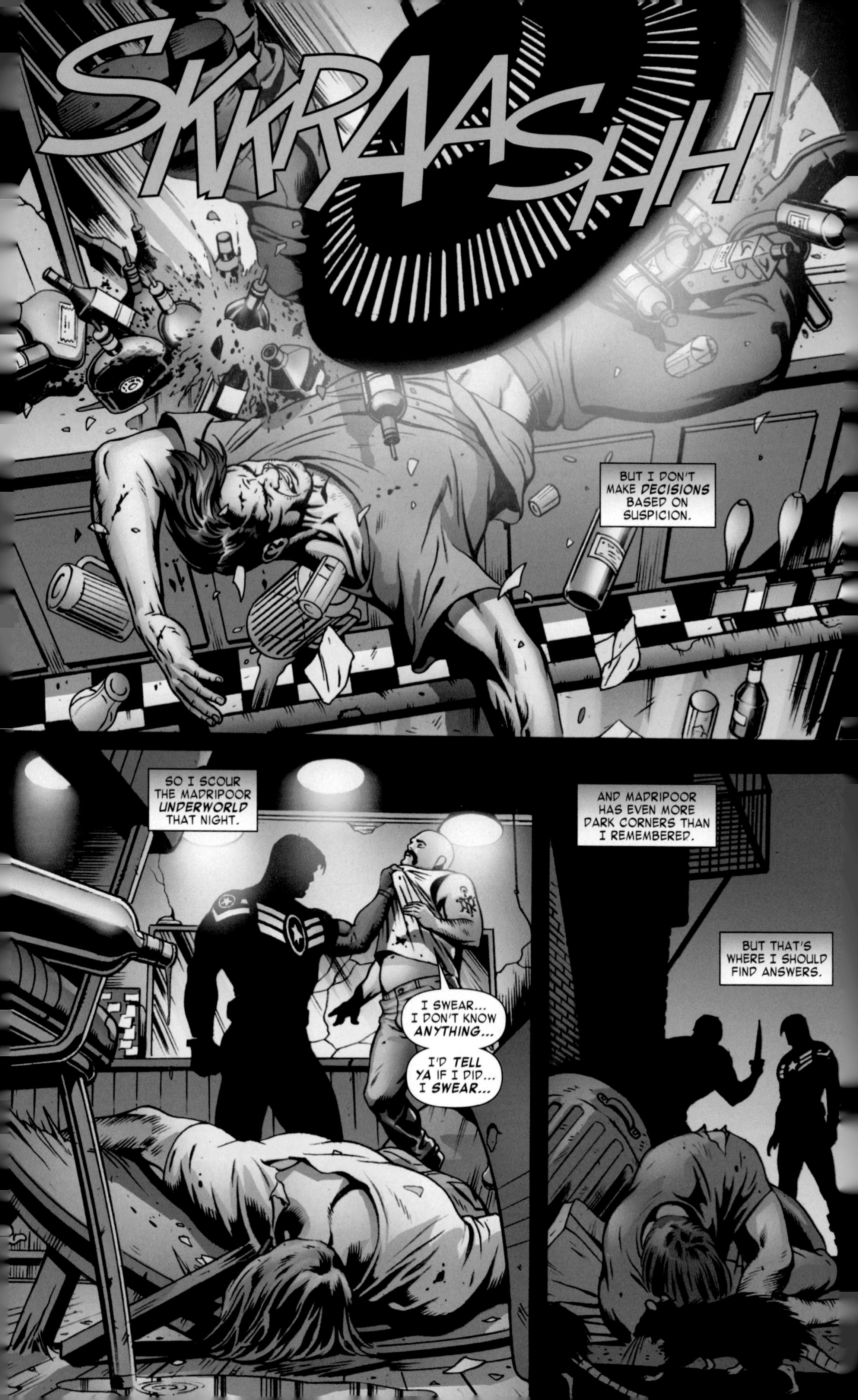
SKKRAASHH
BUT I DON'T MAKE DECISIONS BASED ON SUSPICION.
SO I SCOUR THE MADRIPOOR UNDERWORLD THAT NIGHT.
AND MADRIPOOR HAS EVEN MORE DARK CORNERS THAN I REMEMBERED.
I SWEAR... I DON'T KNOW ANYTHING...
I'D TELL YA IF I DID... I SWEAR...
BUT THAT'S WHERE I SHOULD FIND ANSWERS.

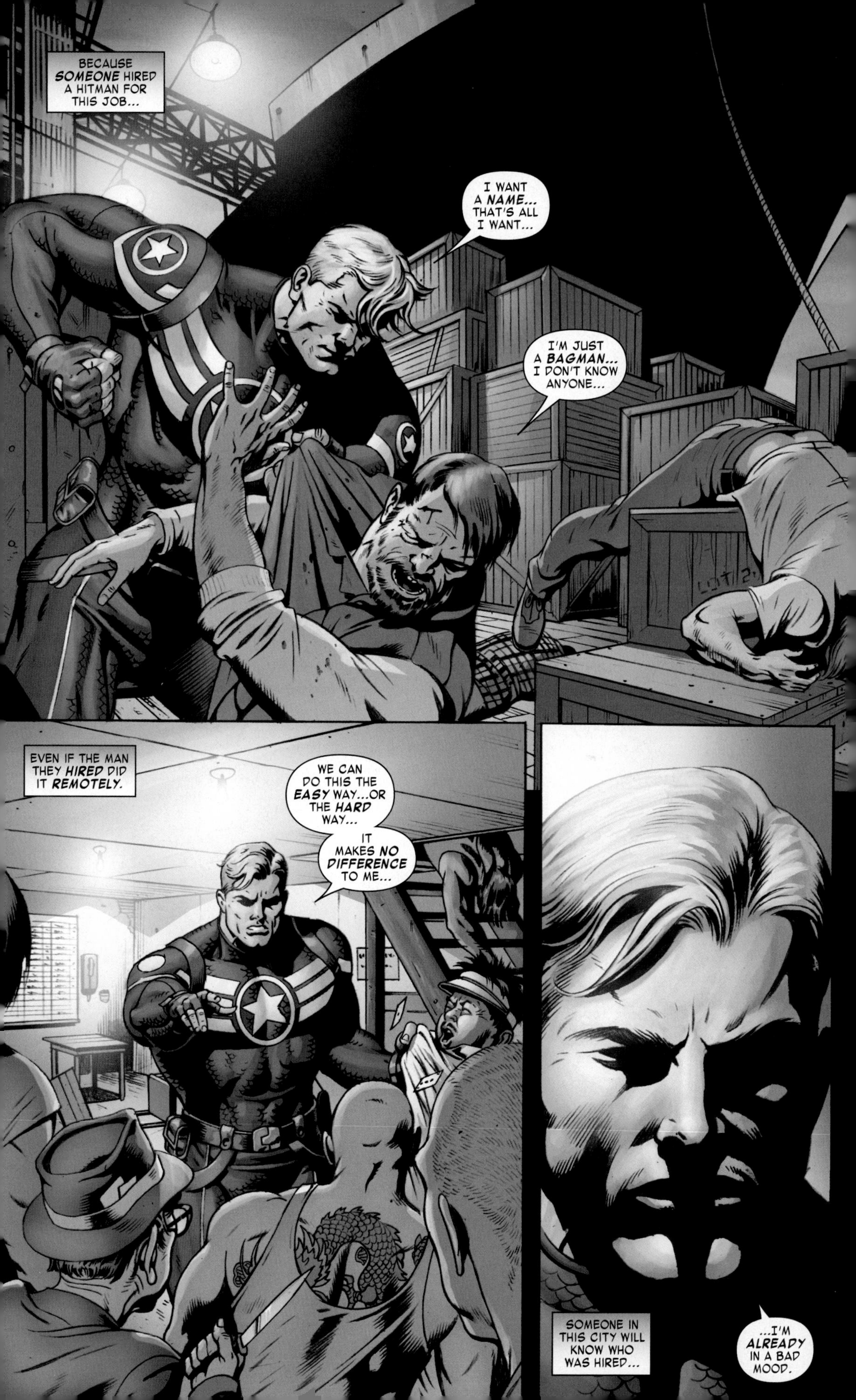
BECAUSE SOMEONE HIRED A HITMAN FOR THIS JOB...
I WANT A NAME... THAT'S ALL I WANT...
I'M JUST A BAGMAN... I DON'T KNOW ANYONE...
EVEN IF THE MAN THEY HIRED DID IT REMOTELY.
WE CAN DO THIS THE EASY WAY...OR THE HARD WAY...
IT MAKES NO DIFFERENCE TO ME...
SOMEONE IN THIS CITY WILL KNOW WHO WAS HIRED...
...I'M ALREADY IN A BAD MOOD.

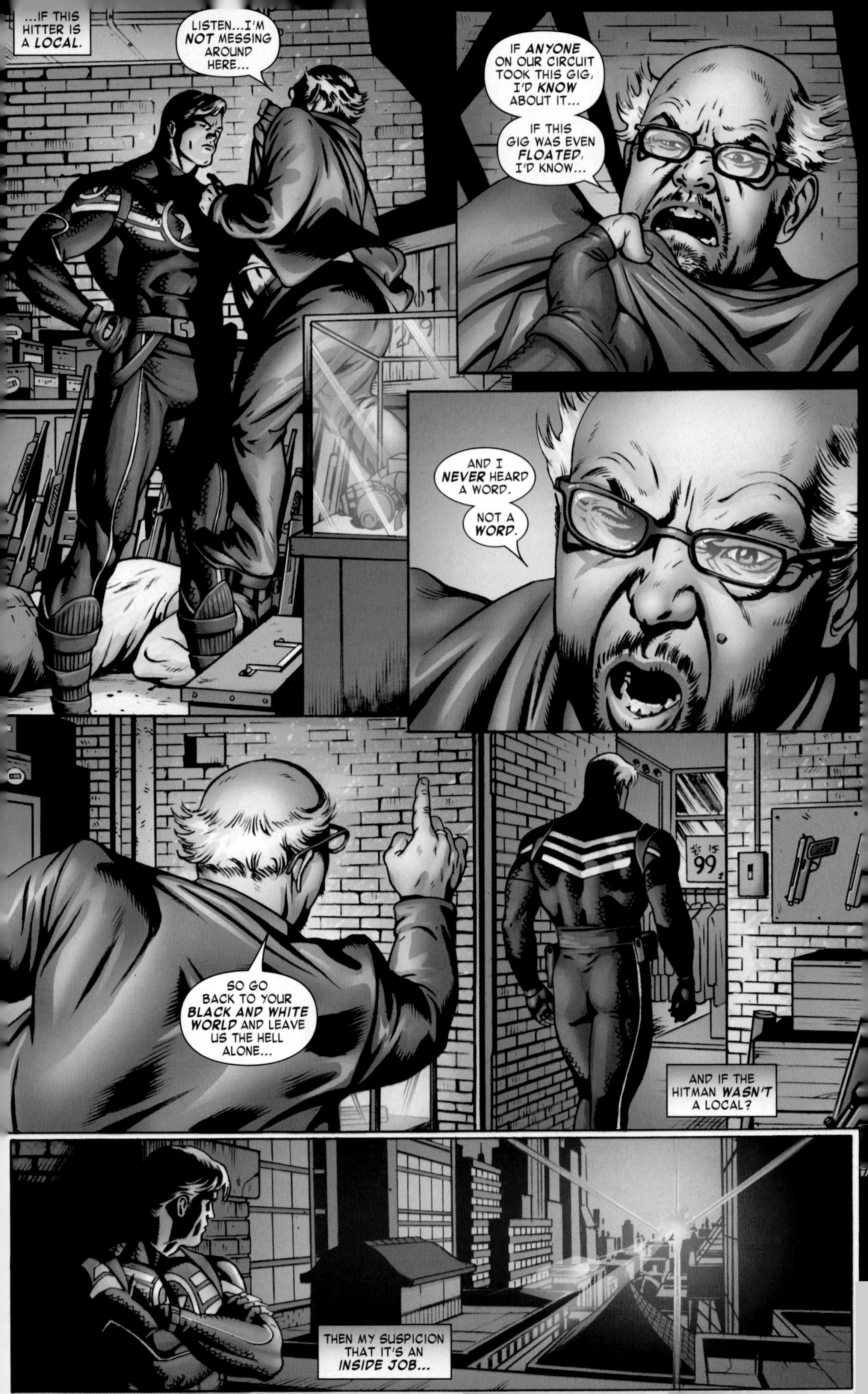
...IF THIS HITTER IS A LOCAL.
LISTEN...I'M NOT MESSING AROUND HERE...
IF ANYONE ON OUR CIRCUIT TOOK THIS GIG, I'D KNOW ABOUT IT...
IF THIS GIG WAS EVEN FLOATED, I'D KNOW...
AND I NEVER HEARD A WORD.
NOT A WORD.
SO GO BACK TO YOUR BLACK AND WHITE WORLD AND LEAVE US THE HELL ALONE...
99
AND IF THE HITMAN WASN'T A LOCAL?
THEN MY SUSPICION THAT IT'S AN INSIDE JOB...

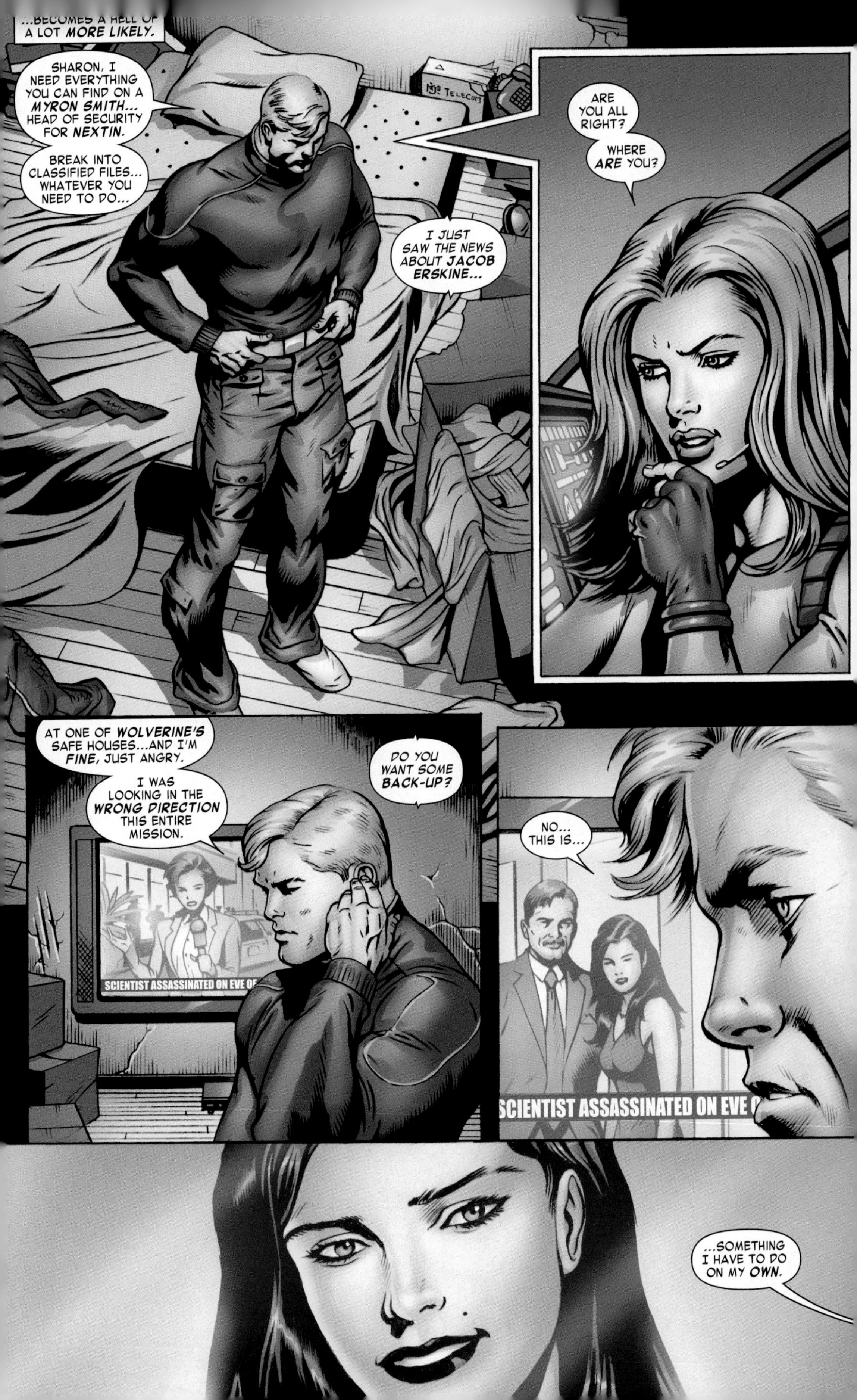
...BECOMES A HELL OF A LOT MORE LIKELY.
SHARON, I NEED EVERYTHING YOU CAN FIND ON A MYRON SMITH... HEAD OF SECURITY FOR NEXTIN.
BREAK INTO CLASSIFIED FILES... WHATEVER YOU NEED TO DO...
TELECOM
ARE YOU ALL RIGHT?
WHERE ARE YOU?
I JUST SAW THE NEWS ABOUT JACOB ERSKINE...
AT ONE OF WOLVERINE'S SAFE HOUSES...AND I'M FINE, JUST ANGRY.
I WAS LOOKING IN THE WRONG DIRECTION THIS ENTIRE MISSION.
DO YOU WANT SOME BACK-UP?
SCIENTIST ASSASSINATED ON EVE O
NO... THIS IS...
SCIENTIST ASSASSINATED ON EVE O
...SOMETHING I HAVE TO DO ON MY OWN.

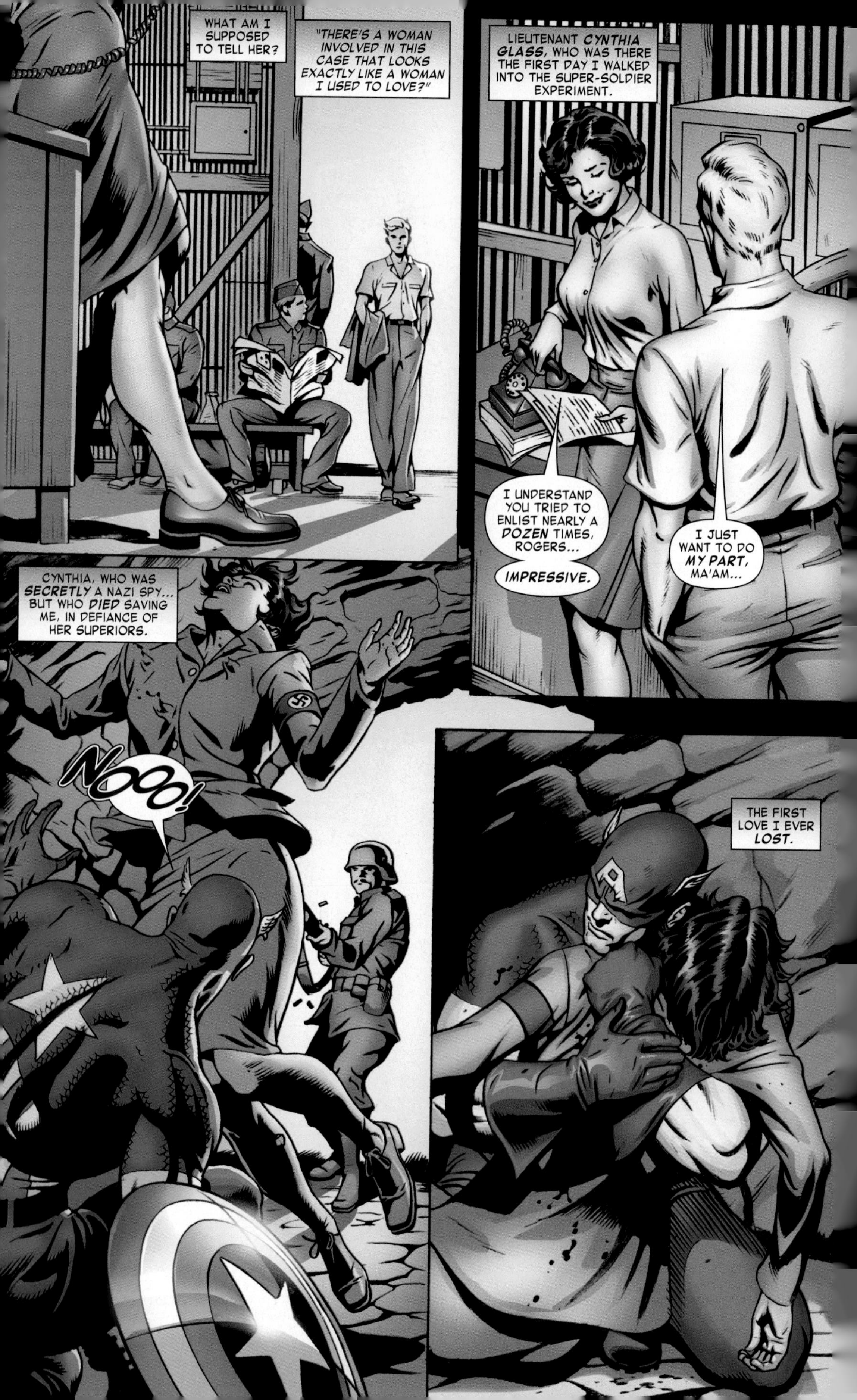
WHAT AM I SUPPOSED TO TELL HER?
"THERE'S A WOMAN INVOLVED IN THIS CASE THAT LOOKS EXACTLY LIKE A WOMAN I USED TO LOVE?"
LIEUTENANT CYNTHIA GLASS, WHO WAS THERE THE FIRST DAY I WALKED INTO THE SUPER-SOLDIER EXPERIMENT.
I UNDERSTAND YOU TRIED TO ENLIST NEARLY A DOZEN TIMES, ROGERS...
IMPRESSIVE.
I JUST WANT TO DO MY PART, MA'AM...
CYNTHIA, WHO WAS SECRETLY A NAZI SPY... BUT WHO DIED SAVING ME, IN DEFIANCE OF HER SUPERIORS.
NOOO!
THE FIRST LOVE I EVER LOST.

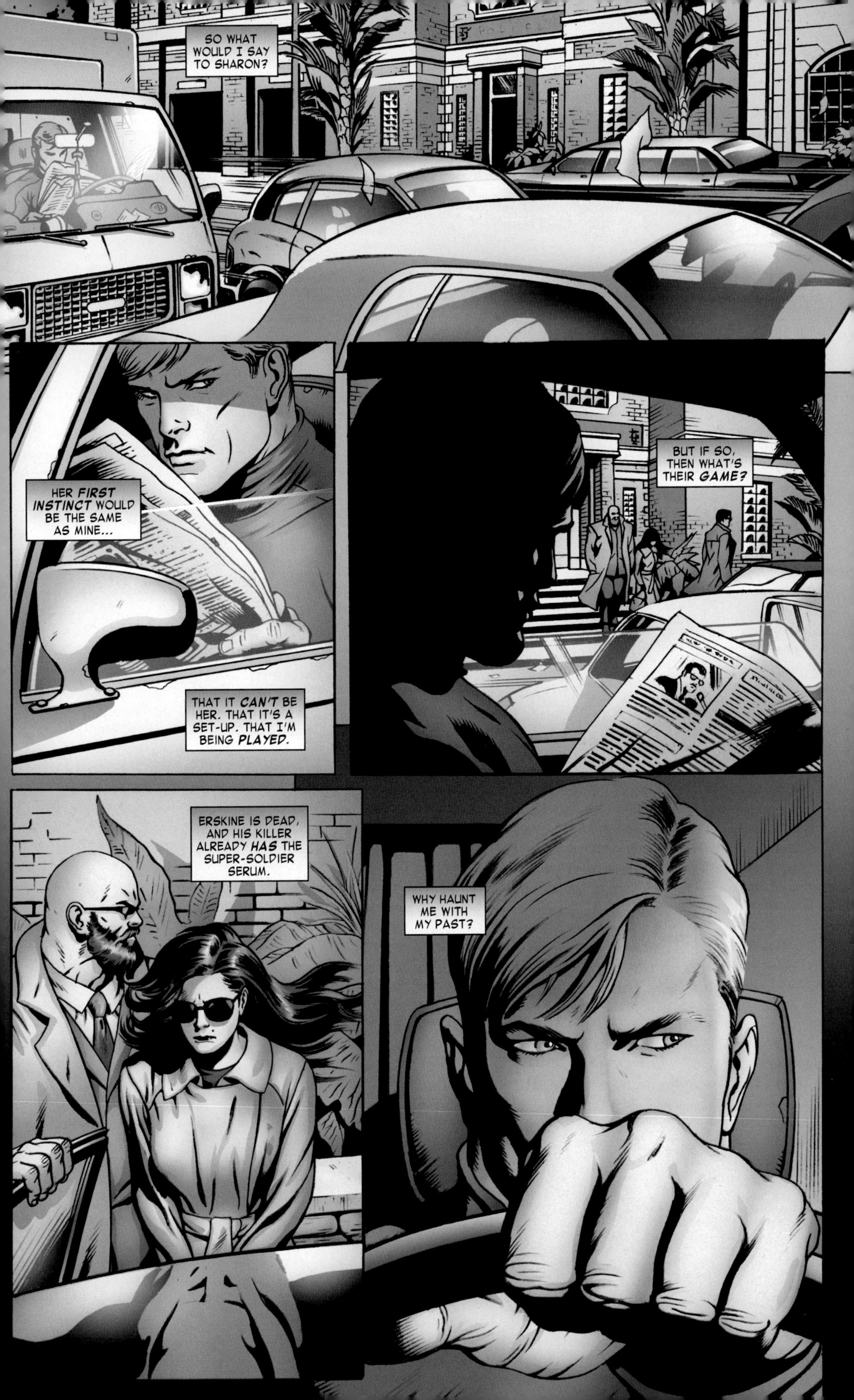
SO WHAT WOULD I SAY TO SHARON?
HER FIRST INSTINCT WOULD BE THE SAME AS MINE...
THAT IT CAN'T BE HER. THAT IT'S A SET-UP. THAT I'M BEING PLAYED.
BUT IF SO, THEN WHAT'S THEIR GAME?
ERSKINE IS DEAD, AND HIS KILLER ALREADY HAS THE SUPER-SOLDIER SERUM.
WHY HAUNT ME WITH MY PAST?

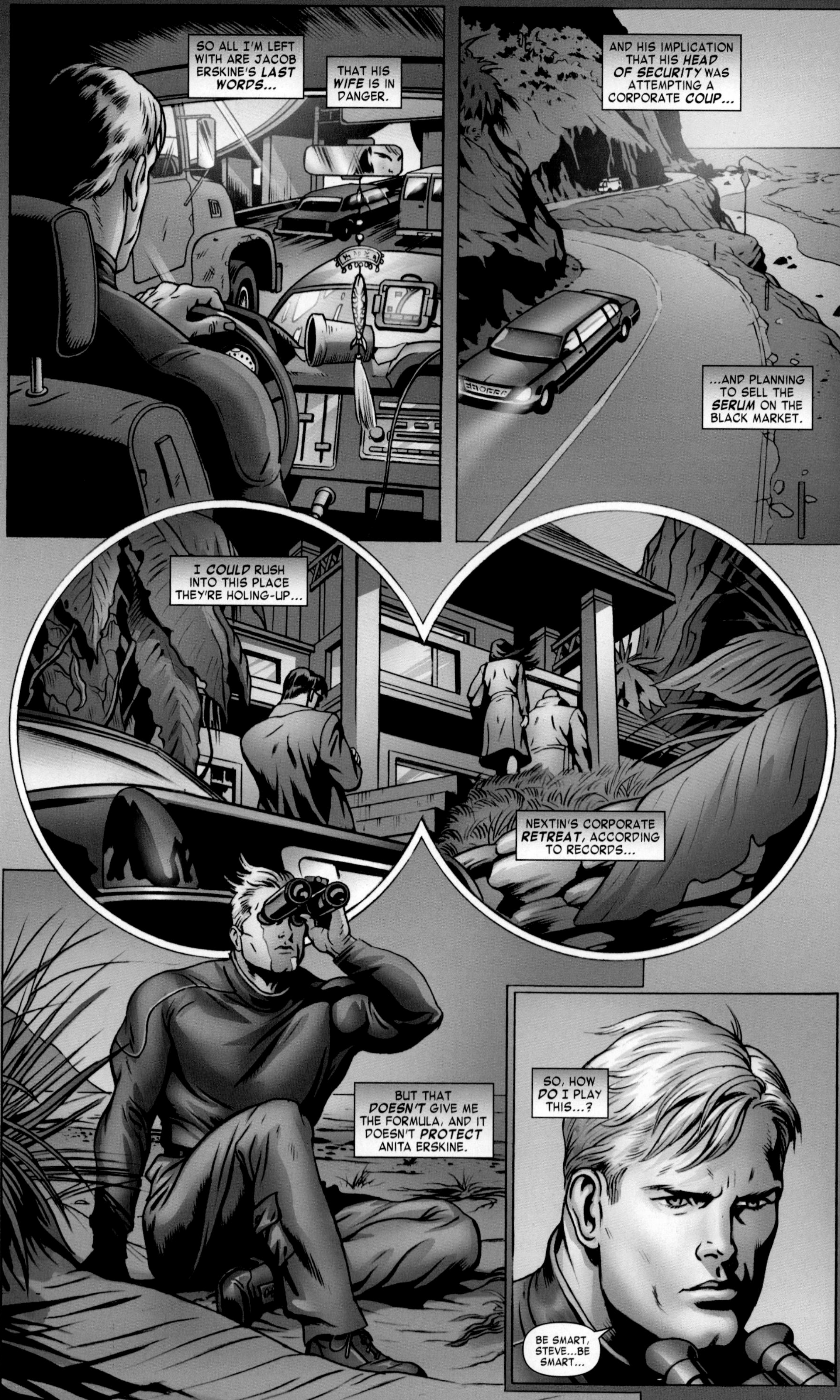
SO ALL I'M LEFT WITH ARE JACOB ERSKINE'S LAST WORDS...
THAT HIS WIFE IS IN DANGER.
AND HIS IMPLICATION THAT HIS HEAD OF SECURITY WAS ATTEMPTING A CORPORATE COUP...
...AND PLANNING TO SELL THE SERUM ON THE BLACK MARKET.
I COULD RUSH INTO THIS PLACE THEY'RE HOLING-UP...
NEXTIN'S CORPORATE RETREAT, ACCORDING TO RECORDS...
BUT THAT DOESN'T GIVE ME THE FORMULA, AND IT DOESN'T PROTECT ANITA ERSKINE.
SO, HOW DO I PLAY THIS...?
BE SMART, STEVE...BE SMART...

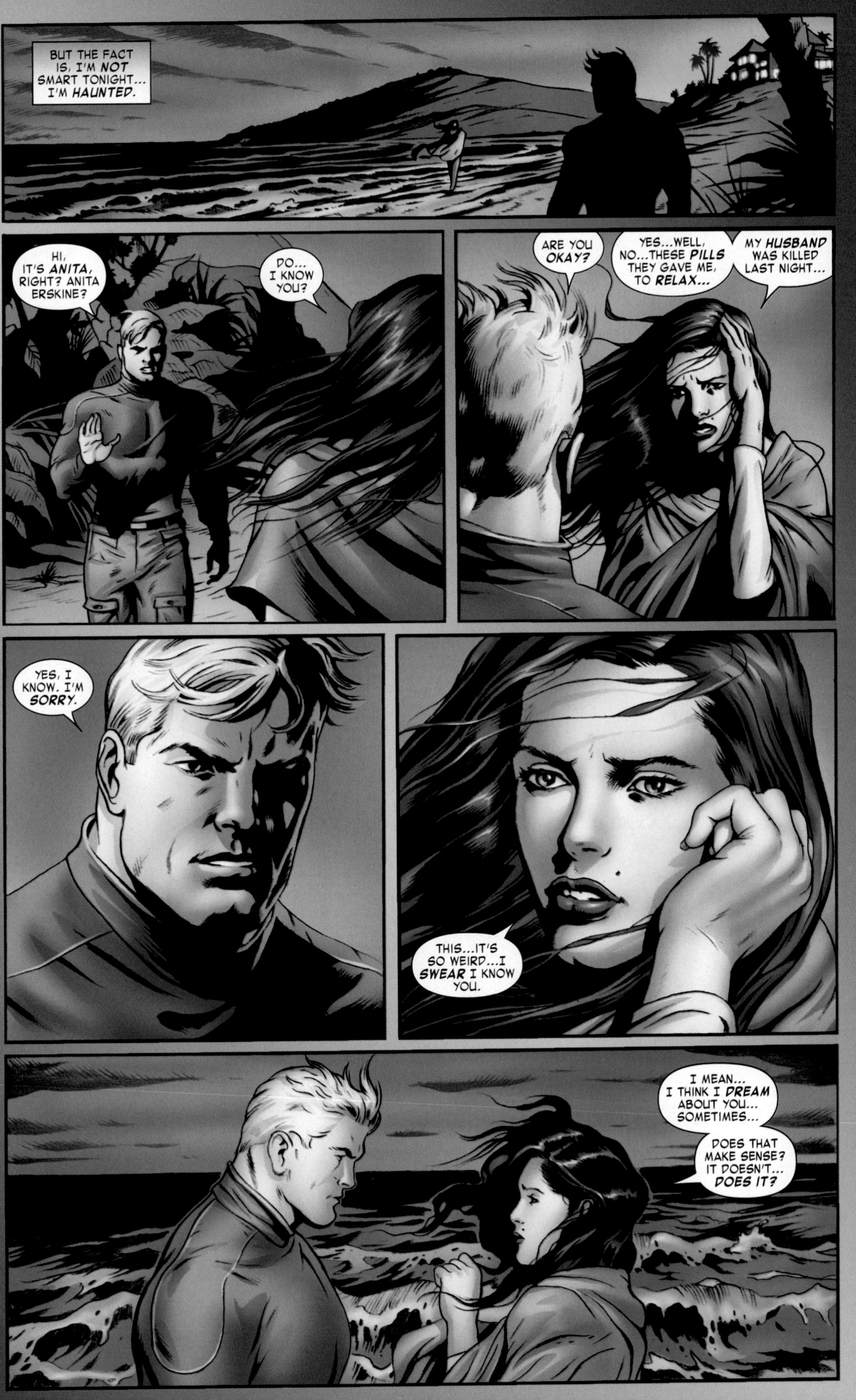
BUT THE FACT IS, I'M NOT SMART TONIGHT... I'M HAUNTED.
HI, IT'S ANITA, RIGHT? ANITA ERSKINE?
DO... I KNOW YOU?
ARE YOU OKAY?
YES...WELL, NO...THESE PILLS THEY GAVE ME, TO RELAX...
MY HUSBAND WAS KILLED LAST NIGHT...
YES, I KNOW. I'M SORRY.
THIS...IT'S SO WEIRD...I SWEAR I KNOW YOU.
I MEAN... I THINK I DREAM ABOUT YOU... SOMETIMES...
DOES THAT MAKE SENSE? IT DOESN'T... DOES IT?

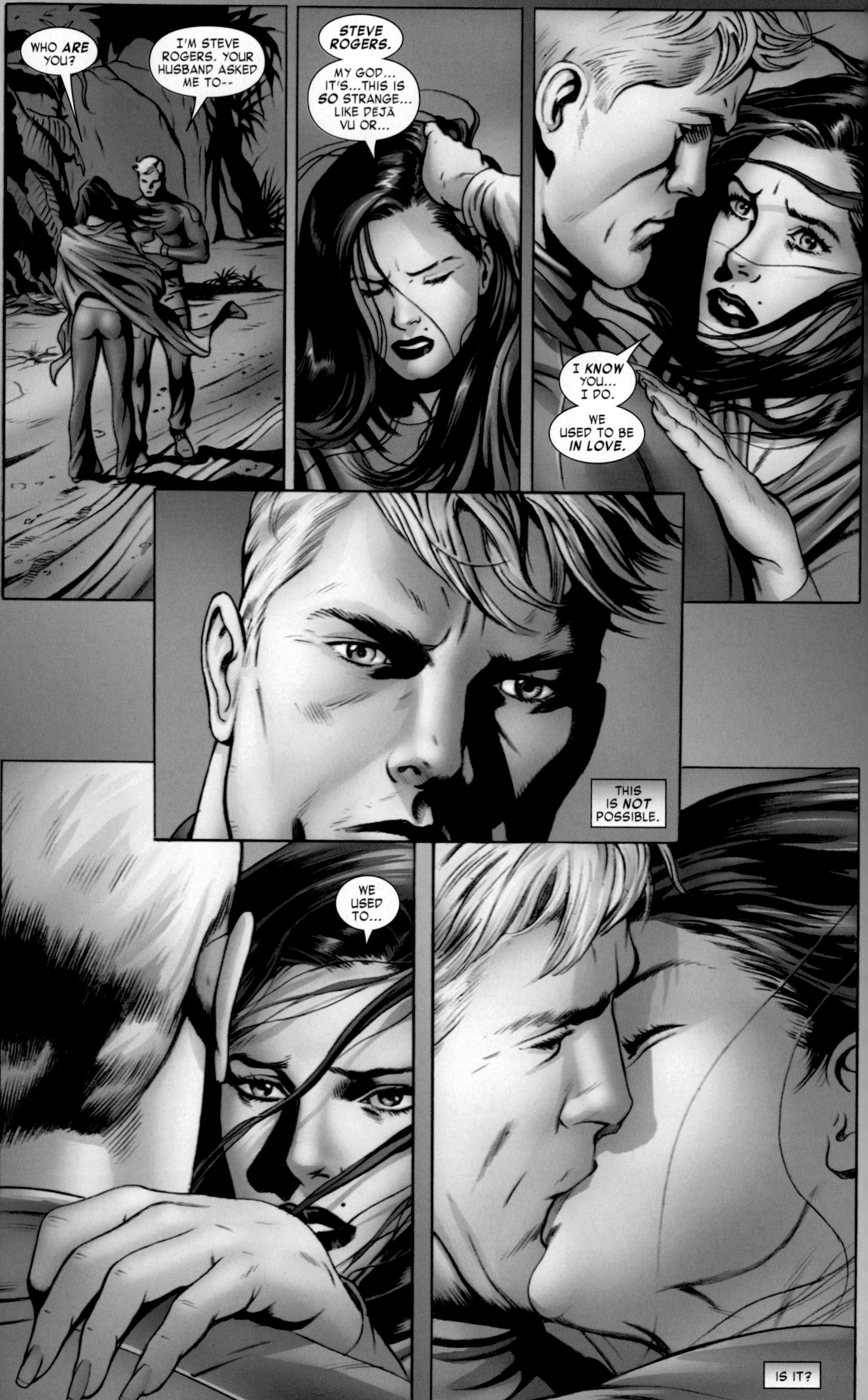
WHO ARE YOU?
I'M STEVE ROGERS. YOUR HUSBAND ASKED ME TO--
STEVE ROGERS.
MY GOD... IT'S...THIS IS SO STRANGE... LIKE DEJÀ VU OR...
I KNOW YOU... I DO.
WE USED TO BE IN LOVE.
THIS IS NOT POSSIBLE.
WE USED TO...
IS IT?

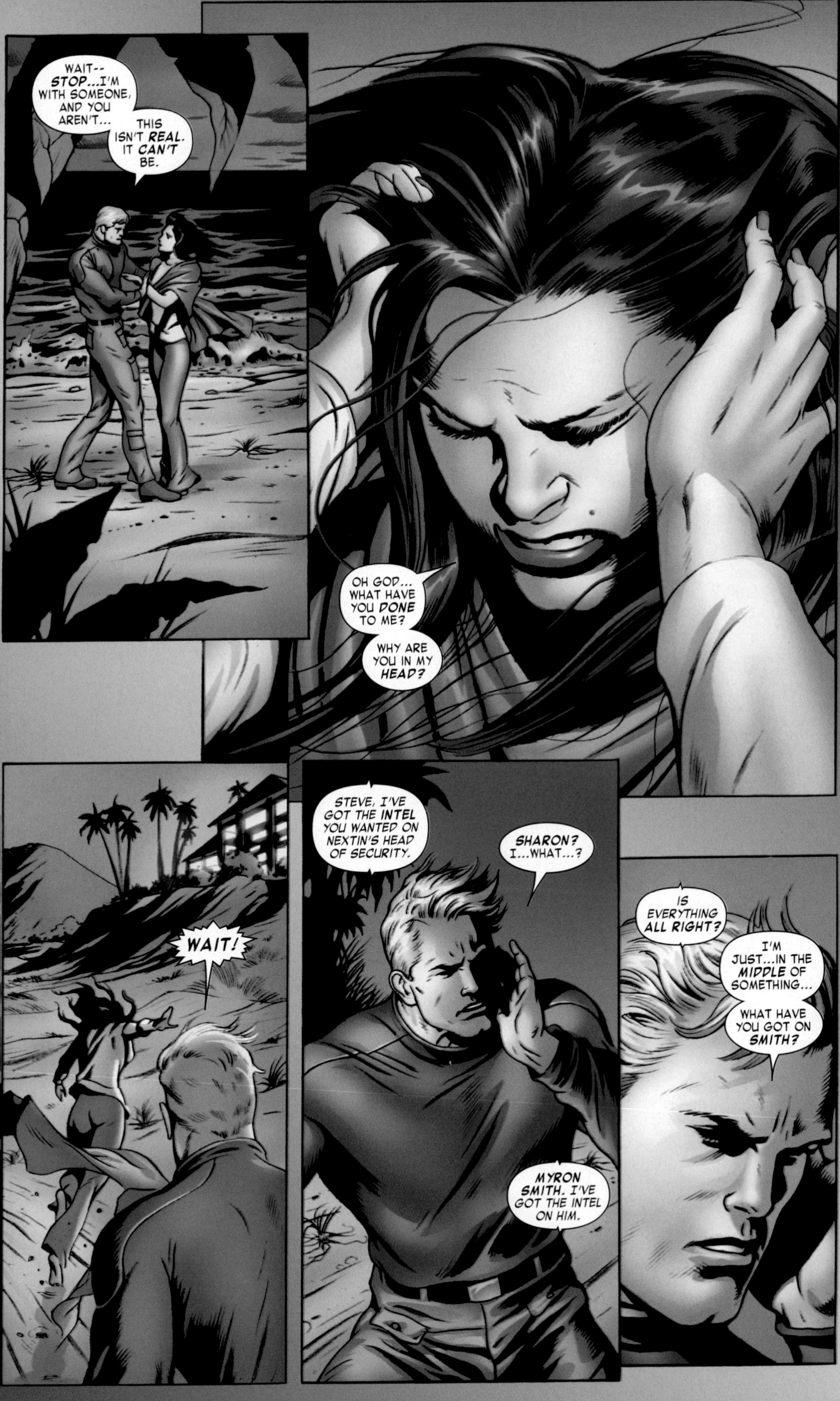
WAIT-- STOP...I'M WITH SOMEONE, AND YOU AREN'T...
THIS ISN'T REAL. IT CAN'T BE.
OH GOD... WHAT HAVE YOU DONE TO ME?
WHY ARE YOU IN MY HEAD?
WAIT!
STEVE, I'VE GOT THE INTEL YOU WANTED ON NEXTIN'S HEAD OF SECURITY.
SHARON? I...WHAT...?
IS EVERYTHING ALL RIGHT?
I'M JUST...IN THE MIDDLE OF SOMETHING...
WHAT HAVE YOU GOT ON SMITH?
MYRON SMITH. I'VE GOT THE INTEL ON HIM.

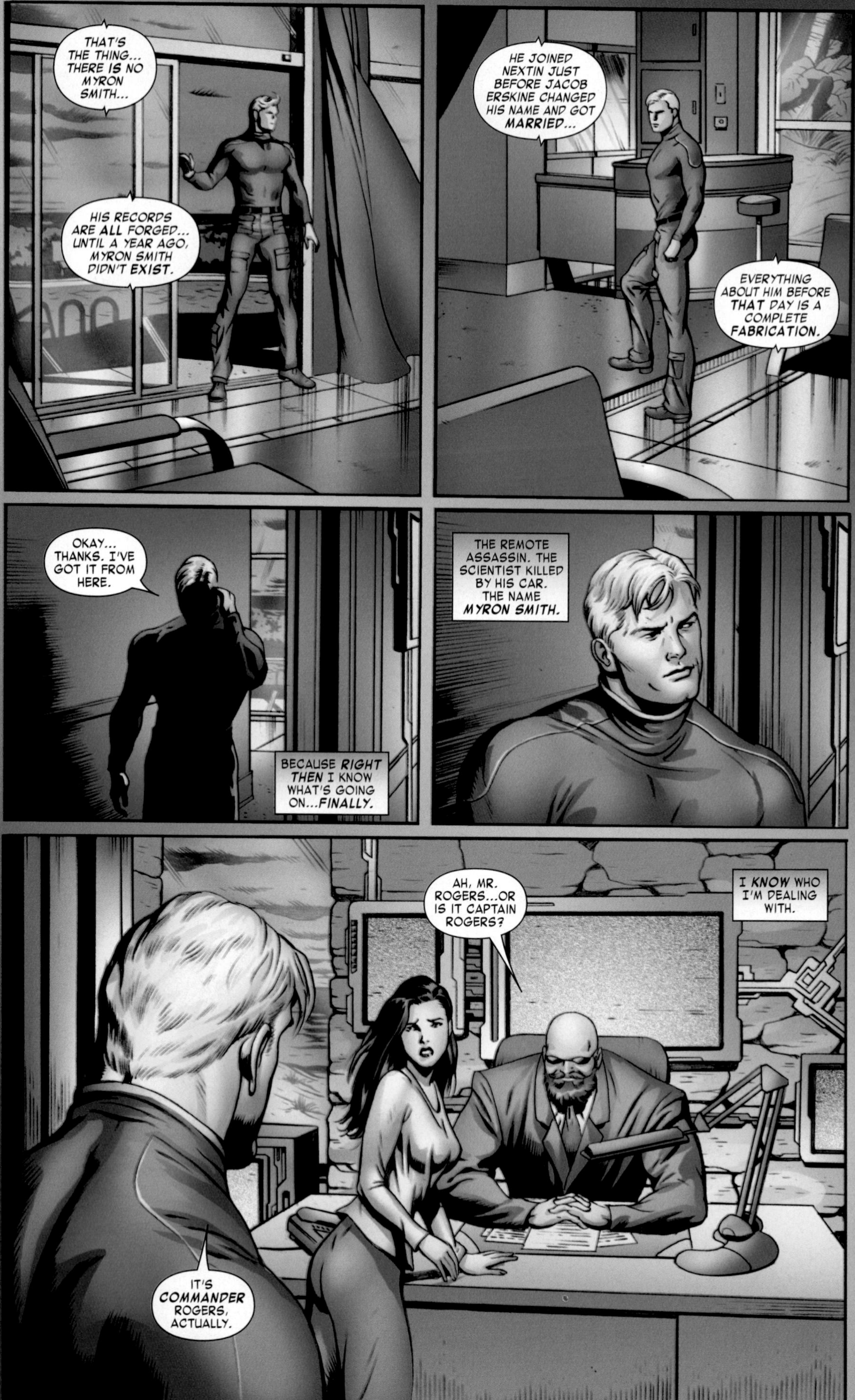
THAT'S THE THING... THERE IS NO MYRON SMITH...
HIS RECORDS ARE ALL FORGED... UNTIL A YEAR AGO, MYRON SMITH DIDN'T EXIST.
HE JOINED NEXTIN JUST BEFORE JACOB ERSKINE CHANGED HIS NAME AND GOT MARRIED...
EVERYTHING ABOUT HIM BEFORE THAT DAY IS A COMPLETE FABRICATION.
OKAY... THANKS. I'VE GOT IT FROM HERE.
BECAUSE RIGHT THEN I KNOW WHAT'S GOING ON...FINALLY.
THE REMOTE ASSASSIN. THE SCIENTIST KILLED BY HIS CAR. THE NAME MYRON SMITH.
AH, MR. ROGERS...OR IS IT CAPTAIN ROGERS?
I KNOW WHO I'M DEALING WITH.
IT'S COMMANDER ROGERS, ACTUALLY.

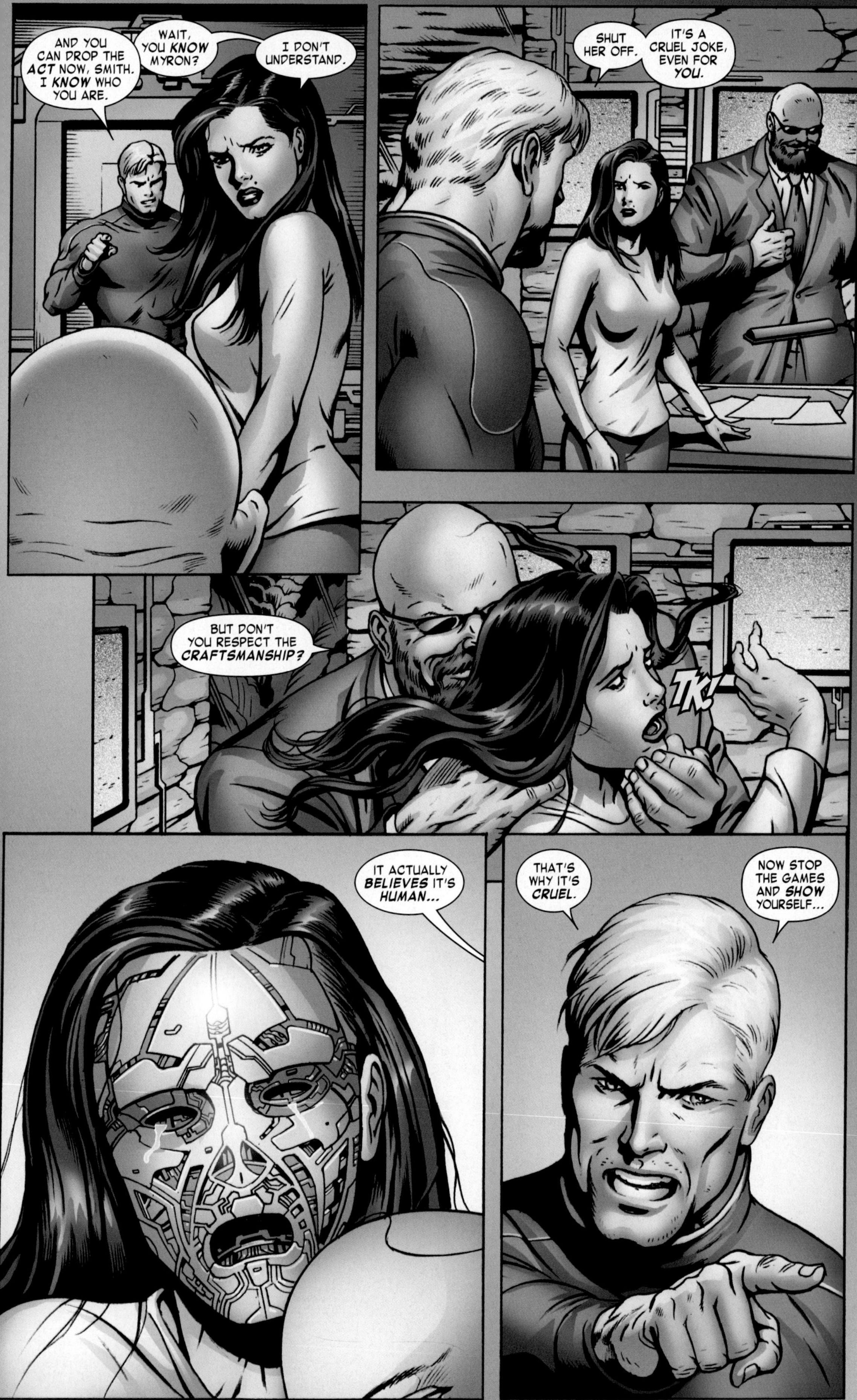
AND YOU CAN DROP THE ACT NOW, SMITH. I KNOW WHO YOU ARE.
WAIT, YOU KNOW MYRON?
I DON'T UNDERSTAND.
SHUT HER OFF.
IT'S A CRUEL JOKE, EVEN FOR YOU.
BUT DON'T YOU RESPECT THE CRAFTSMANSHIP?
TK!
IT ACTUALLY BELIEVES IT'S HUMAN...
THAT'S WHY IT'S CRUEL.
NOW STOP THE GAMES AND SHOW YOURSELF...

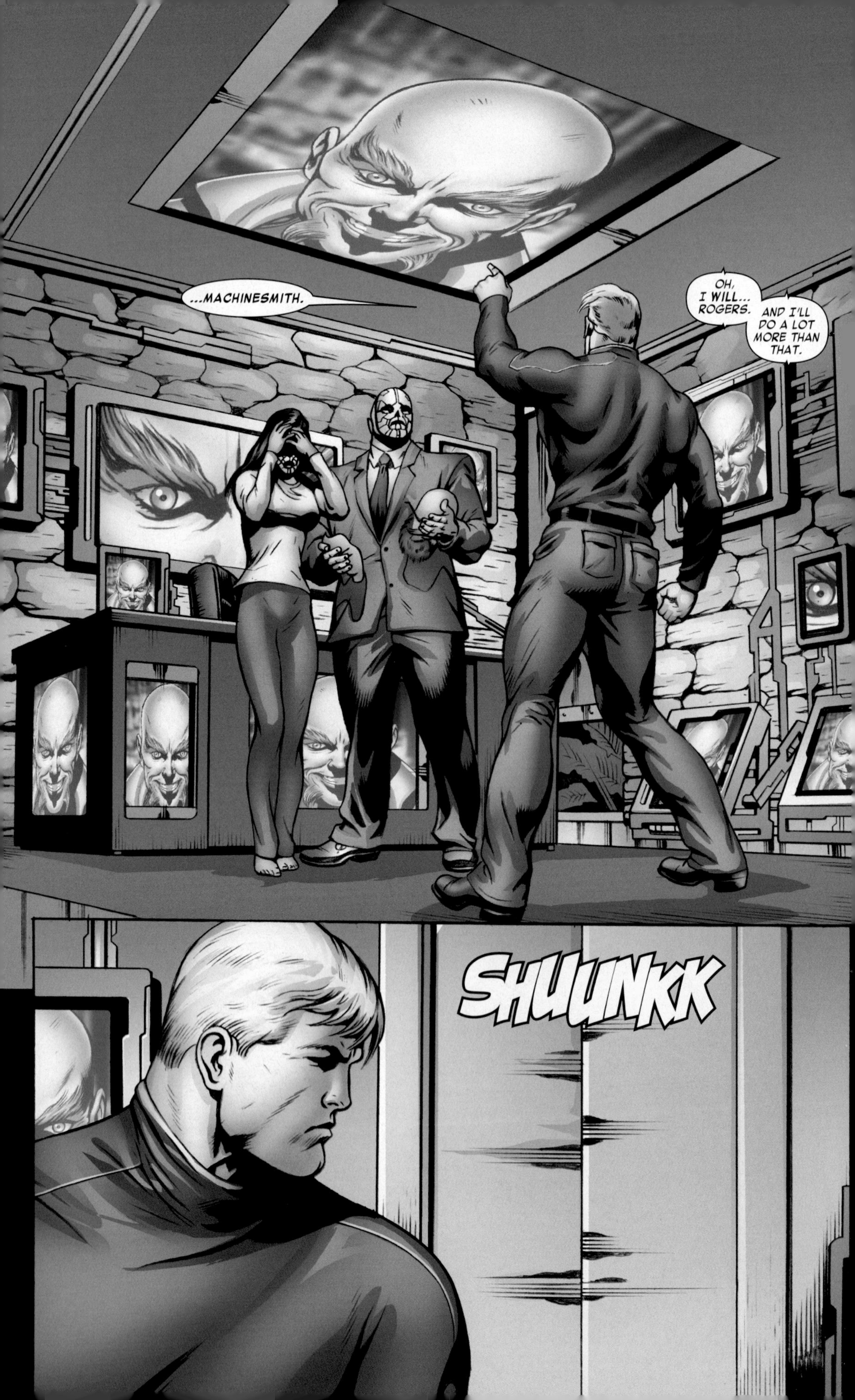
...MACHINESMITH.
OH, I WILL... ROGERS.
AND I'LL DO A LOT MORE THAN THAT.
SHUUNKK

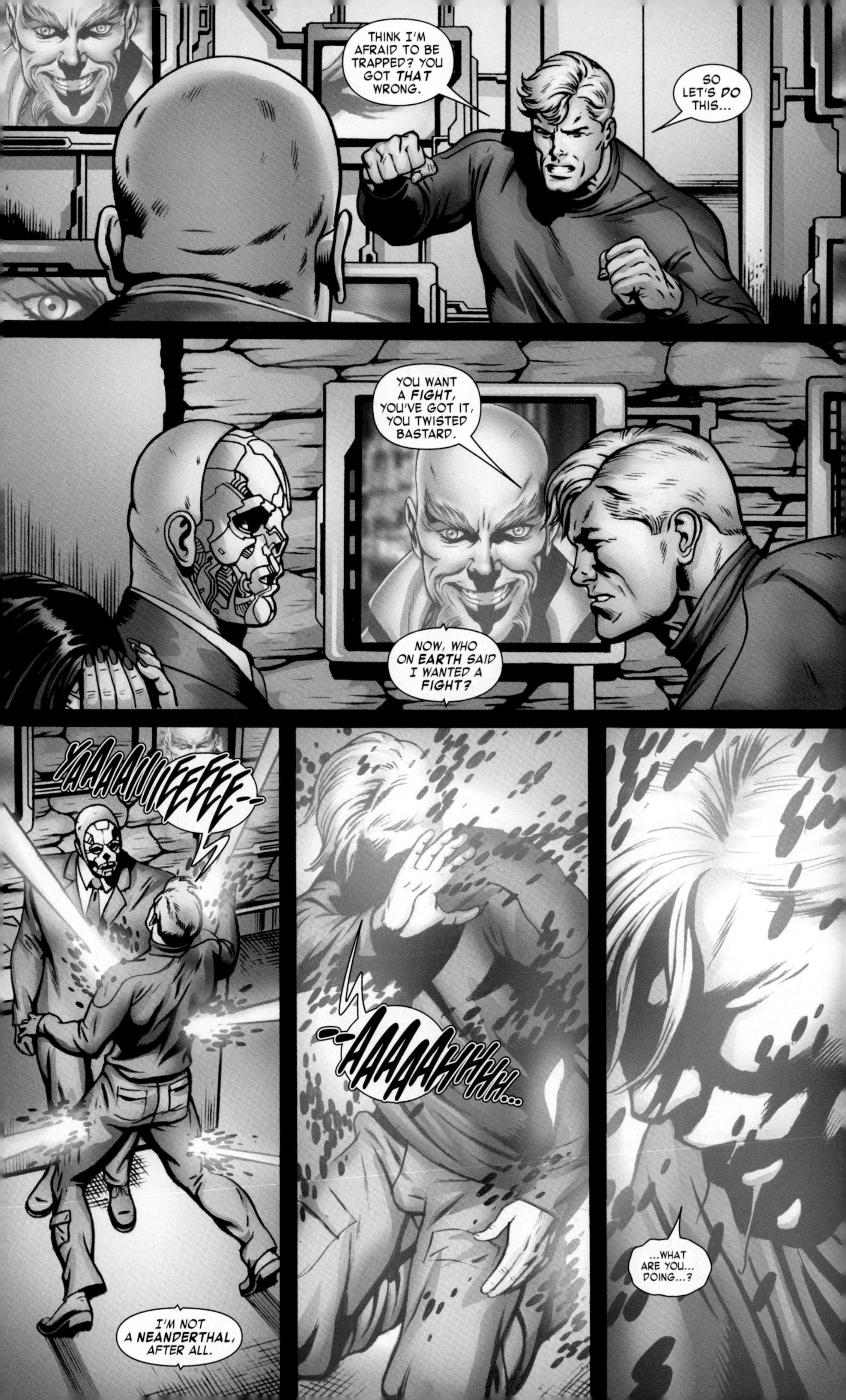
THINK I'M AFRAID TO BE TRAPPED? YOU GOT THAT WRONG.
SO LET'S DO THIS...
YOU WANT A FIGHT, YOU'VE GOT IT, YOU TWISTED BASTARD.
NOW, WHO ON EARTH SAID I WANTED A FIGHT?
YAAAAAIIIEEEEE--
I'M NOT A NEANDERTHAL, AFTER ALL.
--AAAAAHHHHH...
...WHAT ARE YOU... DOING...?

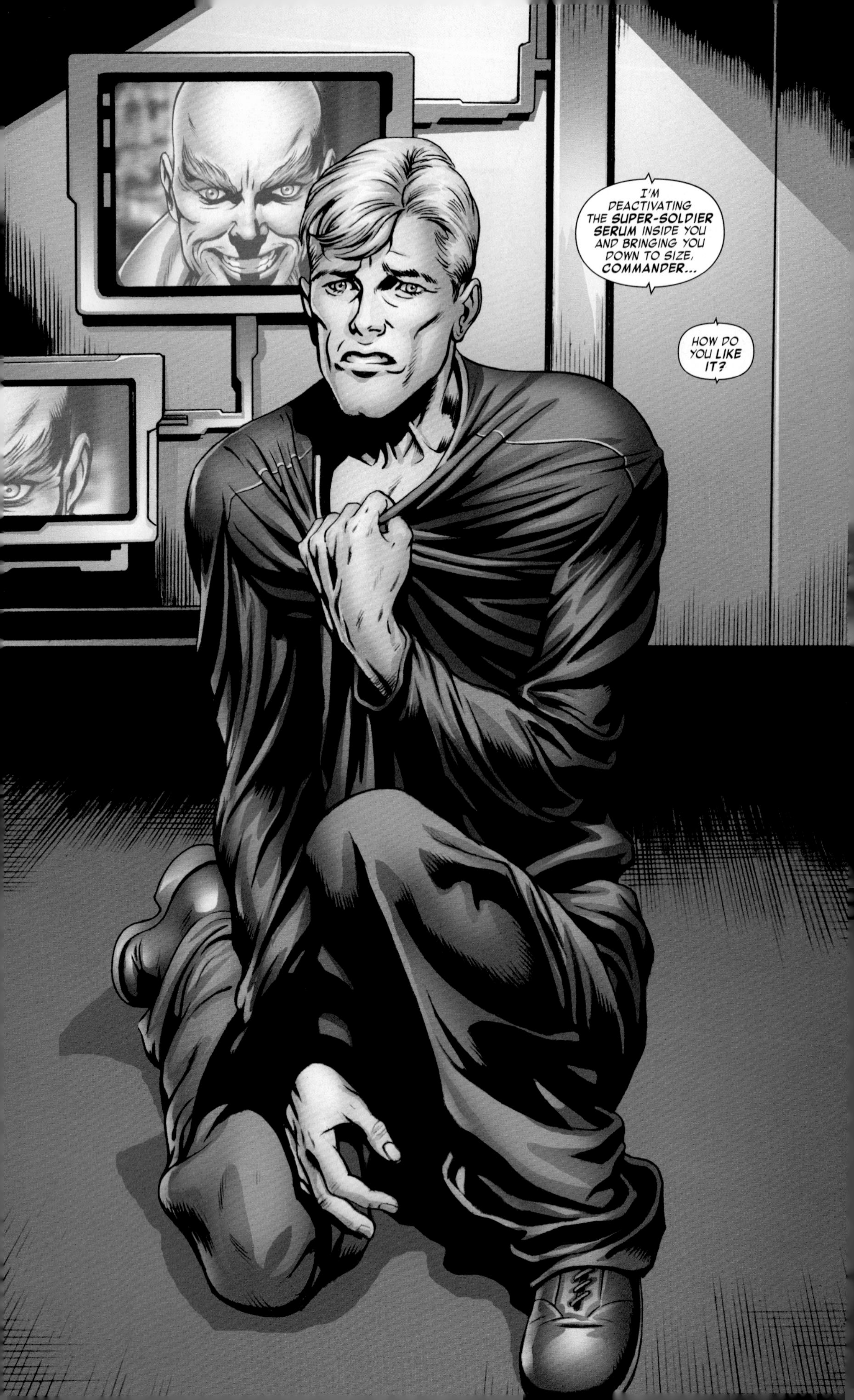
I'M DEACTIVATING THE SUPER-SOLDIER SERUM INSIDE YOU AND BRINGING YOU DOWN TO SIZE, COMMANDER...
HOW DO YOU LIKE IT?

3

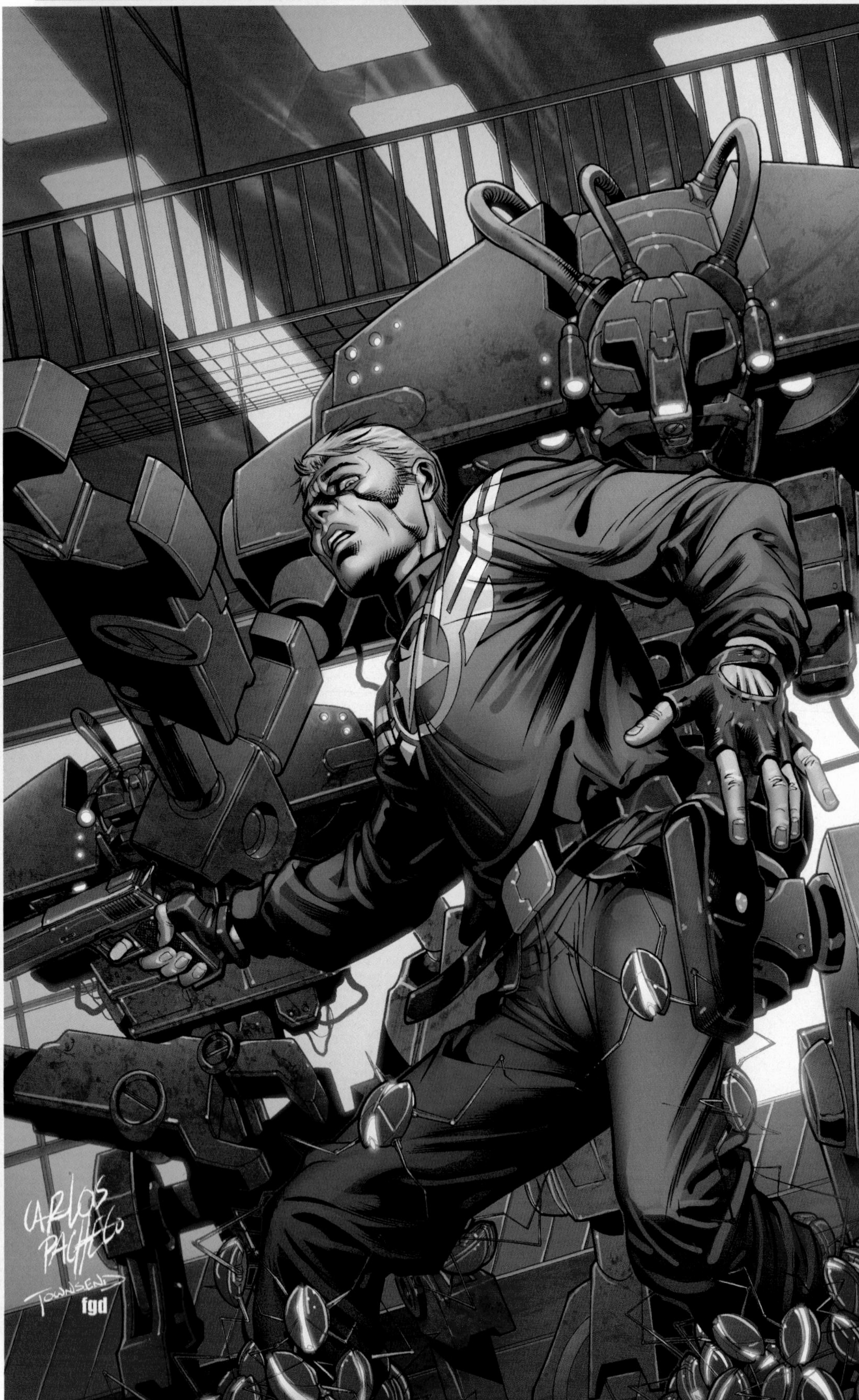
CARLOS PACHECO
TOWNSEND
fgd

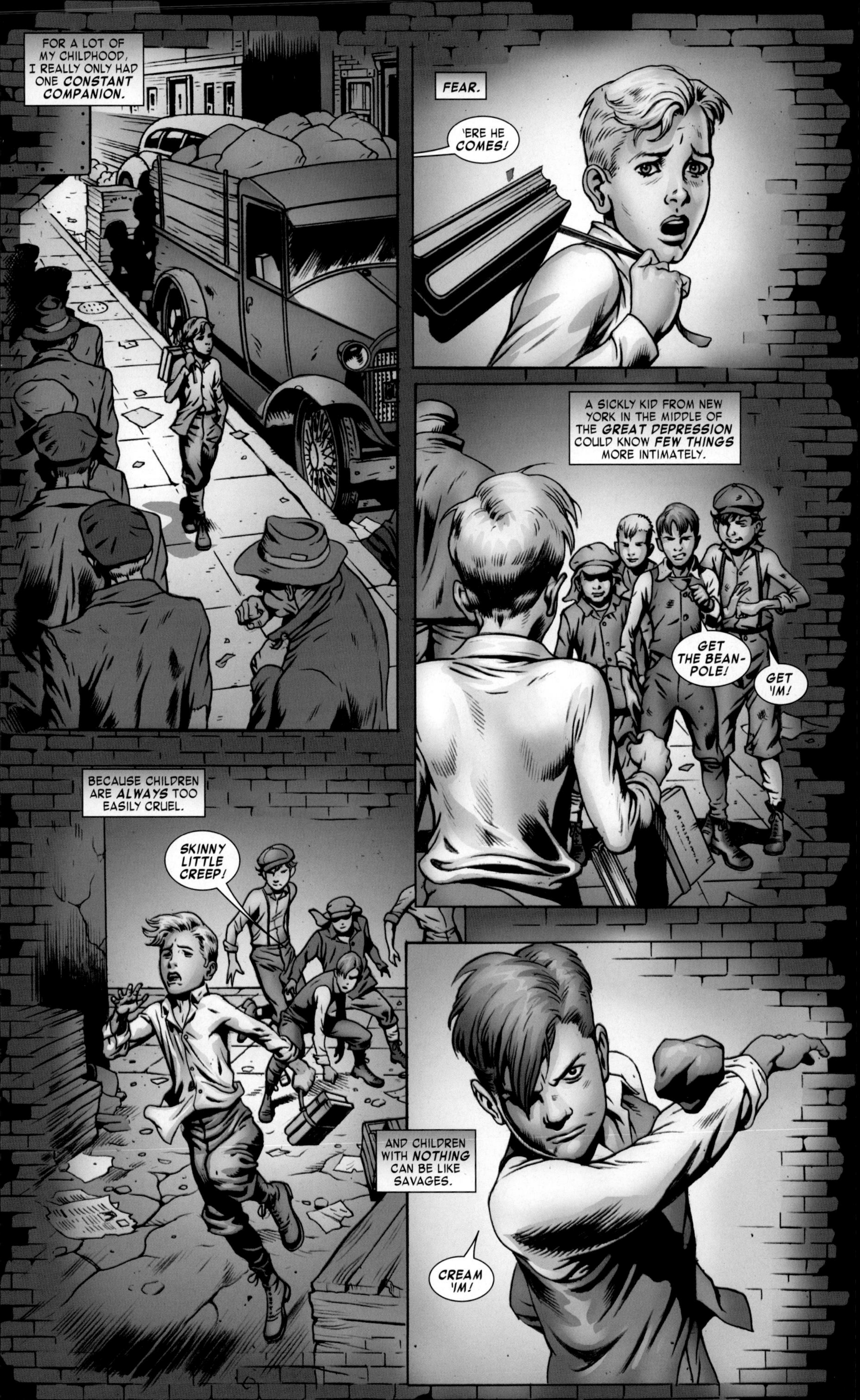
FOR A LOT OF MY CHILDHOOD, I REALLY ONLY HAD ONE CONSTANT COMPANION.
FEAR.
'ERE HE COMES!
A SICKLY KID FROM NEW YORK IN THE MIDDLE OF THE GREAT DEPRESSION COULD KNOW FEW THINGS MORE INTIMATELY.
GET THE BEAN-POLE!
GET 'IM!
BECAUSE CHILDREN ARE ALWAYS TOO EASILY CRUEL.
SKINNY LITTLE CREEP!
AND CHILDREN WITH NOTHING CAN BE LIKE SAVAGES.
CREAM 'IM!

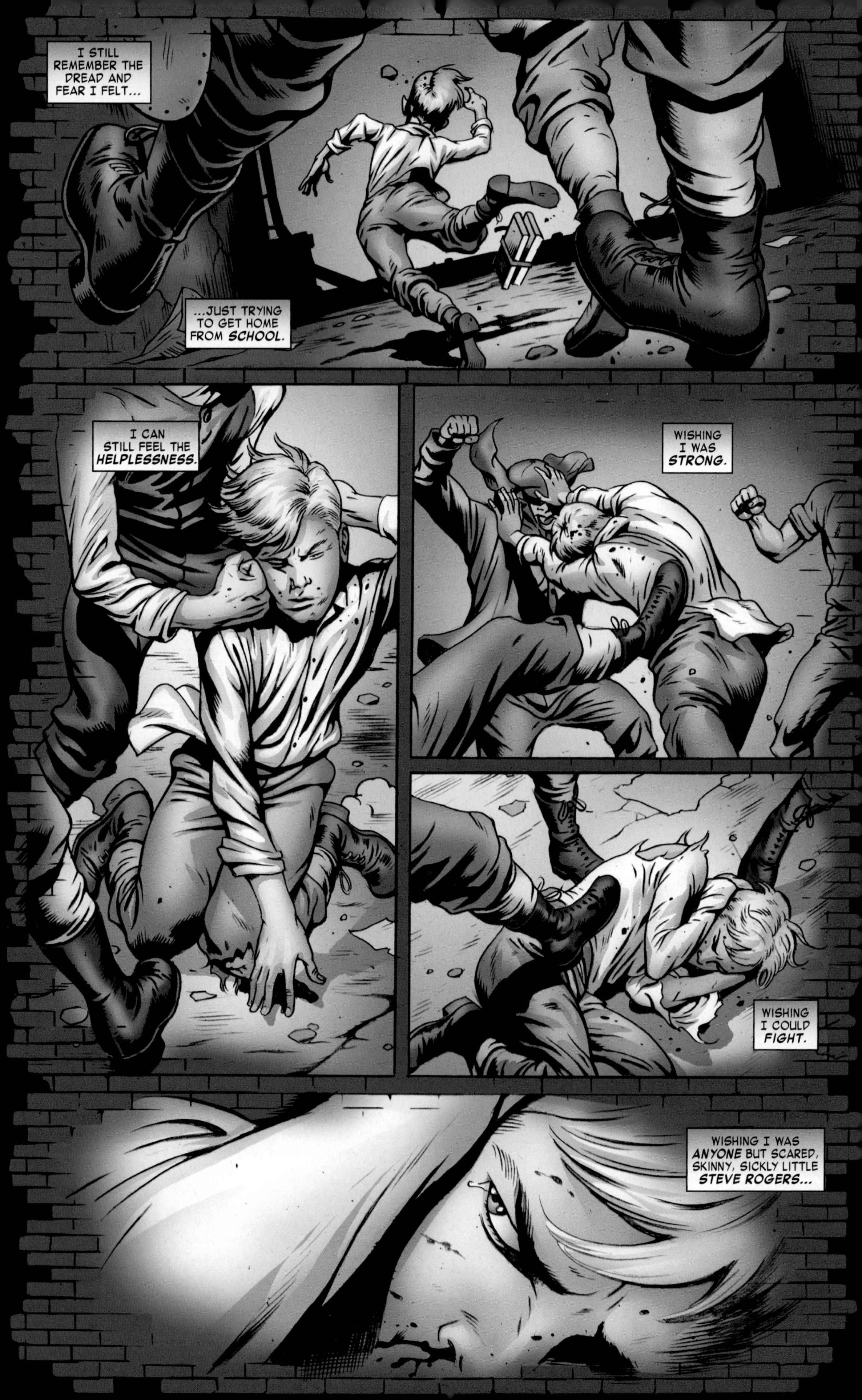
I STILL REMEMBER THE DREAD AND FEAR I FELT...
...JUST TRYING TO GET HOME FROM SCHOOL.
I CAN STILL FEEL THE HELPLESSNESS.
WISHING I WAS STRONG.
WISHING I COULD FIGHT.
WISHING I WAS ANYONE BUT SCARED, SKINNY, SICKLY LITTLE STEVE ROGERS...

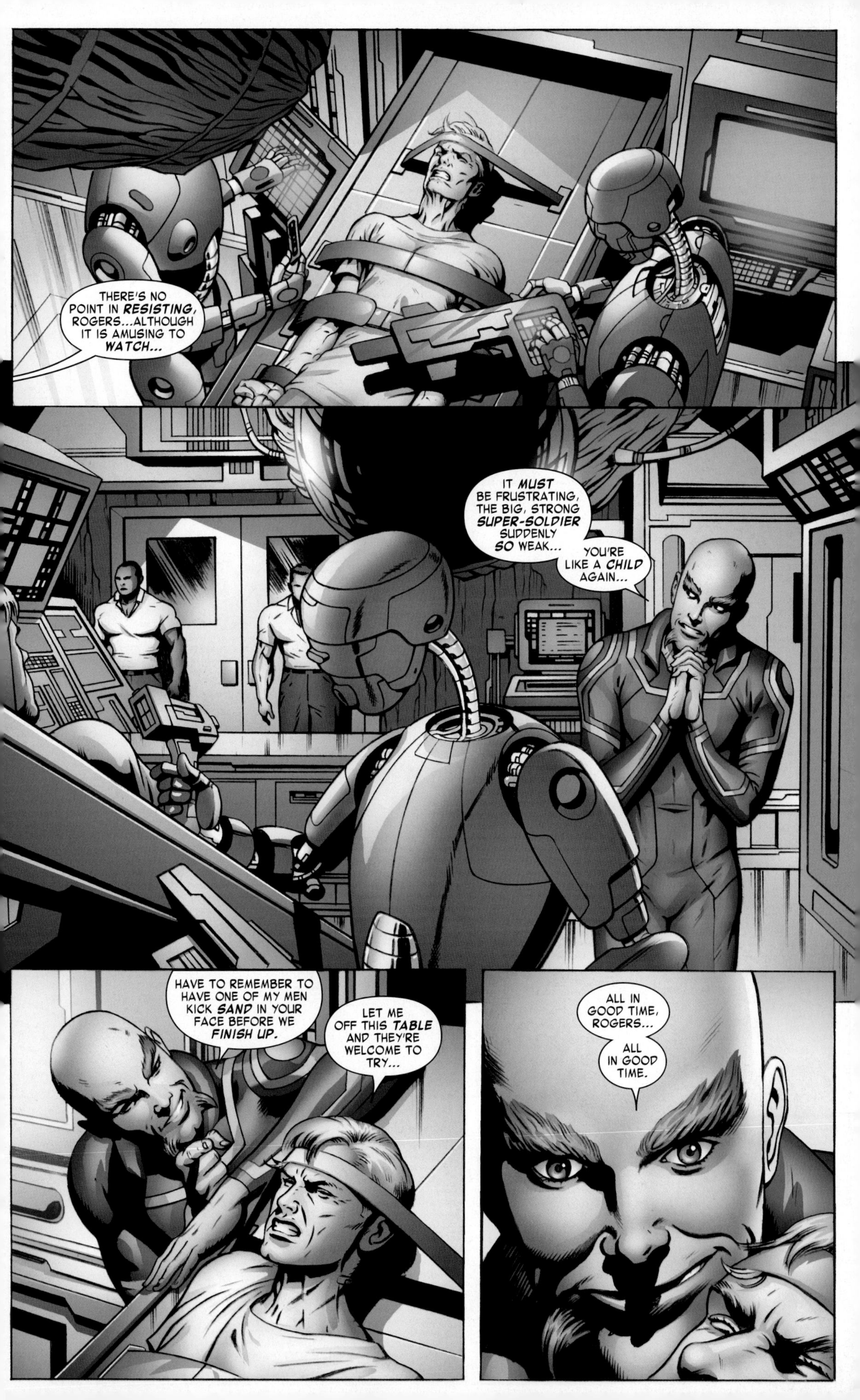
THERE'S NO POINT IN RESISTING, ROGERS...ALTHOUGH IT IS AMUSING TO WATCH...
IT MUST BE FRUSTRATING, THE BIG, STRONG SUPER-SOLDIER SUDDENLY SO WEAK...
YOU'RE LIKE A CHILD AGAIN...
HAVE TO REMEMBER TO HAVE ONE OF MY MEN KICK SAND IN YOUR FACE BEFORE WE FINISH UP.
LET ME OFF THIS TABLE AND THEY'RE WELCOME TO TRY...
ALL IN GOOD TIME, ROGERS...
ALL IN GOOD TIME.

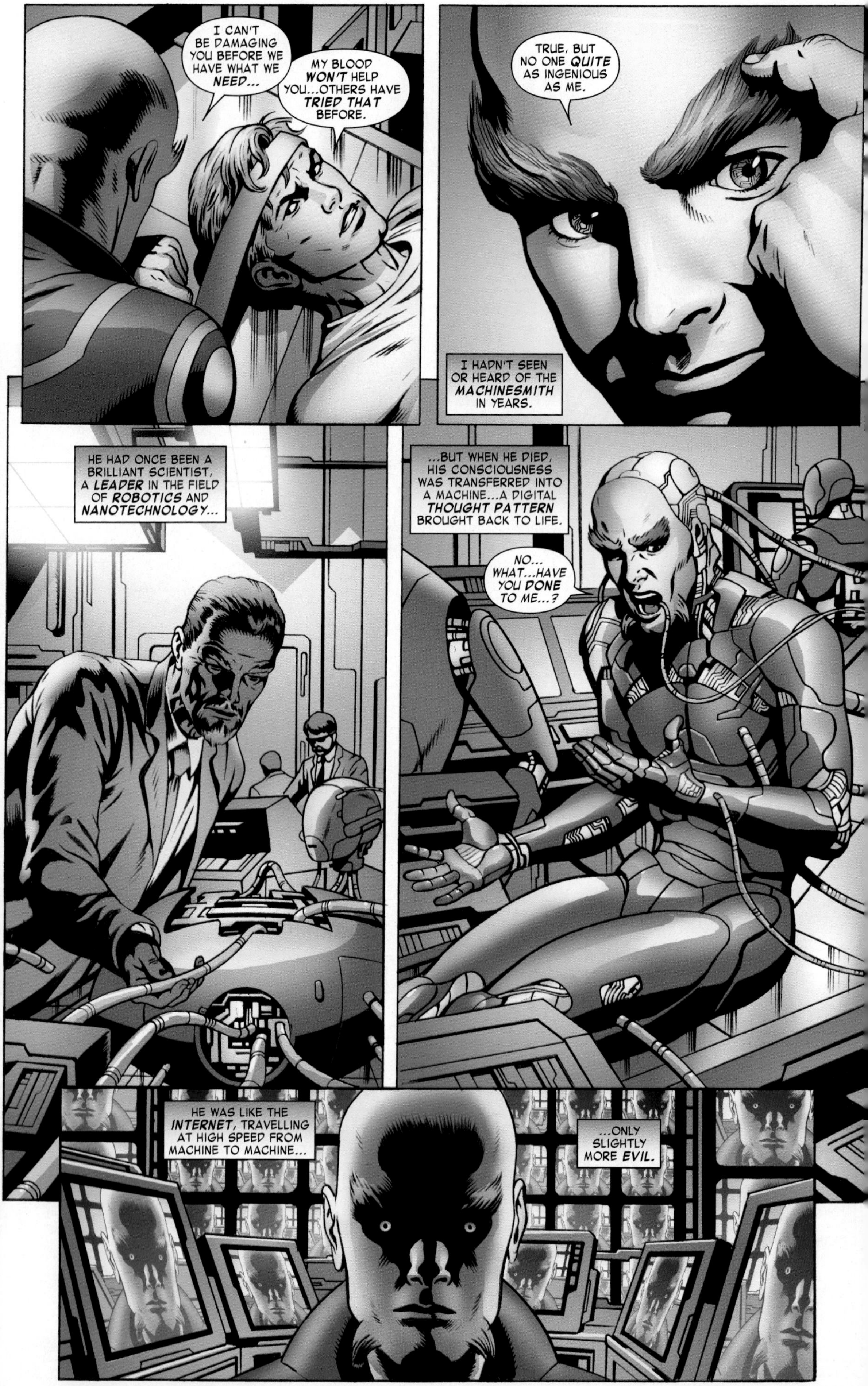
I CAN'T BE DAMAGING YOU BEFORE WE HAVE WHAT WE NEED...
MY BLOOD WON'T HELP YOU...OTHERS HAVE TRIED THAT BEFORE.
TRUE, BUT NO ONE QUITE AS INGENIOUS AS ME.
I HADN'T SEEN OR HEARD OF THE MACHINESMITH IN YEARS.
HE HAD ONCE BEEN A BRILLIANT SCIENTIST, A LEADER IN THE FIELD OF ROBOTICS AND NANOTECHNOLOGY...
...BUT WHEN HE DIED, HIS CONSCIOUSNESS WAS TRANSFERRED INTO A MACHINE...A DIGITAL THOUGHT PATTERN BROUGHT BACK TO LIFE.
NO... WHAT...HAVE YOU DONE TO ME...?
HE WAS LIKE THE INTERNET, TRAVELLING AT HIGH SPEED FROM MACHINE TO MACHINE...
...ONLY SLIGHTLY MORE EVIL.

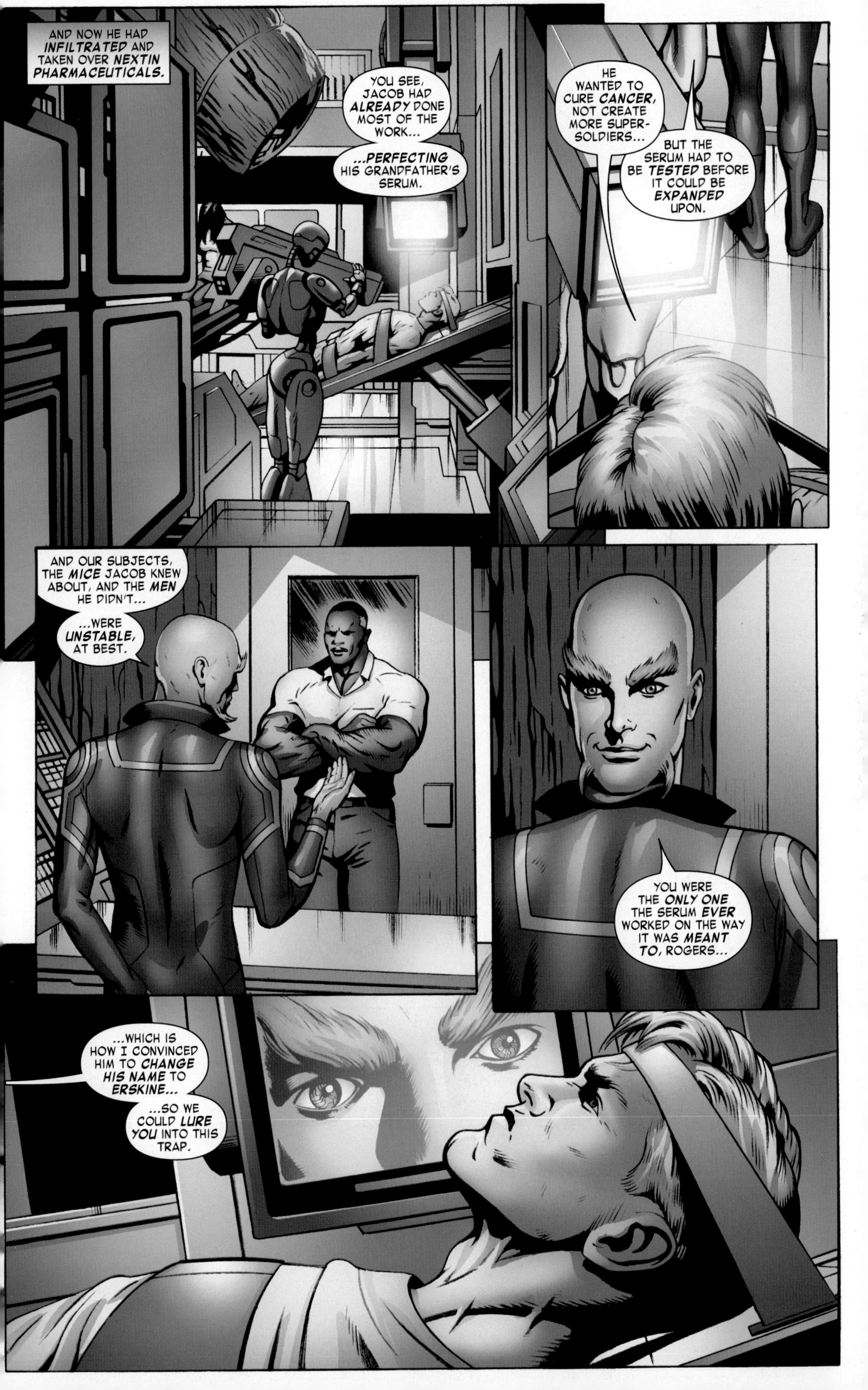
AND NOW HE HAD INFILTRATED AND TAKEN OVER NEXTIN PHARMACEUTICALS.
YOU SEE, JACOB HAD ALREADY DONE MOST OF THE WORK...
...PERFECTING HIS GRANDFATHER'S SERUM.
HE WANTED TO CURE CANCER, NOT CREATE MORE SUPER-SOLDIERS...
BUT THE SERUM HAD TO BE TESTED BEFORE IT COULD BE EXPANDED UPON.
AND OUR SUBJECTS, THE MICE JACOB KNEW ABOUT, AND THE MEN HE DIDN'T...
...WERE UNSTABLE, AT BEST.
YOU WERE THE ONLY ONE THE SERUM EVER WORKED ON THE WAY IT WAS MEANT TO, ROGERS...
...WHICH IS HOW I CONVINCED HIM TO CHANGE HIS NAME TO ERSKINE...
...SO WE COULD LURE YOU INTO THIS TRAP.

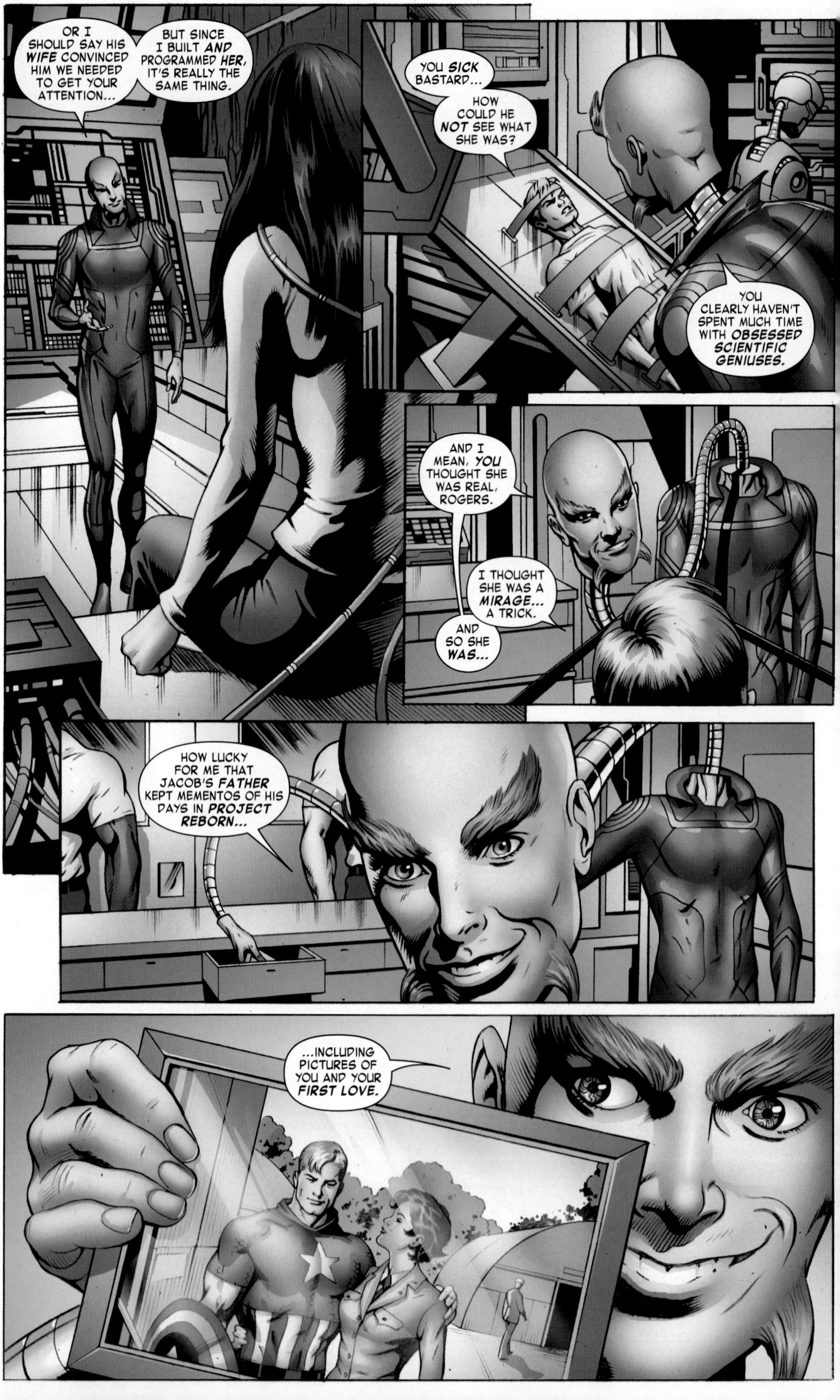
OR I SHOULD SAY HIS WIFE CONVINCED HIM WE NEEDED TO GET YOUR ATTENTION...
BUT SINCE I BUILT AND PROGRAMMED HER, IT'S REALLY THE SAME THING.
YOU SICK BASTARD...
HOW COULD HE NOT SEE WHAT SHE WAS?
YOU CLEARLY HAVEN'T SPENT MUCH TIME WITH OBSESSED SCIENTIFIC GENIUSES.
AND I MEAN, YOU THOUGHT SHE WAS REAL, ROGERS.
I THOUGHT SHE WAS A MIRAGE... A TRICK.
AND SO SHE WAS...
HOW LUCKY FOR ME THAT JACOB'S FATHER KEPT MEMENTOS OF HIS DAYS IN PROJECT REBORN...
...INCLUDING PICTURES OF YOU AND YOUR FIRST LOVE.

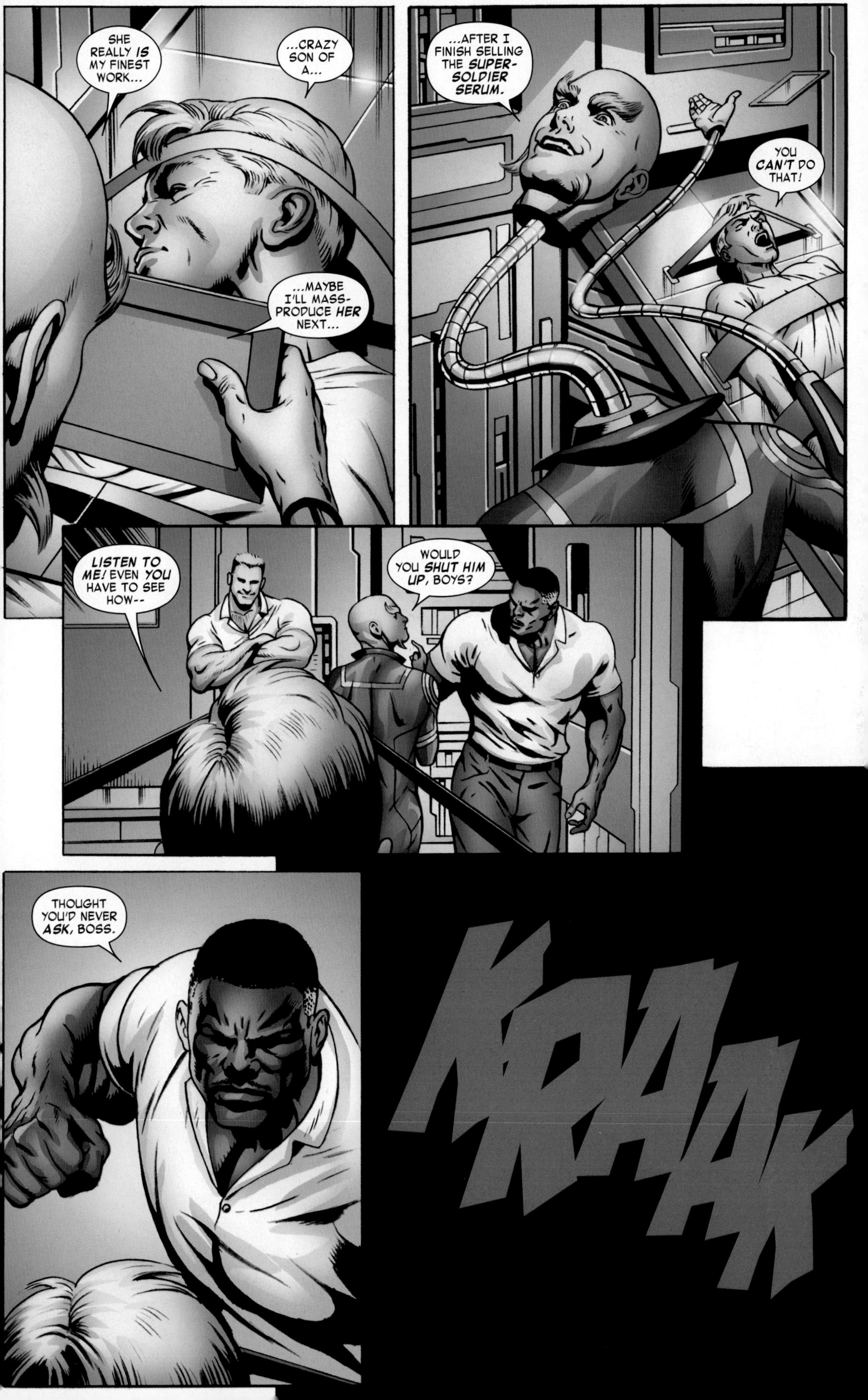
SHE REALLY IS MY FINEST WORK...
...CRAZY SON OF A...
...MAYBE I'LL MASS-PRODUCE HER NEXT...
...AFTER I FINISH SELLING THE SUPER-SOLDIER SERUM.
YOU CAN'T DO THAT!
LISTEN TO ME! EVEN YOU HAVE TO SEE HOW--
WOULD YOU SHUT HIM UP, BOYS?
THOUGHT YOU'D NEVER ASK, BOSS.
KRAAK

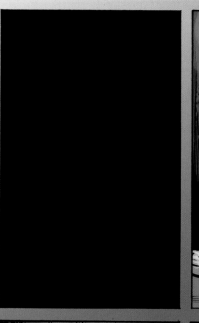

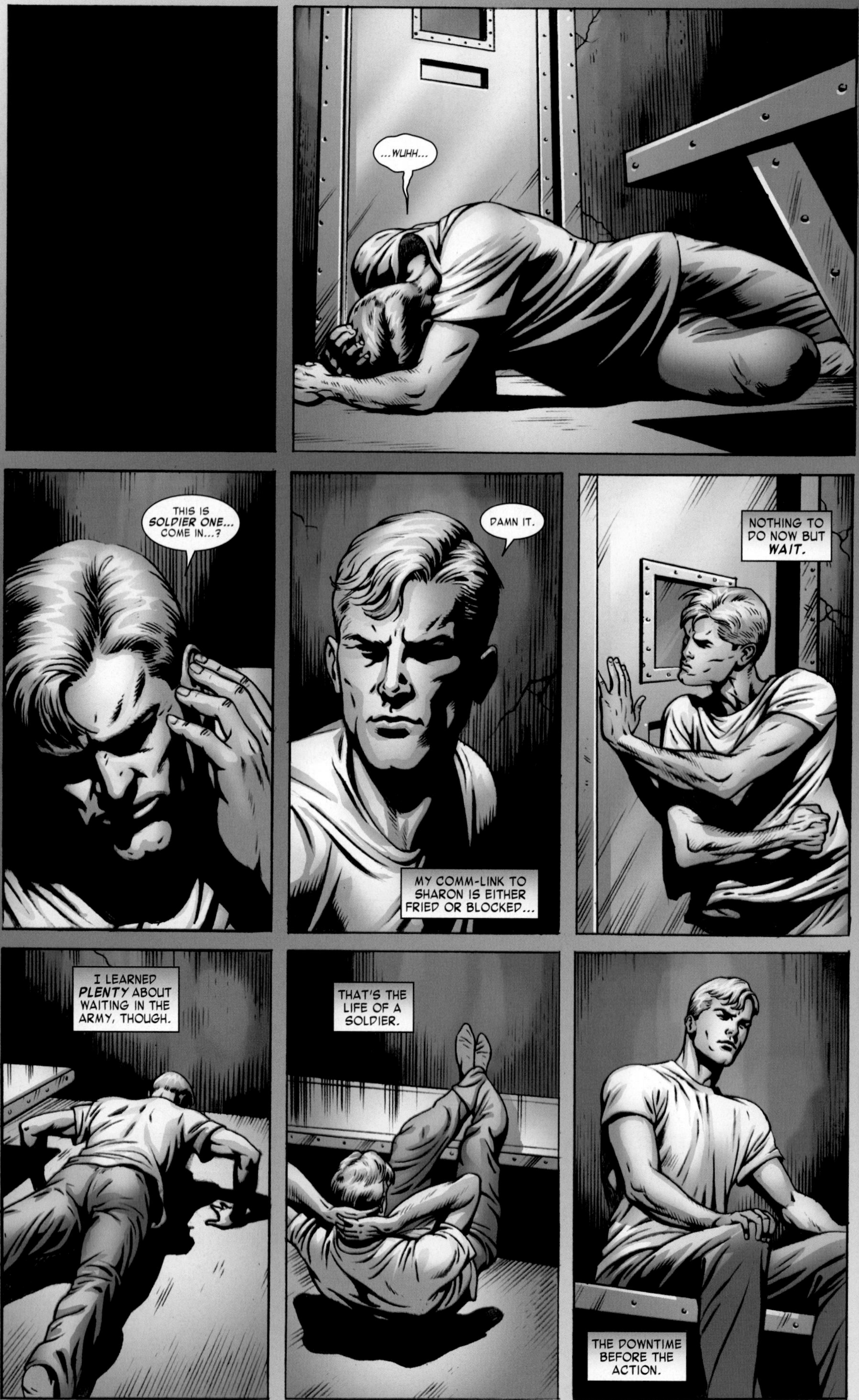
...WUHH...
THIS IS SOLDIER ONE... COME IN...?
DAMN IT.
MY COMM-LINK TO SHARON IS EITHER FRIED OR BLOCKED...
NOTHING TO DO NOW BUT WAIT.
I LEARNED PLENTY ABOUT WAITING IN THE ARMY, THOUGH.
THAT'S THE LIFE OF A SOLDIER.
THE DOWNTIME BEFORE THE ACTION.

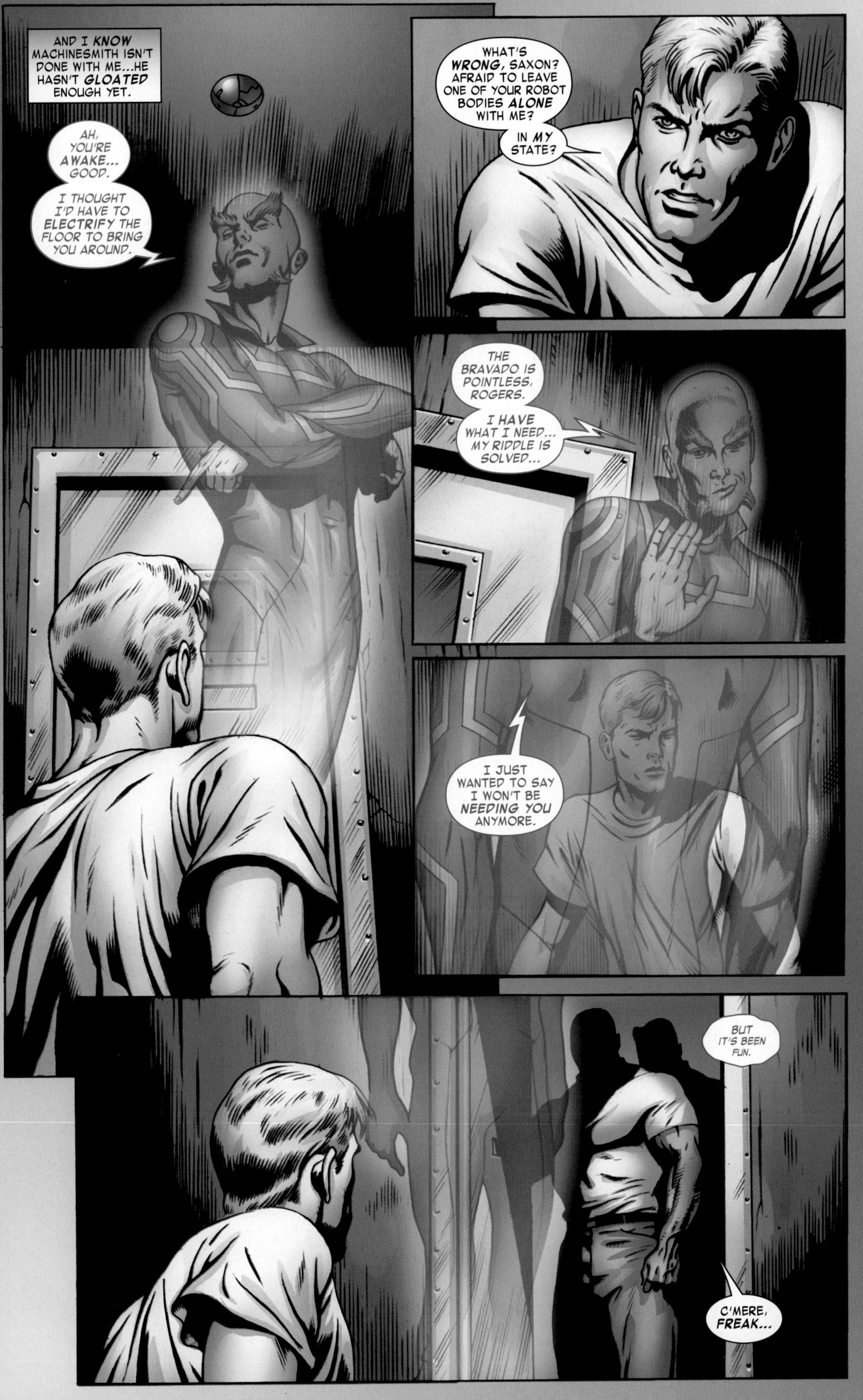
AND I KNOW MACHINESMITH ISN'T DONE WITH ME...HE HASN'T GLOATED ENOUGH YET.
AH, YOU'RE AWAKE... GOOD.
I THOUGHT I'D HAVE TO ELECTRIFY THE FLOOR TO BRING YOU AROUND.
WHAT'S WRONG, SAXON? AFRAID TO LEAVE ONE OF YOUR ROBOT BODIES ALONE WITH ME?
IN MY STATE?
THE BRAVADO IS POINTLESS, ROGERS.
I HAVE WHAT I NEED... MY RIDDLE IS SOLVED...
I JUST WANTED TO SAY I WON'T BE NEEDING YOU ANYMORE.
BUT IT'S BEEN FUN.
C'MERE, FREAK...

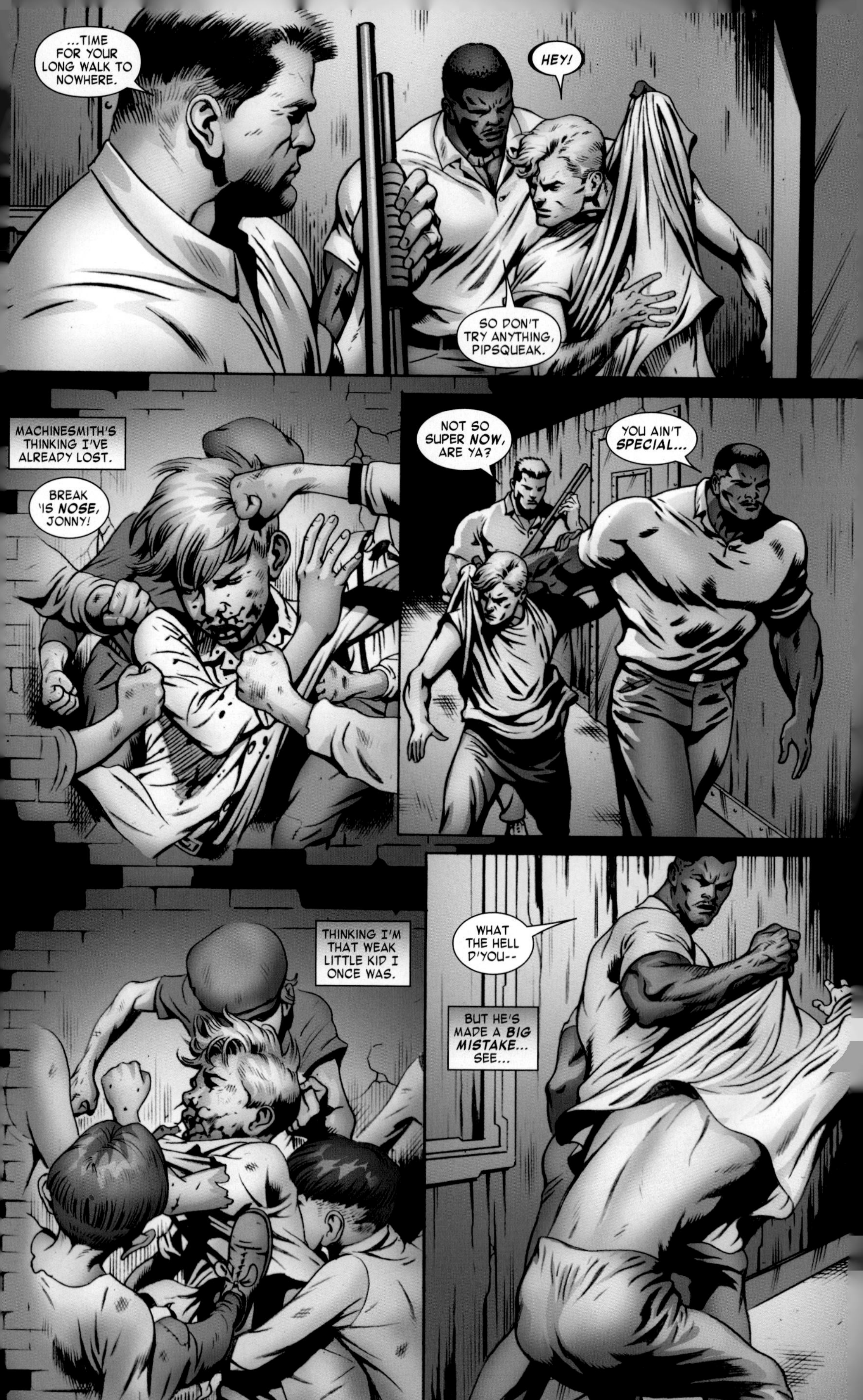
...TIME FOR YOUR LONG WALK TO NOWHERE.
HEY!
SO DON'T TRY ANYTHING, PIPSQUEAK.
MACHINESMITH'S THINKING I'VE ALREADY LOST.
BREAK 'IS NOSE, JONNY!
NOT SO SUPER NOW, ARE YA?
YOU AIN'T SPECIAL...
THINKING I'M THAT WEAK LITTLE KID I ONCE WAS.
WHAT THE HELL D'YOU--
BUT HE'S MADE A BIG MISTAKE... SEE...

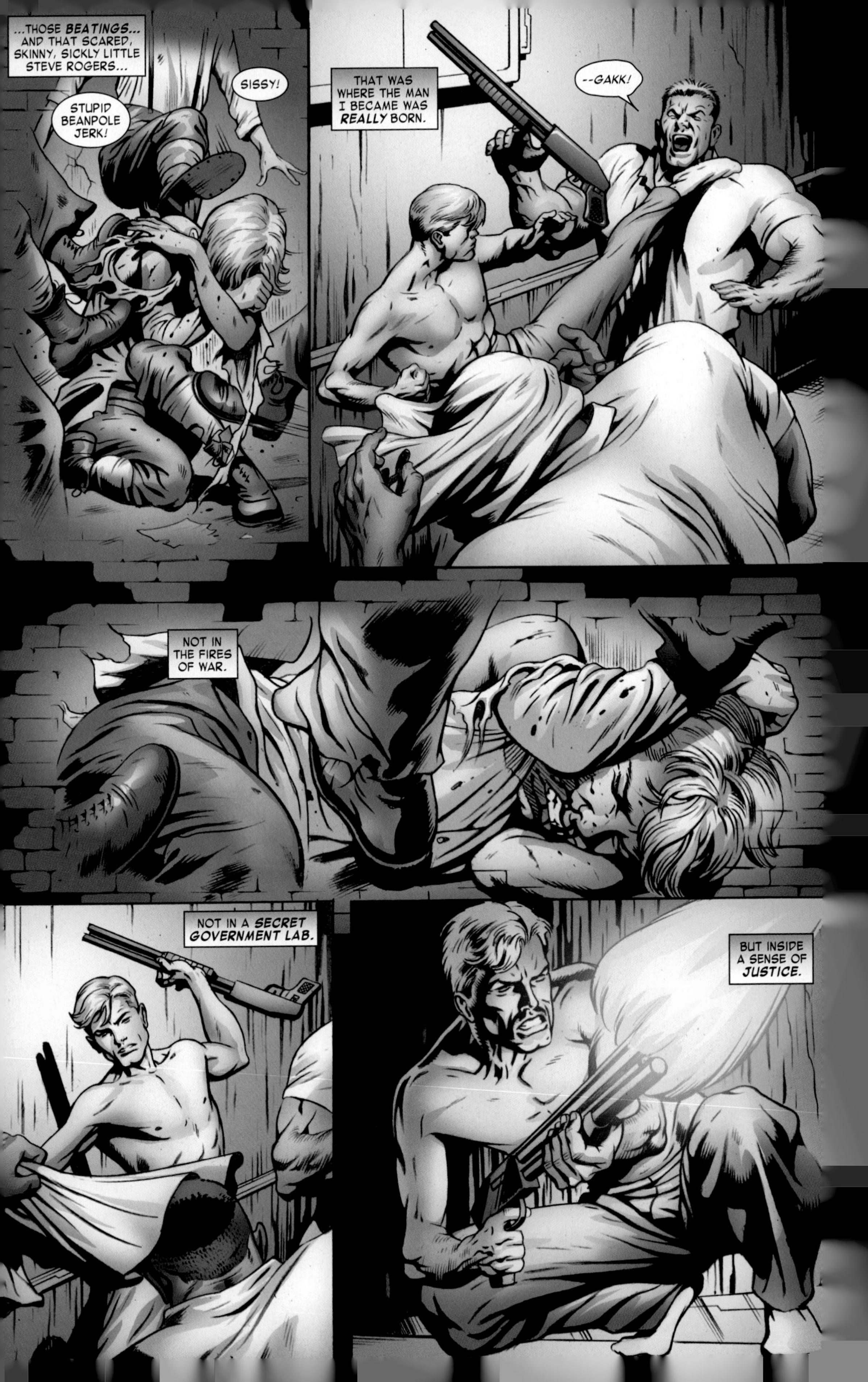
...THOSE BEATINGS... AND THAT SCARED, SKINNY, SICKLY LITTLE STEVE ROGERS...
SISSY!
STUPID BEANPOLE JERK!
THAT WAS WHERE THE MAN I BECAME WAS REALLY BORN.
--GAKK!
NOT IN THE FIRES OF WAR.
NOT IN A SECRET GOVERNMENT LAB.
BUT INSIDE A SENSE OF JUSTICE.

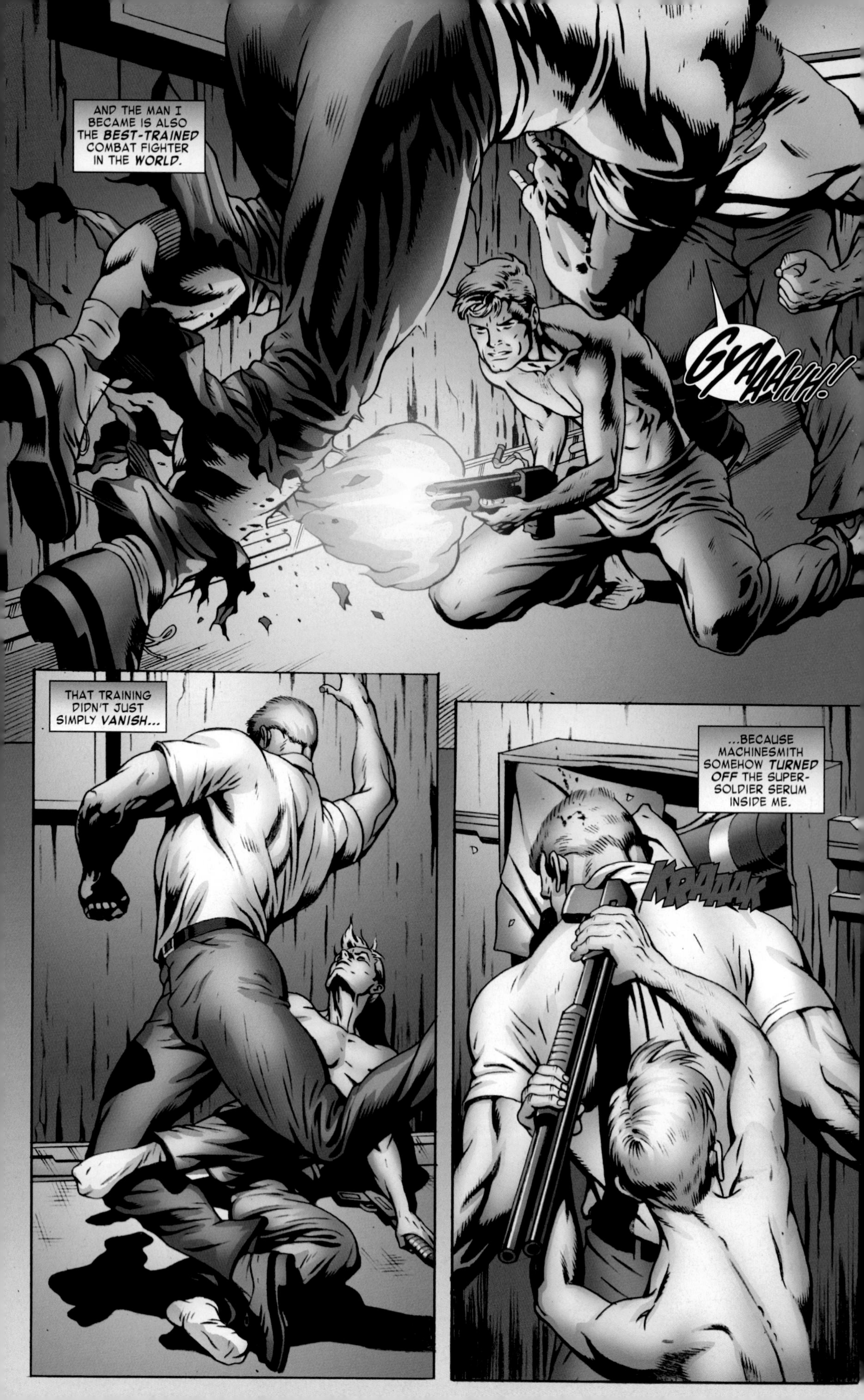
AND THE MAN I BECAME IS ALSO THE BEST-TRAINED COMBAT FIGHTER IN THE WORLD.
GYAAAHH!
THAT TRAINING DIDN'T JUST SIMPLY VANISH...
...BECAUSE MACHINESMITH SOMEHOW TURNED OFF THE SUPER-SOLDIER SERUM INSIDE ME.
KRAAAK

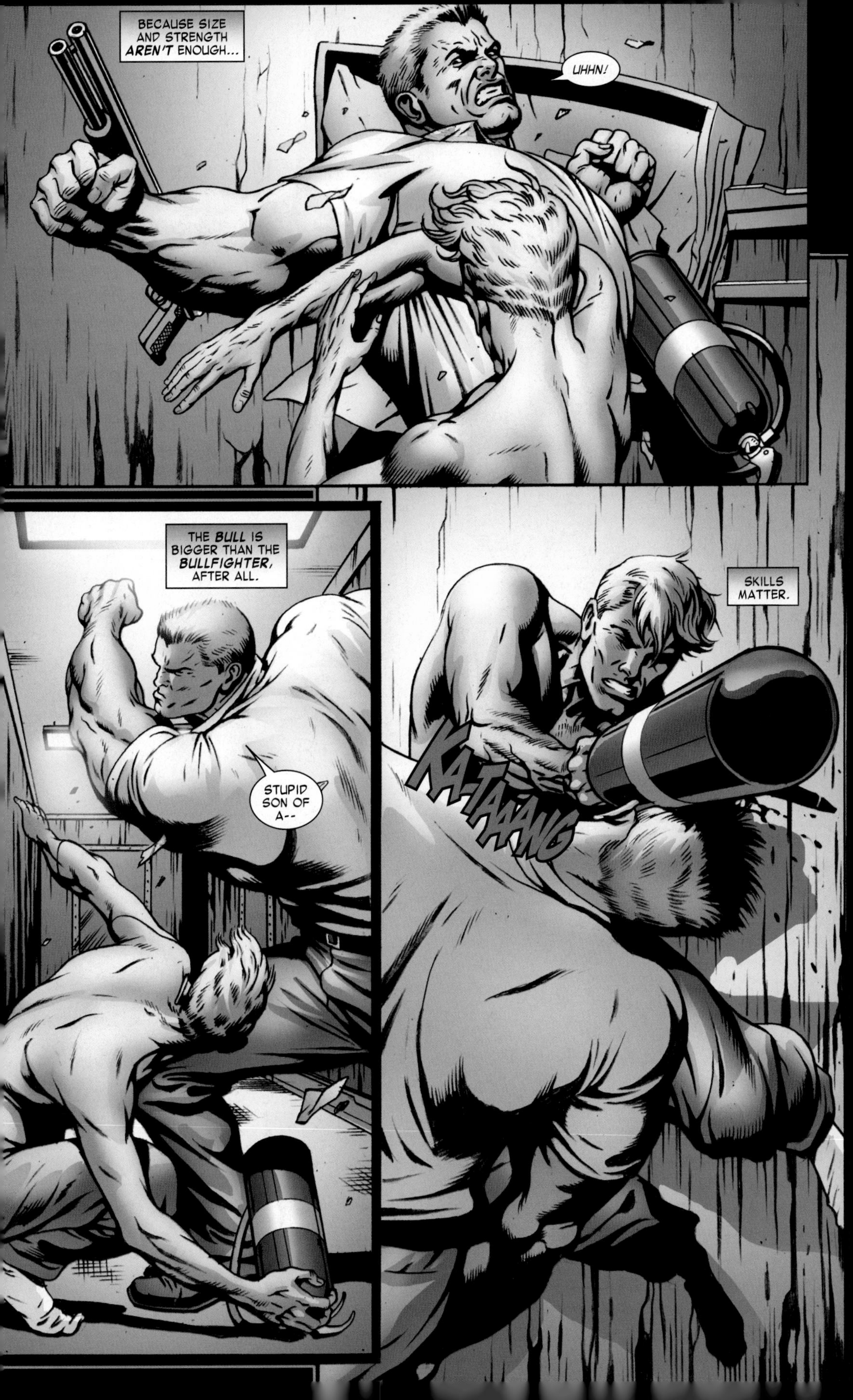
BECAUSE SIZE AND STRENGTH AREN'T ENOUGH...
UHHN!
THE BULL IS BIGGER THAN THE BULLFIGHTER, AFTER ALL.
STUPID SON OF A--
SKILLS MATTER.
KA-TAAANG

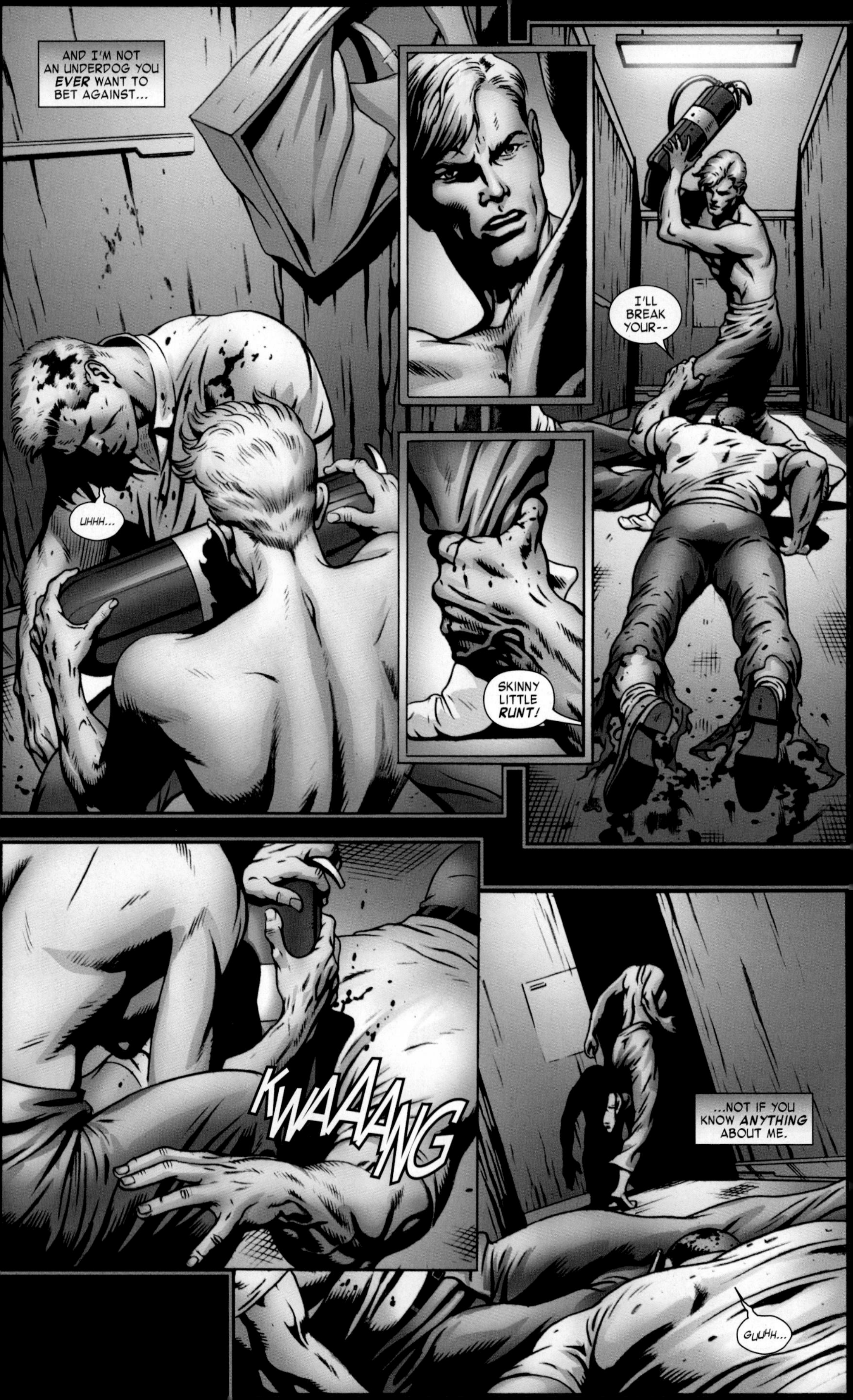
AND I'M NOT AN UNDERDOG YOU *EVER* WANT TO BET AGAINST...
UHHH...
I'LL BREAK YOUR--
SKINNY LITTLE *RUNT!*
KWAAAANG
...NOT IF YOU KNOW *ANYTHING* ABOUT ME.
GUUHH...

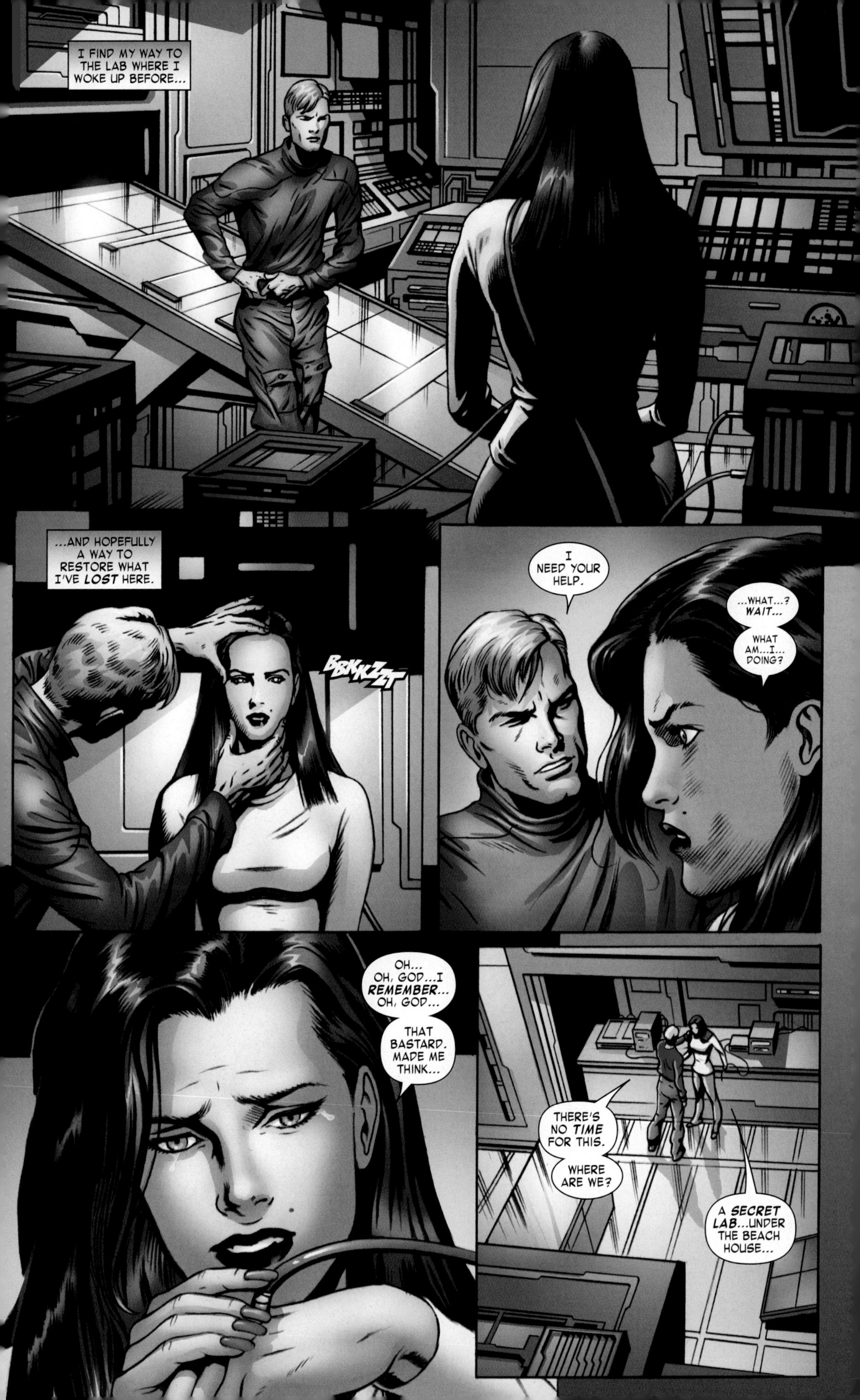
I FIND MY WAY TO THE LAB WHERE I WOKE UP BEFORE...
...AND HOPEFULLY A WAY TO RESTORE WHAT I'VE LOST HERE.
BBKKZZT
I NEED YOUR HELP.
...WHAT...? WAIT...
WHAT AM...I... DOING?
OH... OH, GOD...I REMEMBER... OH, GOD...
THAT BASTARD. MADE ME THINK...
THERE'S NO TIME FOR THIS.
WHERE ARE WE?
A SECRET LAB...UNDER THE BEACH HOUSE...

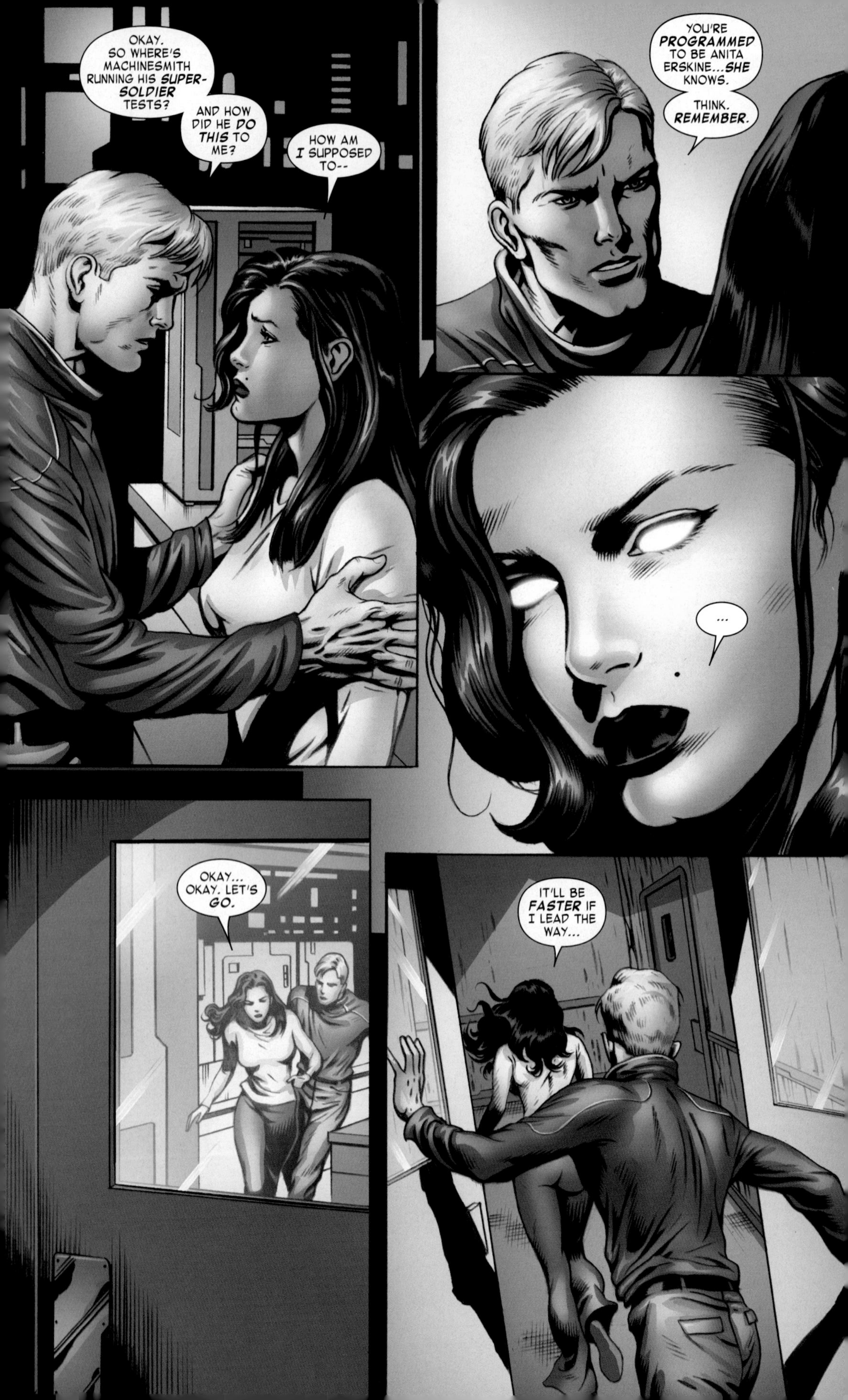
OKAY. SO WHERE'S MACHINESMITH RUNNING HIS SUPER-SOLDIER TESTS?
AND HOW DID HE DO THIS TO ME?
HOW AM I SUPPOSED TO--
YOU'RE PROGRAMMED TO BE ANITA ERSKINE...SHE KNOWS.
THINK. REMEMBER.
...
OKAY... OKAY. LET'S GO.
IT'LL BE FASTER IF I LEAD THE WAY...

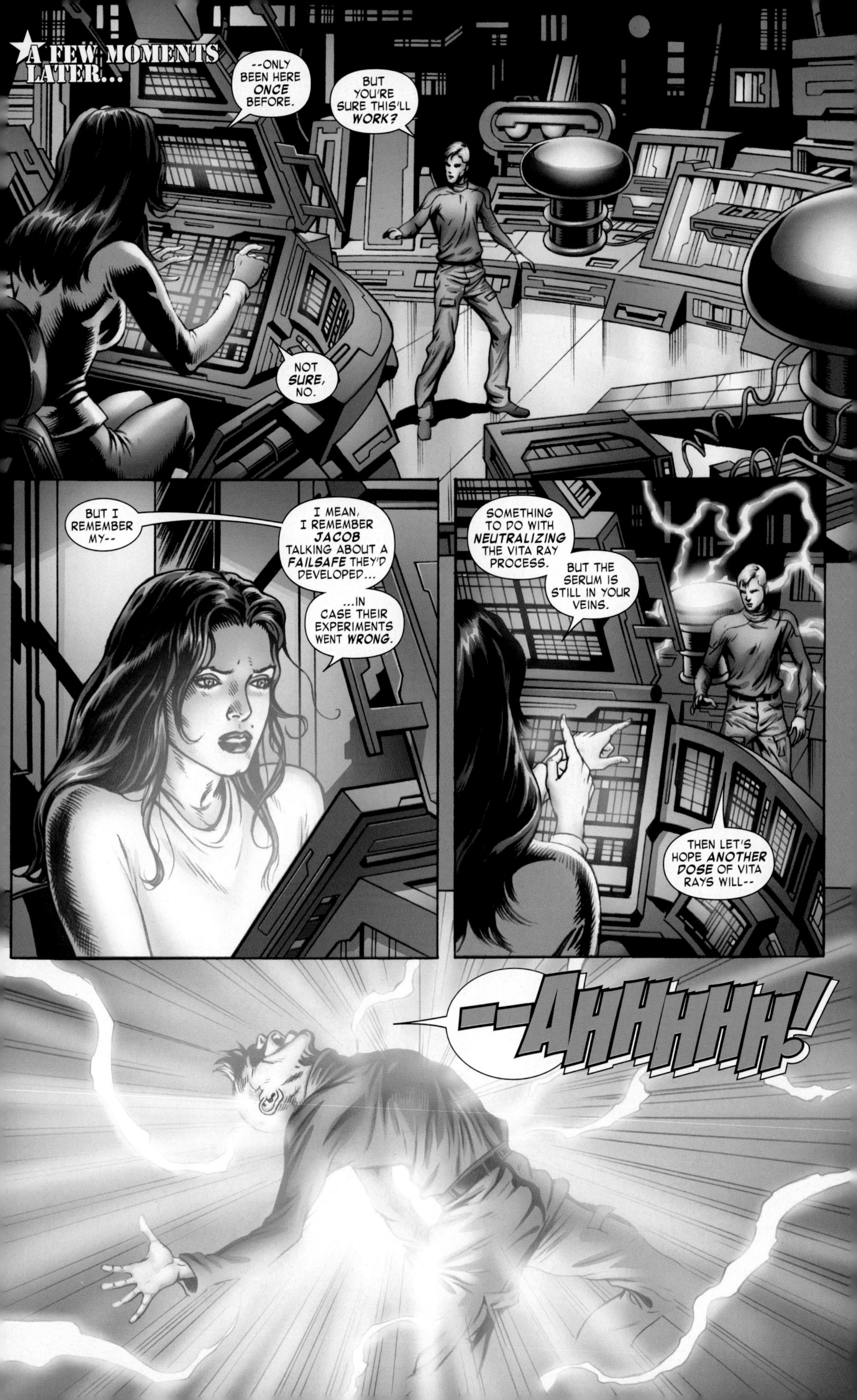
A FEW MOMENTS LATER...
--ONLY BEEN HERE ONCE BEFORE.
BUT YOU'RE SURE THIS'LL WORK?
NOT SURE, NO.
BUT I REMEMBER MY--
I MEAN, I REMEMBER JACOB TALKING ABOUT A FAILSAFE THEY'D DEVELOPED...
...IN CASE THEIR EXPERIMENTS WENT WRONG.
SOMETHING TO DO WITH NEUTRALIZING THE VITA RAY PROCESS.
BUT THE SERUM IS STILL IN YOUR VEINS.
THEN LET'S HOPE ANOTHER DOSE OF VITA RAYS WILL--
--AHHHHH!

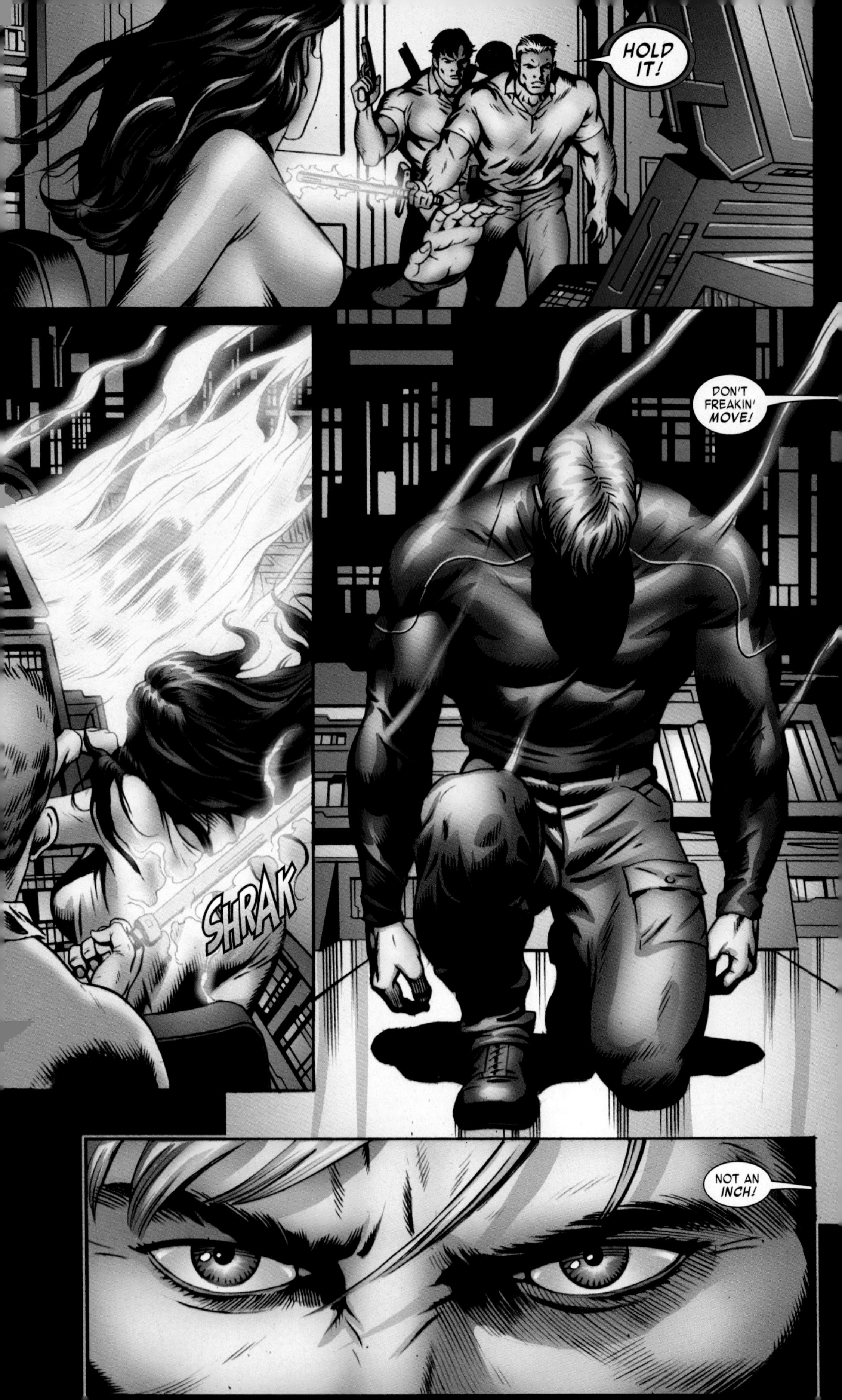
HOLD IT!
SHRAK
DON'T FREAKIN' MOVE!
NOT AN INCH!

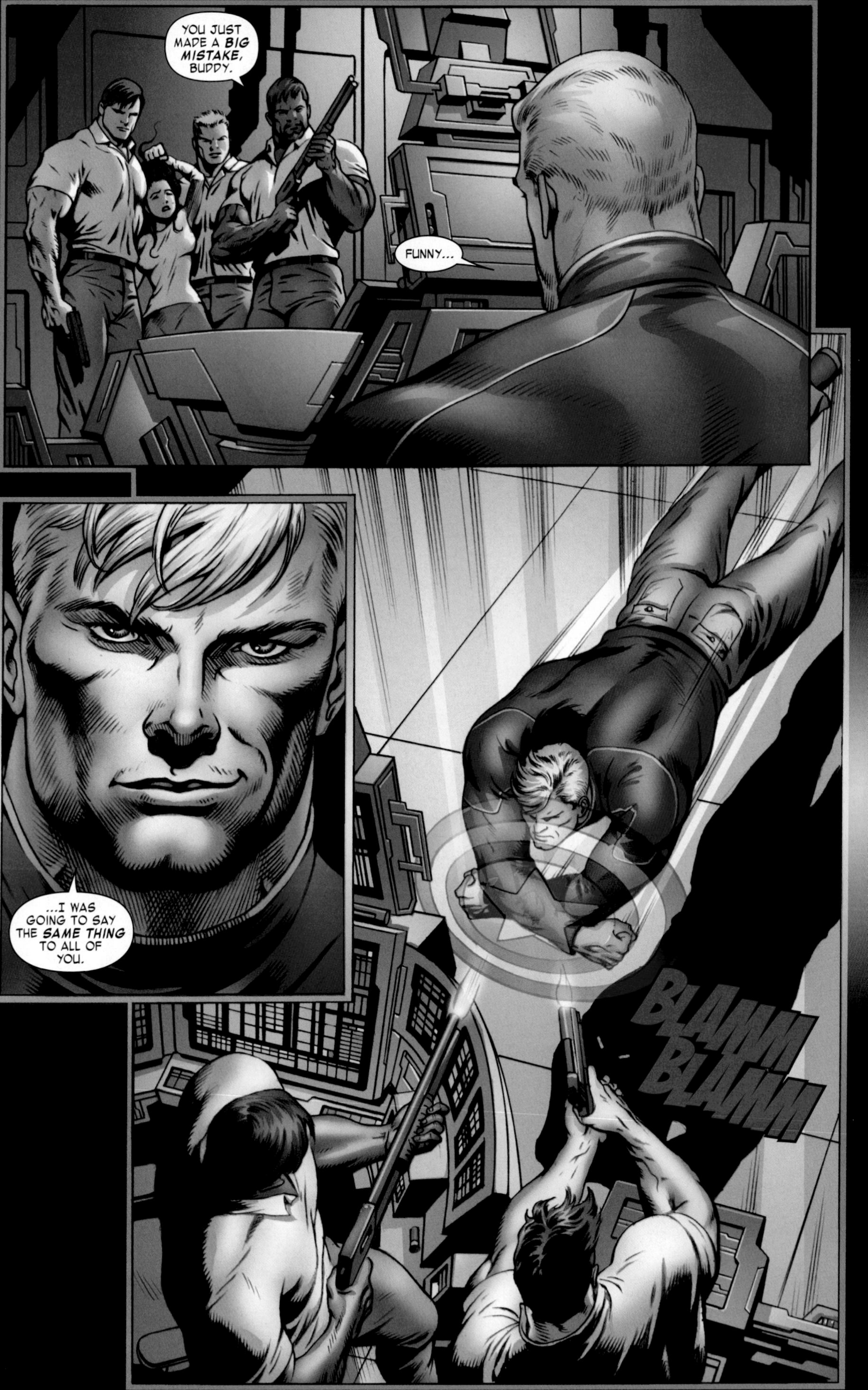
YOU JUST MADE A BIG MISTAKE, BUDDY.
FUNNY...
...I WAS GOING TO SAY THE SAME THING TO ALL OF YOU.
BLAMM
BLAMM

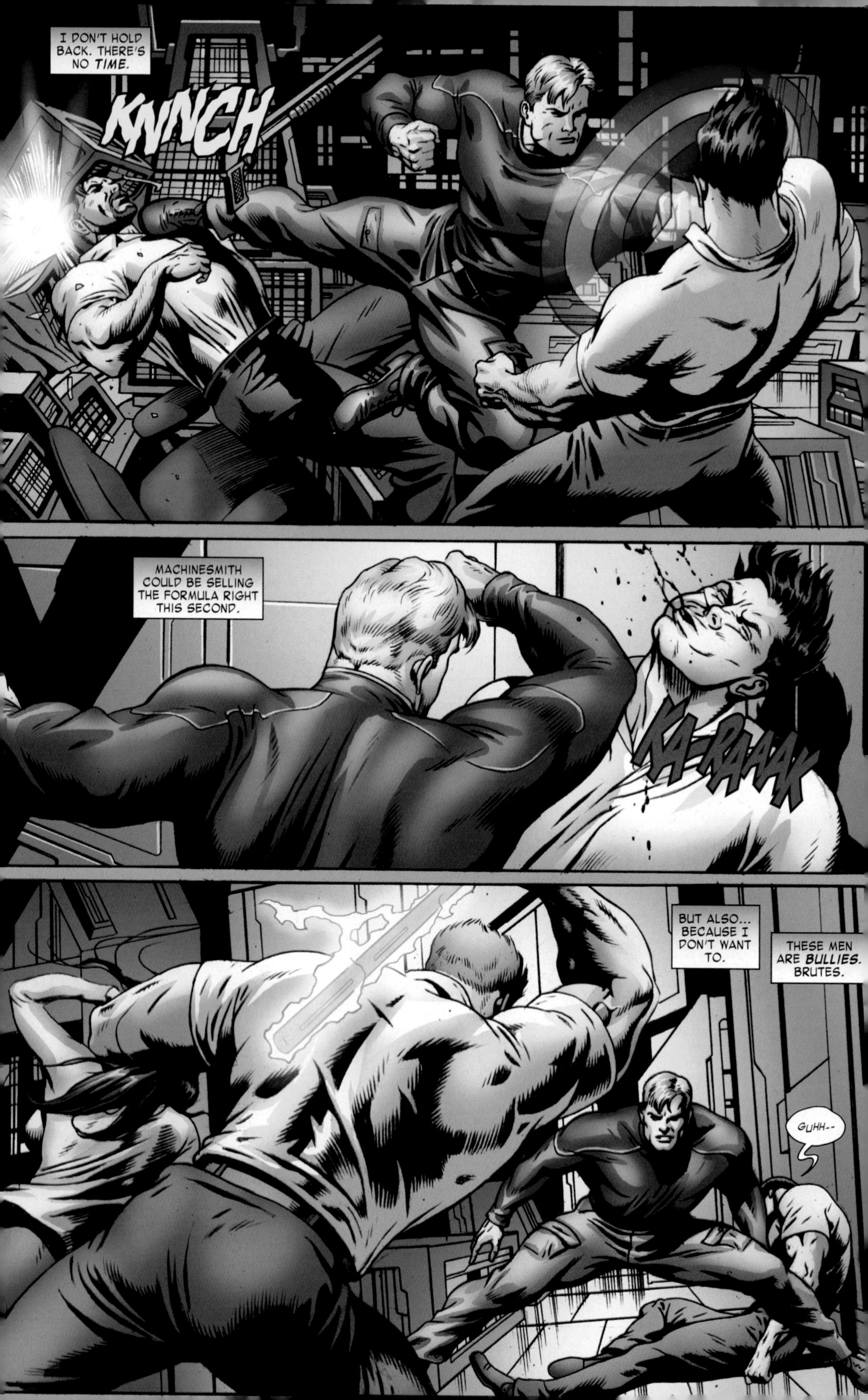
I DON'T HOLD BACK. THERE'S NO TIME.
KNNCH
MACHINESMITH COULD BE SELLING THE FORMULA RIGHT THIS SECOND.
KA-RAAAK
BUT ALSO... BECAUSE I DON'T WANT TO.
THESE MEN ARE BULLIES. BRUTES.
GUHH--

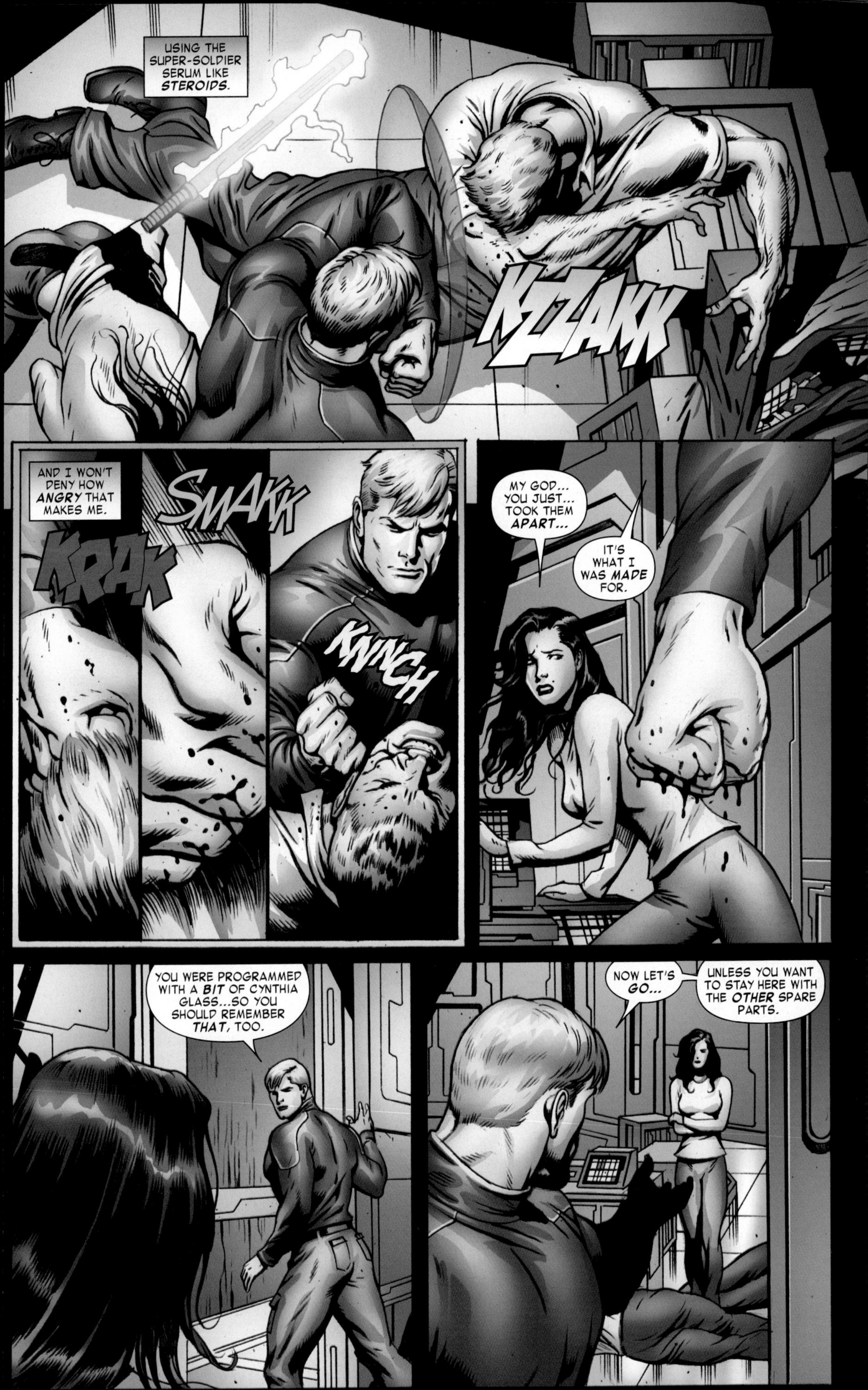

USING THE SUPER-SOLDIER SERUM LIKE STEROIDS.
KZZAKK
AND I WON'T DENY HOW ANGRY THAT MAKES ME.
SMAKK
KRAK
KNNCH
MY GOD... YOU JUST... TOOK THEM APART...
IT'S WHAT I WAS MADE FOR.
YOU WERE PROGRAMMED WITH A BIT OF CYNTHIA GLASS...SO YOU SHOULD REMEMBER THAT, TOO.
NOW LET'S GO...
UNLESS YOU WANT TO STAY HERE WITH THE OTHER SPARE PARTS.

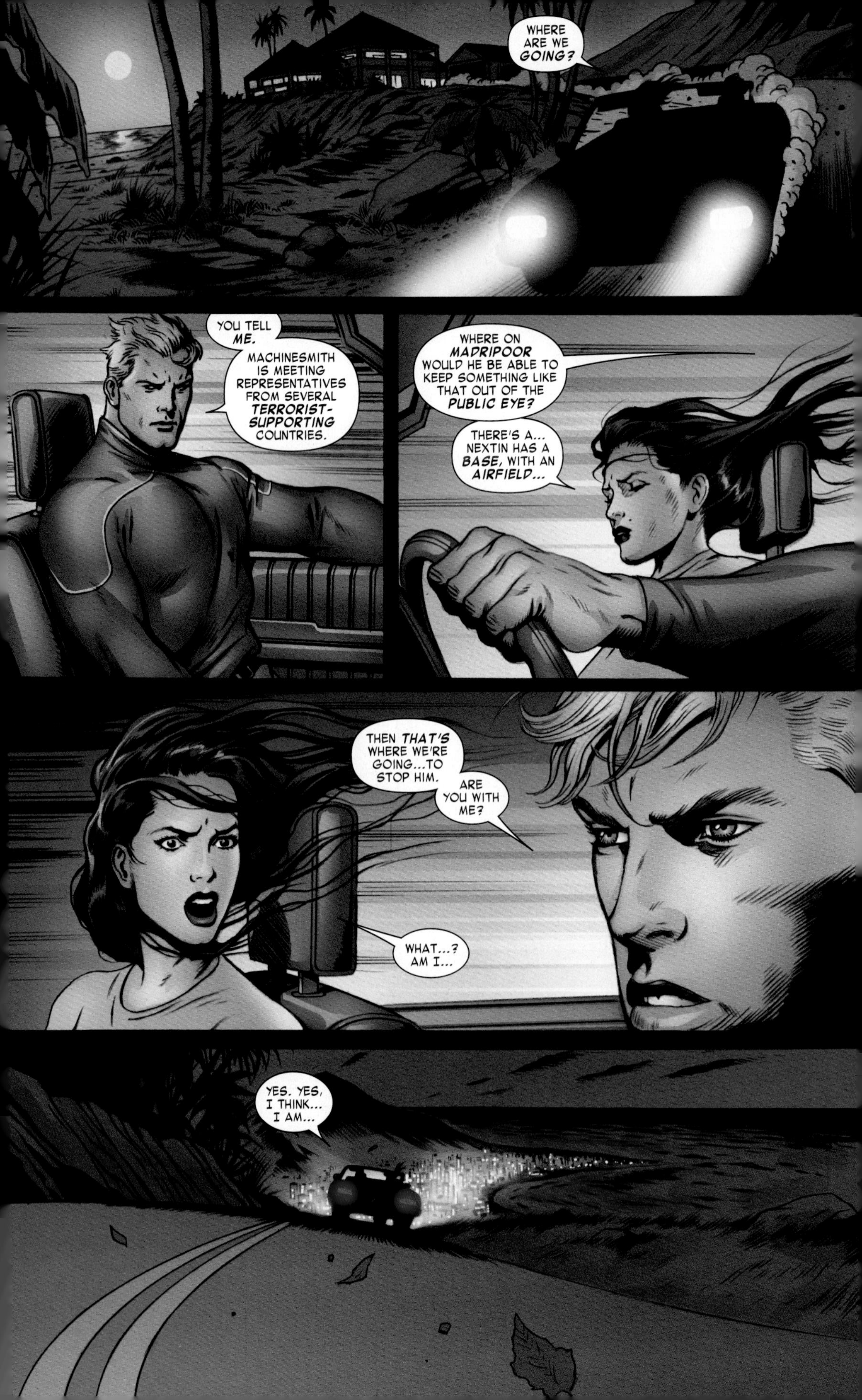

WHERE ARE WE GOING?
YOU TELL ME.
MACHINESMITH IS MEETING REPRESENTATIVES FROM SEVERAL TERRORIST-SUPPORTING COUNTRIES.
WHERE ON MADRIPOOR WOULD HE BE ABLE TO KEEP SOMETHING LIKE THAT OUT OF THE PUBLIC EYE?
THERE'S A... NEXTIN HAS A BASE, WITH AN AIRFIELD...
THEN THAT'S WHERE WE'RE GOING...TO STOP HIM.
ARE YOU WITH ME?
WHAT...? AM I...
YES. YES, I THINK... I AM...

4

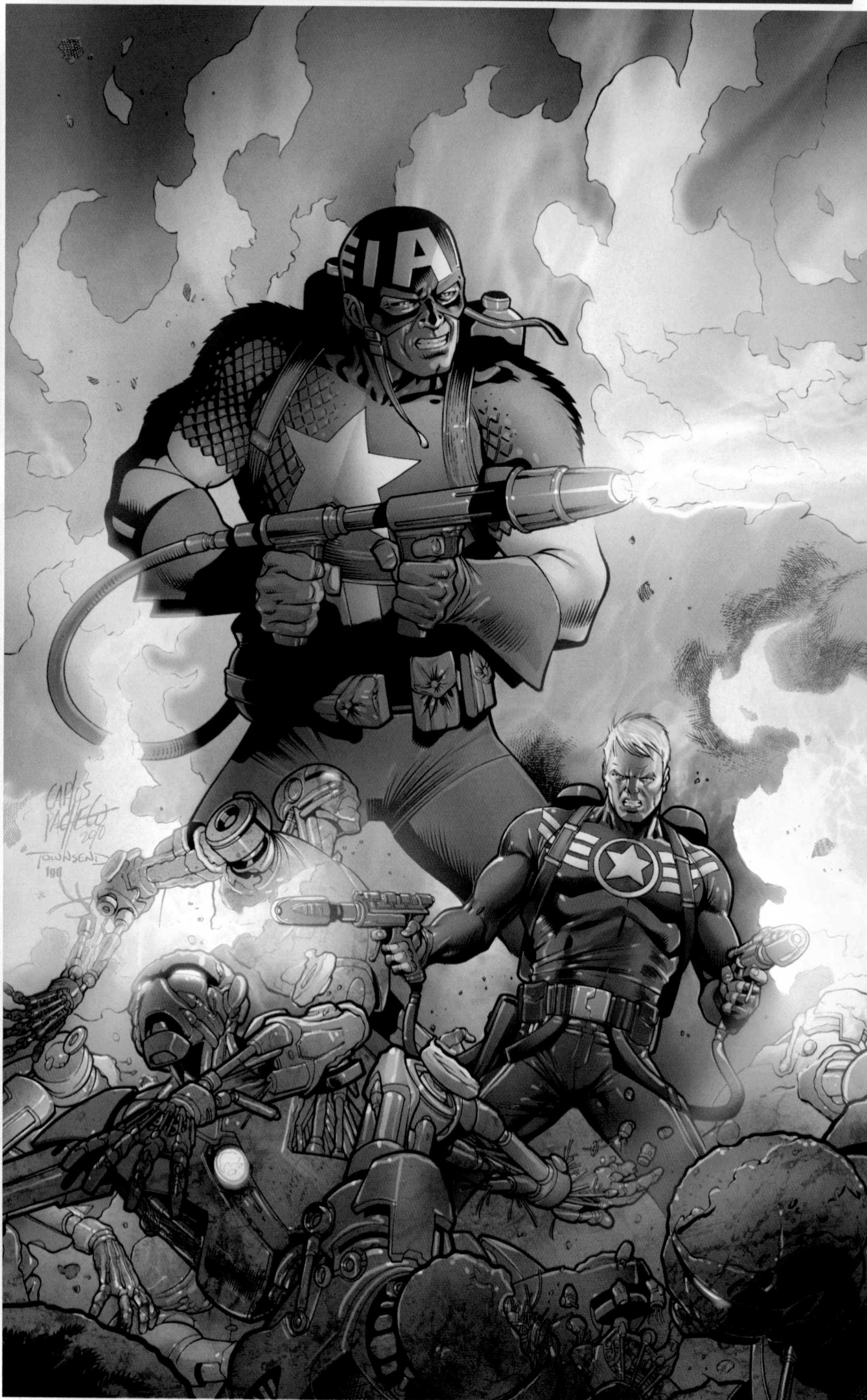
TOWNSEND

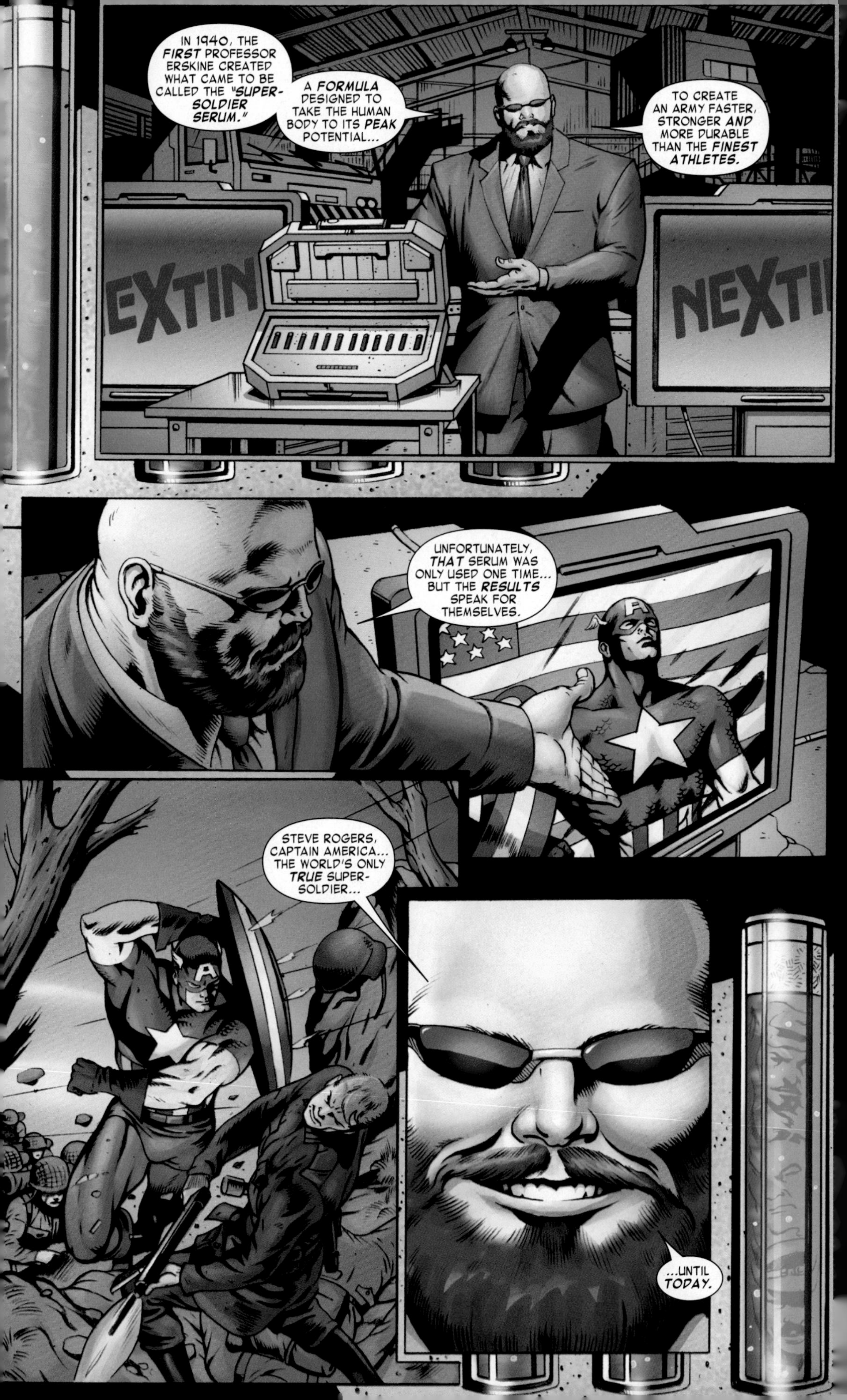
IN 1940, THE FIRST PROFESSOR ERSKINE CREATED WHAT CAME TO BE CALLED THE "SUPER-SOLDIER SERUM."
A FORMULA DESIGNED TO TAKE THE HUMAN BODY TO ITS PEAK POTENTIAL...
TO CREATE AN ARMY FASTER, STRONGER AND MORE DURABLE THAN THE FINEST ATHLETES.
NEXTIN
NEXTIN
UNFORTUNATELY, THAT SERUM WAS ONLY USED ONE TIME... BUT THE RESULTS SPEAK FOR THEMSELVES.
STEVE ROGERS, CAPTAIN AMERICA... THE WORLD'S ONLY TRUE SUPER-SOLDIER...
...UNTIL TODAY.

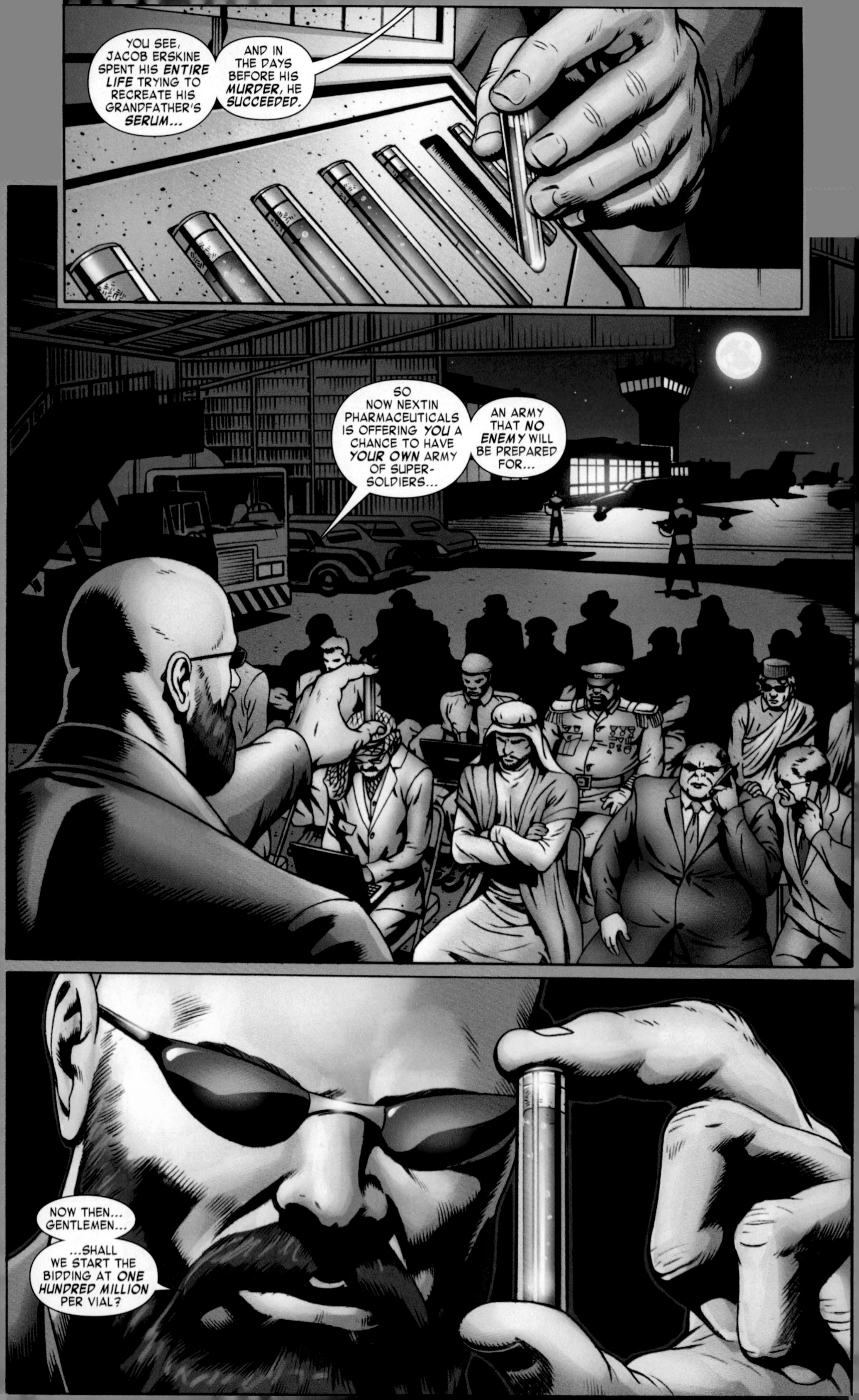
YOU SEE, JACOB ERSKINE SPENT HIS ENTIRE LIFE TRYING TO RECREATE HIS GRANDFATHER'S SERUM...
AND IN THE DAYS BEFORE HIS MURDER, HE SUCCEEDED.
SO NOW NEXTIN PHARMACEUTICALS IS OFFERING YOU A CHANCE TO HAVE YOUR OWN ARMY OF SUPER-SOLDIERS...
AN ARMY THAT NO ENEMY WILL BE PREPARED FOR...
NOW THEN... GENTLEMEN...
...SHALL WE START THE BIDDING AT ONE HUNDRED MILLION PER VIAL?

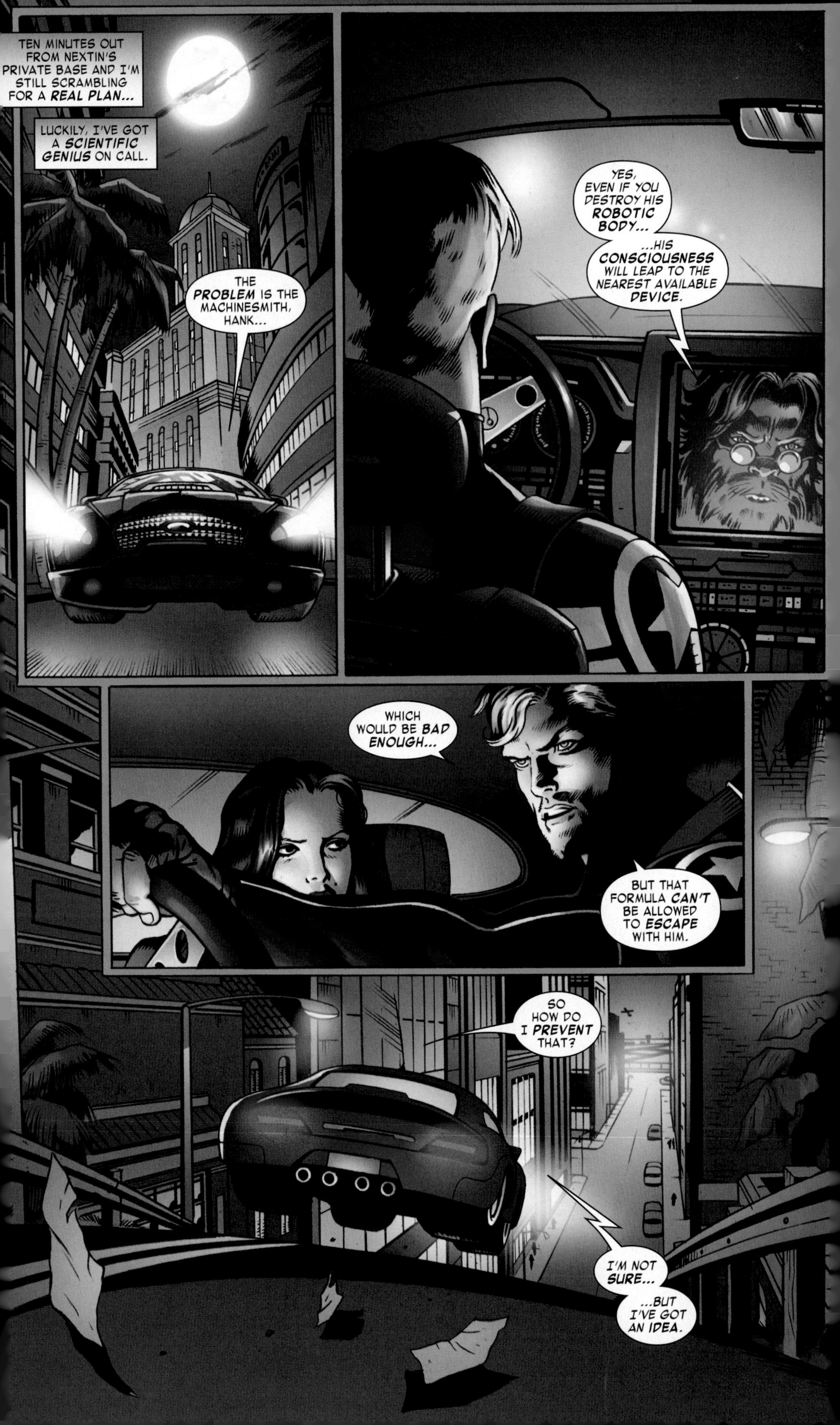
TEN MINUTES OUT FROM NEXTIN'S PRIVATE BASE AND I'M STILL SCRAMBLING FOR A REAL PLAN...
LUCKILY, I'VE GOT A SCIENTIFIC GENIUS ON CALL.
THE PROBLEM IS THE MACHINESMITH, HANK...
YES, EVEN IF YOU DESTROY HIS ROBOTIC BODY...
...HIS CONSCIOUSNESS WILL LEAP TO THE NEAREST AVAILABLE DEVICE.
WHICH WOULD BE BAD ENOUGH...
BUT THAT FORMULA CAN'T BE ALLOWED TO ESCAPE WITH HIM.
SO HOW DO I PREVENT THAT?
I'M NOT SURE...
...BUT I'VE GOT AN IDEA.

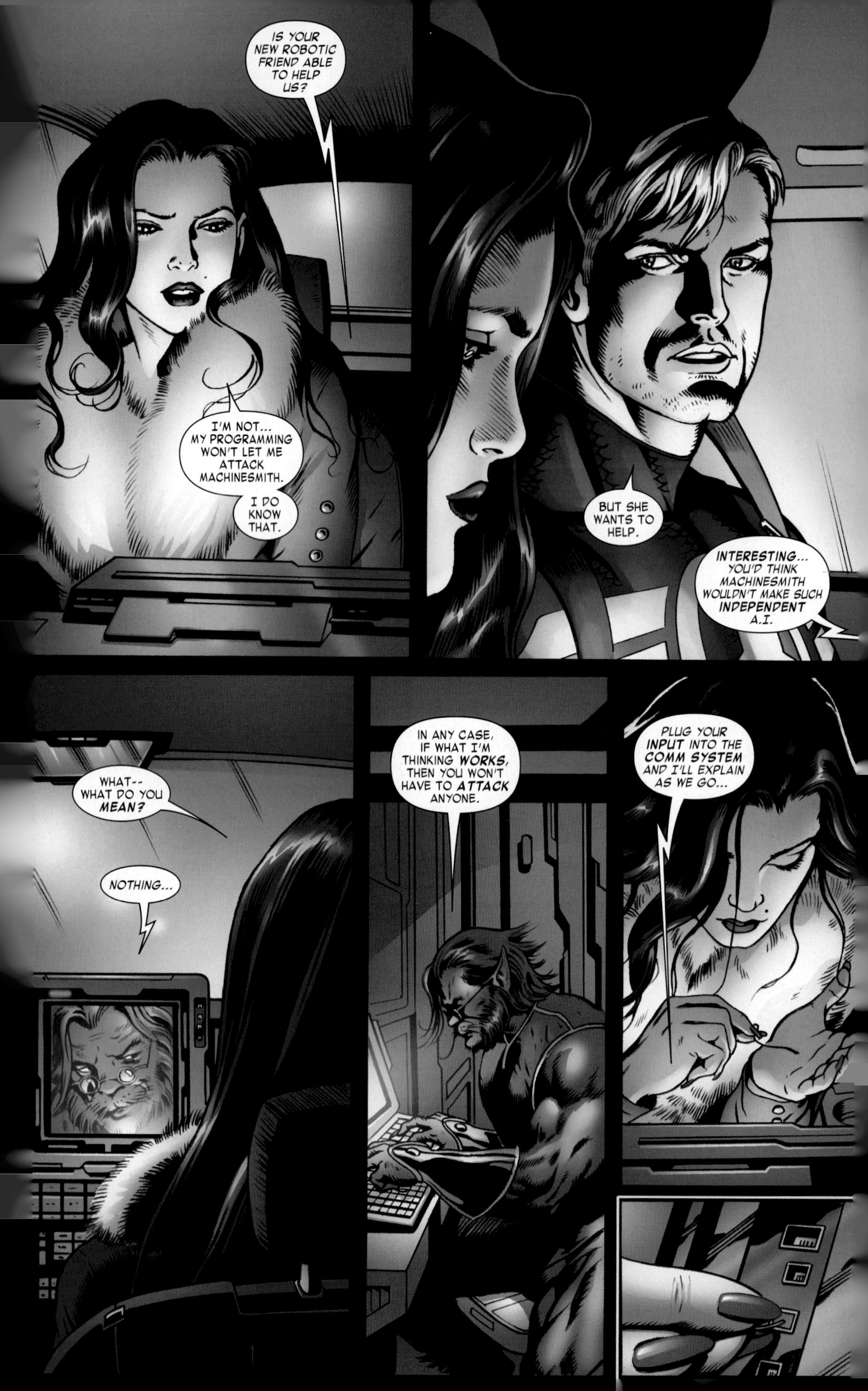
IS YOUR NEW ROBOTIC FRIEND ABLE TO HELP US?
I'M NOT... MY PROGRAMMING WON'T LET ME ATTACK MACHINESMITH.
I DO KNOW THAT.
BUT SHE WANTS TO HELP.
INTERESTING... YOU'D THINK MACHINESMITH WOULDN'T MAKE SUCH INDEPENDENT A.I.
WHAT-- WHAT DO YOU MEAN?
NOTHING...
IN ANY CASE, IF WHAT I'M THINKING WORKS, THEN YOU WON'T HAVE TO ATTACK ANYONE.
PLUG YOUR INPUT INTO THE COMM SYSTEM AND I'LL EXPLAIN AS WE GO...

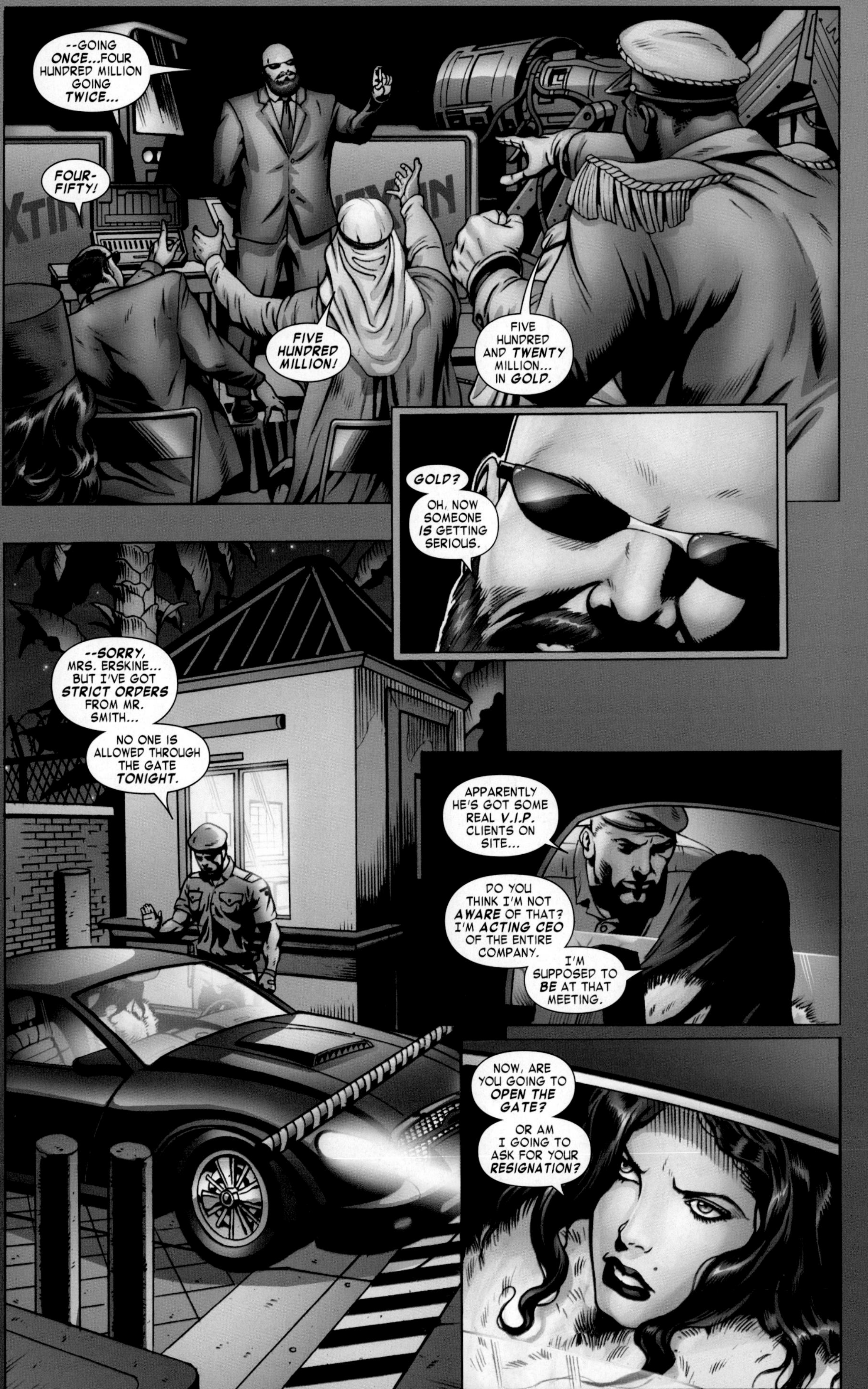

--GOING ONCE...FOUR HUNDRED MILLION GOING TWICE...
FOUR-FIFTY!
FIVE HUNDRED MILLION!
FIVE HUNDRED AND TWENTY MILLION... IN GOLD.
GOLD?
OH, NOW SOMEONE IS GETTING SERIOUS.
--SORRY, MRS. ERSKINE... BUT I'VE GOT STRICT ORDERS FROM MR. SMITH...
NO ONE IS ALLOWED THROUGH THE GATE TONIGHT.
APPARENTLY HE'S GOT SOME REAL V.I.P. CLIENTS ON SITE...
DO YOU THINK I'M NOT AWARE OF THAT? I'M ACTING CEO OF THE ENTIRE COMPANY.
I'M SUPPOSED TO BE AT THAT MEETING.
NOW, ARE YOU GOING TO OPEN THE GATE?
OR AM I GOING TO ASK FOR YOUR RESIGNATION?

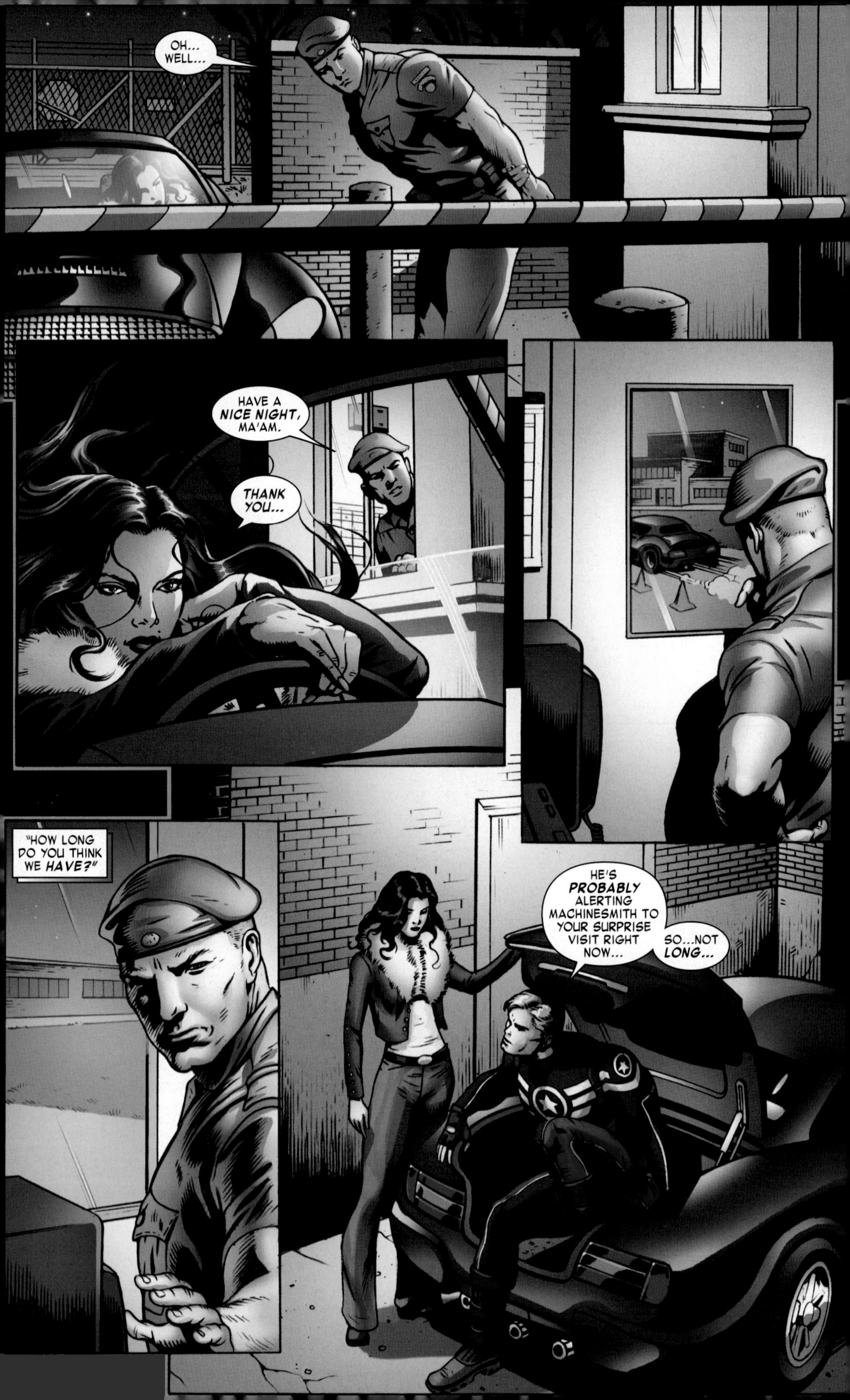
OH... WELL...
HAVE A NICE NIGHT, MA'AM.
THANK YOU...
"HOW LONG DO YOU THINK WE HAVE?"
HE'S PROBABLY ALERTING MACHINESMITH TO YOUR SURPRISE VISIT RIGHT NOW...
SO...NOT LONG...

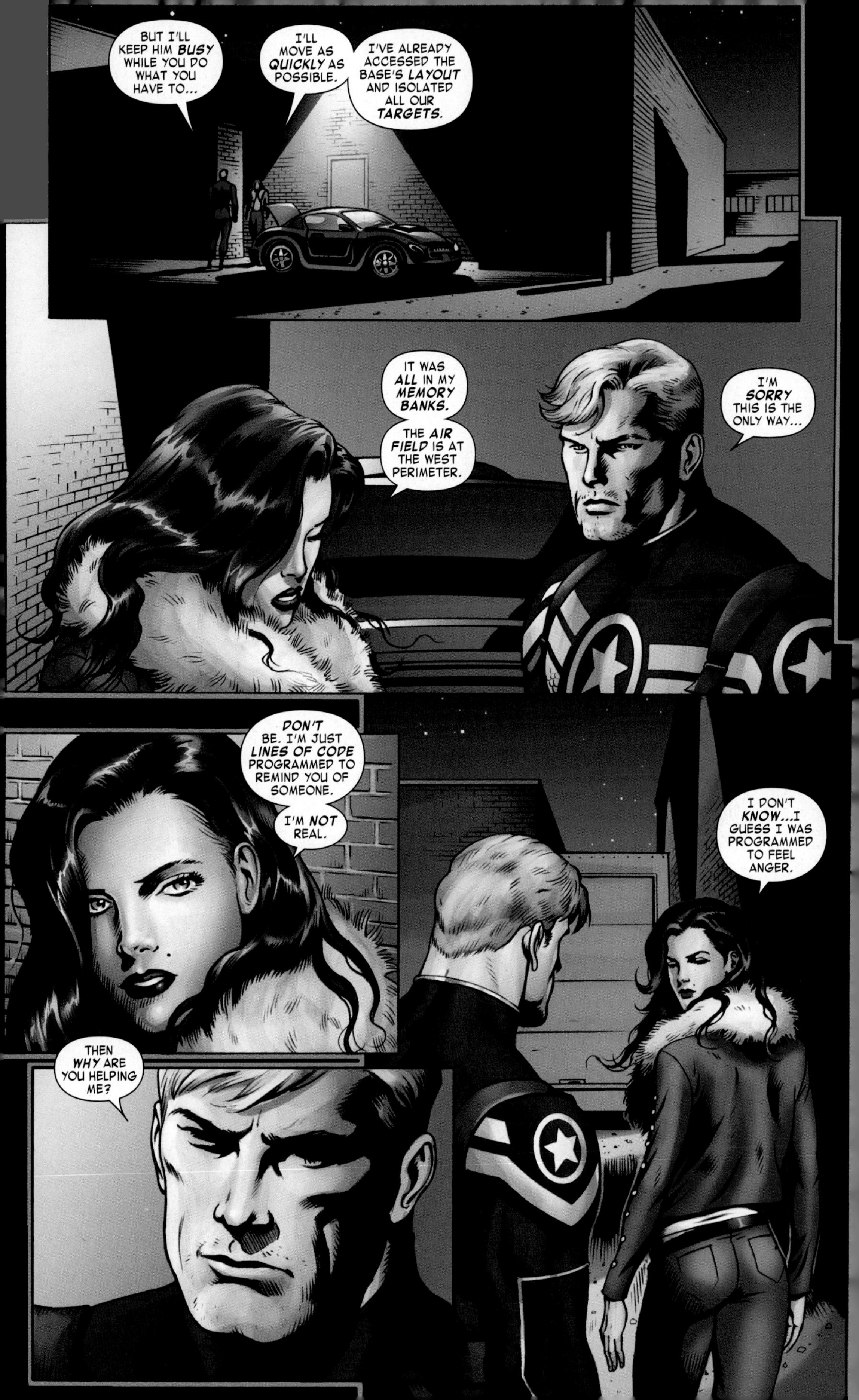
BUT I'LL KEEP HIM BUSY WHILE YOU DO WHAT YOU HAVE TO...
I'LL MOVE AS QUICKLY AS POSSIBLE.
I'VE ALREADY ACCESSED THE BASE'S LAYOUT AND ISOLATED ALL OUR TARGETS.
IT WAS ALL IN MY MEMORY BANKS.
THE AIR FIELD IS AT THE WEST PERIMETER.
I'M SORRY THIS IS THE ONLY WAY...
DON'T BE. I'M JUST LINES OF CODE PROGRAMMED TO REMIND YOU OF SOMEONE.
I'M NOT REAL.
THEN WHY ARE YOU HELPING ME?
I DON'T KNOW...I GUESS I WAS PROGRAMMED TO FEEL ANGER.

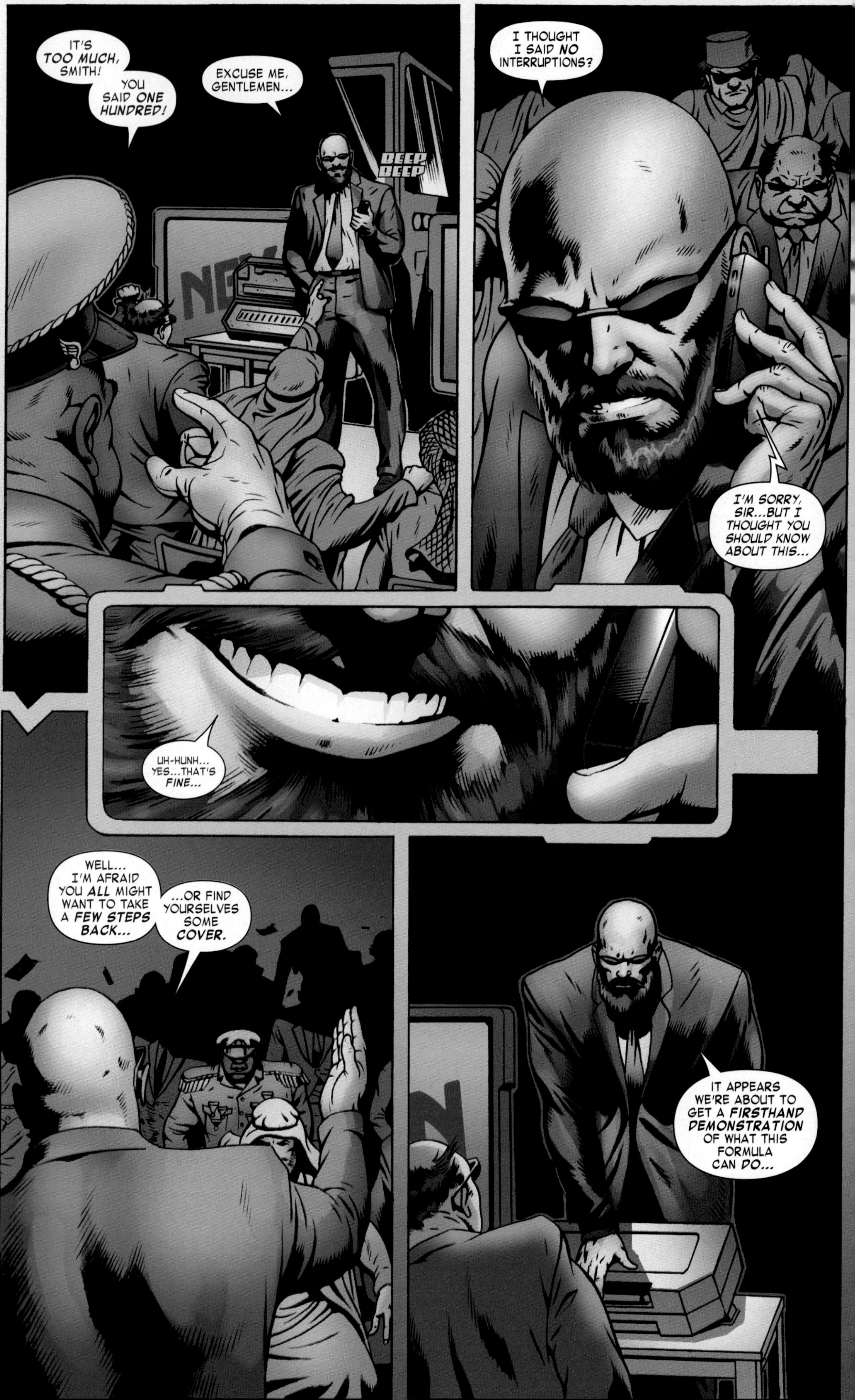
IT'S TOO MUCH, SMITH!
YOU SAID ONE HUNDRED!
EXCUSE ME, GENTLEMEN...
BEEP BEEP
I THOUGHT I SAID NO INTERRUPTIONS?
I'M SORRY, SIR...BUT I THOUGHT YOU SHOULD KNOW ABOUT THIS...
UH-HUNH... YES...THAT'S FINE...
WELL... I'M AFRAID YOU ALL MIGHT WANT TO TAKE A FEW STEPS BACK...
...OR FIND YOURSELVES SOME COVER.
IT APPEARS WE'RE ABOUT TO GET A FIRSTHAND DEMONSTRATION OF WHAT THIS FORMULA CAN DO...

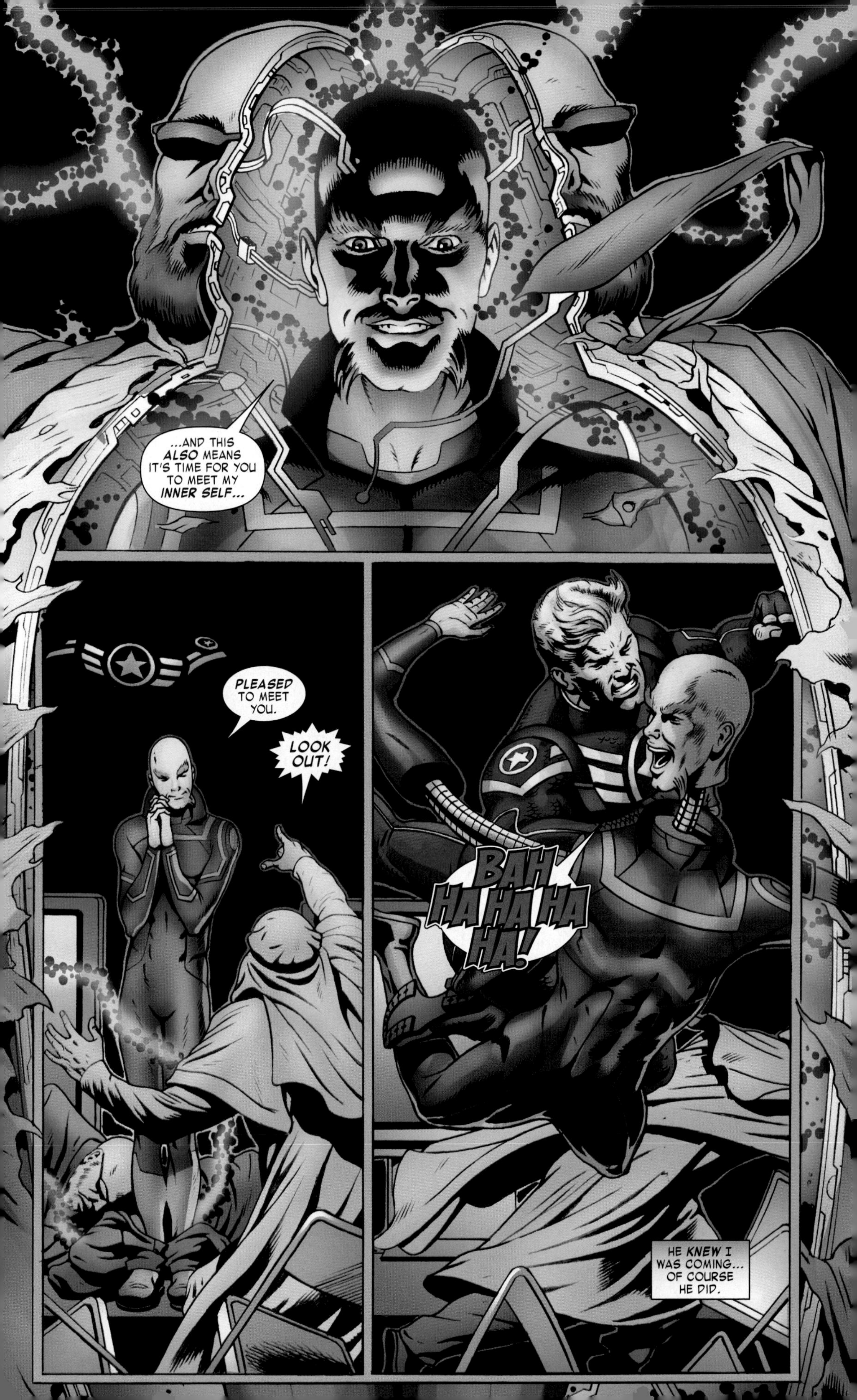
...AND THIS ALSO MEANS IT'S TIME FOR YOU TO MEET MY INNER SELF...
PLEASED TO MEET YOU.
LOOK OUT!
BAH HA HA HA HA!
HE KNEW I WAS COMING... OF COURSE HE DID.

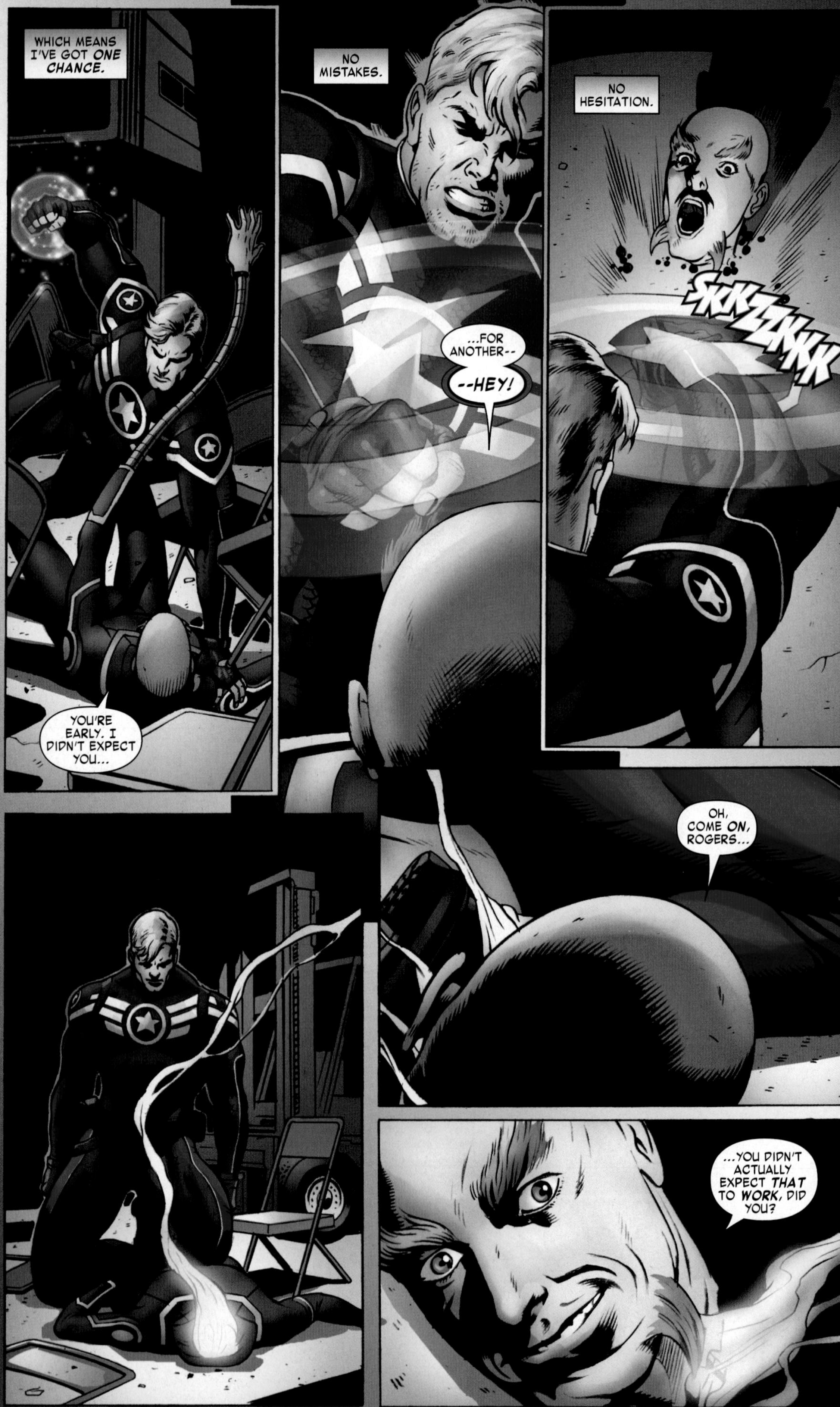
WHICH MEANS I'VE GOT ONE CHANCE.
NO MISTAKES.
NO HESITATION.
YOU'RE EARLY. I DIDN'T EXPECT YOU...
...FOR ANOTHER--
--HEY!
SKKZZNKKK
OH, COME ON, ROGERS...
...YOU DIDN'T ACTUALLY EXPECT THAT TO WORK, DID YOU?

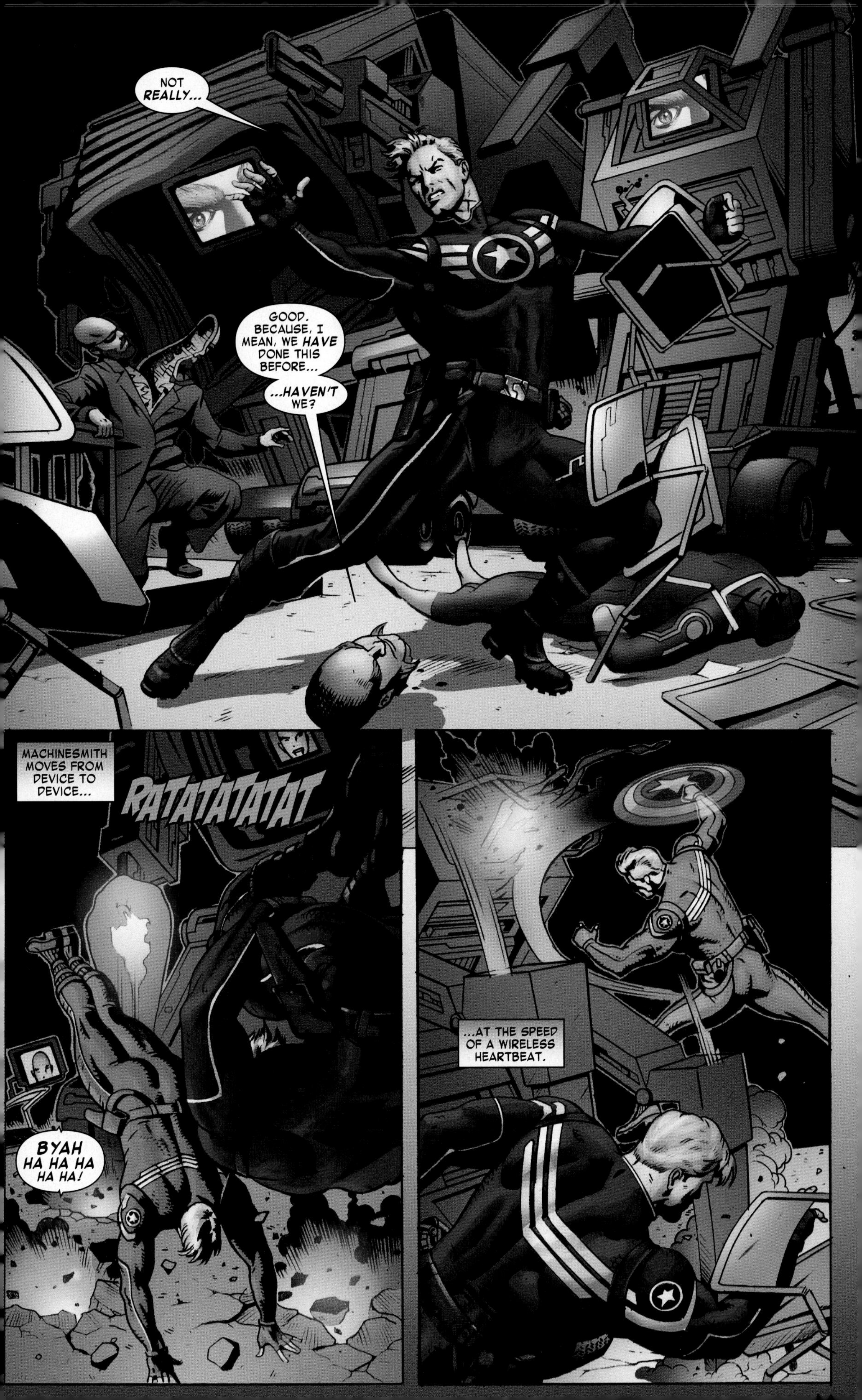
NOT REALLY...
GOOD. BECAUSE, I MEAN, WE HAVE DONE THIS BEFORE...
...HAVEN'T WE?
MACHINESMITH MOVES FROM DEVICE TO DEVICE...
RATATATATAT
BYAH HA HA HA HA HA!
...AT THE SPEED OF A WIRELESS HEARTBEAT.

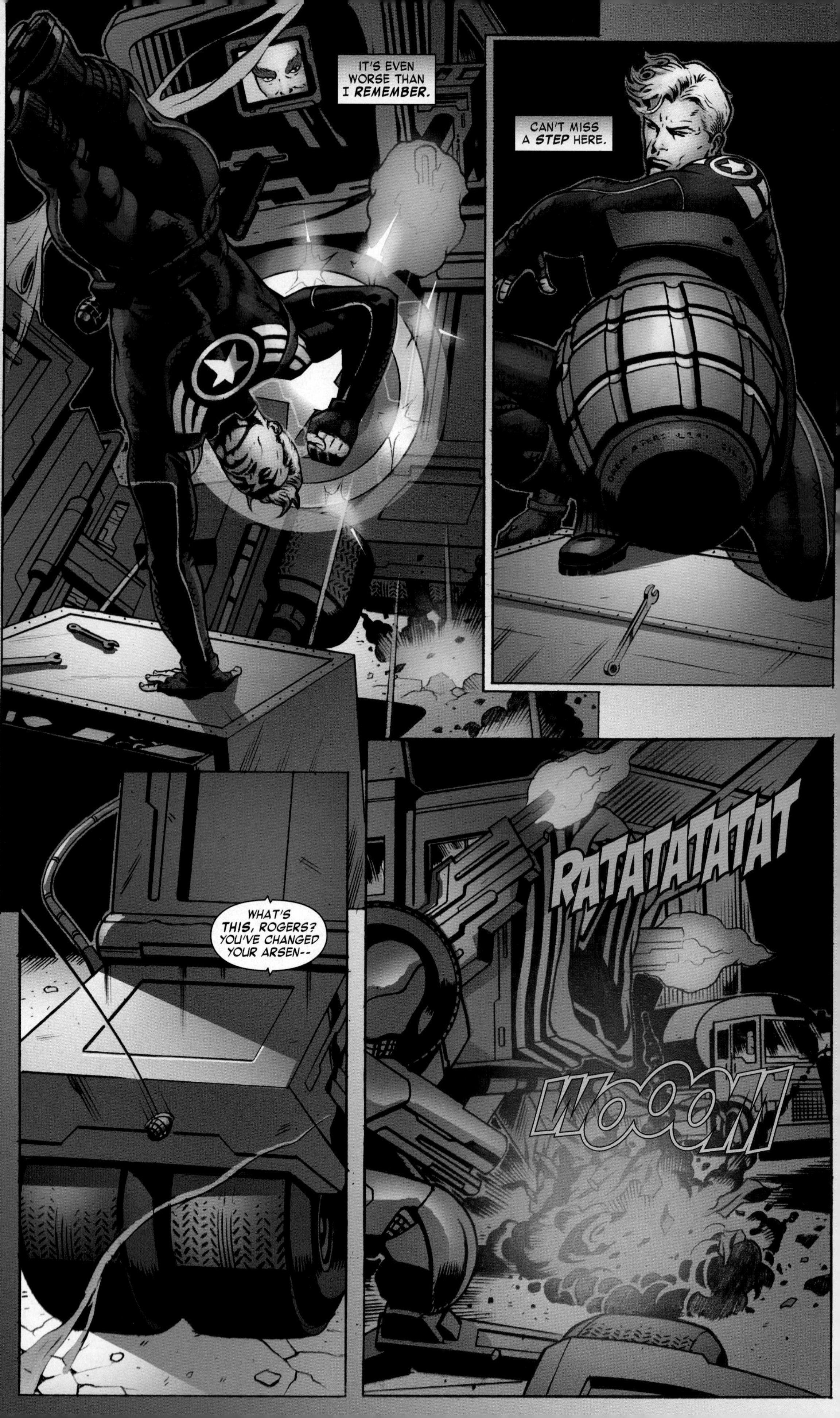
IT'S EVEN WORSE THAN I REMEMBER.
CAN'T MISS A STEP HERE.
WHAT'S THIS, ROGERS? YOU'VE CHANGED YOUR ARSEN--
RATATATATAT
WOOOM

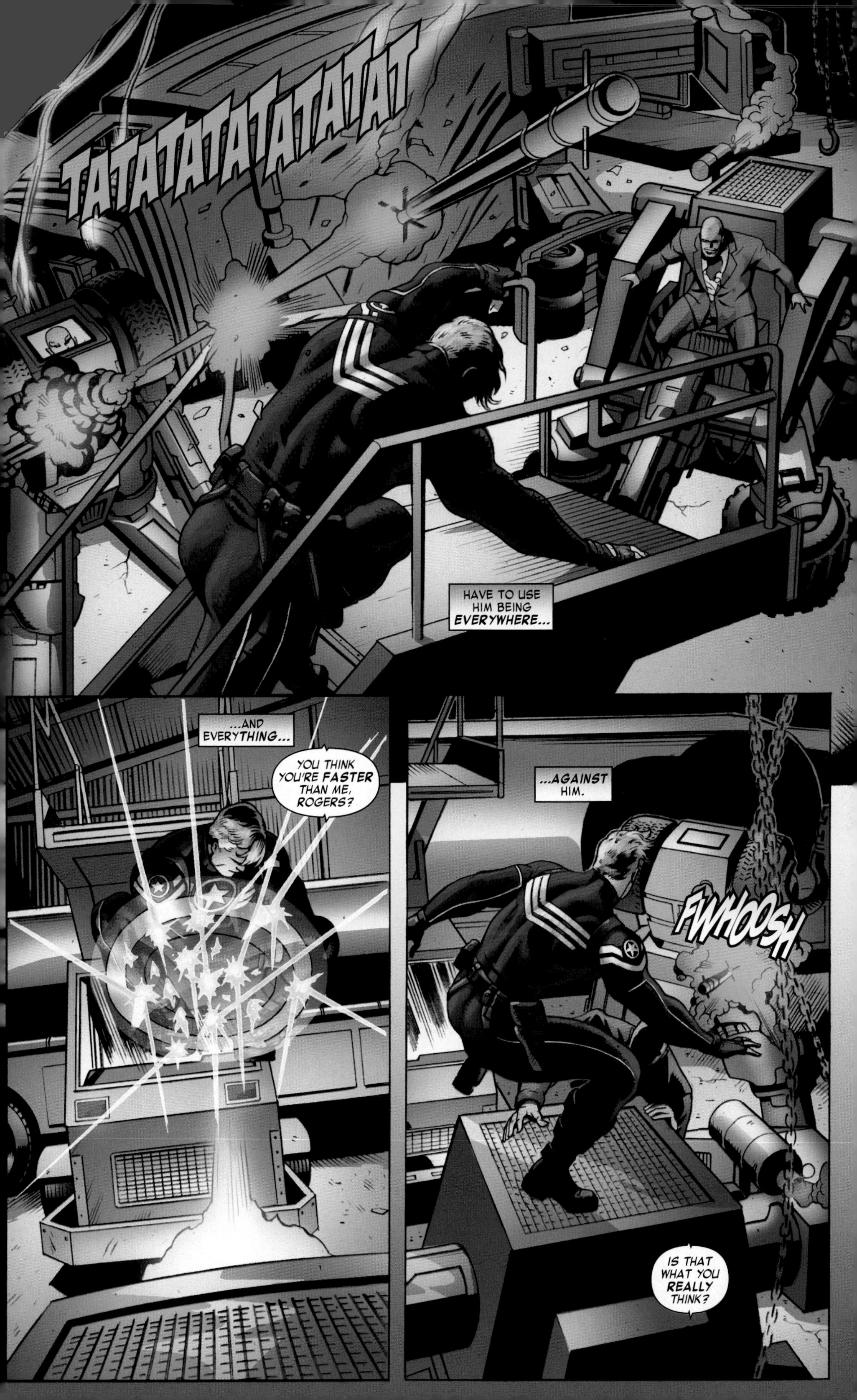
TATATATATATATAT
HAVE TO USE HIM BEING EVERYWHERE...
...AND EVERYTHING...
YOU THINK YOU'RE FASTER THAN ME, ROGERS?
...AGAINST HIM.
FWHOOSH
IS THAT WHAT YOU REALLY THINK?

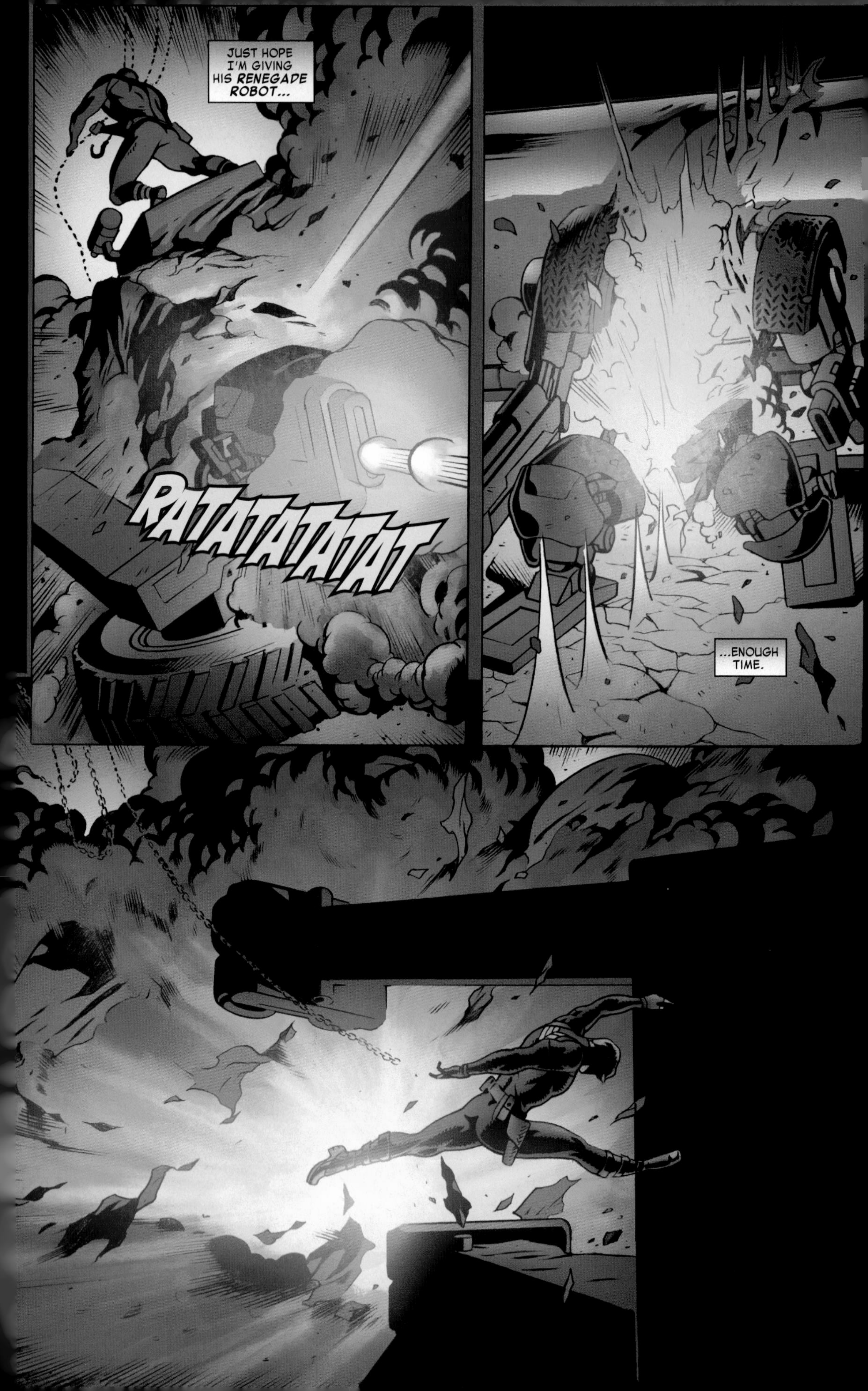
JUST HOPE I'M GIVING HIS *RENEGADE ROBOT*...
RATATATATATAT
...ENOUGH TIME.

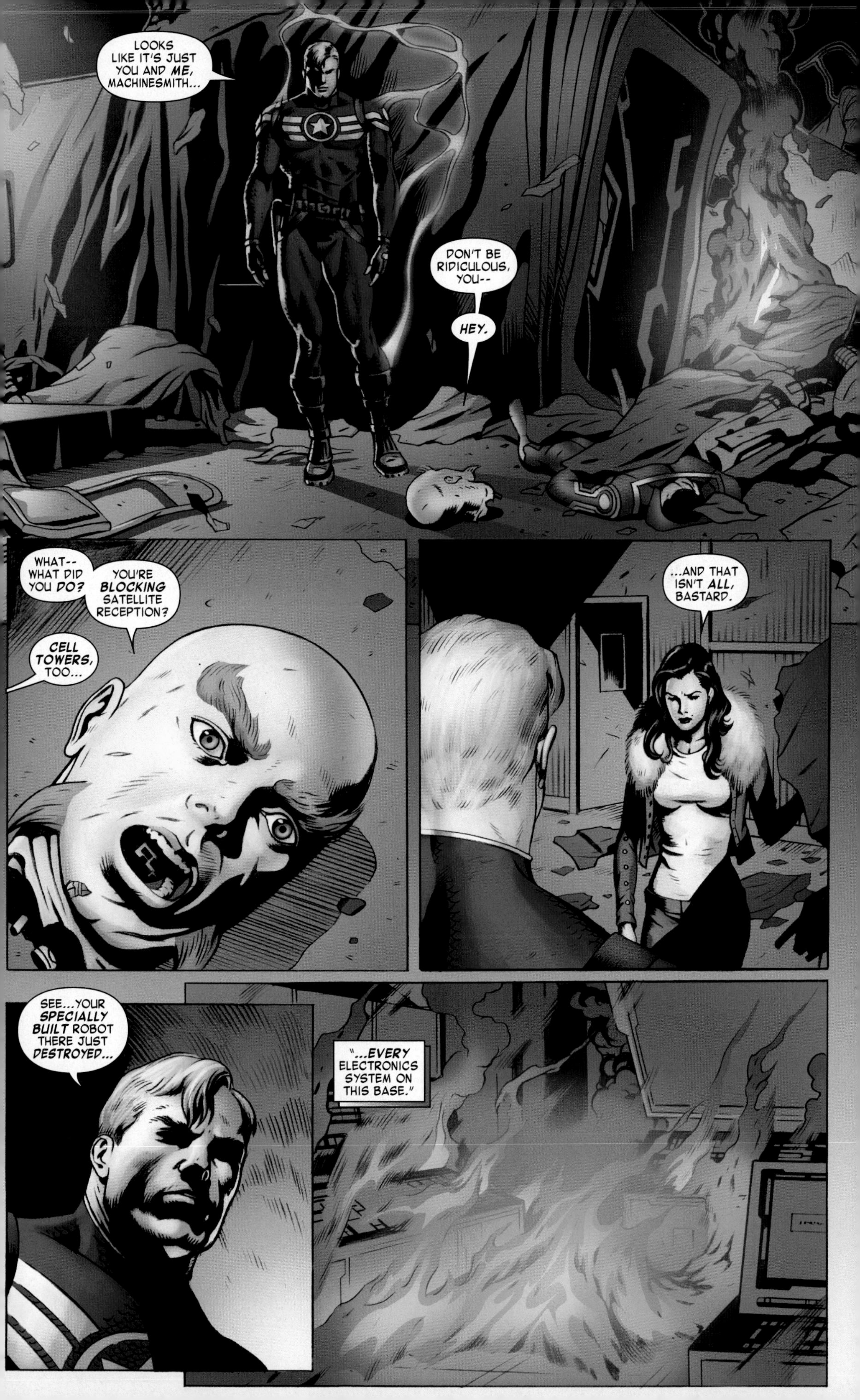
LOOKS LIKE IT'S JUST YOU AND ME, MACHINESMITH...
DON'T BE RIDICULOUS, YOU--
HEY.
WHAT-- WHAT DID YOU DO?
YOU'RE BLOCKING SATELLITE RECEPTION?
CELL TOWERS, TOO...
...AND THAT ISN'T ALL, BASTARD.
SEE...YOUR SPECIALLY BUILT ROBOT THERE JUST DESTROYED...
"...EVERY ELECTRONICS SYSTEM ON THIS BASE."

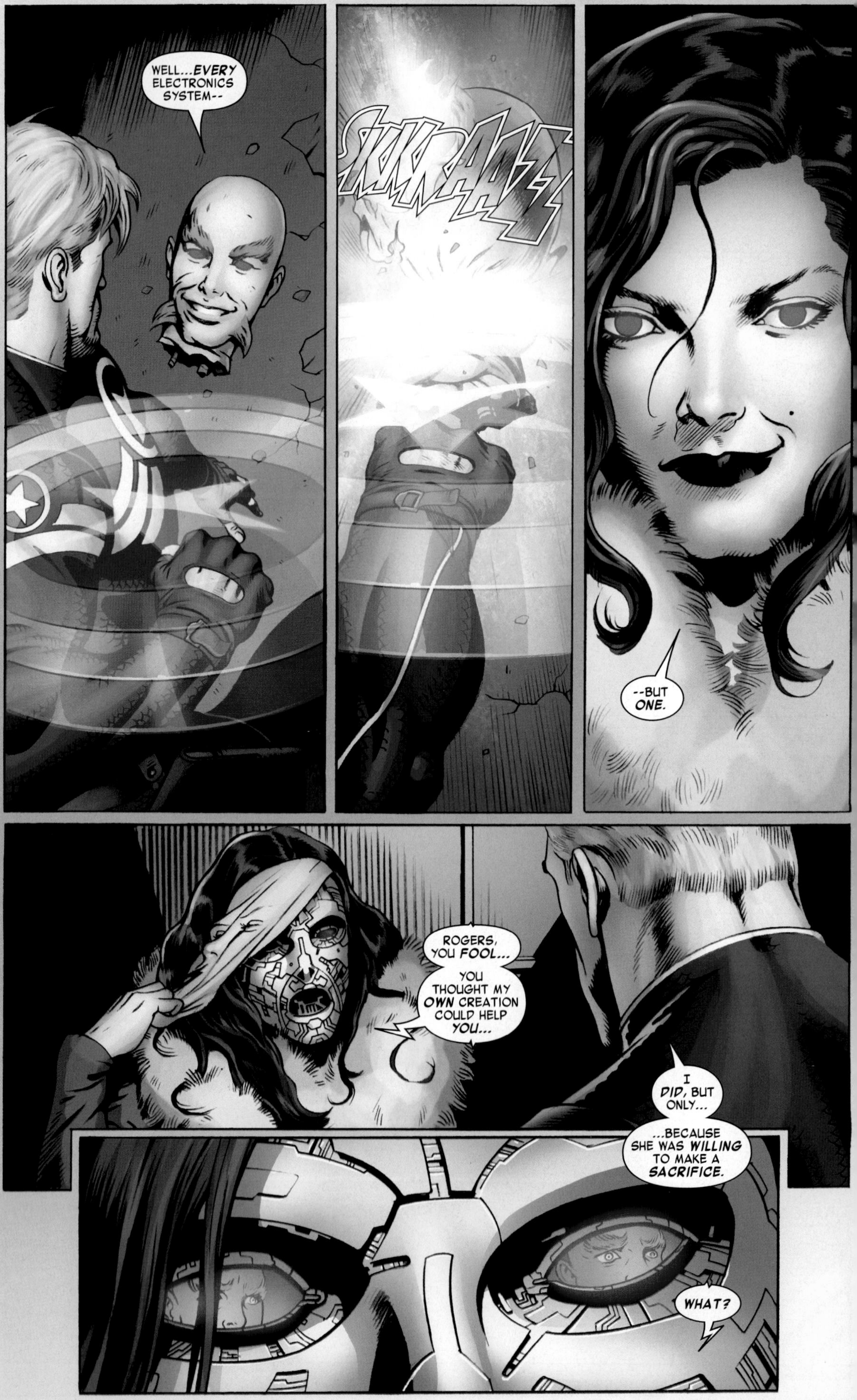
WELL...EVERY ELECTRONICS SYSTEM--
SKKRAAKK
--BUT ONE.
ROGERS, YOU FOOL...
YOU THOUGHT MY OWN CREATION COULD HELP YOU...
I DID, BUT ONLY...
...BECAUSE SHE WAS WILLING TO MAKE A SACRIFICE.
WHAT?

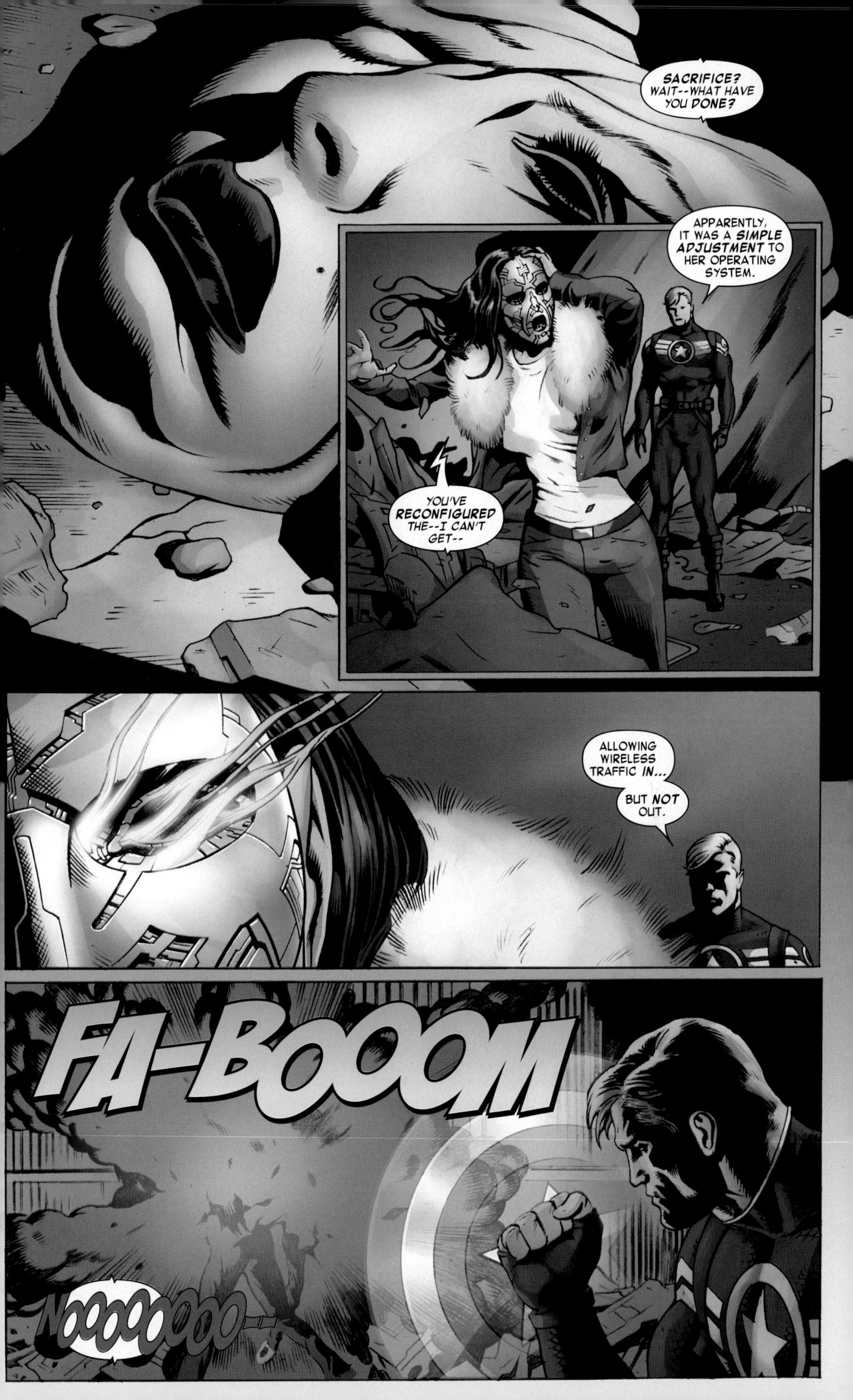
SACRIFICE? WAIT--WHAT HAVE YOU DONE?
APPARENTLY, IT WAS A SIMPLE ADJUSTMENT TO HER OPERATING SYSTEM.
YOU'VE RECONFIGURED THE--I CAN'T GET--
ALLOWING WIRELESS TRAFFIC IN...
BUT NOT OUT.
FA-BOOOM
NOOOOOOOO--!

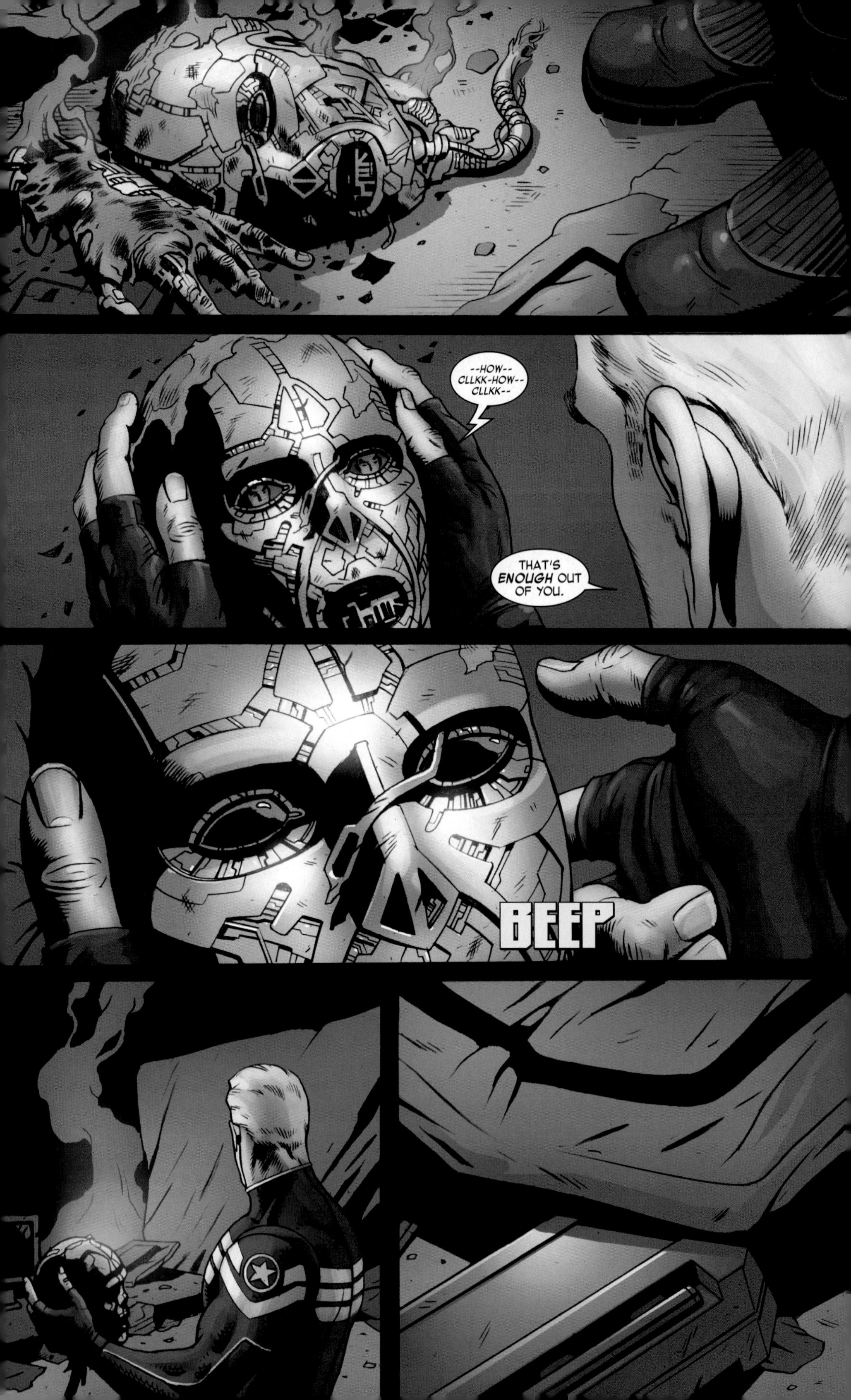
--HOW--
CLLKK-HOW--
CLLKK--
THAT'S ENOUGH OUT OF YOU.
BEEP

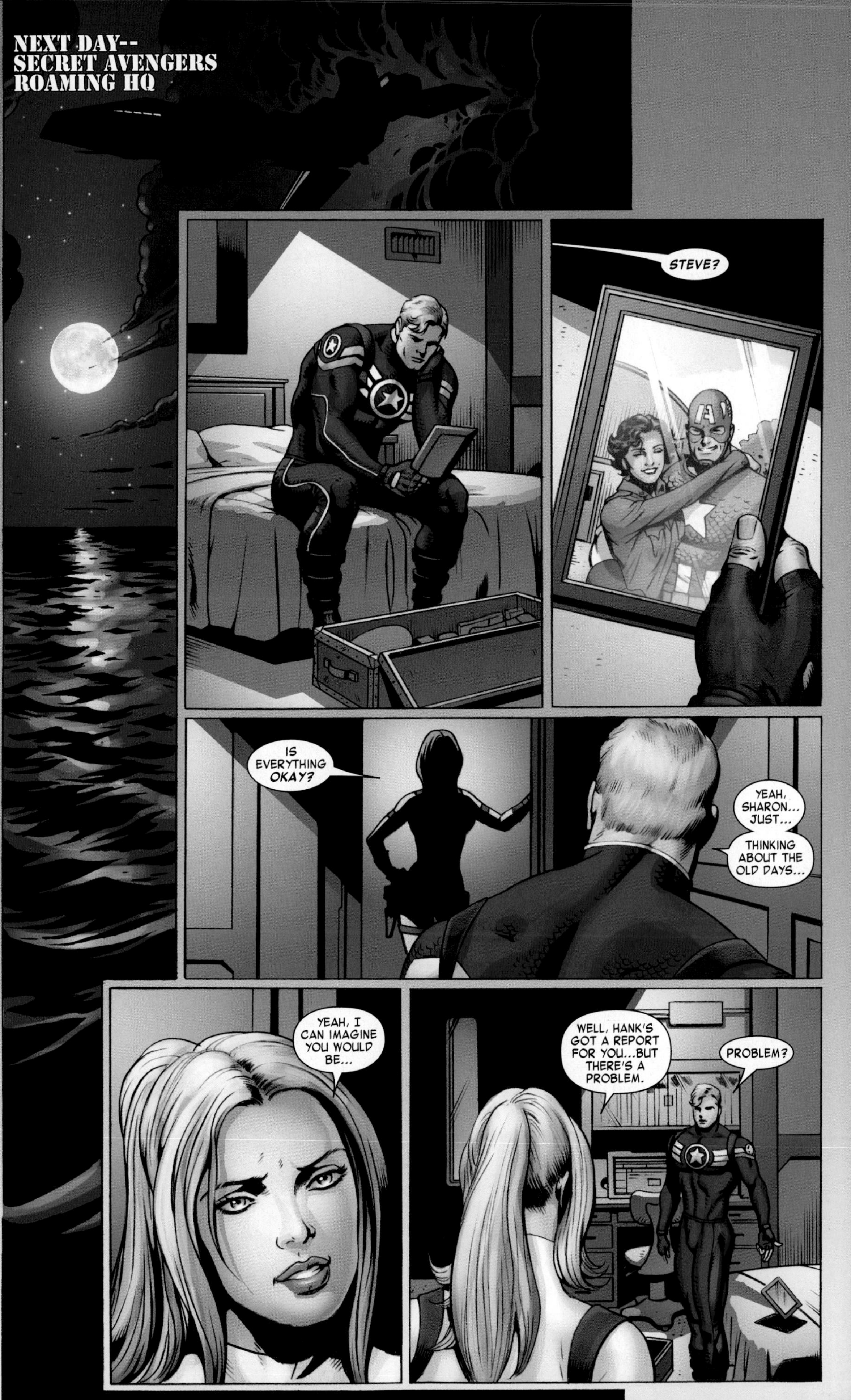
NEXT DAY--
SECRET AVENGERS
ROAMING HQ
STEVE?
IS EVERYTHING OKAY?
YEAH, SHARON... JUST...
THINKING ABOUT THE OLD DAYS...
YEAH, I CAN IMAGINE YOU WOULD BE...
WELL, HANK'S GOT A REPORT FOR YOU...BUT THERE'S A PROBLEM.
PROBLEM?

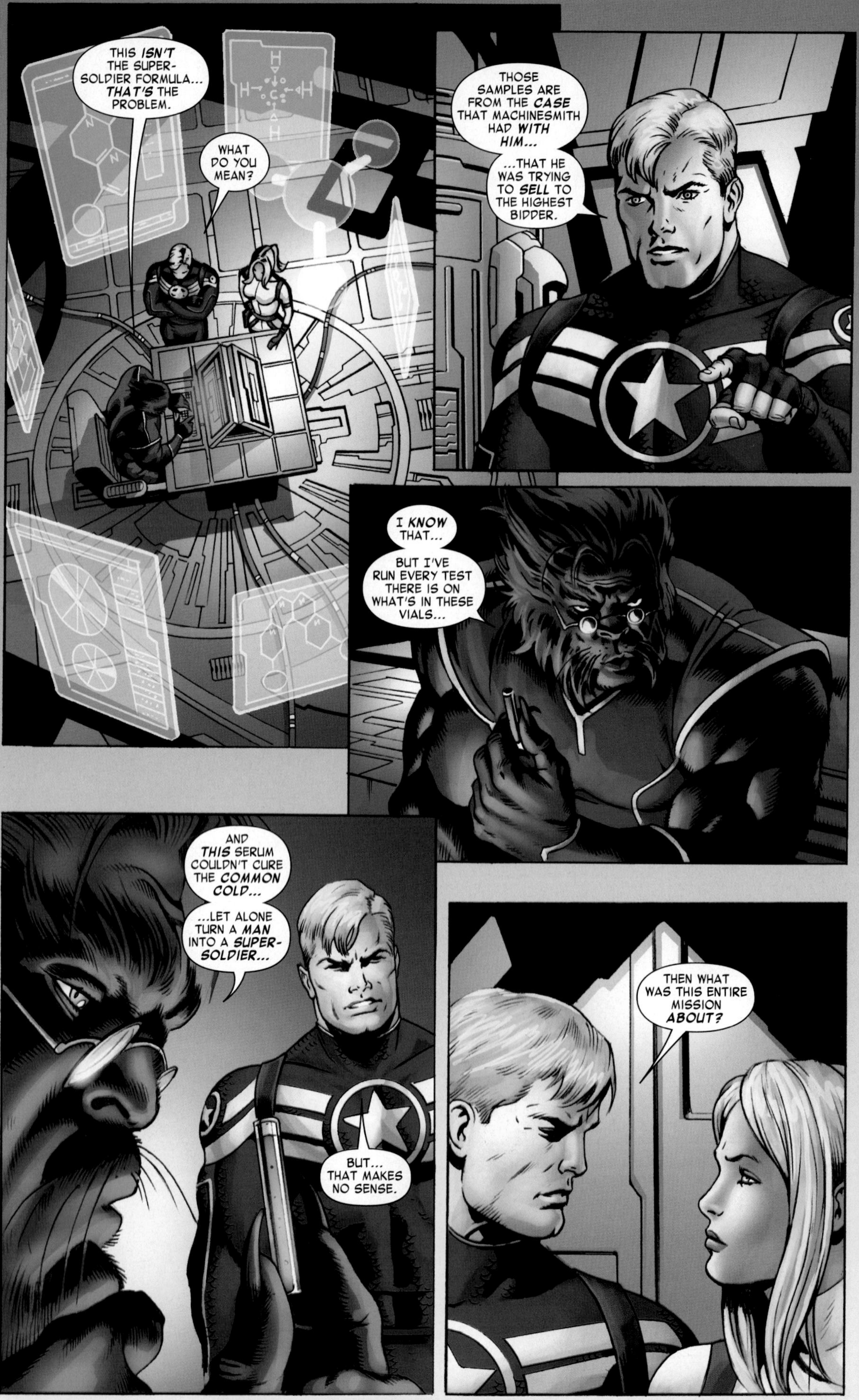
THIS ISN'T THE SUPER-SOLDIER FORMULA... THAT'S THE PROBLEM.
WHAT DO YOU MEAN?
THOSE SAMPLES ARE FROM THE CASE THAT MACHINESMITH HAD WITH HIM...
...THAT HE WAS TRYING TO SELL TO THE HIGHEST BIDDER.
I KNOW THAT...
BUT I'VE RUN EVERY TEST THERE IS ON WHAT'S IN THESE VIALS...
AND THIS SERUM COULDN'T CURE THE COMMON COLD...
...LET ALONE TURN A MAN INTO A SUPER-SOLDIER...
BUT... THAT MAKES NO SENSE.
THEN WHAT WAS THIS ENTIRE MISSION ABOUT?

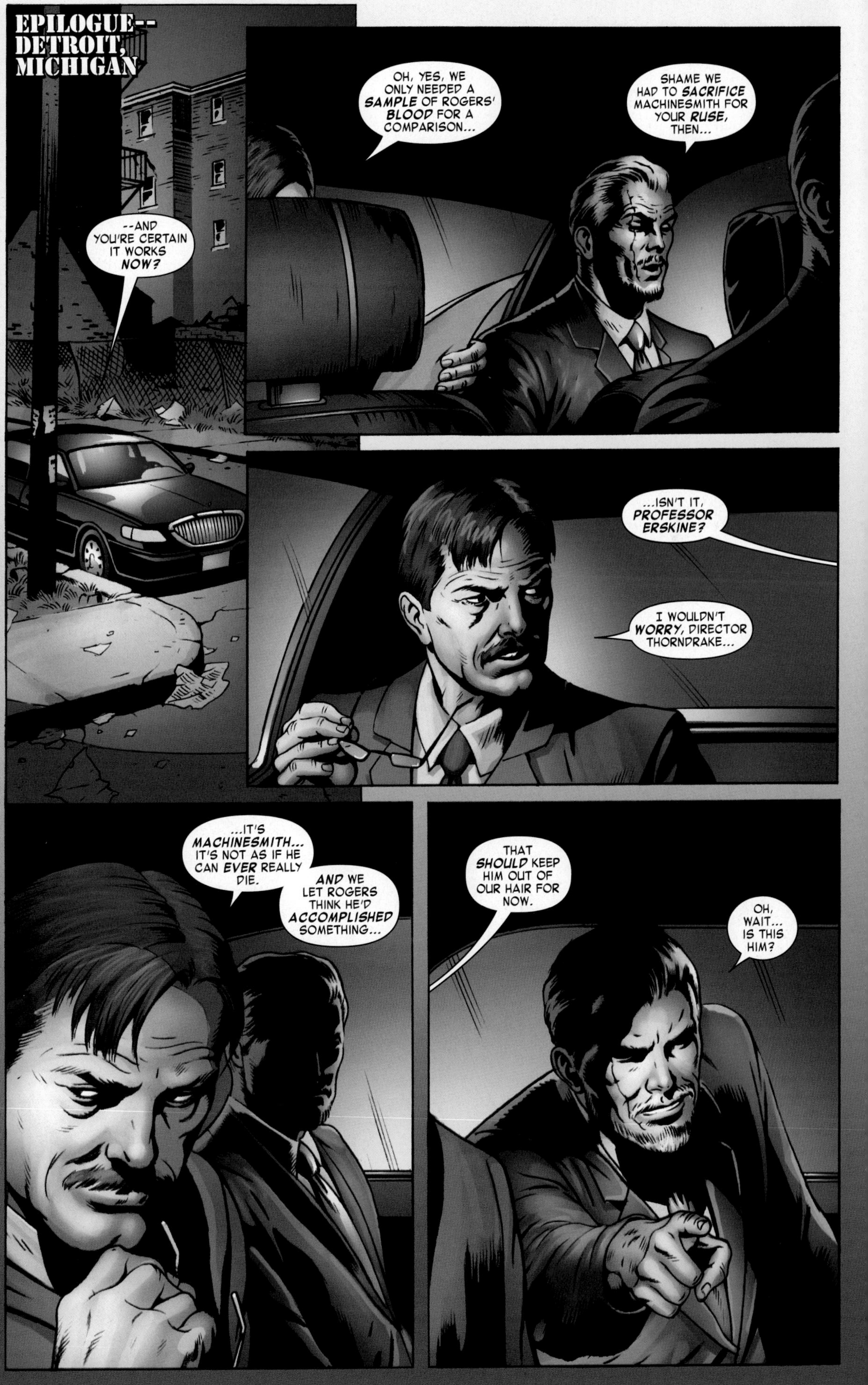
EPILOGUE-- DETROIT, MICHIGAN
--AND YOU'RE CERTAIN IT WORKS NOW?
OH, YES, WE ONLY NEEDED A SAMPLE OF ROGERS' BLOOD FOR A COMPARISON...
SHAME WE HAD TO SACRIFICE MACHINESMITH FOR YOUR RUSE, THEN...
...ISN'T IT, PROFESSOR ERSKINE?
I WOULDN'T WORRY, DIRECTOR THORNDRAKE...
...IT'S MACHINESMITH... IT'S NOT AS IF HE CAN EVER REALLY DIE.
AND WE LET ROGERS THINK HE'D ACCOMPLISHED SOMETHING...
THAT SHOULD KEEP HIM OUT OF OUR HAIR FOR NOW.
OH, WAIT... IS THIS HIM?

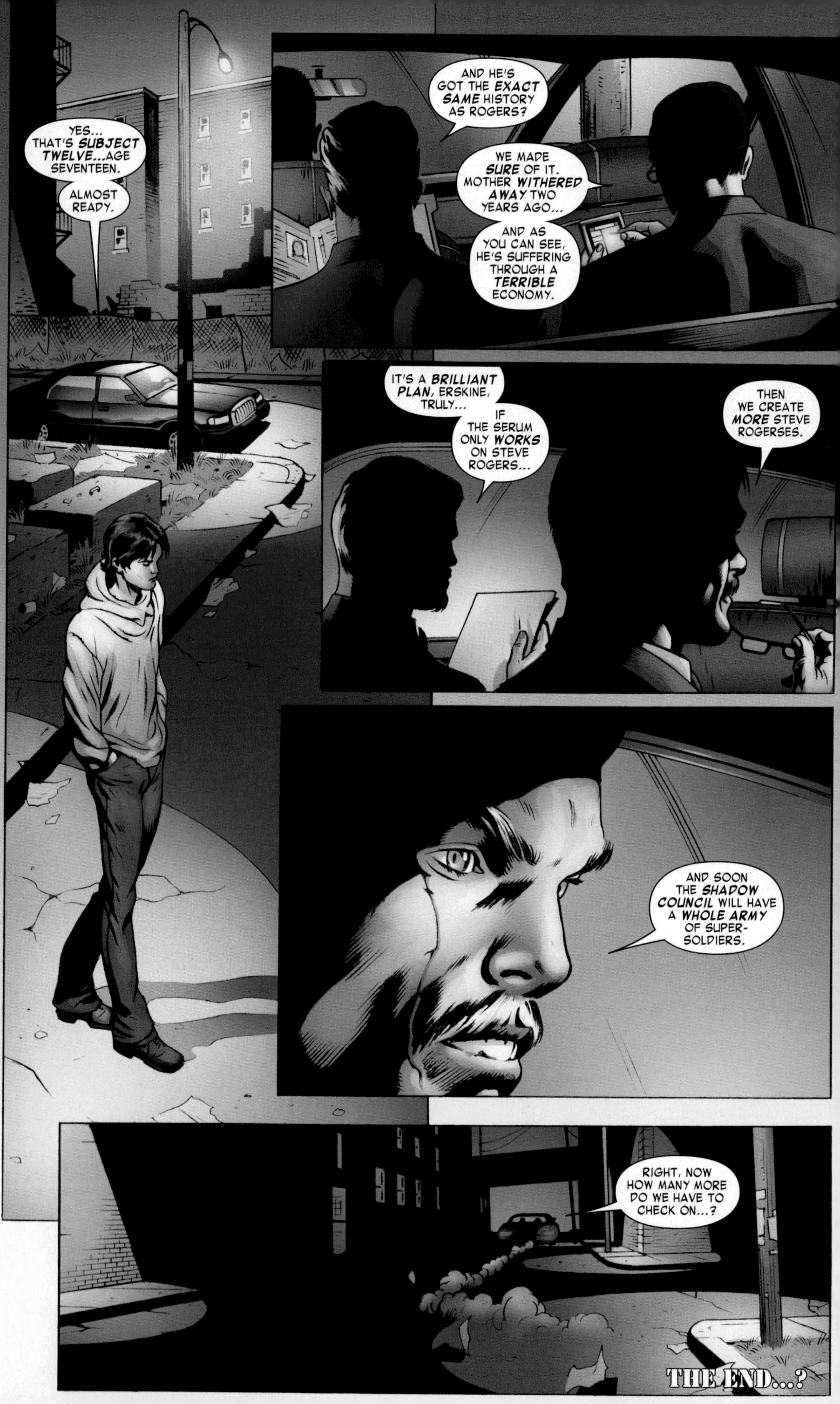

YES... THAT'S SUBJECT TWELVE...AGE SEVENTEEN.
ALMOST READY.
AND HE'S GOT THE EXACT SAME HISTORY AS ROGERS?
WE MADE SURE OF IT. MOTHER WITHERED AWAY TWO YEARS AGO...
AND AS YOU CAN SEE, HE'S SUFFERING THROUGH A TERRIBLE ECONOMY.
IT'S A BRILLIANT PLAN, ERSKINE, TRULY...
IF THE SERUM ONLY WORKS ON STEVE ROGERS...
THEN WE CREATE MORE STEVE ROGERSES.
AND SOON THE SHADOW COUNCIL WILL HAVE A WHOLE ARMY OF SUPER-SOLDIERS.
RIGHT, NOW HOW MANY MORE DO WE HAVE TO CHECK ON...?
THE END...?

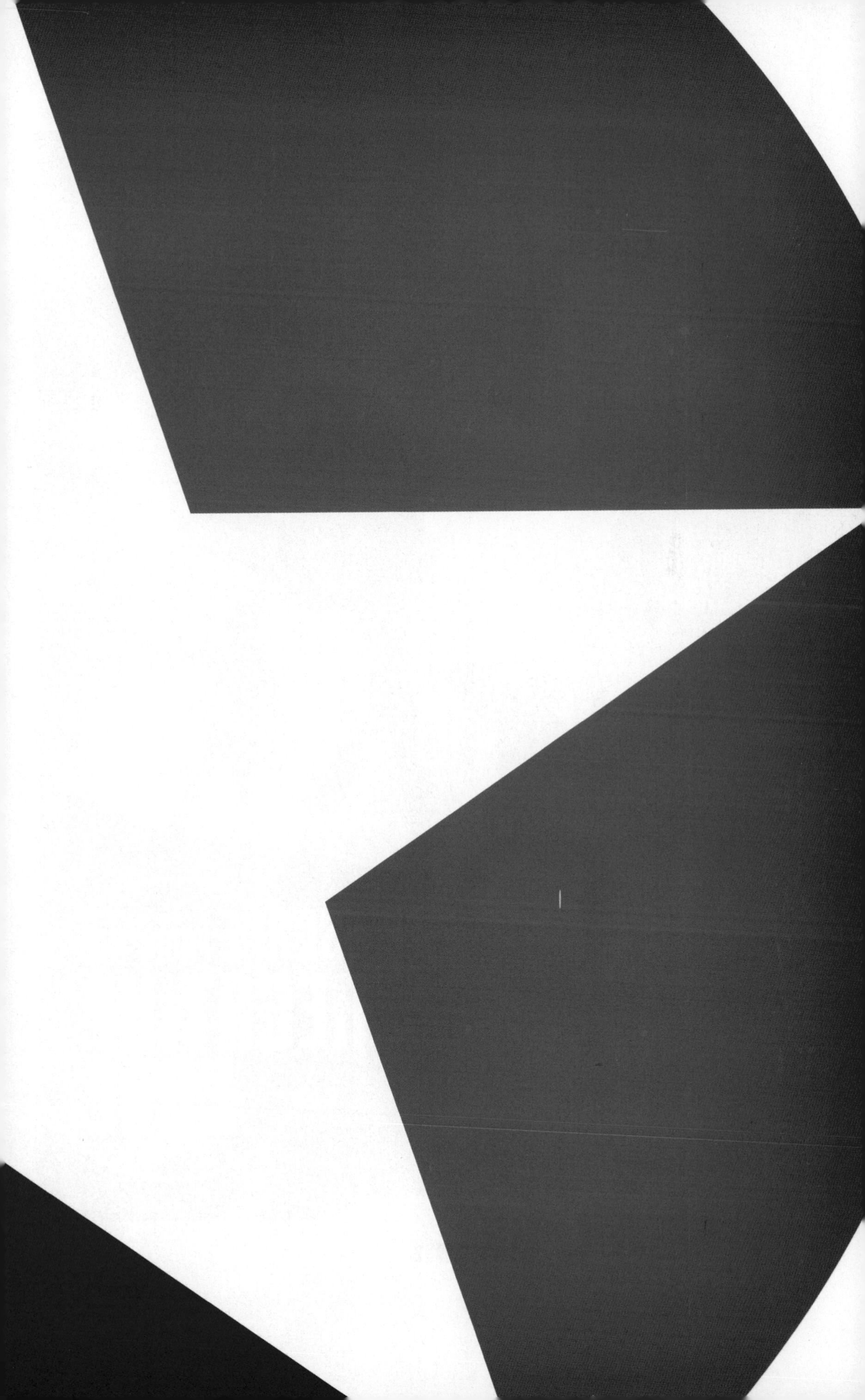

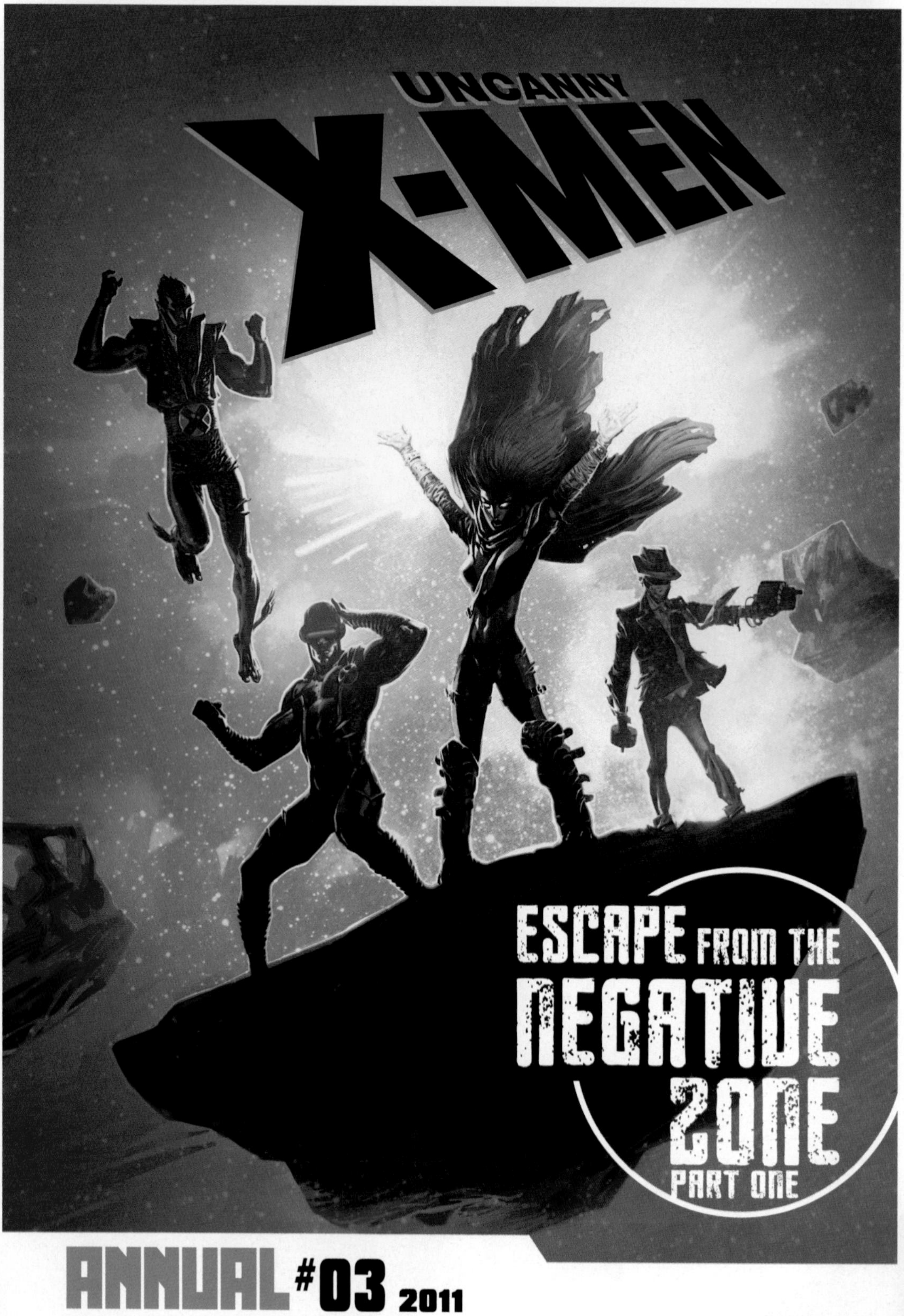
UNCANNY
X-MEN
ESCAPE FROM THE
NEGATIVE
ZONE
PART ONE

ANNUAL #03 2011

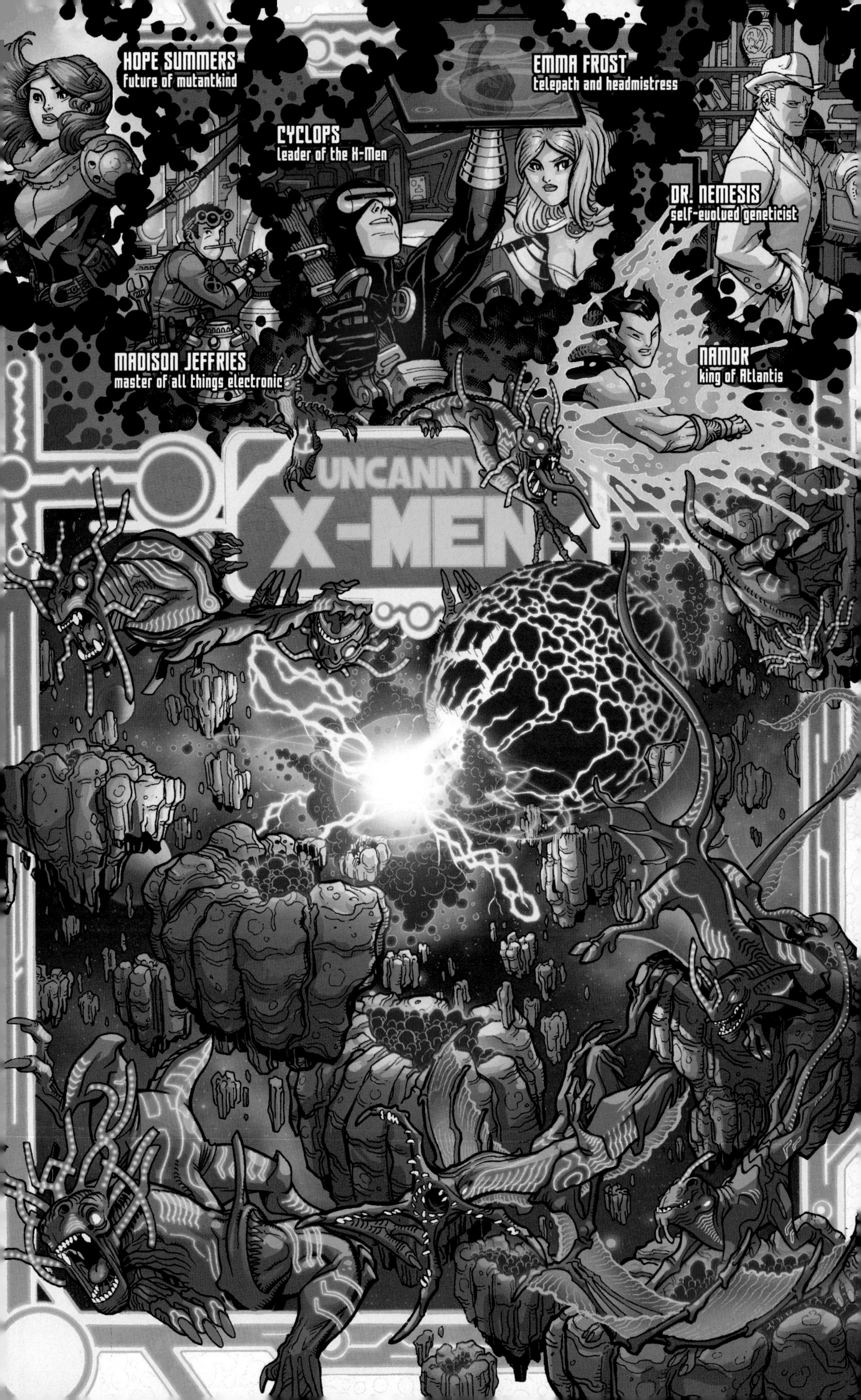
HOPE SUMMERS
future of mutantkind
EMMA FROST
telepath and headmistress
CYCLOPS
leader of the X-Men
DR. NEMESIS
self-evolved geneticist
MADISON JEFFRIES
master of all things electronic
NAMOR
king of Atlantis
UNCANNY
X-MEN

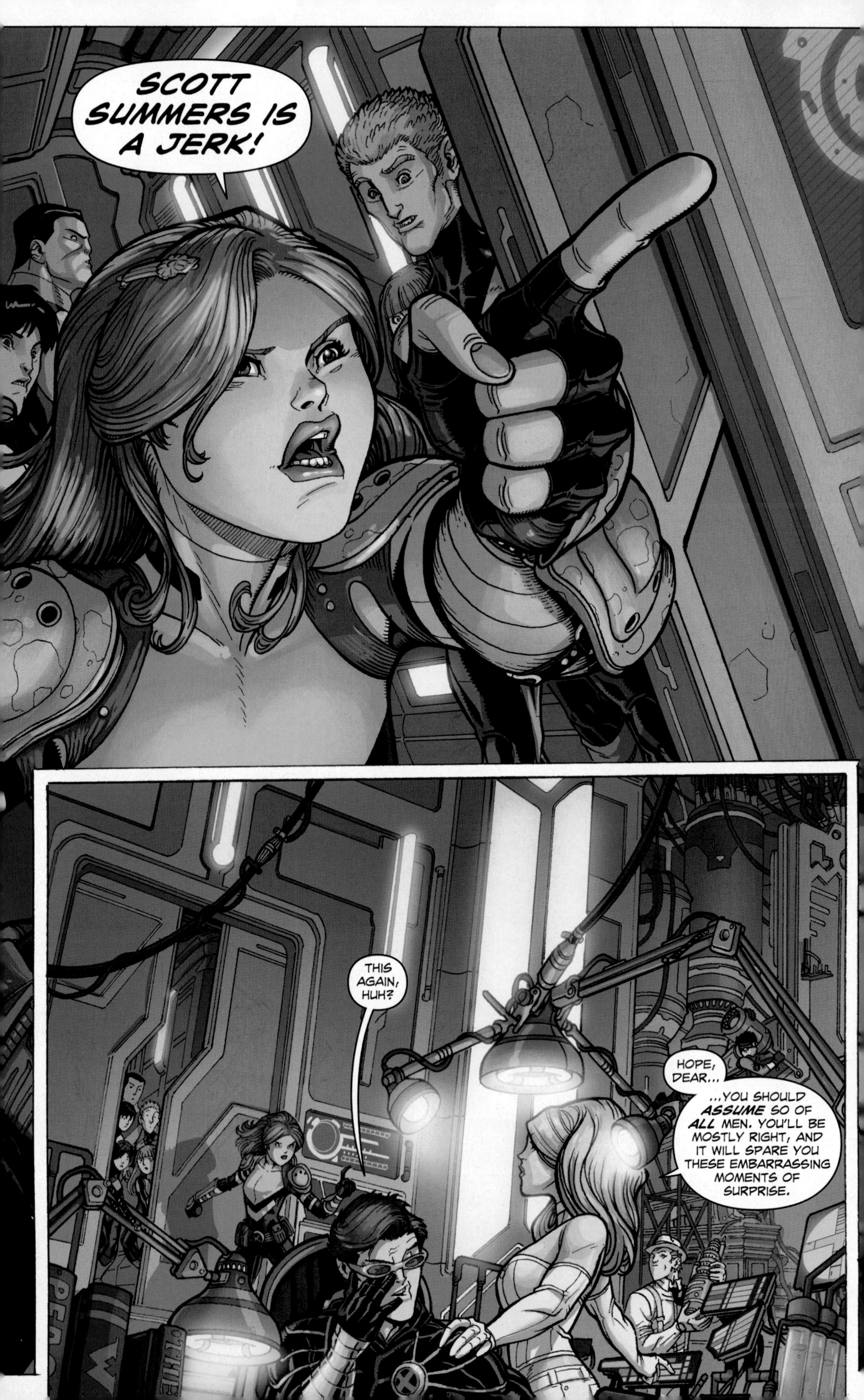
SCOTT SUMMERS IS A JERK!
THIS AGAIN, HUH?
HOPE, DEAR...
...YOU SHOULD ASSUME SO OF ALL MEN. YOU'LL BE MOSTLY RIGHT, AND IT WILL SPARE YOU THESE EMBARRASSING MOMENTS OF SURPRISE.

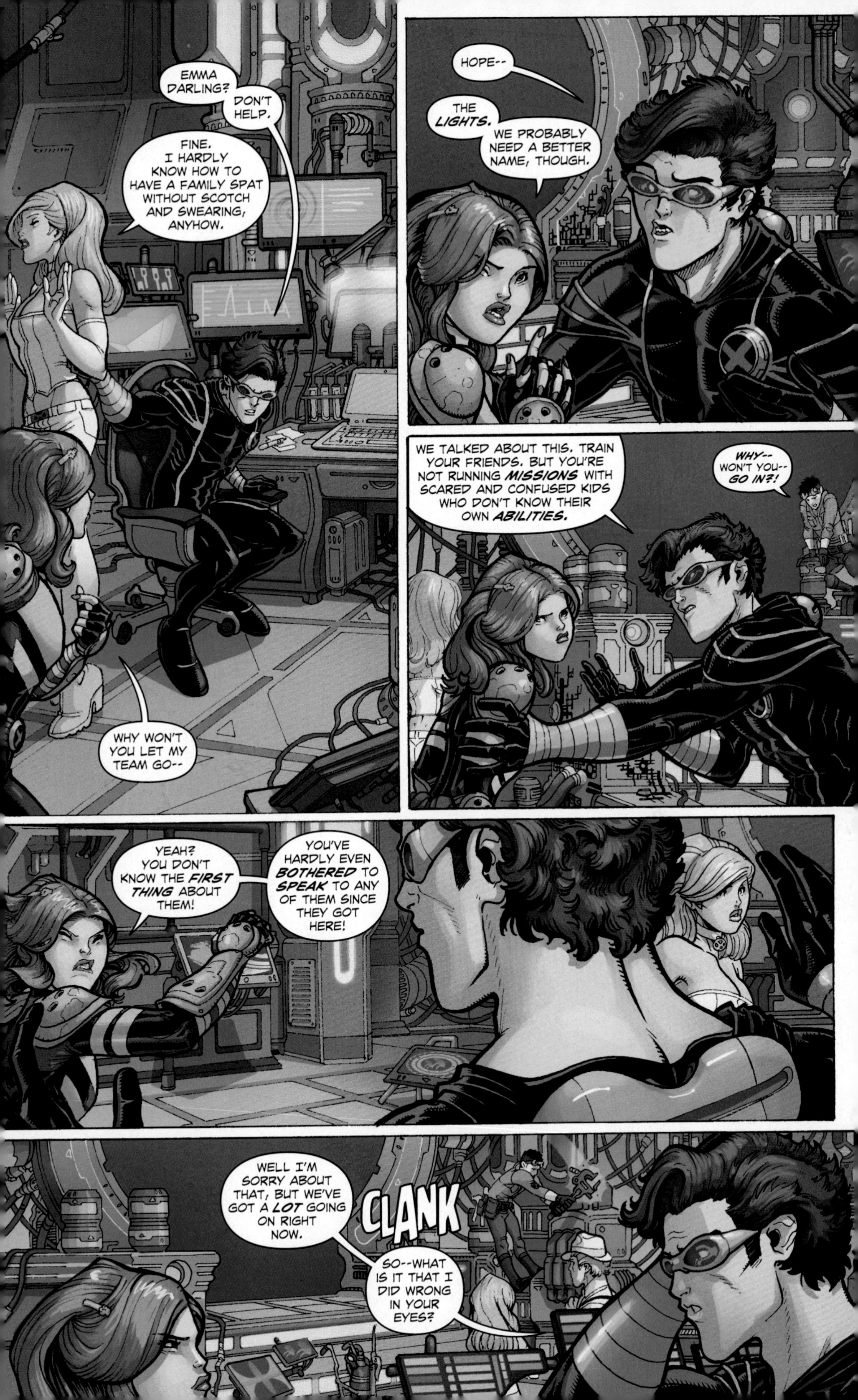
EMMA DARLING?
DON'T HELP.
FINE. I HARDLY KNOW HOW TO HAVE A FAMILY SPAT WITHOUT SCOTCH AND SWEARING, ANYHOW.
WHY WON'T YOU LET MY TEAM GO--
HOPE--
THE LIGHTS.
WE PROBABLY NEED A BETTER NAME, THOUGH.
WE TALKED ABOUT THIS. TRAIN YOUR FRIENDS. BUT YOU'RE NOT RUNNING MISSIONS WITH SCARED AND CONFUSED KIDS WHO DON'T KNOW THEIR OWN ABILITIES.
WHY-- WON'T YOU-- GO IN?!
YEAH? YOU DON'T KNOW THE FIRST THING ABOUT THEM!
YOU'VE HARDLY EVEN BOTHERED TO SPEAK TO ANY OF THEM SINCE THEY GOT HERE!
WELL I'M SORRY ABOUT THAT, BUT WE'VE GOT A LOT GOING ON RIGHT NOW.
CLANK
SO--WHAT IS IT THAT I DID WRONG IN YOUR EYES?

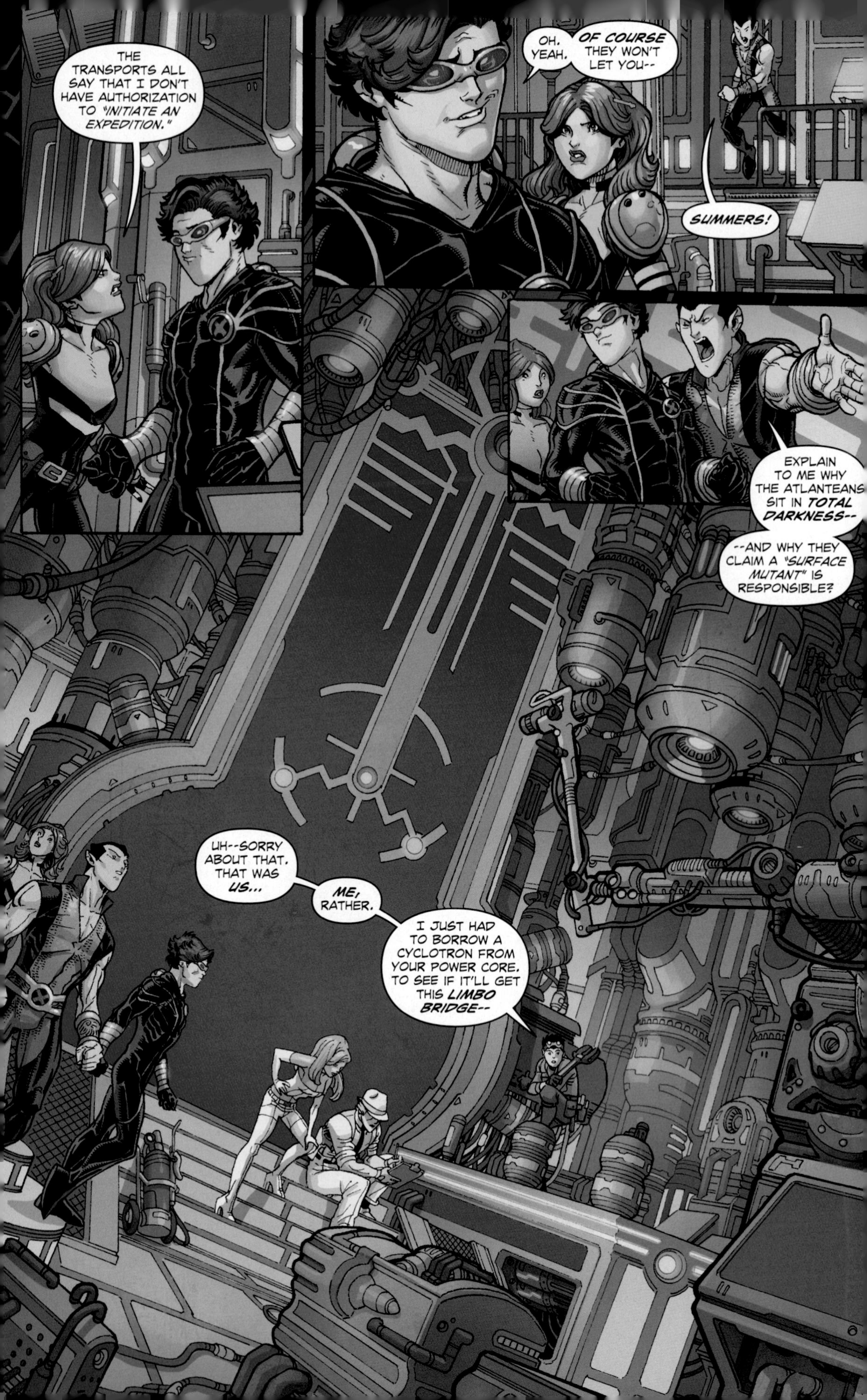
THE TRANSPORTS ALL SAY THAT I DON'T HAVE AUTHORIZATION TO "INITIATE AN EXPEDITION."
OH. YEAH.
OF COURSE THEY WON'T LET YOU--
SUMMERS!
EXPLAIN TO ME WHY THE ATLANTEANS SIT IN TOTAL DARKNESS--
--AND WHY THEY CLAIM A "SURFACE MUTANT" IS RESPONSIBLE?
UH--SORRY ABOUT THAT. THAT WAS US...
ME, RATHER.
I JUST HAD TO BORROW A CYCLOTRON FROM YOUR POWER CORE. TO SEE IF IT'LL GET THIS LIMBO BRIDGE--

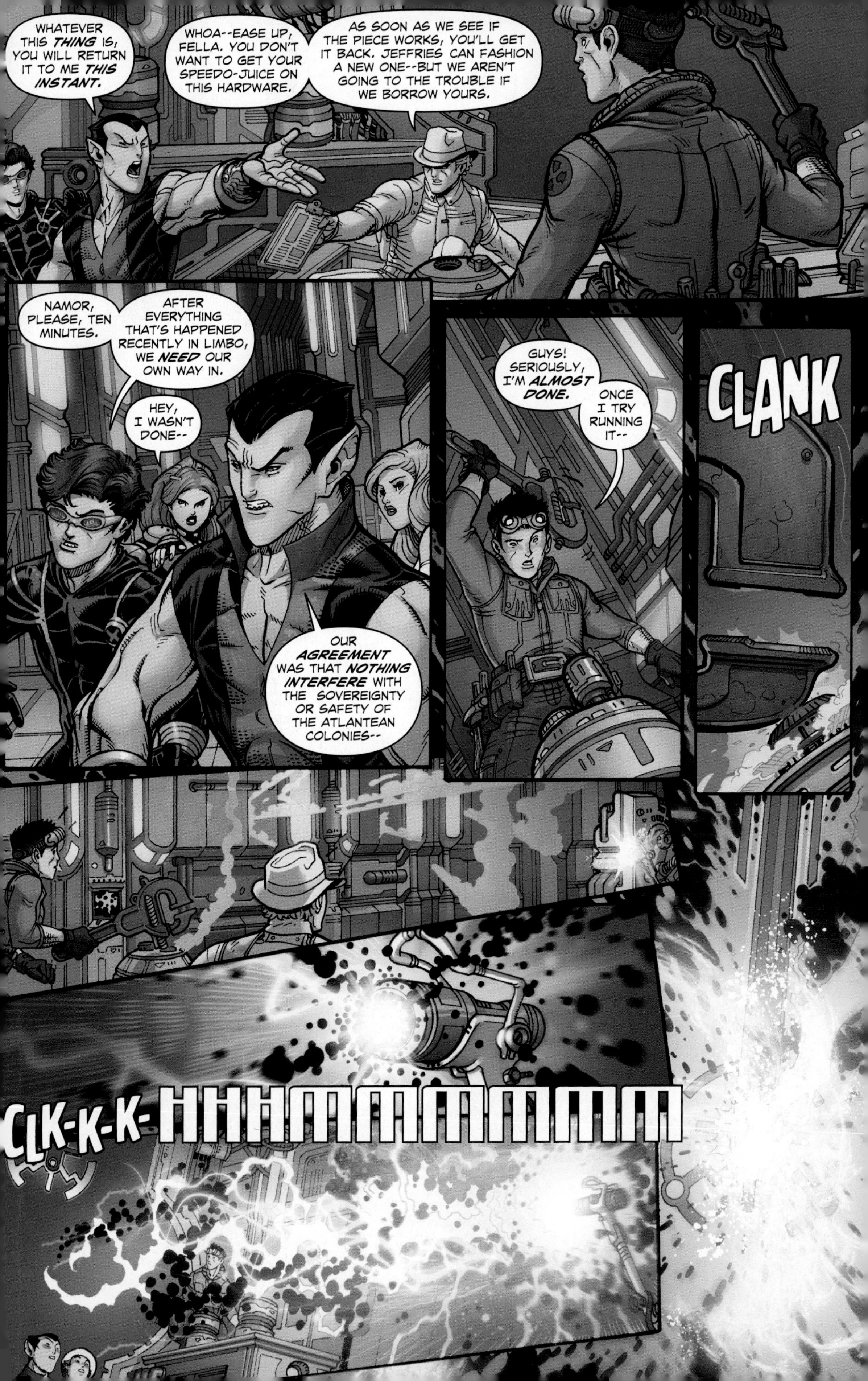
WHATEVER THIS THING IS, YOU WILL RETURN IT TO ME THIS INSTANT.
WHOA--EASE UP, FELLA. YOU DON'T WANT TO GET YOUR SPEEDO-JUICE ON THIS HARDWARE.
AS SOON AS WE SEE IF THE PIECE WORKS, YOU'LL GET IT BACK. JEFFRIES CAN FASHION A NEW ONE--BUT WE AREN'T GOING TO THE TROUBLE IF WE BORROW YOURS.
NAMOR, PLEASE, TEN MINUTES.
AFTER EVERYTHING THAT'S HAPPENED RECENTLY IN LIMBO, WE NEED OUR OWN WAY IN.
HEY, I WASN'T DONE--
OUR AGREEMENT WAS THAT NOTHING INTERFERE WITH THE SOVEREIGNTY OR SAFETY OF THE ATLANTEAN COLONIES--
GUYS! SERIOUSLY, I'M ALMOST DONE.
ONCE I TRY RUNNING IT--
CLANK
CLK-K-K-HHHMMMMMMMM

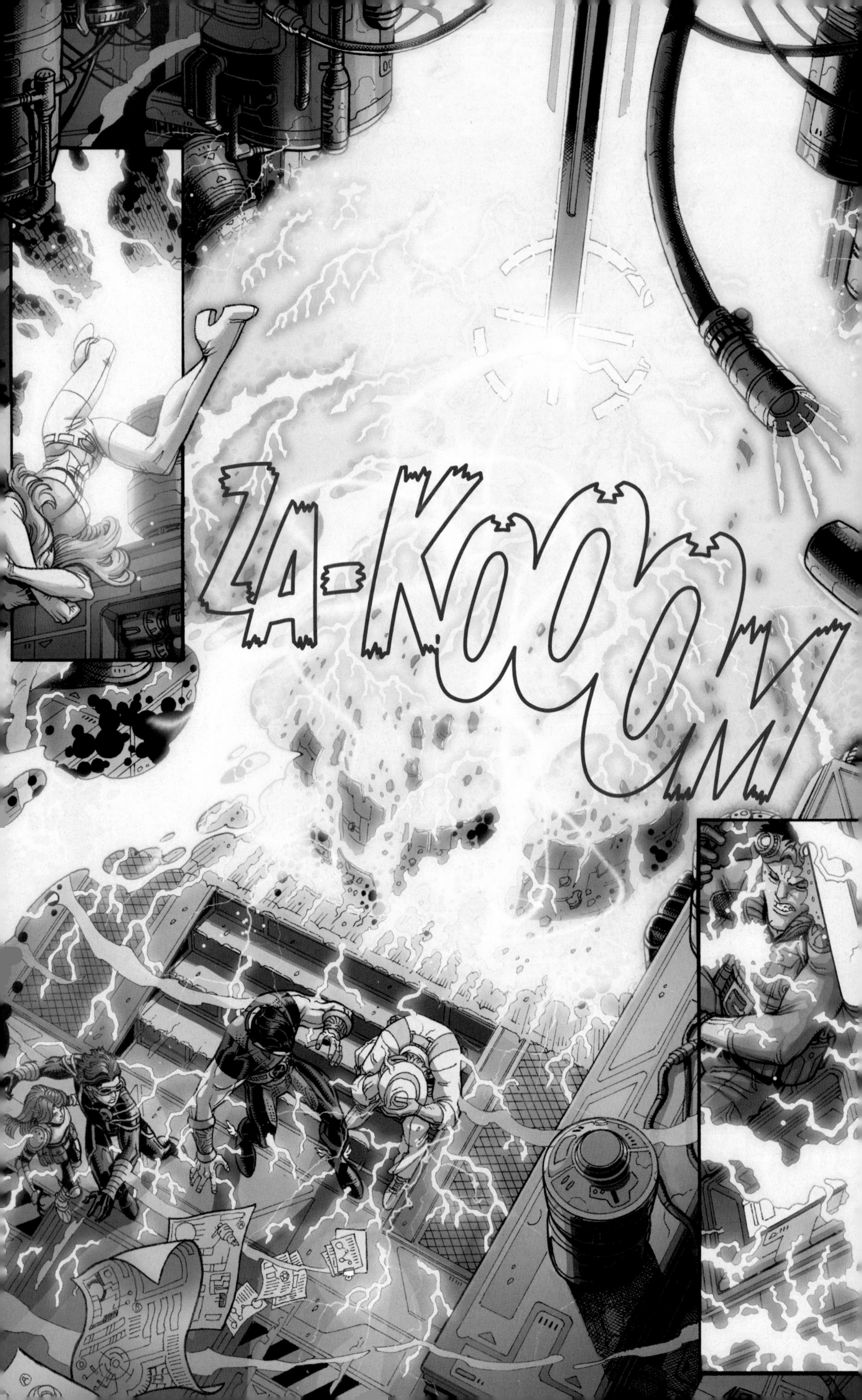
ZA-KOOOOM

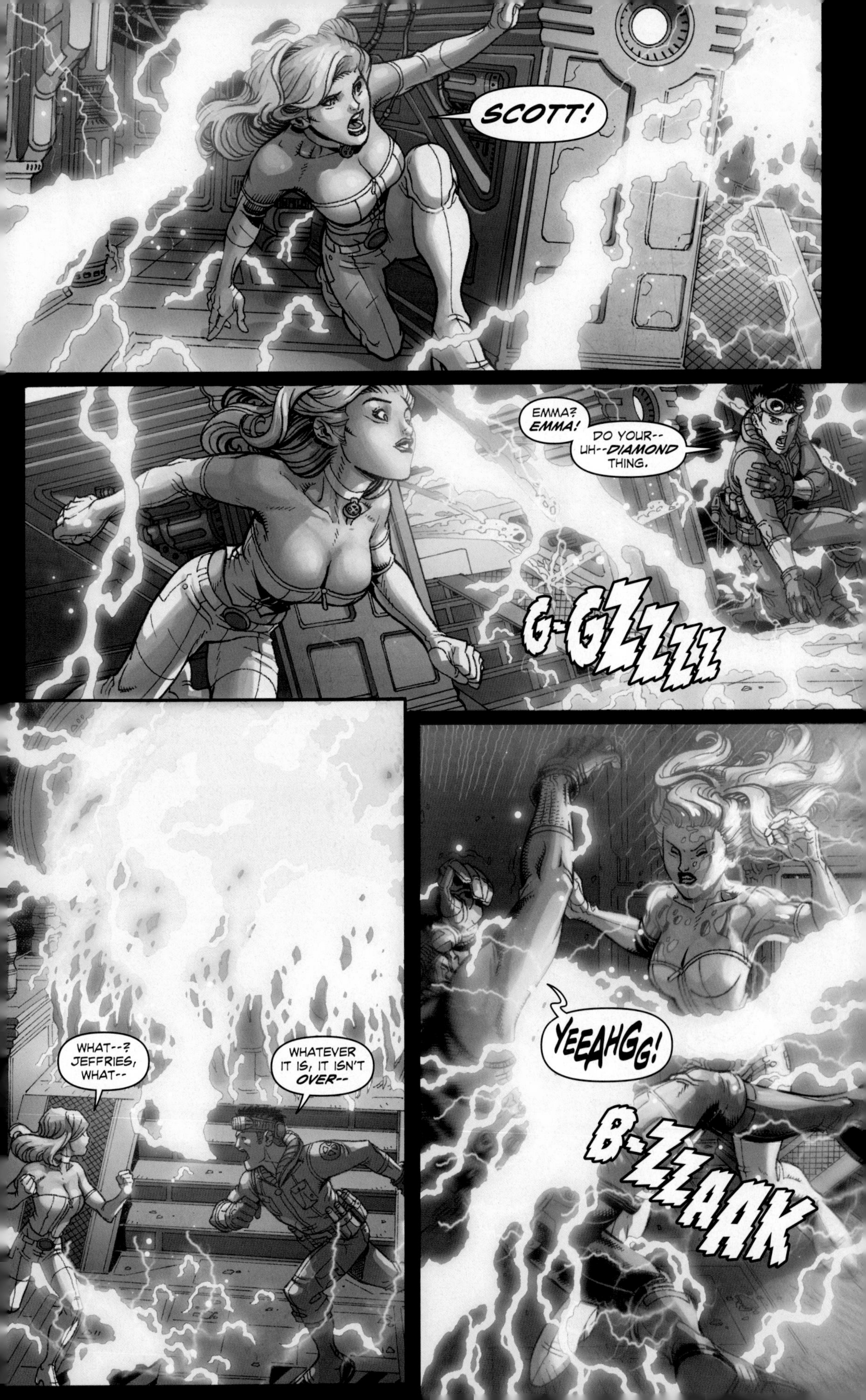
SCOTT!
EMMA? EMMA!
DO YOUR--UH--DIAMOND THING.
G-GZZZZ
WHAT--? JEFFRIES, WHAT--
WHATEVER IT IS, IT ISN'T OVER--
YEEAHGG!
B-ZZAAK

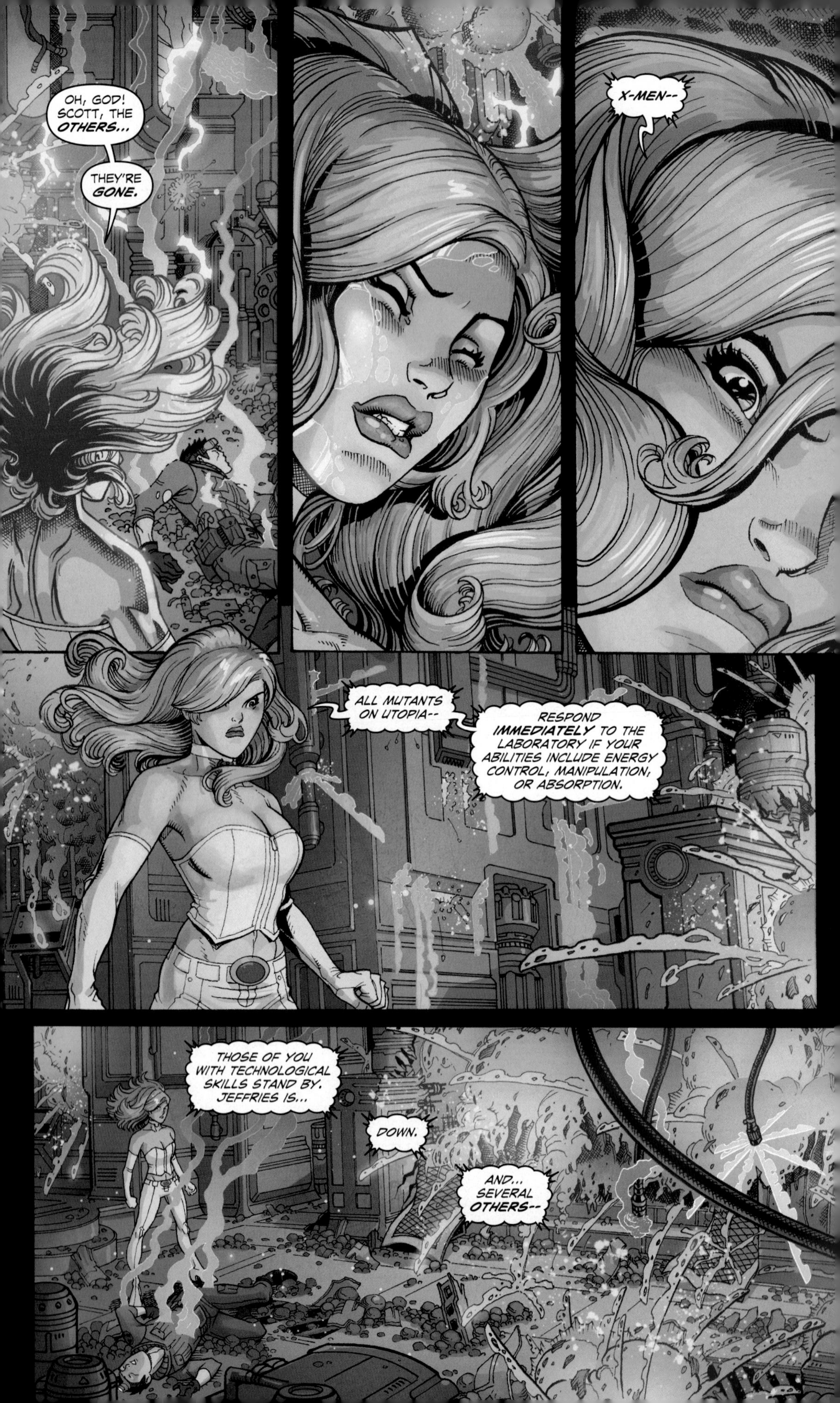
OH, GOD! SCOTT, THE OTHERS...
THEY'RE GONE.
X-MEN--
ALL MUTANTS ON UTOPIA--
RESPOND IMMEDIATELY TO THE LABORATORY IF YOUR ABILITIES INCLUDE ENERGY CONTROL, MANIPULATION, OR ABSORPTION.
THOSE OF YOU WITH TECHNOLOGICAL SKILLS STAND BY. JEFFRIES IS...
DOWN.
AND... SEVERAL OTHERS--

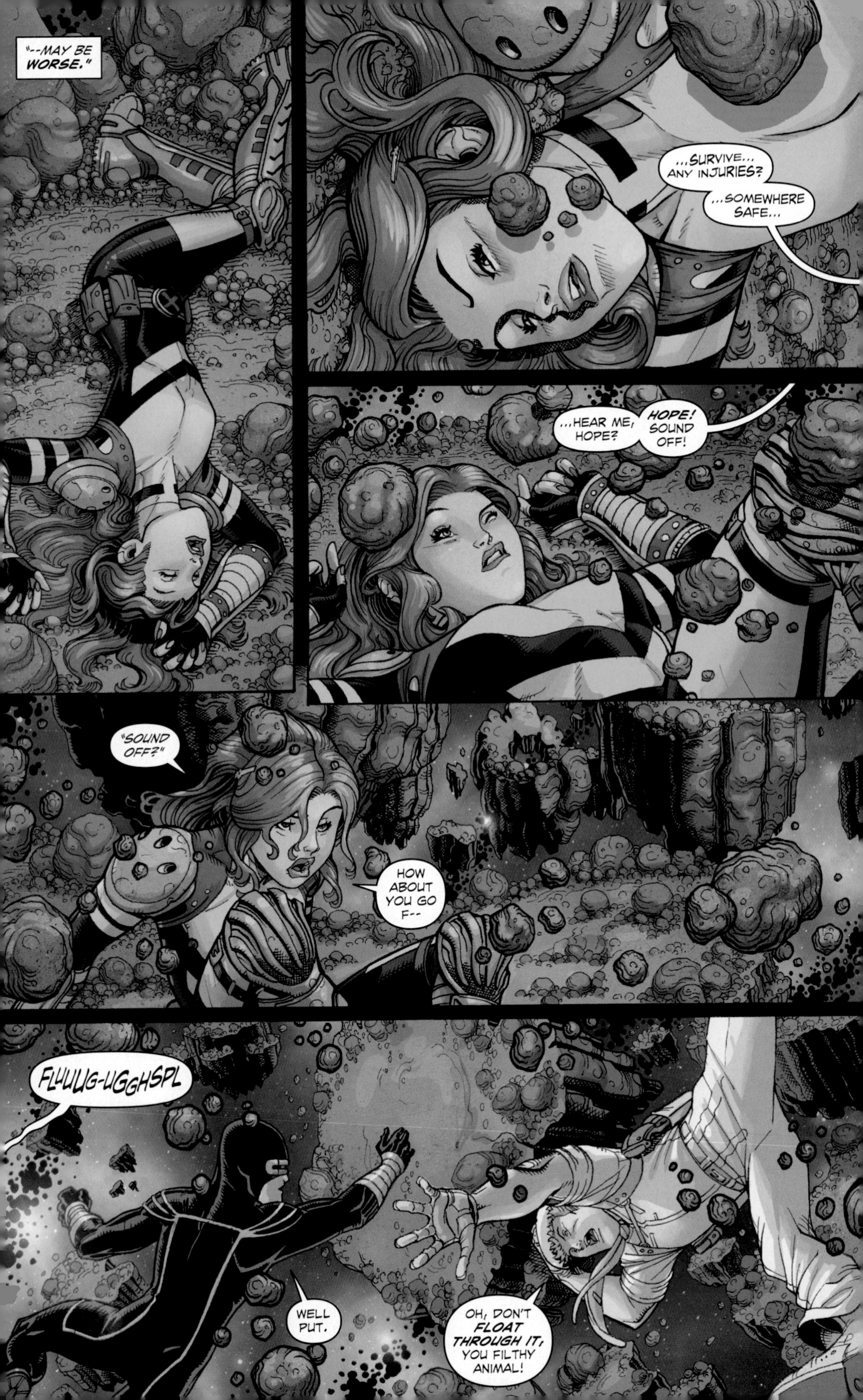
"--MAY BE WORSE."
...SURVIVE... ANY INJURIES?
...SOMEWHERE SAFE...
...HEAR ME, HOPE?
HOPE! SOUND OFF!
"SOUND OFF?"
HOW ABOUT YOU GO F--
FLUUUG-UGGHSPL
WELL PUT.
OH, DON'T FLOAT THROUGH IT, YOU FILTHY ANIMAL!

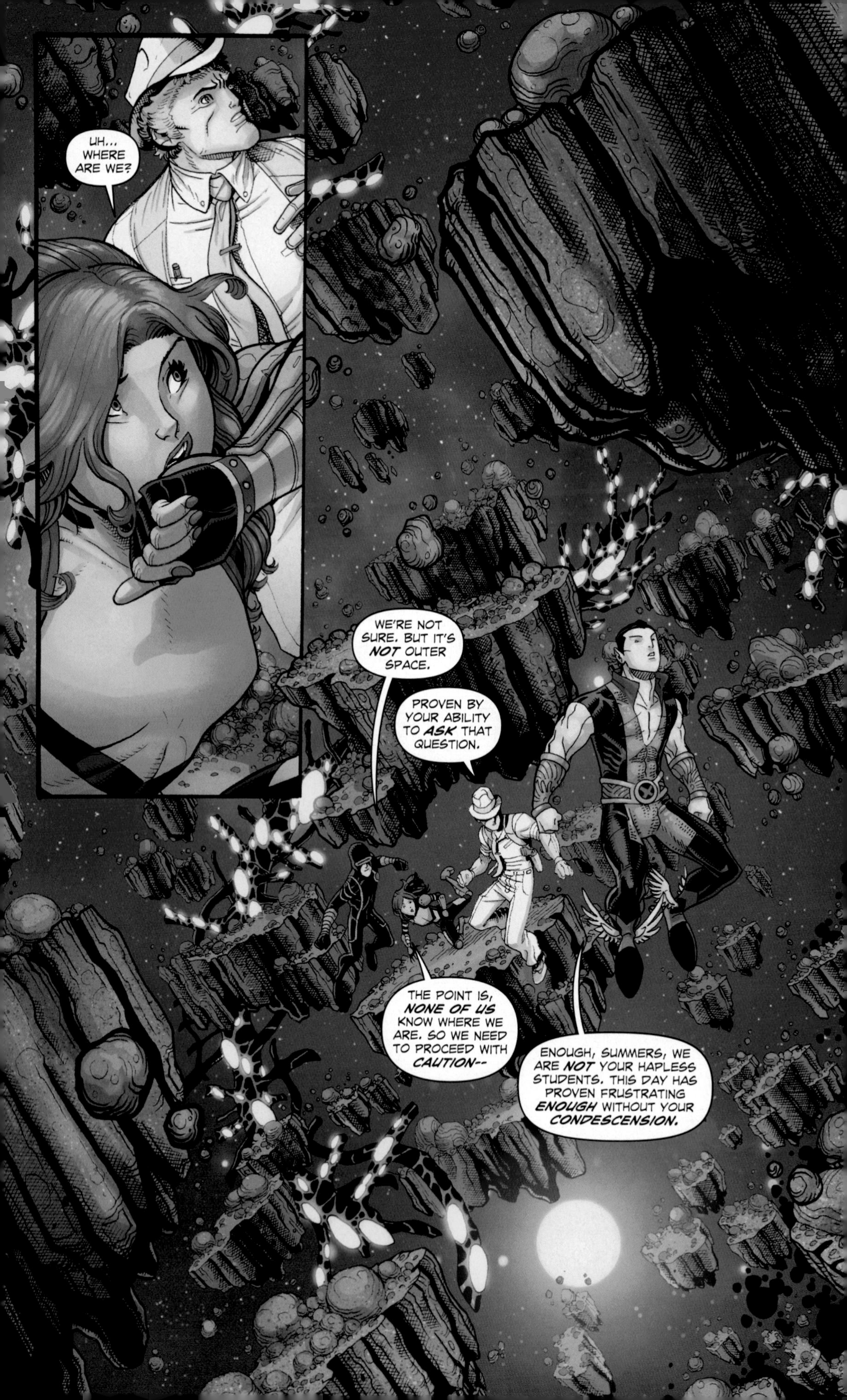
UH... WHERE ARE WE?
WE'RE NOT SURE. BUT IT'S NOT OUTER SPACE.
PROVEN BY YOUR ABILITY TO ASK THAT QUESTION.
THE POINT IS, NONE OF US KNOW WHERE WE ARE. SO WE NEED TO PROCEED WITH CAUTION--
ENOUGH, SUMMERS, WE ARE NOT YOUR HAPLESS STUDENTS. THIS DAY HAS PROVEN FRUSTRATING ENOUGH WITHOUT YOUR CONDESCENSION.

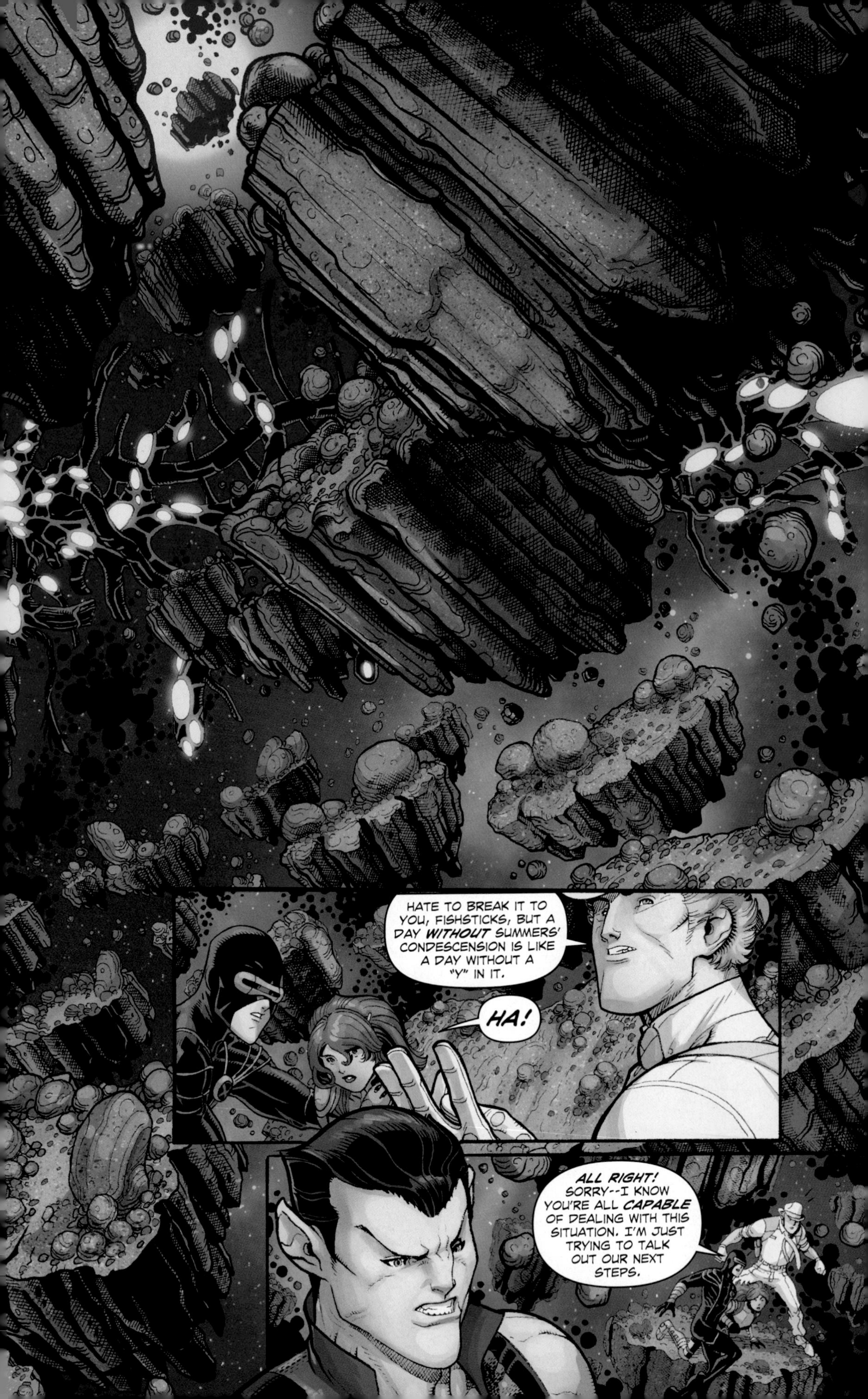
HATE TO BREAK IT TO YOU, FISHSTICKS, BUT A DAY WITHOUT SUMMERS' CONDESCENSION IS LIKE A DAY WITHOUT A "Y" IN IT.
HA!
ALL RIGHT! SORRY--I KNOW YOU'RE ALL CAPABLE OF DEALING WITH THIS SITUATION. I'M JUST TRYING TO TALK OUT OUR NEXT STEPS.

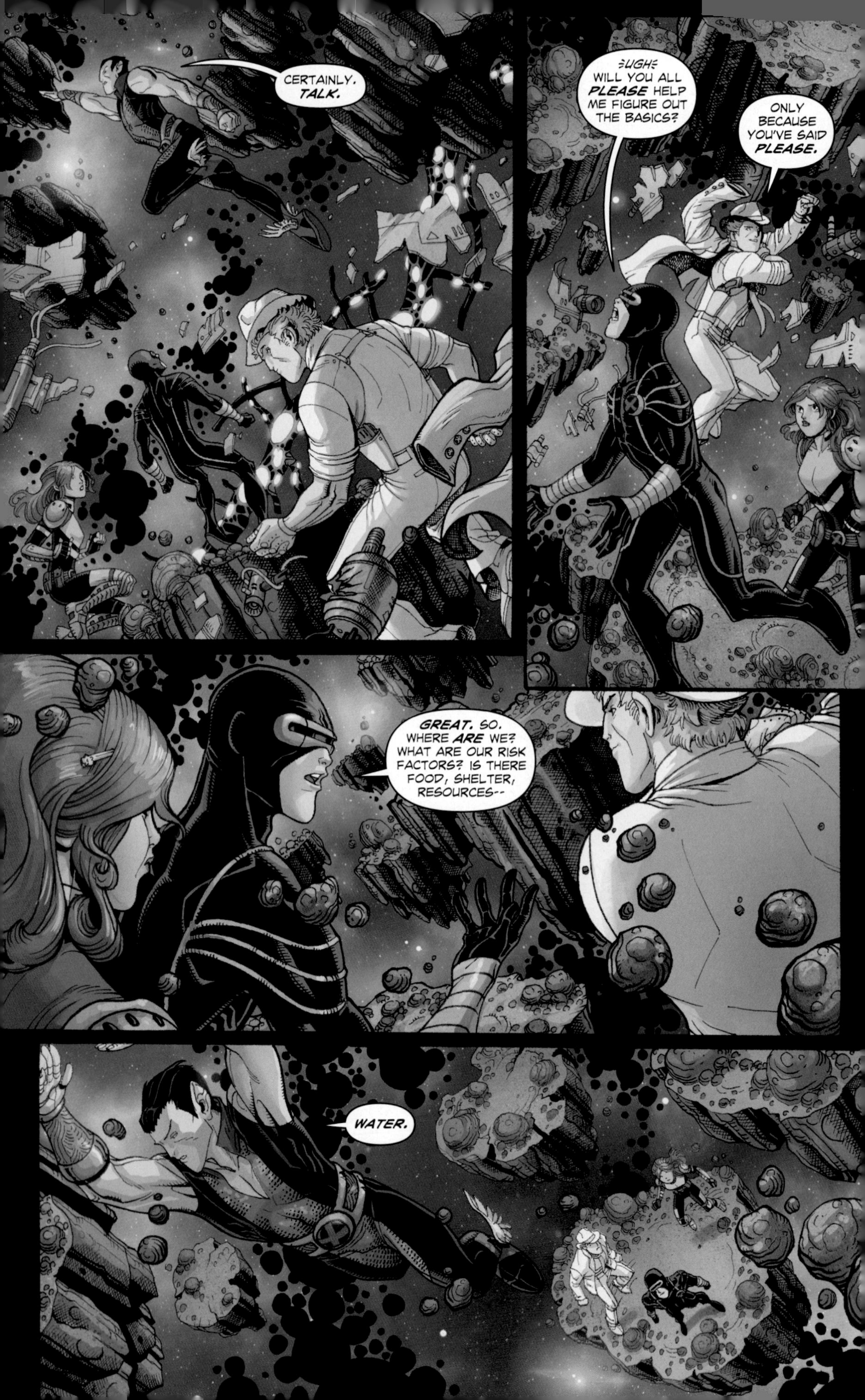
CERTAINLY. TALK.
UGH WILL YOU ALL PLEASE HELP ME FIGURE OUT THE BASICS?
ONLY BECAUSE YOU'VE SAID PLEASE.
GREAT. SO. WHERE ARE WE? WHAT ARE OUR RISK FACTORS? IS THERE FOOD, SHELTER, RESOURCES--
WATER.

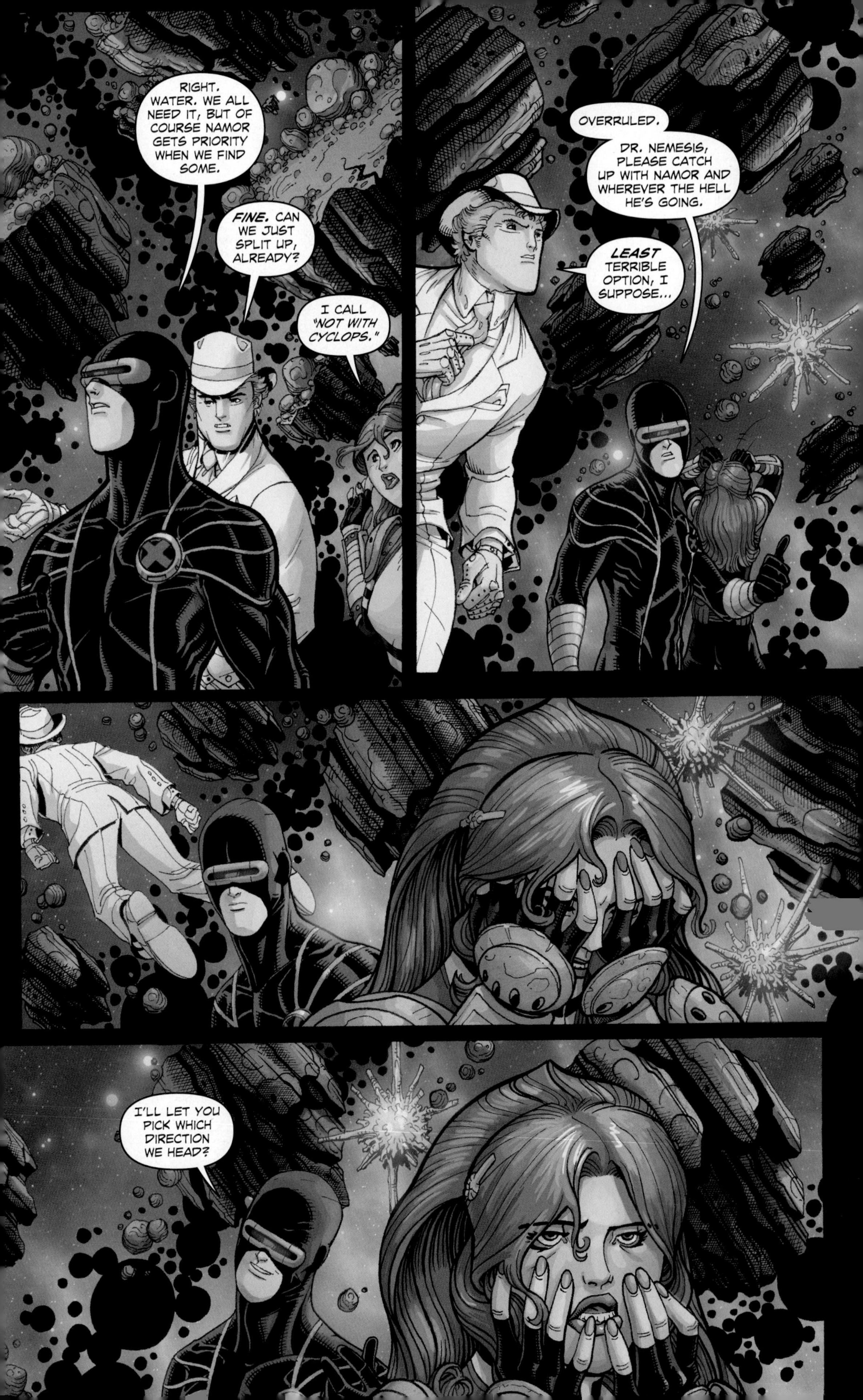
RIGHT. WATER. WE ALL NEED IT, BUT OF COURSE NAMOR GETS PRIORITY WHEN WE FIND SOME.
FINE. CAN WE JUST SPLIT UP, ALREADY?
I CALL "NOT WITH CYCLOPS."
OVERRULED.
DR. NEMESIS, PLEASE CATCH UP WITH NAMOR AND WHEREVER THE HELL HE'S GOING.
LEAST TERRIBLE OPTION, I SUPPOSE...
I'LL LET YOU PICK WHICH DIRECTION WE HEAD?

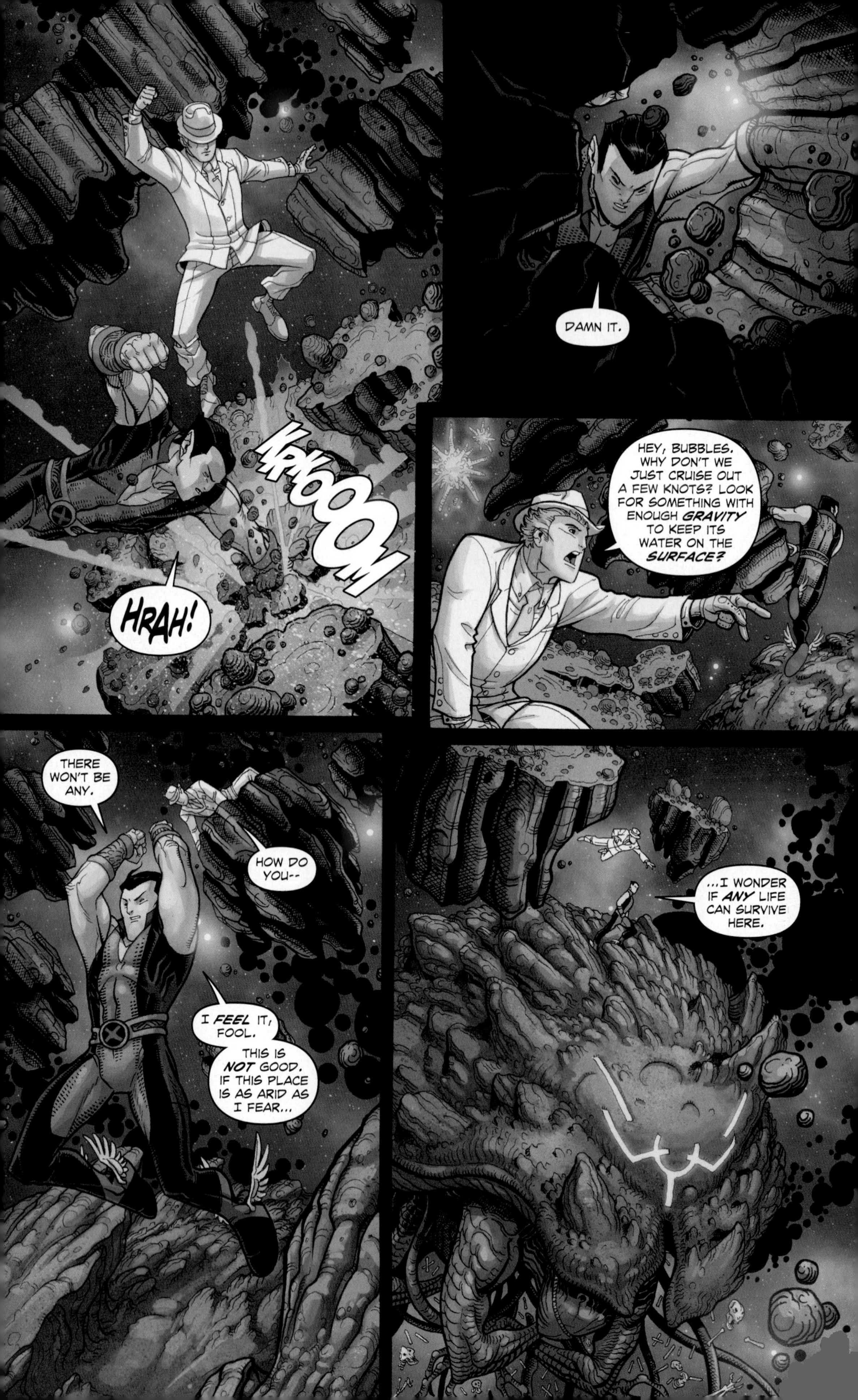
KRKOOOM
HRAH!
DAMN IT.
HEY, BUBBLES. WHY DON'T WE JUST CRUISE OUT A FEW KNOTS? LOOK FOR SOMETHING WITH ENOUGH *GRAVITY* TO KEEP ITS WATER ON THE *SURFACE?*
THERE WON'T BE ANY.
HOW DO YOU--
I *FEEL* IT, FOOL.
THIS IS *NOT* GOOD. IF THIS PLACE IS AS ARID AS I FEAR...
...I WONDER IF *ANY* LIFE CAN SURVIVE HERE.

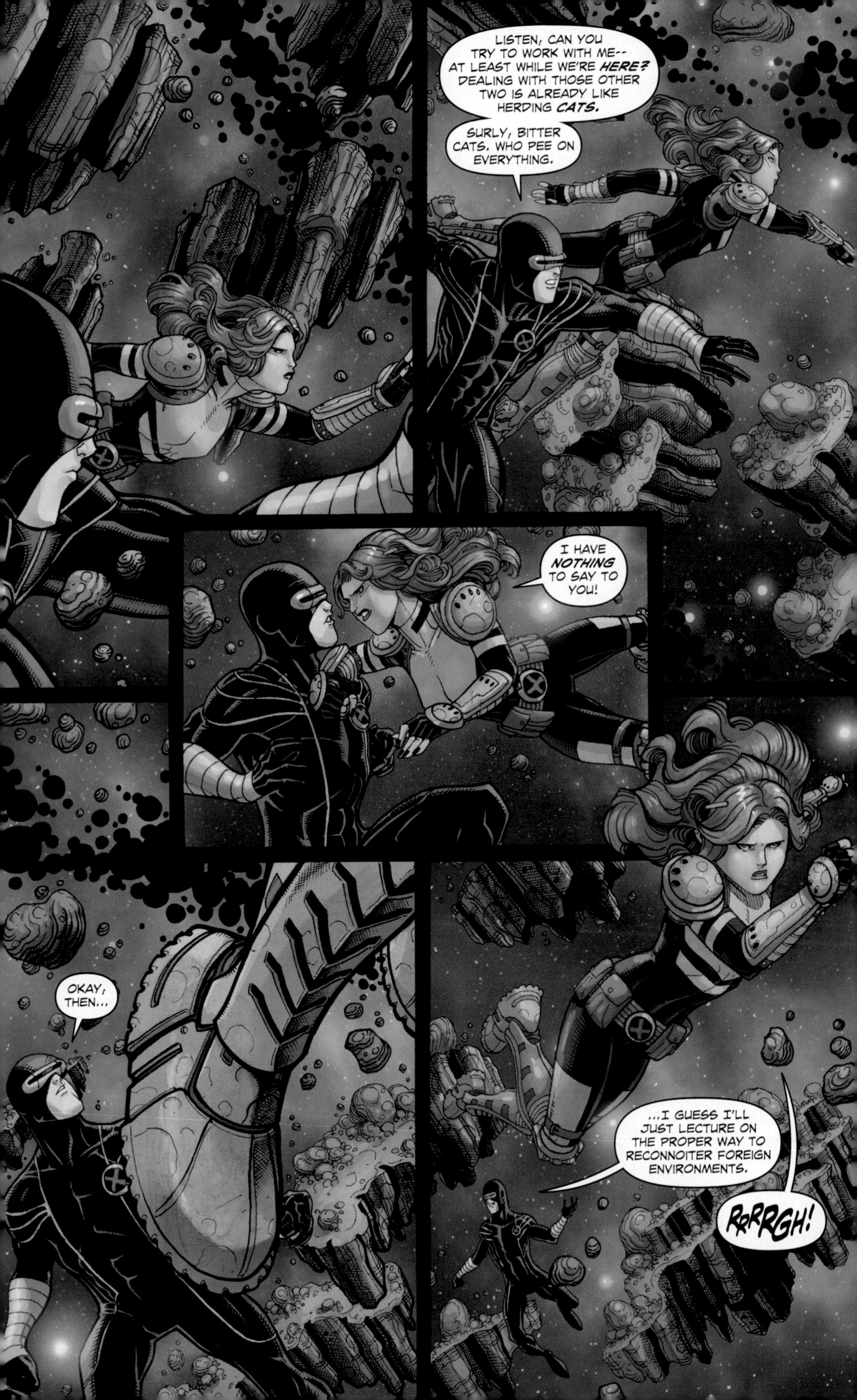
LISTEN, CAN YOU TRY TO WORK WITH ME-- AT LEAST WHILE WE'RE *HERE?* DEALING WITH THOSE OTHER TWO IS ALREADY LIKE HERDING *CATS.*
SURLY, BITTER CATS. WHO PEE ON EVERYTHING.
I HAVE *NOTHING* TO SAY TO YOU!
OKAY, THEN...
...I GUESS I'LL JUST LECTURE ON THE PROPER WAY TO RECONNOITER FOREIGN ENVIRONMENTS.
RRRRGH!

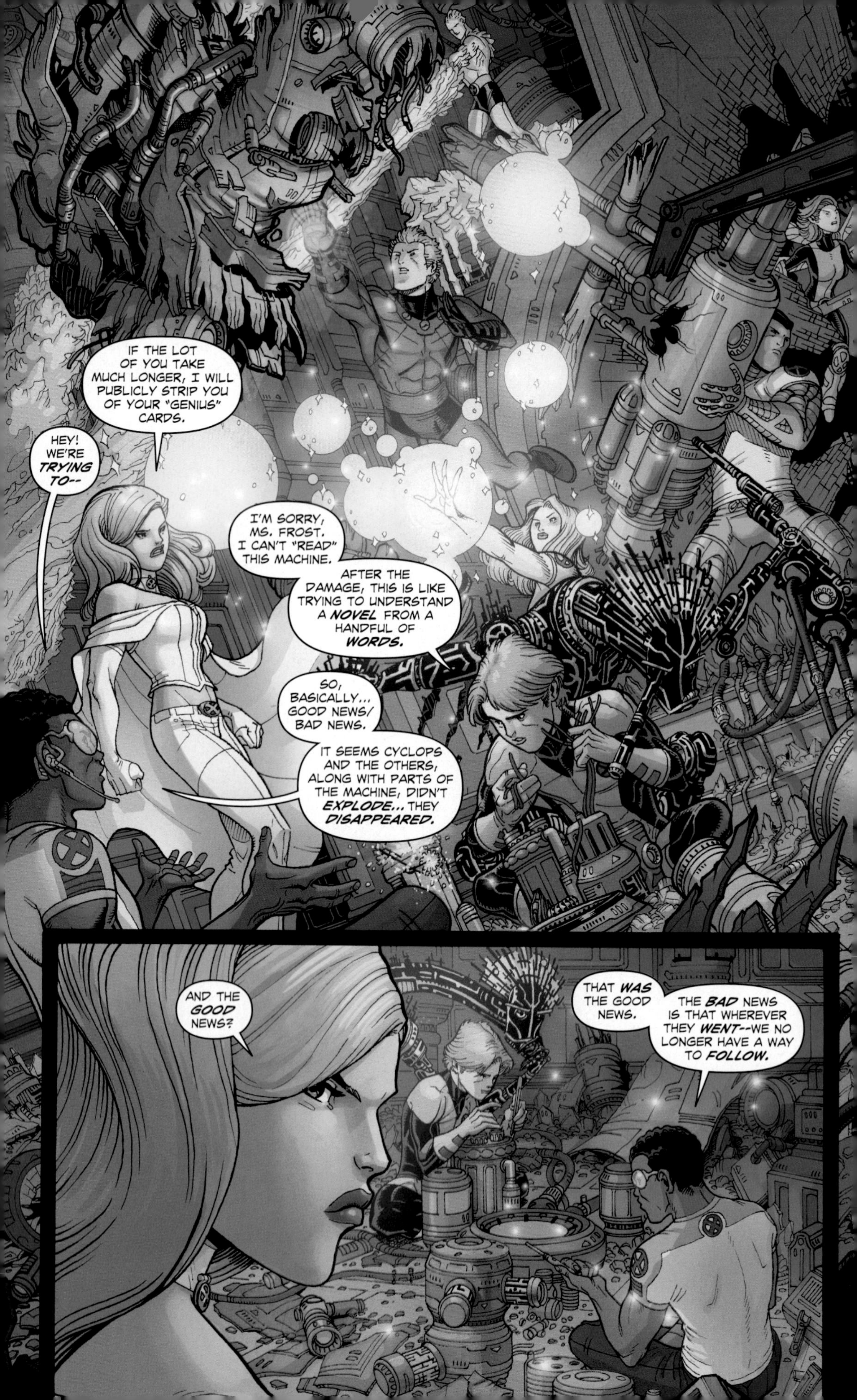
IF THE LOT OF YOU TAKE MUCH LONGER, I WILL PUBLICLY STRIP YOU OF YOUR "GENIUS" CARDS.
HEY! WE'RE *TRYING* TO--
I'M SORRY, MS. FROST. I CAN'T "READ" THIS MACHINE.
AFTER THE DAMAGE, THIS IS LIKE TRYING TO UNDERSTAND A *NOVEL* FROM A HANDFUL OF *WORDS.*
SO, BASICALLY... GOOD NEWS/ BAD NEWS.
IT SEEMS CYCLOPS AND THE OTHERS, ALONG WITH PARTS OF THE MACHINE, DIDN'T *EXPLODE*... THEY *DISAPPEARED.*
AND THE *GOOD* NEWS?
THAT *WAS* THE GOOD NEWS.
THE *BAD* NEWS IS THAT WHEREVER THEY *WENT*--WE NO LONGER HAVE A WAY TO *FOLLOW.*

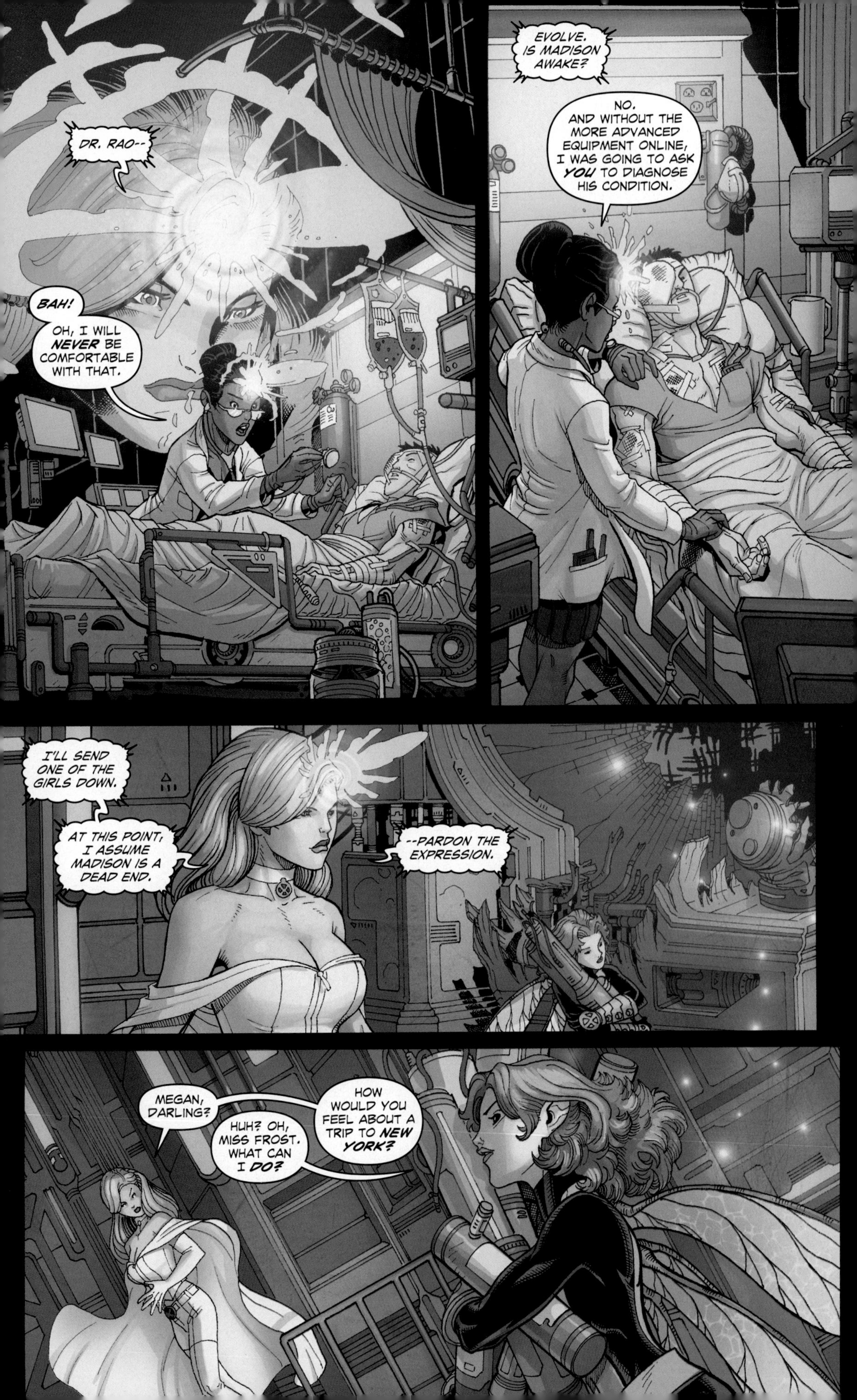
DR. RAO--
BAH!
OH, I WILL NEVER BE COMFORTABLE WITH THAT.
EVOLVE. IS MADISON AWAKE?
NO. AND WITHOUT THE MORE ADVANCED EQUIPMENT ONLINE, I WAS GOING TO ASK YOU TO DIAGNOSE HIS CONDITION.
I'LL SEND ONE OF THE GIRLS DOWN.
AT THIS POINT, I ASSUME MADISON IS A DEAD END.
--PARDON THE EXPRESSION.
MEGAN, DARLING?
HUH? OH, MISS FROST. WHAT CAN I DO?
HOW WOULD YOU FEEL ABOUT A TRIP TO NEW YORK?

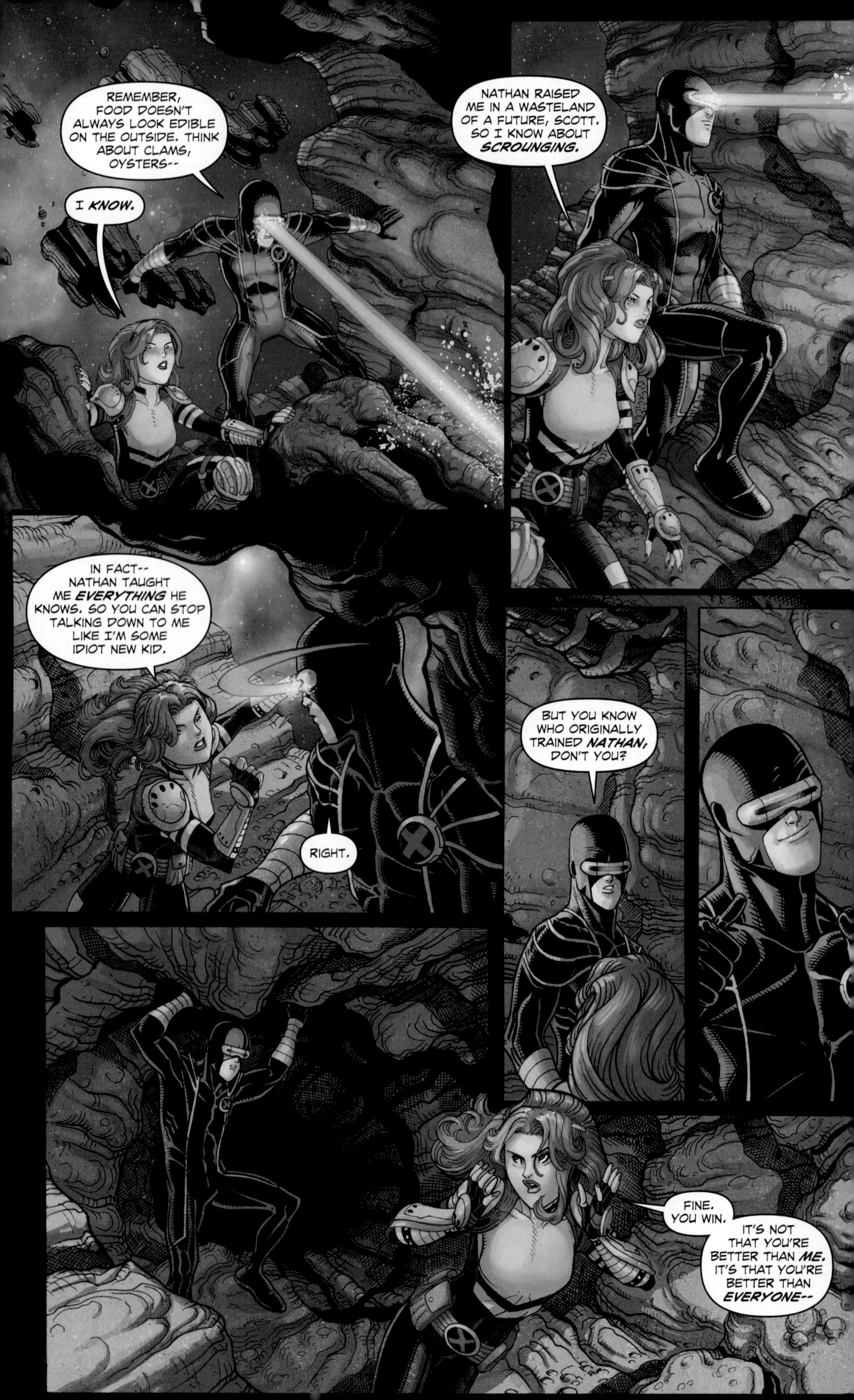
REMEMBER, FOOD DOESN'T ALWAYS LOOK EDIBLE ON THE OUTSIDE. THINK ABOUT CLAMS, OYSTERS--
I KNOW.
NATHAN RAISED ME IN A WASTELAND OF A FUTURE, SCOTT. SO I KNOW ABOUT SCROUNGING.
IN FACT-- NATHAN TAUGHT ME EVERYTHING HE KNOWS. SO YOU CAN STOP TALKING DOWN TO ME LIKE I'M SOME IDIOT NEW KID.
RIGHT.
BUT YOU KNOW WHO ORIGINALLY TRAINED NATHAN, DON'T YOU?
FINE. YOU WIN.
IT'S NOT THAT YOU'RE BETTER THAN ME. IT'S THAT YOU'RE BETTER THAN EVERYONE--

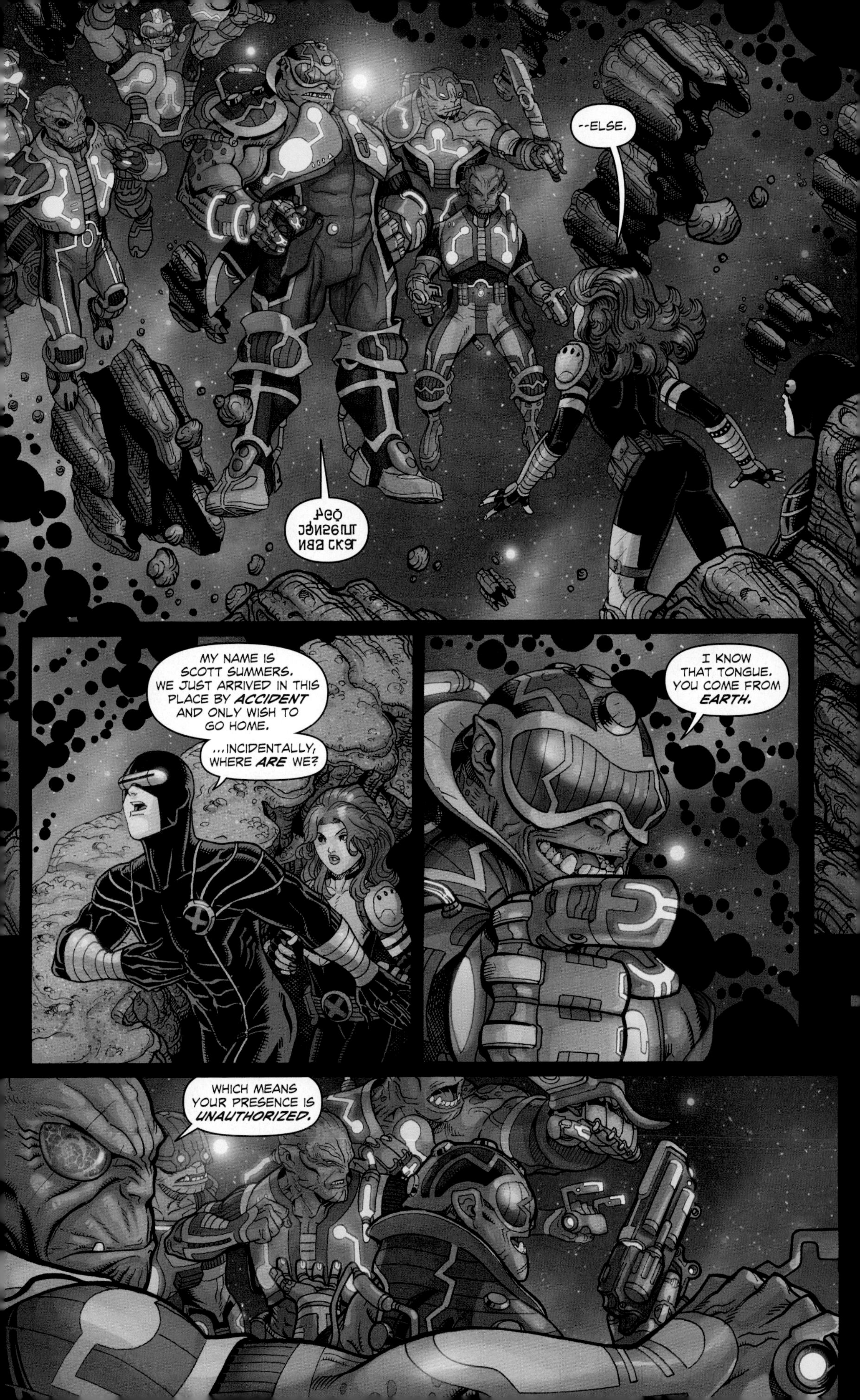
--ELSE.
MY NAME IS SCOTT SUMMERS. WE JUST ARRIVED IN THIS PLACE BY ACCIDENT AND ONLY WISH TO GO HOME.
...INCIDENTALLY, WHERE ARE WE?
I KNOW THAT TONGUE. YOU COME FROM EARTH.
WHICH MEANS YOUR PRESENCE IS UNAUTHORIZED.

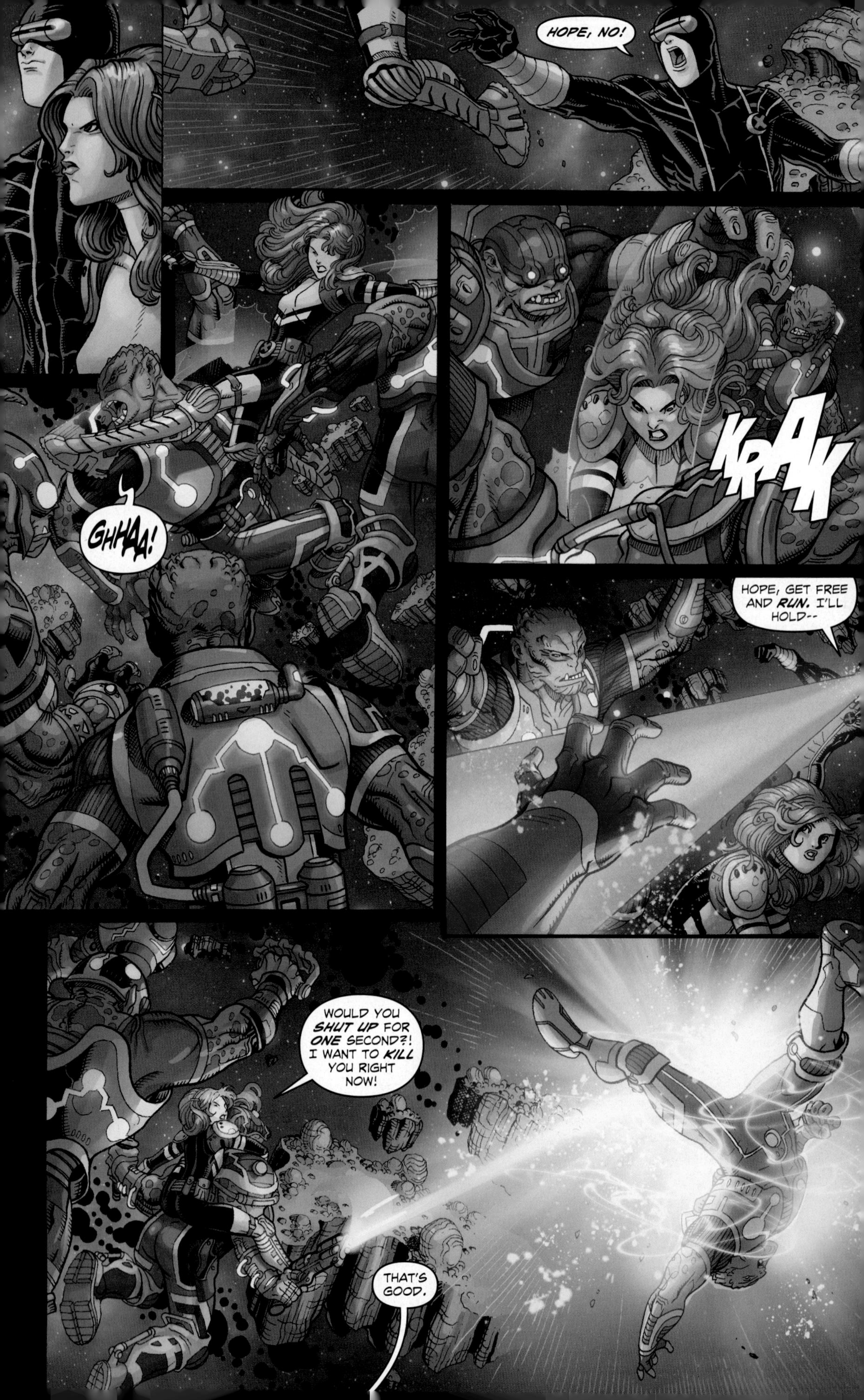
HOPE, NO!
GHHAA!
KRAAK
HOPE, GET FREE AND RUN. I'LL HOLD--
WOULD YOU SHUT UP FOR ONE SECOND?! I WANT TO KILL YOU RIGHT NOW!
THAT'S GOOD.

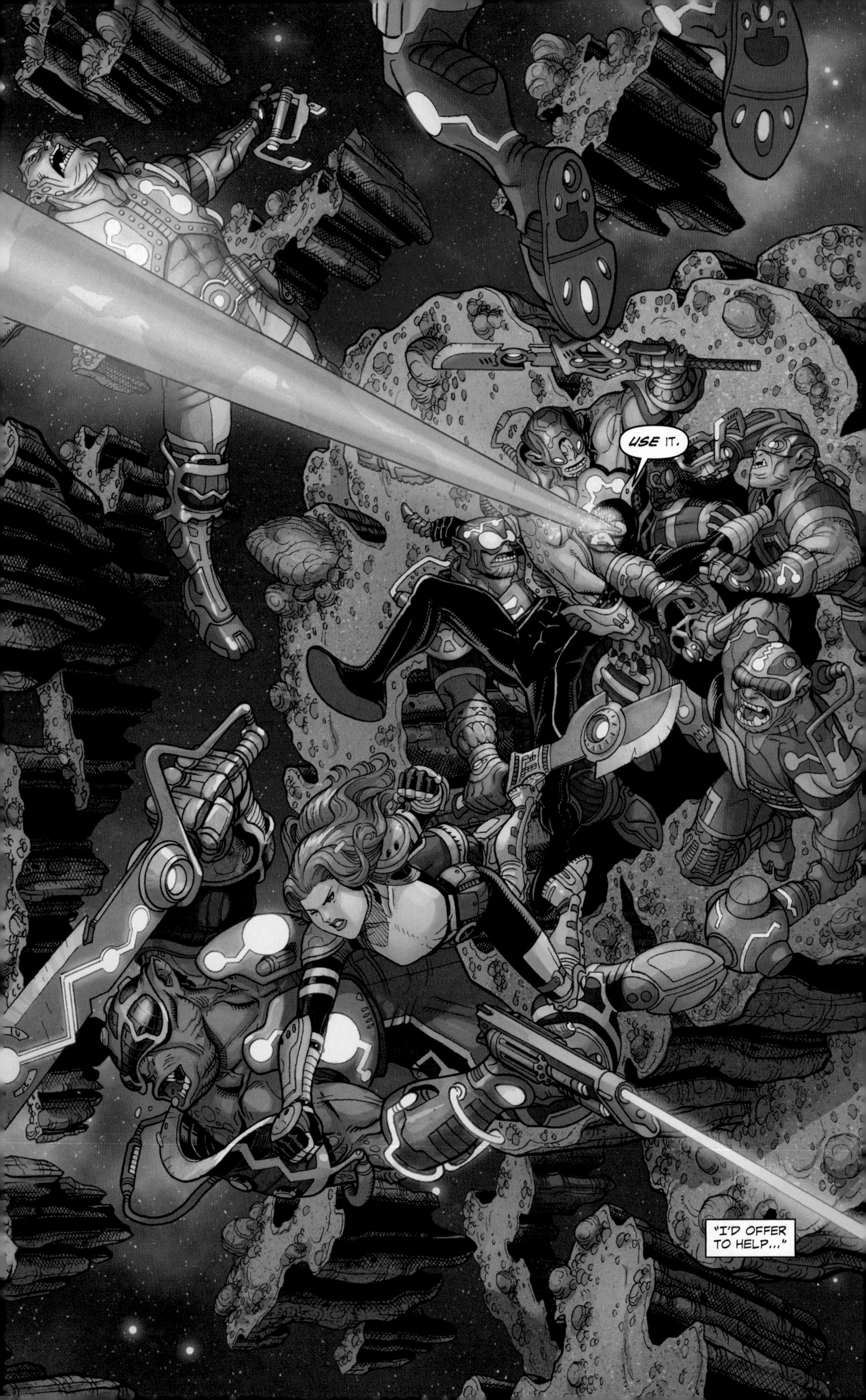
USE IT.
"I'D OFFER TO HELP..."

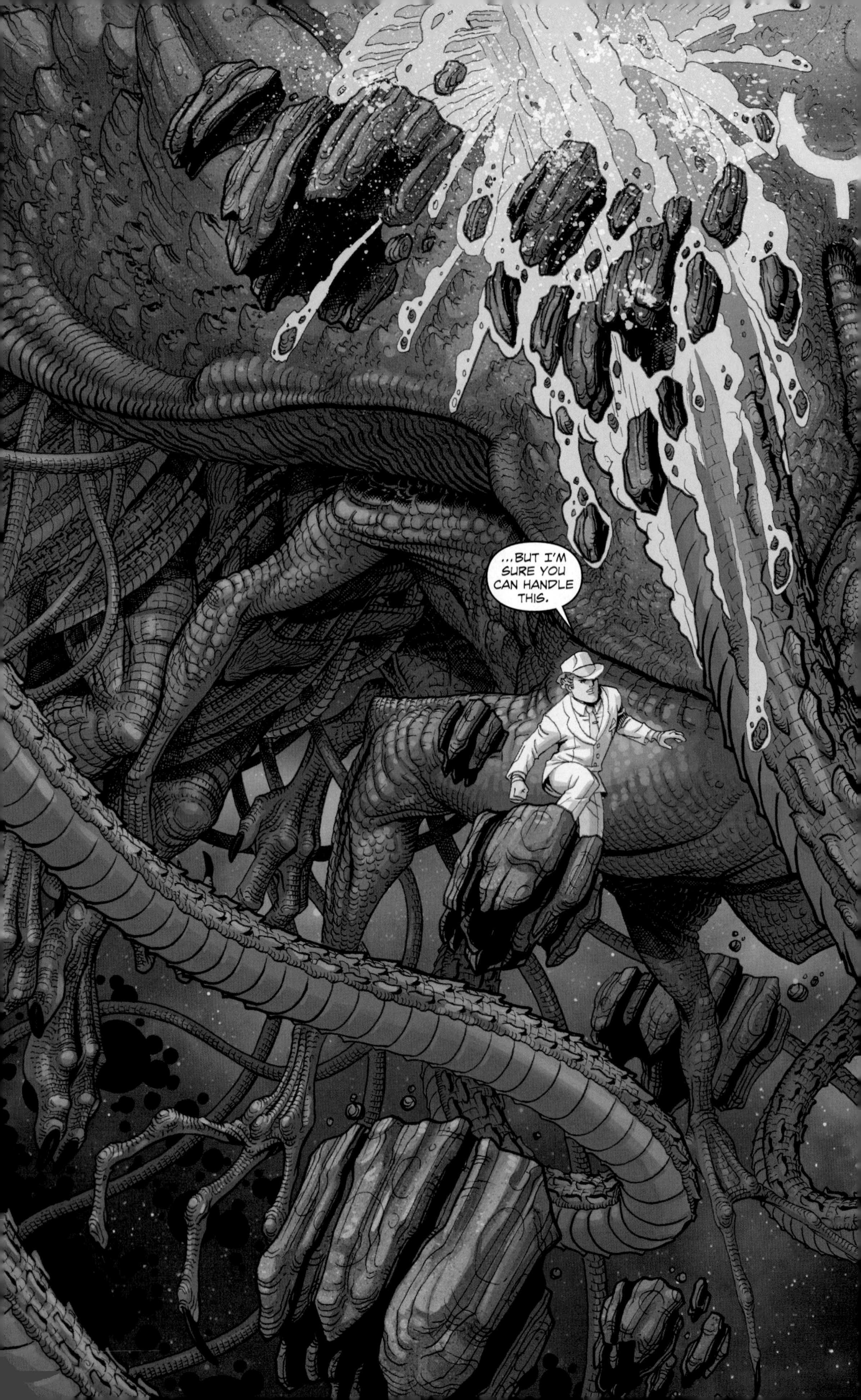
...BUT I'M SURE YOU CAN HANDLE THIS.

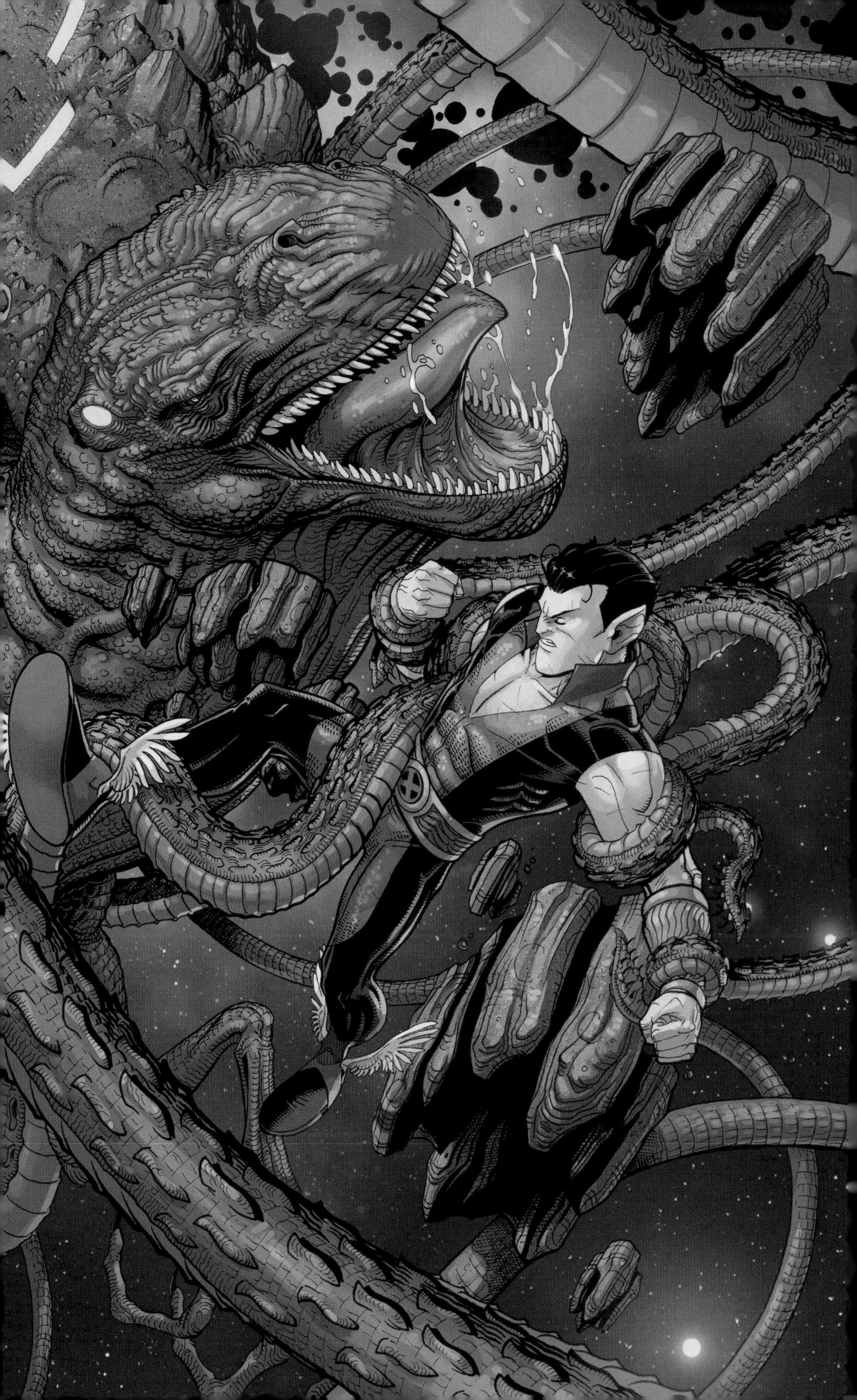

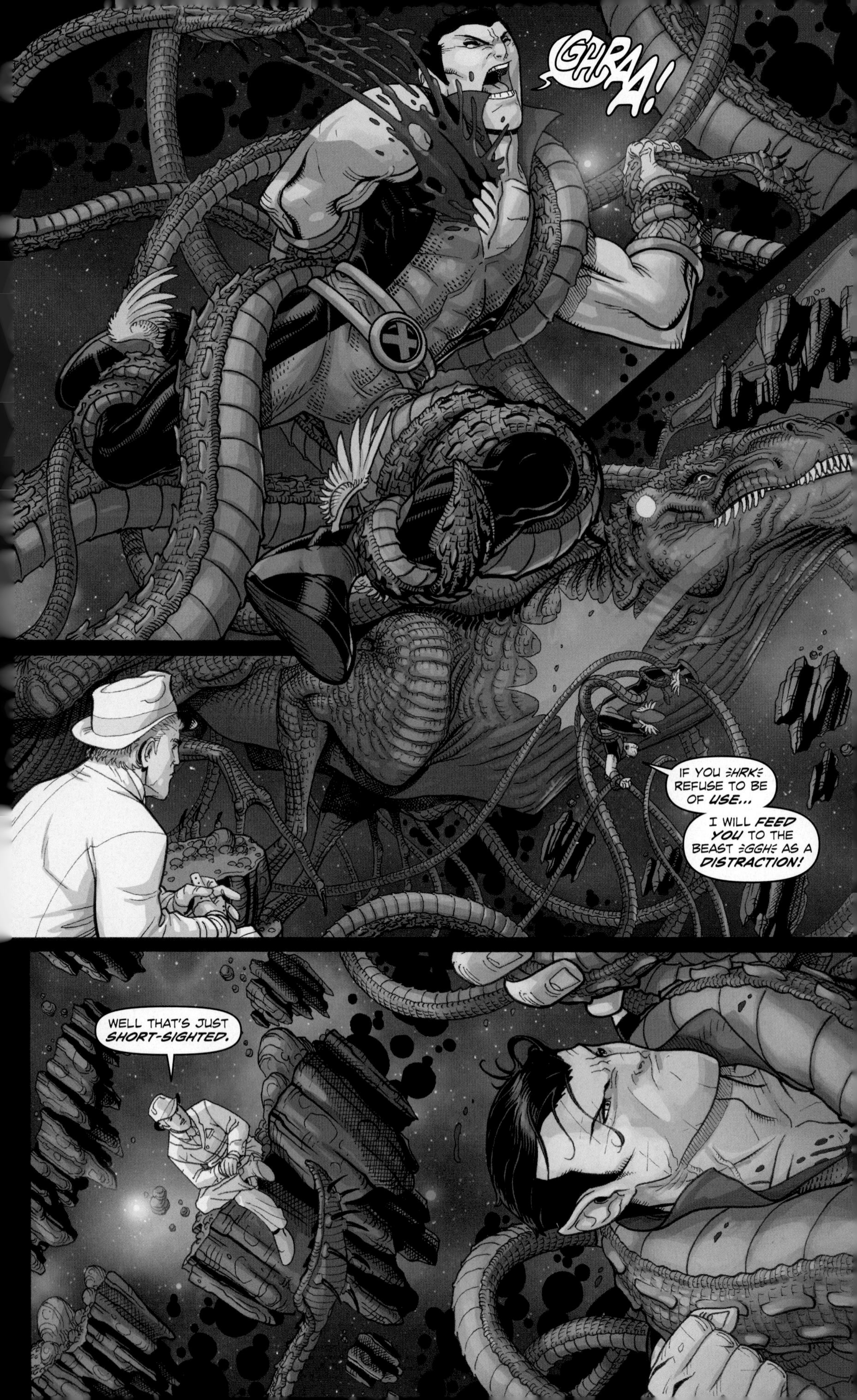
GHRAA!
IF YOU =HRK= REFUSE TO BE OF USE...
I WILL FEED YOU TO THE BEAST =GGH= AS A DISTRACTION!
WELL THAT'S JUST SHORT-SIGHTED.

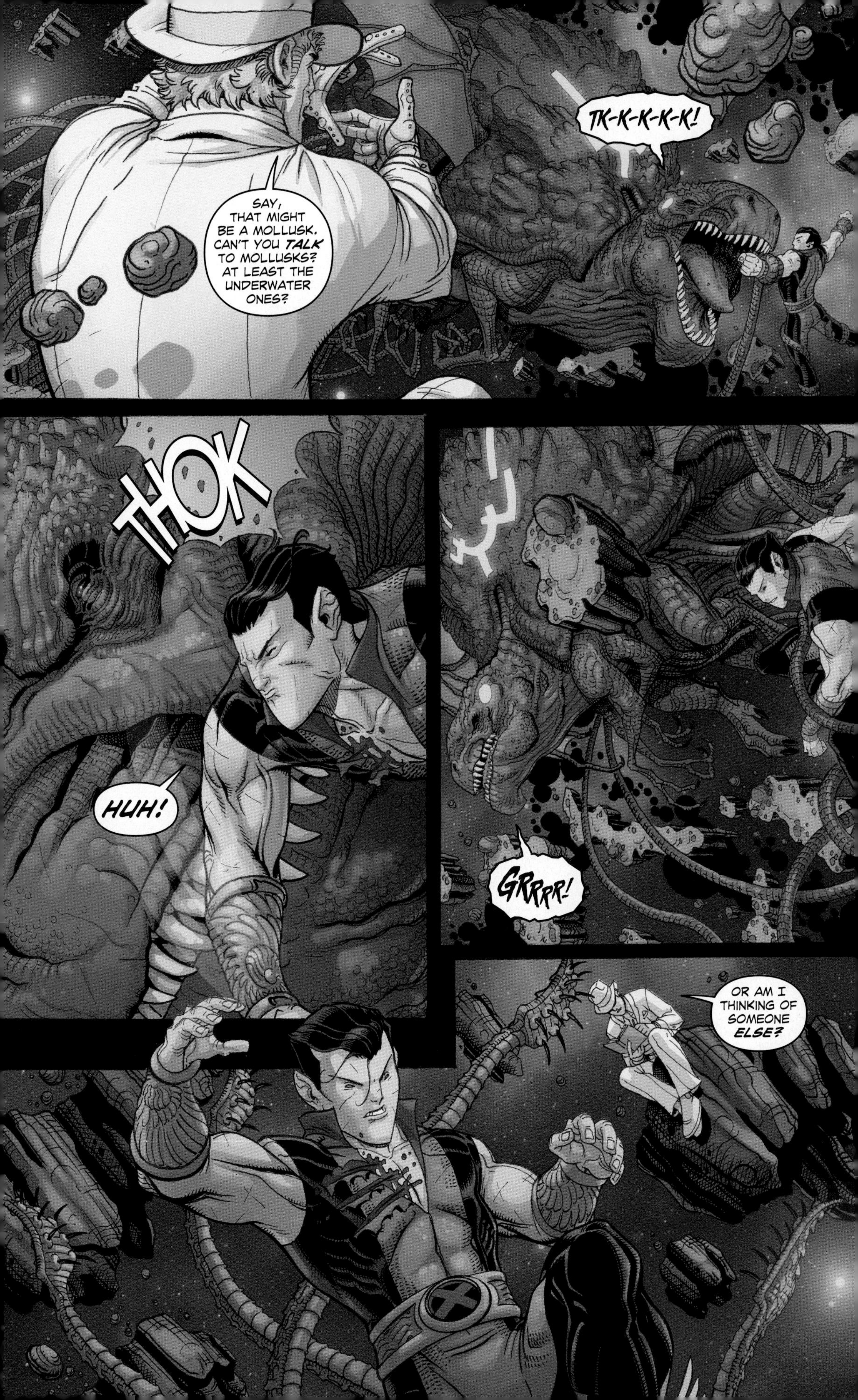
TK-K-K-K-K!
SAY, THAT MIGHT BE A MOLLUSK. CAN'T YOU TALK TO MOLLUSKS? AT LEAST THE UNDERWATER ONES?
THOK
HUH!
GRRRR!
OR AM I THINKING OF SOMEONE ELSE?

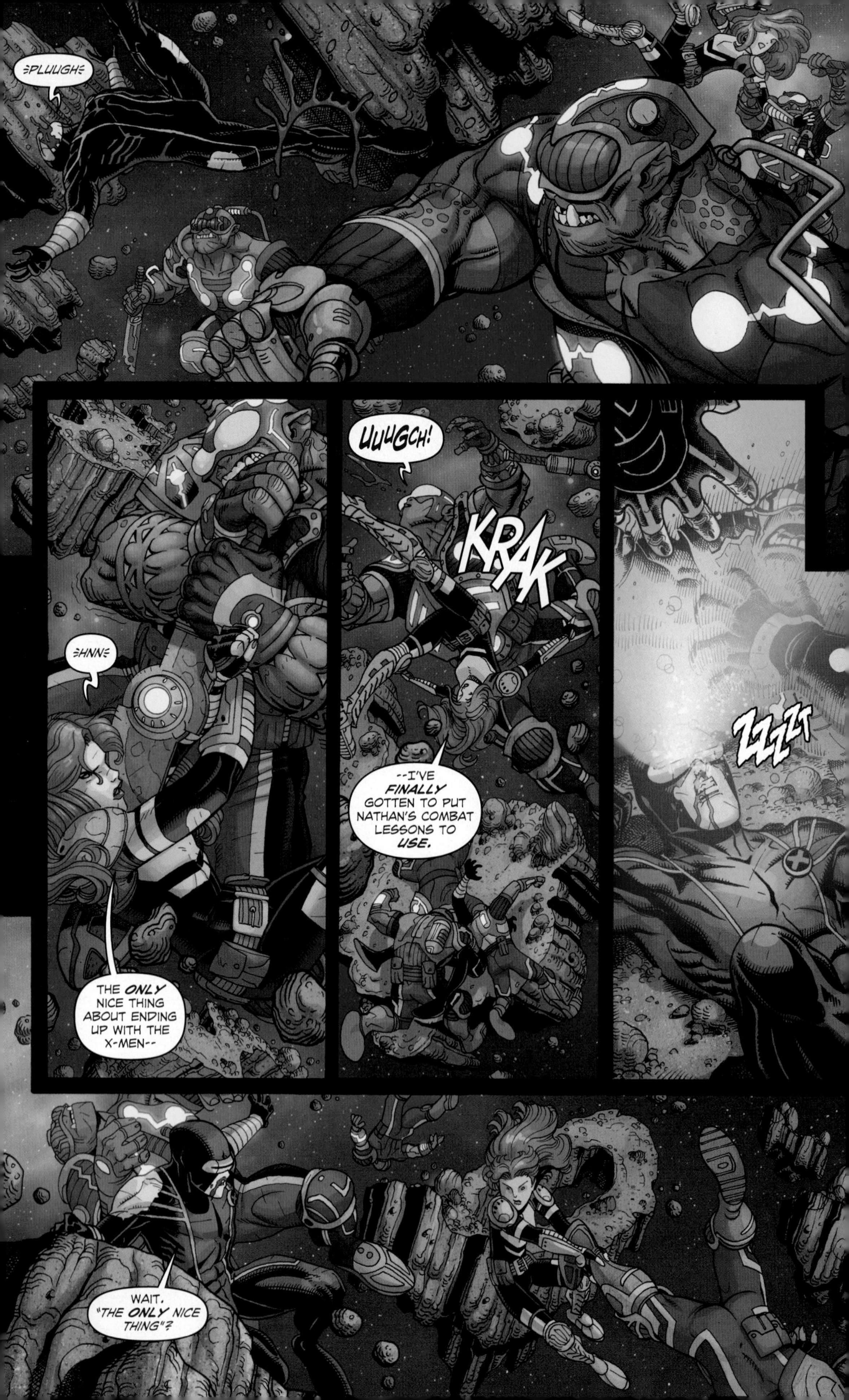
=PLUUGH=
=HNN=
THE ONLY NICE THING ABOUT ENDING UP WITH THE X-MEN--
UUUGCH!
KRAK
--I'VE FINALLY GOTTEN TO PUT NATHAN'S COMBAT LESSONS TO USE.
ZZZZZT
WAIT. "THE ONLY NICE THING"?

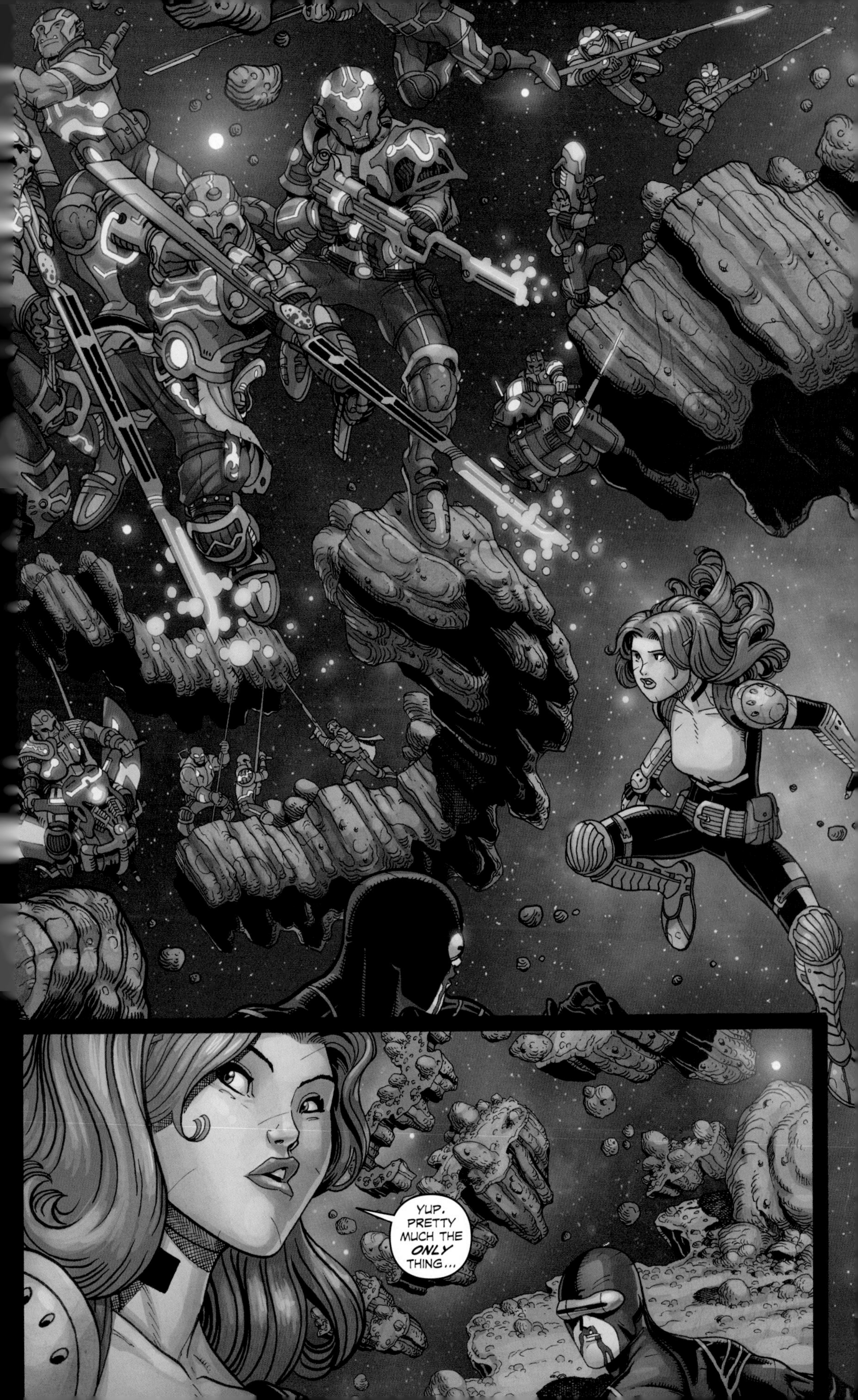
YUP. PRETTY MUCH THE ONLY THING...

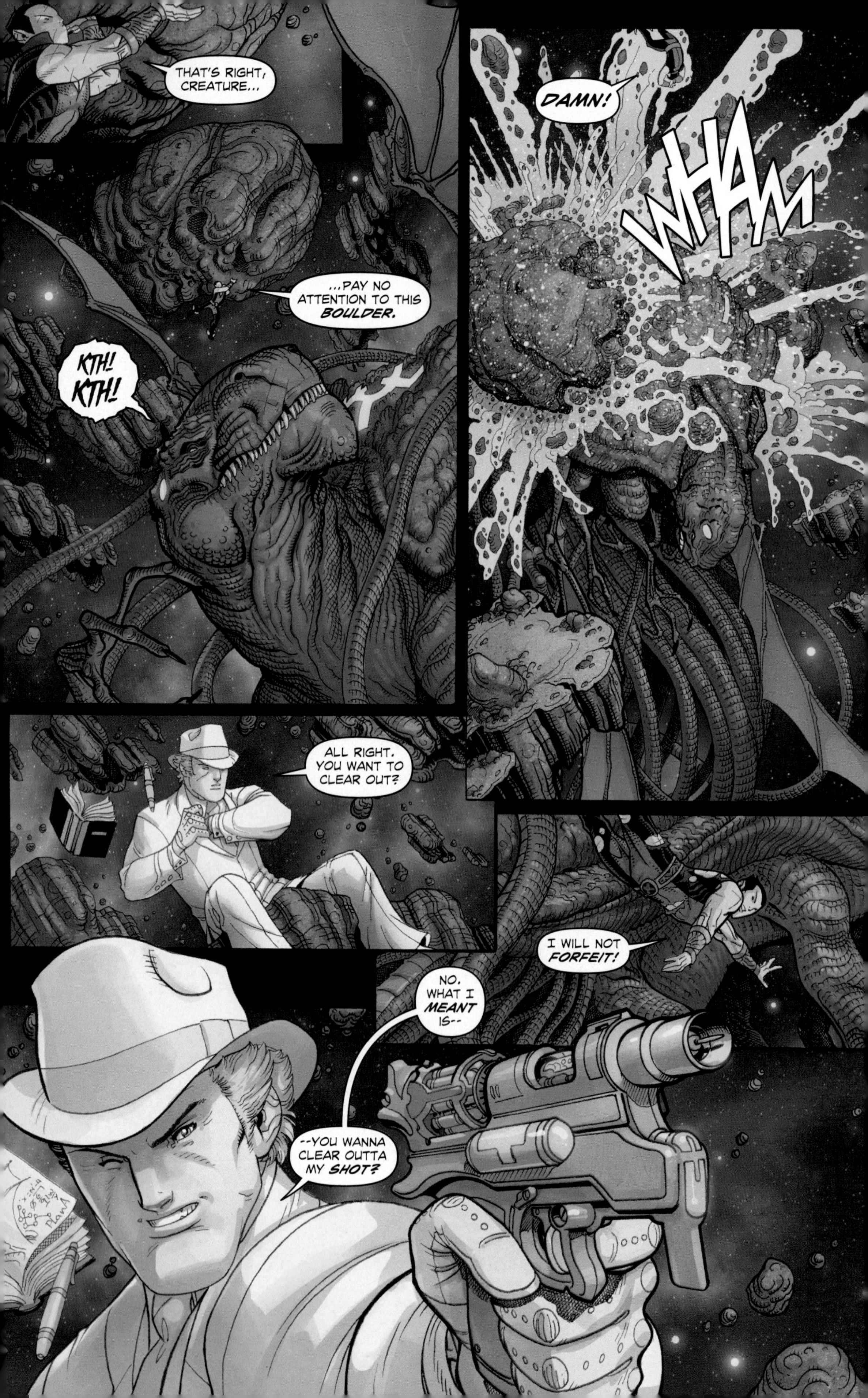
THAT'S RIGHT, CREATURE...
...PAY NO ATTENTION TO THIS BOULDER.
KTH! KTH!
DAMN!
WHAM
ALL RIGHT. YOU WANT TO CLEAR OUT?
I WILL NOT FORFEIT!
NO. WHAT I MEANT IS--
--YOU WANNA CLEAR OUTTA MY SHOT?

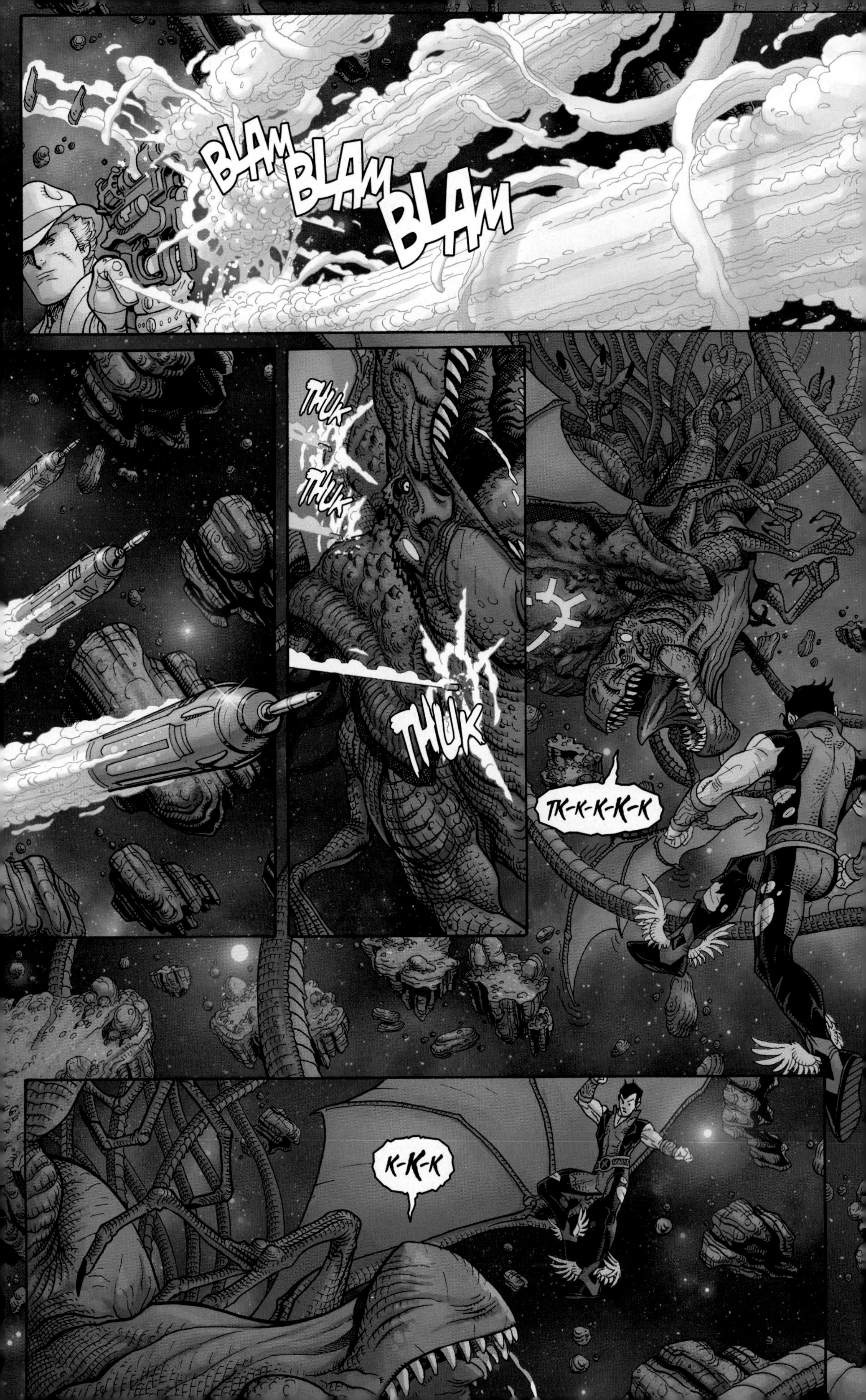
BLAM BLAM BLAM
THUK
THUK
THUK
TK-K-K-K-K
K-K-K

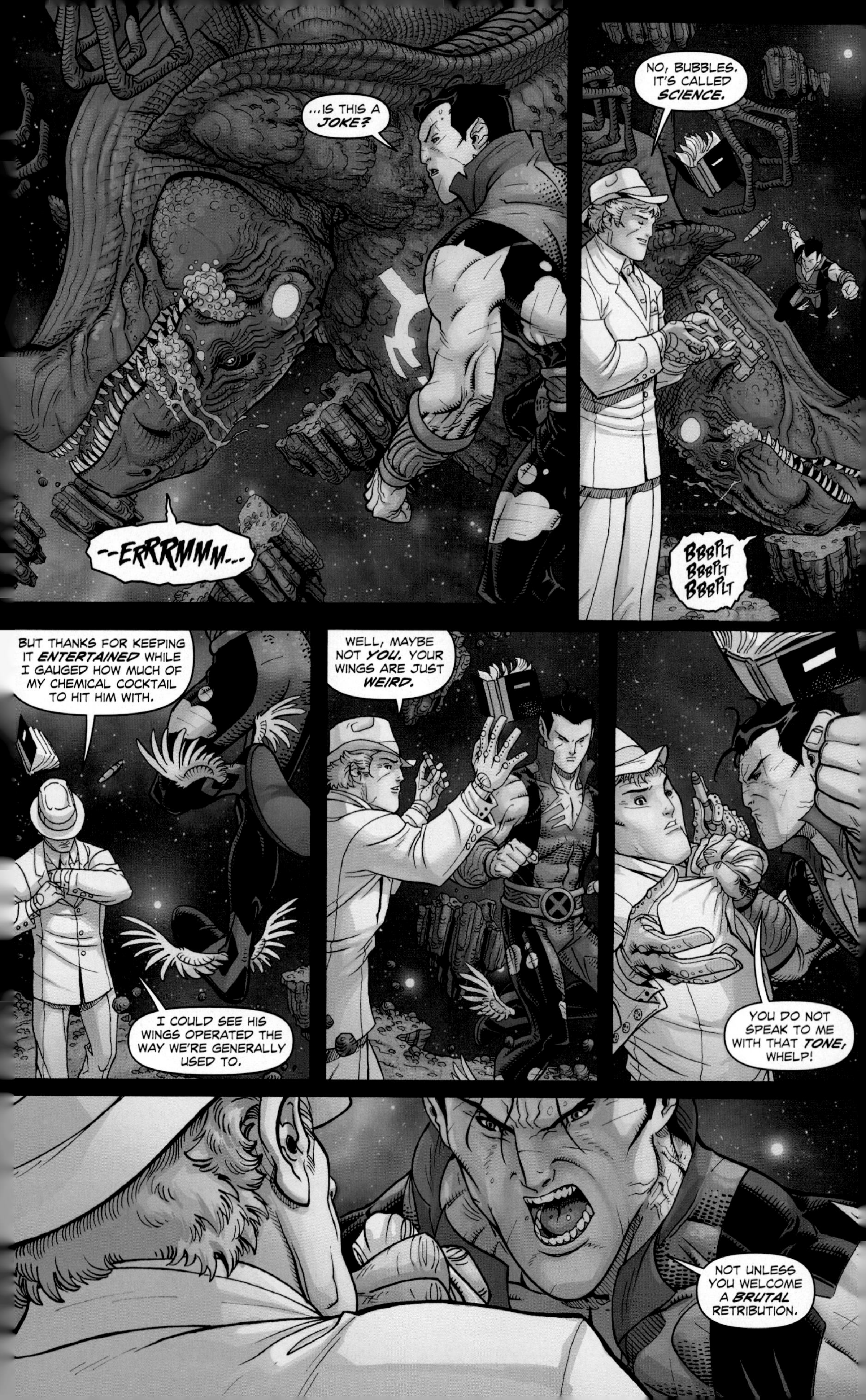
...IS THIS A JOKE?
--ERRRMMM...
NO, BUBBLES. IT'S CALLED SCIENCE.
BBBPLT BBBPLT BBBPLT
BUT THANKS FOR KEEPING IT ENTERTAINED WHILE I GAUGED HOW MUCH OF MY CHEMICAL COCKTAIL TO HIT HIM WITH.
I COULD SEE HIS WINGS OPERATED THE WAY WE'RE GENERALLY USED TO.
WELL, MAYBE NOT YOU. YOUR WINGS ARE JUST WEIRD.
YOU DO NOT SPEAK TO ME WITH THAT TONE, WHELP!
NOT UNLESS YOU WELCOME A BRUTAL RETRIBUTION.

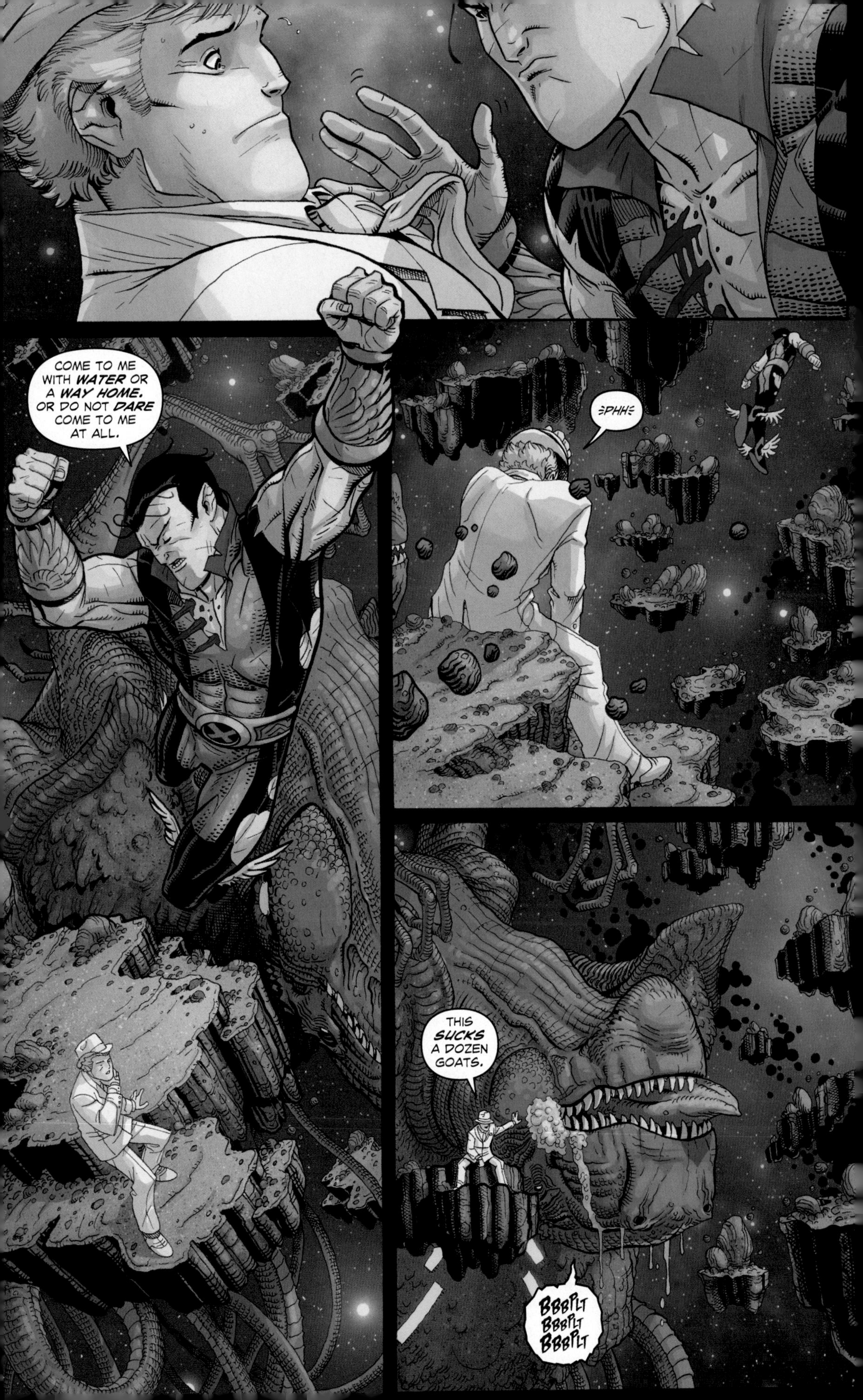
COME TO ME WITH WATER OR A WAY HOME. OR DO NOT DARE COME TO ME AT ALL.
PHH
THIS SUCKS A DOZEN GOATS.
BBBPLT BBBPLT BBBPLT

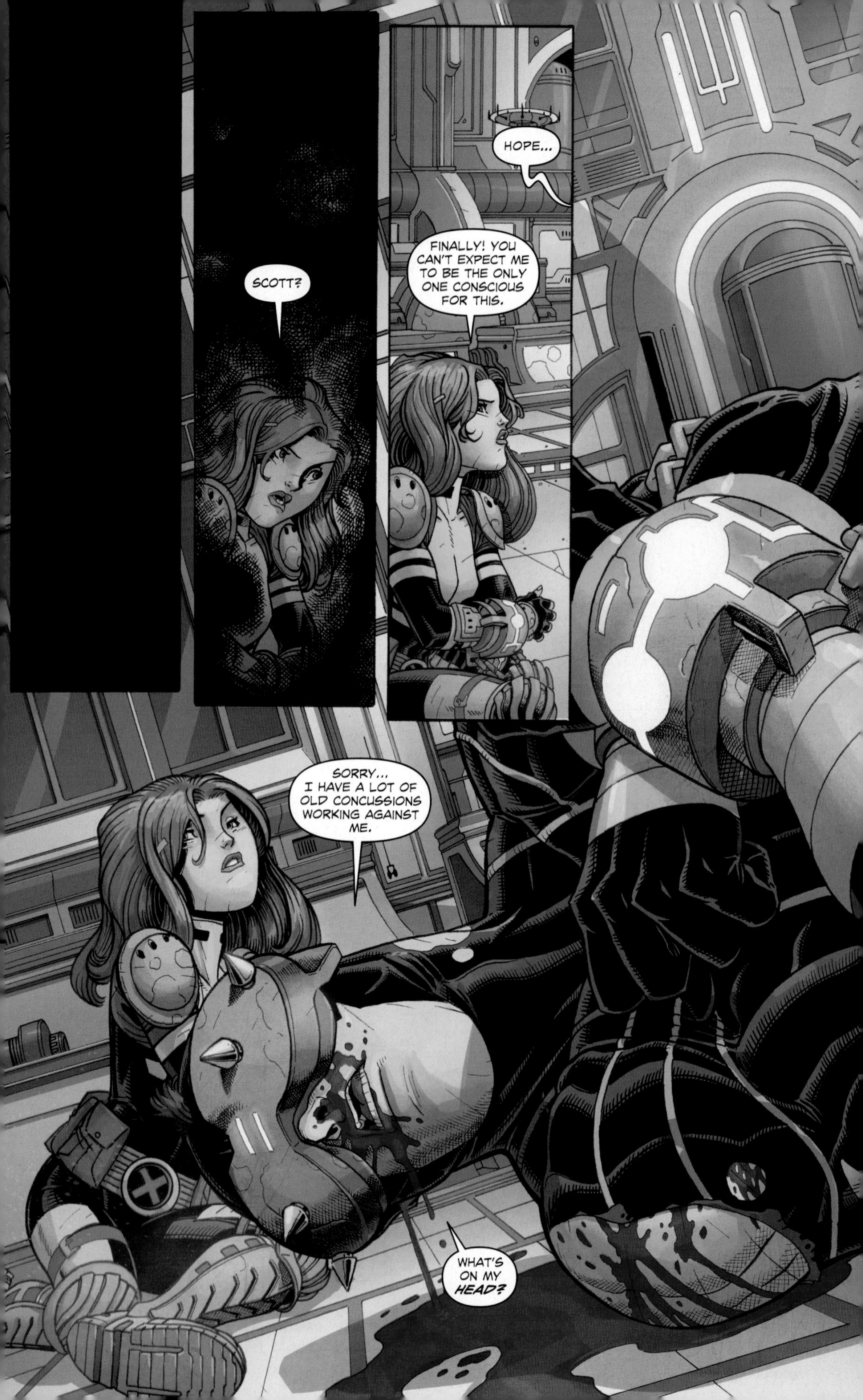
SCOTT?
HOPE...
FINALLY! YOU CAN'T EXPECT ME TO BE THE ONLY ONE CONSCIOUS FOR THIS.
SORRY... I HAVE A LOT OF OLD CONCUSSIONS WORKING AGAINST ME.
WHAT'S ON MY *HEAD?*

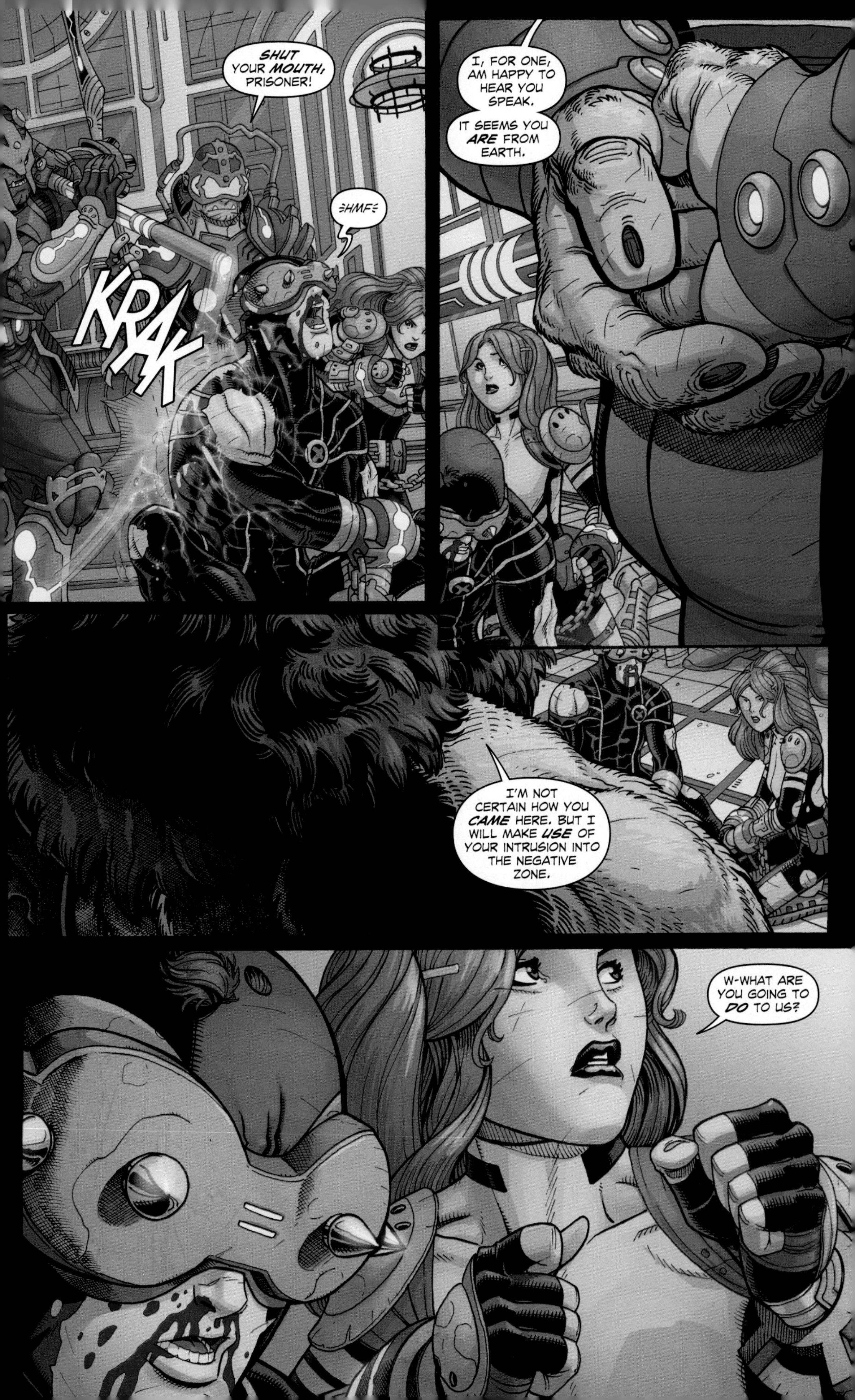
SHUT YOUR MOUTH, PRISONER!
HMF
KRAK
I, FOR ONE, AM HAPPY TO HEAR YOU SPEAK.
IT SEEMS YOU ARE FROM EARTH.
I'M NOT CERTAIN HOW YOU CAME HERE. BUT I WILL MAKE USE OF YOUR INTRUSION INTO THE NEGATIVE ZONE.
W-WHAT ARE YOU GOING TO DO TO US?

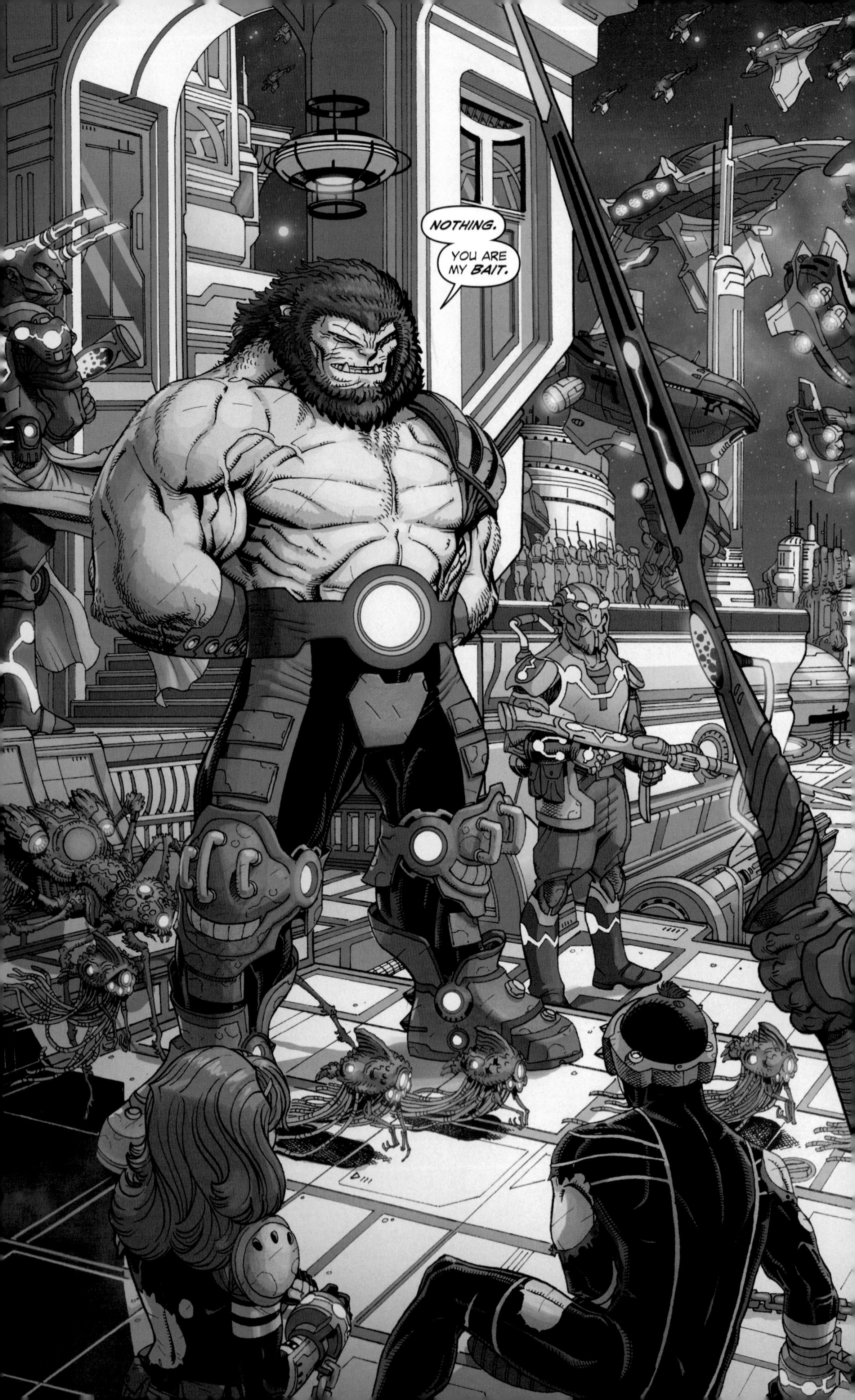
NOTHING.
YOU ARE MY BAIT.

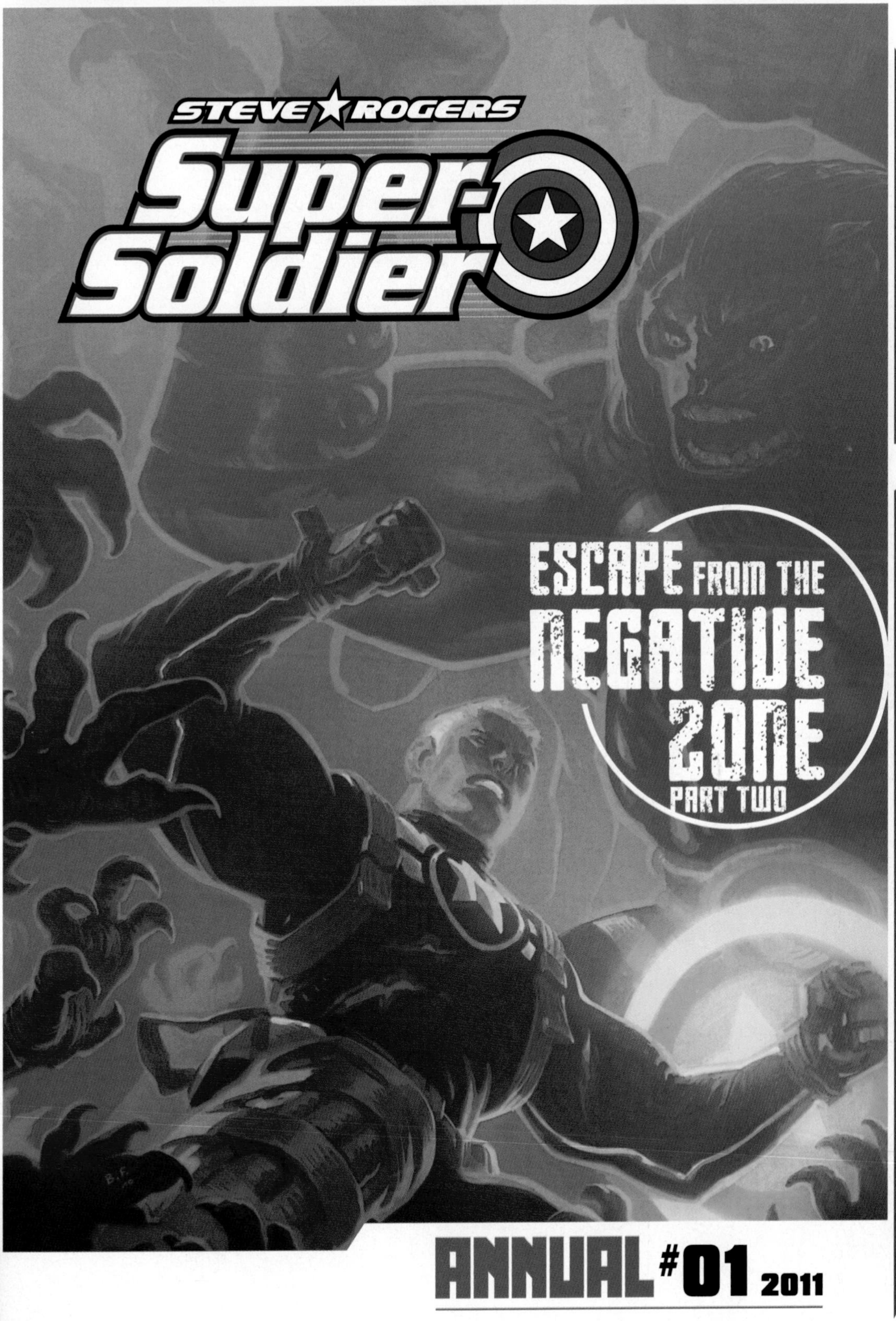

ANNUAL #01 2011

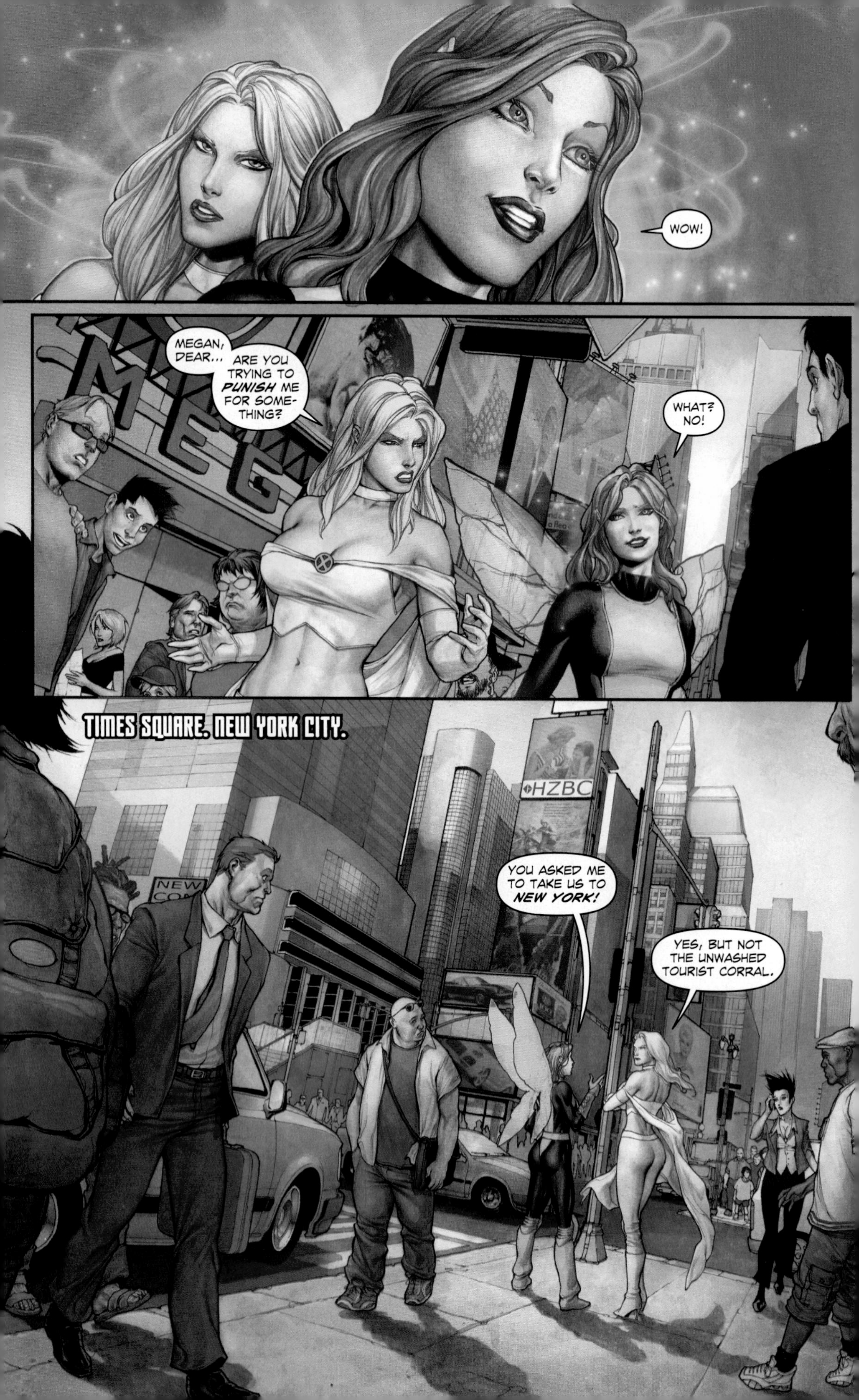
WOW!
MEGAN, DEAR...
ARE YOU TRYING TO PUNISH ME FOR SOME-THING?
WHAT? NO!
TIMES SQUARE. NEW YORK CITY.
HZBC
YOU ASKED ME TO TAKE US TO NEW YORK!
YES, BUT NOT THE UNWASHED TOURIST CORRAL.

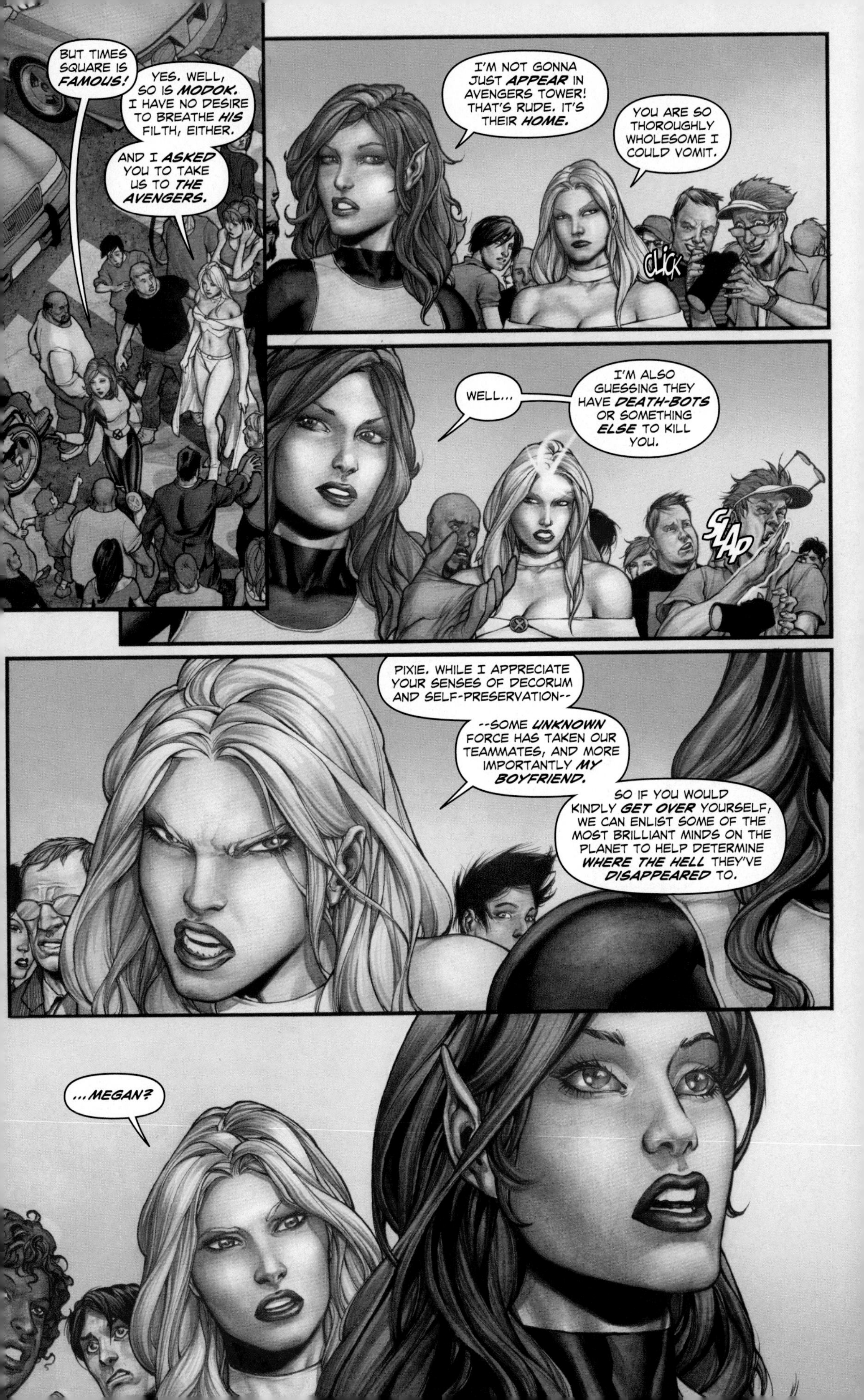

BUT TIMES SQUARE IS FAMOUS!
YES. WELL, SO IS MODOK. I HAVE NO DESIRE TO BREATHE HIS FILTH, EITHER.
AND I ASKED YOU TO TAKE US TO THE AVENGERS.
I'M NOT GONNA JUST APPEAR IN AVENGERS TOWER! THAT'S RUDE. IT'S THEIR HOME.
YOU ARE SO THOROUGHLY WHOLESOME I COULD VOMIT.
CLICK
WELL...
I'M ALSO GUESSING THEY HAVE DEATH-BOTS OR SOMETHING ELSE TO KILL YOU.
SLAP
PIXIE. WHILE I APPRECIATE YOUR SENSES OF DECORUM AND SELF-PRESERVATION--
--SOME UNKNOWN FORCE HAS TAKEN OUR TEAMMATES, AND MORE IMPORTANTLY MY BOYFRIEND.
SO IF YOU WOULD KINDLY GET OVER YOURSELF, WE CAN ENLIST SOME OF THE MOST BRILLIANT MINDS ON THE PLANET TO HELP DETERMINE WHERE THE HELL THEY'VE DISAPPEARED TO.
...MEGAN?

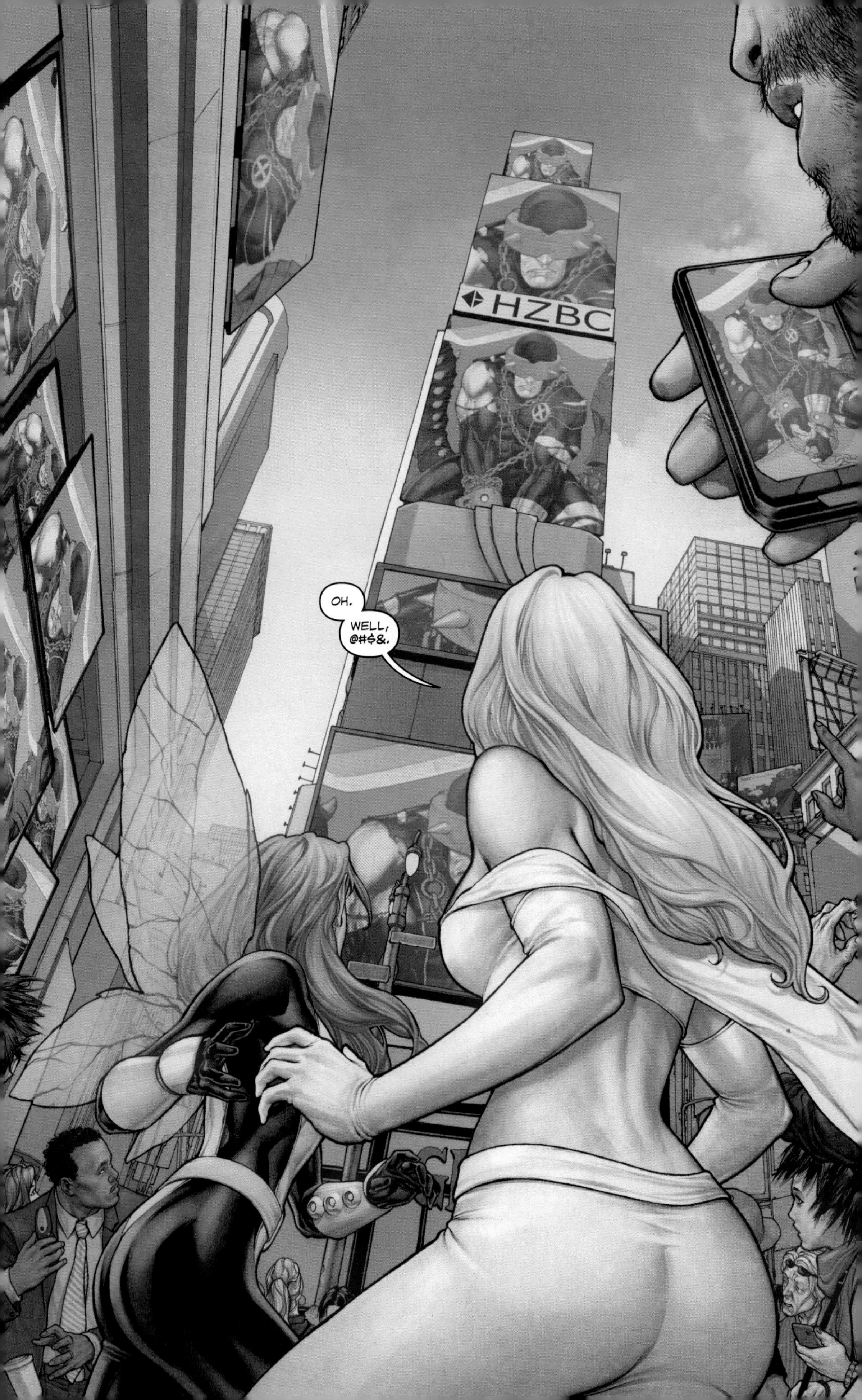
HZBC
OH.
WELL, @#$&.

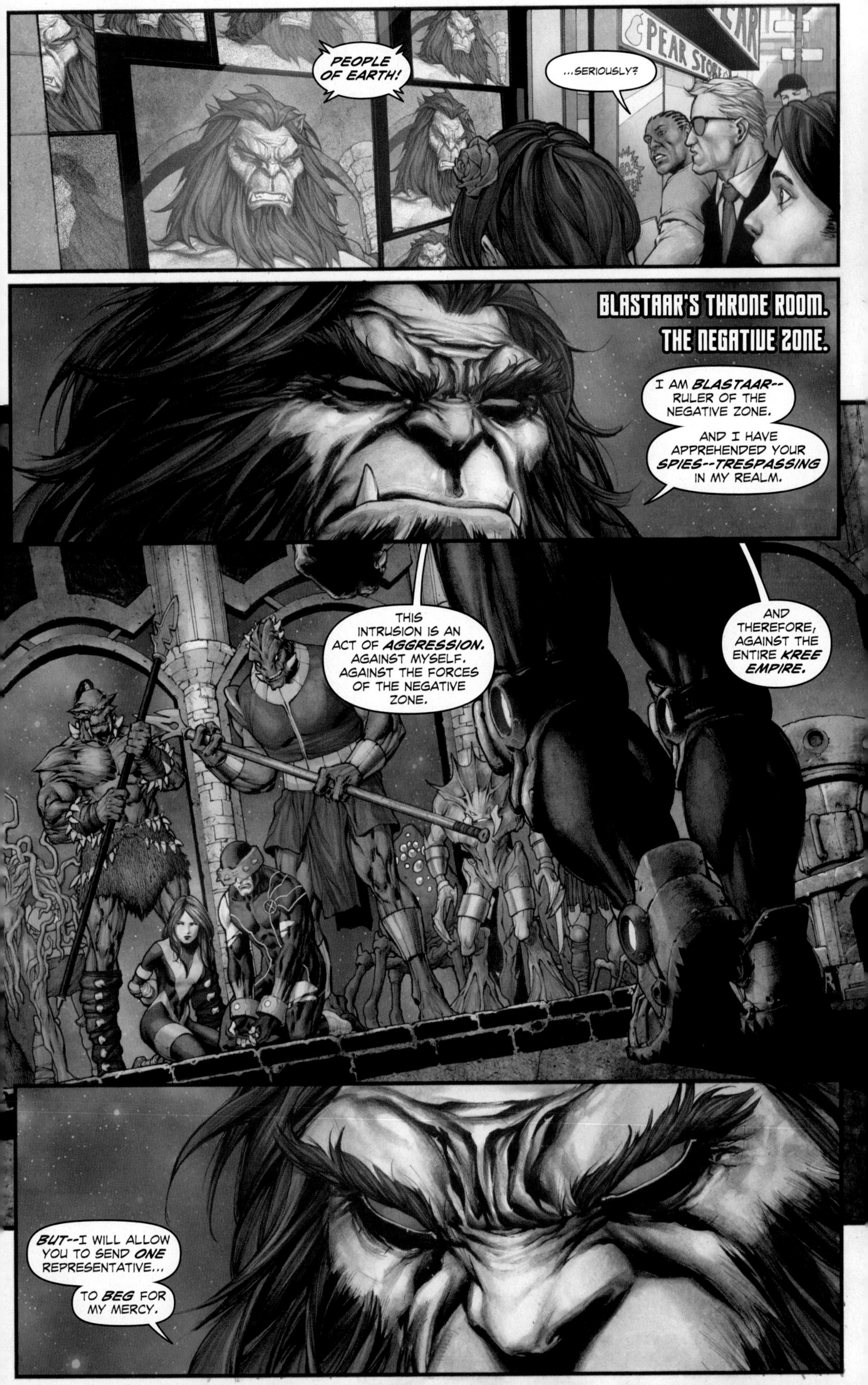
PEOPLE OF EARTH!
...SERIOUSLY?
PEAR STORE
BLASTAAR'S THRONE ROOM.
THE NEGATIVE ZONE.
I AM BLASTAAR-- RULER OF THE NEGATIVE ZONE.
AND I HAVE APPREHENDED YOUR SPIES--TRESPASSING IN MY REALM.
THIS INTRUSION IS AN ACT OF AGGRESSION. AGAINST MYSELF. AGAINST THE FORCES OF THE NEGATIVE ZONE.
AND THEREFORE, AGAINST THE ENTIRE KREE EMPIRE.
BUT--I WILL ALLOW YOU TO SEND ONE REPRESENTATIVE...
TO BEG FOR MY MERCY.

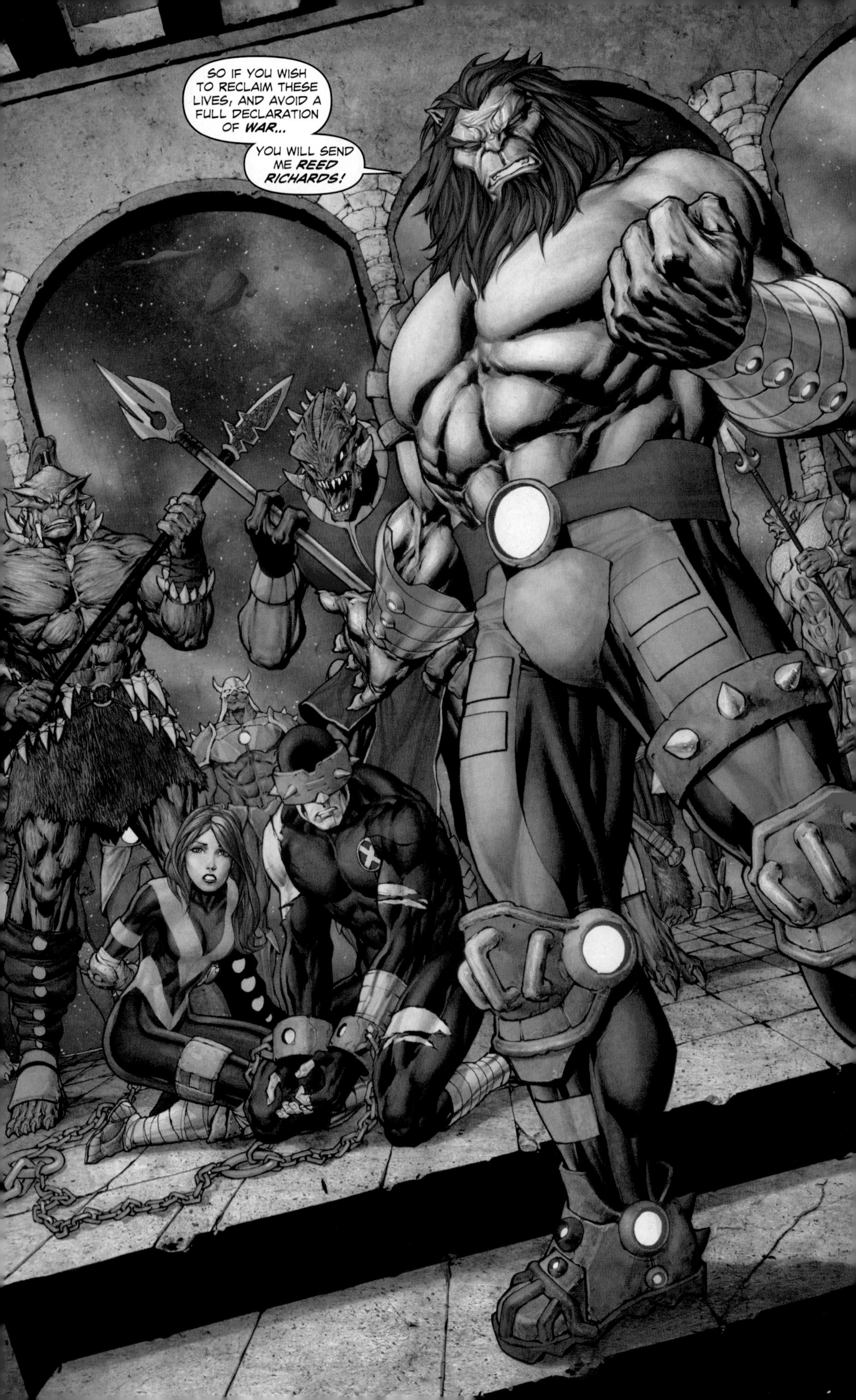
SO IF YOU WISH TO RECLAIM THESE LIVES, AND AVOID A FULL DECLARATION OF WAR...
YOU WILL SEND ME REED RICHARDS!

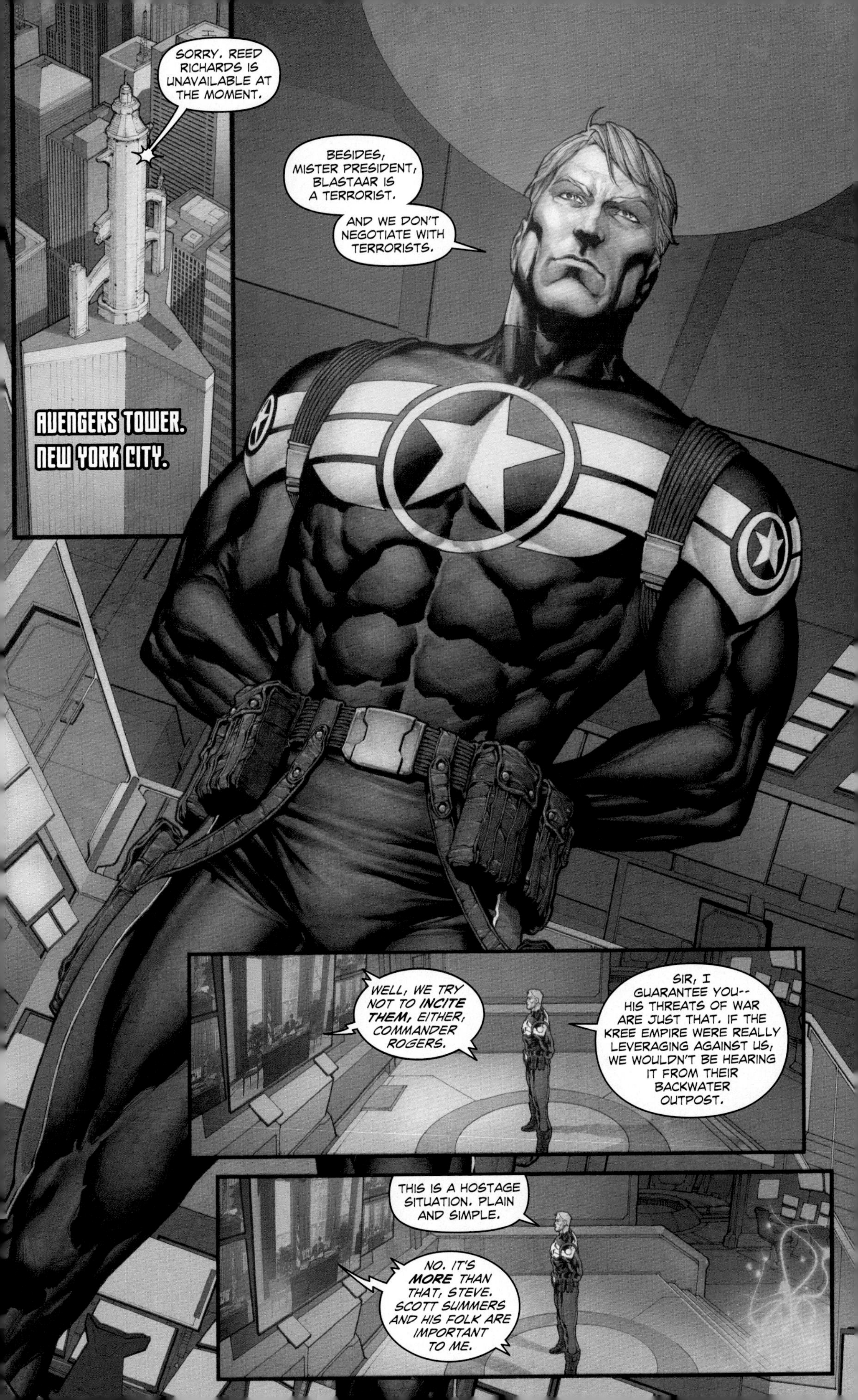

SORRY. REED RICHARDS IS UNAVAILABLE AT THE MOMENT.
AVENGERS TOWER. NEW YORK CITY.
BESIDES, MISTER PRESIDENT, BLASTAAR IS A TERRORIST.
AND WE DON'T NEGOTIATE WITH TERRORISTS.
WELL, WE TRY NOT TO INCITE THEM, EITHER, COMMANDER ROGERS.
SIR, I GUARANTEE YOU-- HIS THREATS OF WAR ARE JUST THAT. IF THE KREE EMPIRE WERE REALLY LEVERAGING AGAINST US, WE WOULDN'T BE HEARING IT FROM THEIR BACKWATER OUTPOST.
THIS IS A HOSTAGE SITUATION. PLAIN AND SIMPLE.
NO. IT'S MORE THAN THAT, STEVE. SCOTT SUMMERS AND HIS FOLK ARE IMPORTANT TO ME.

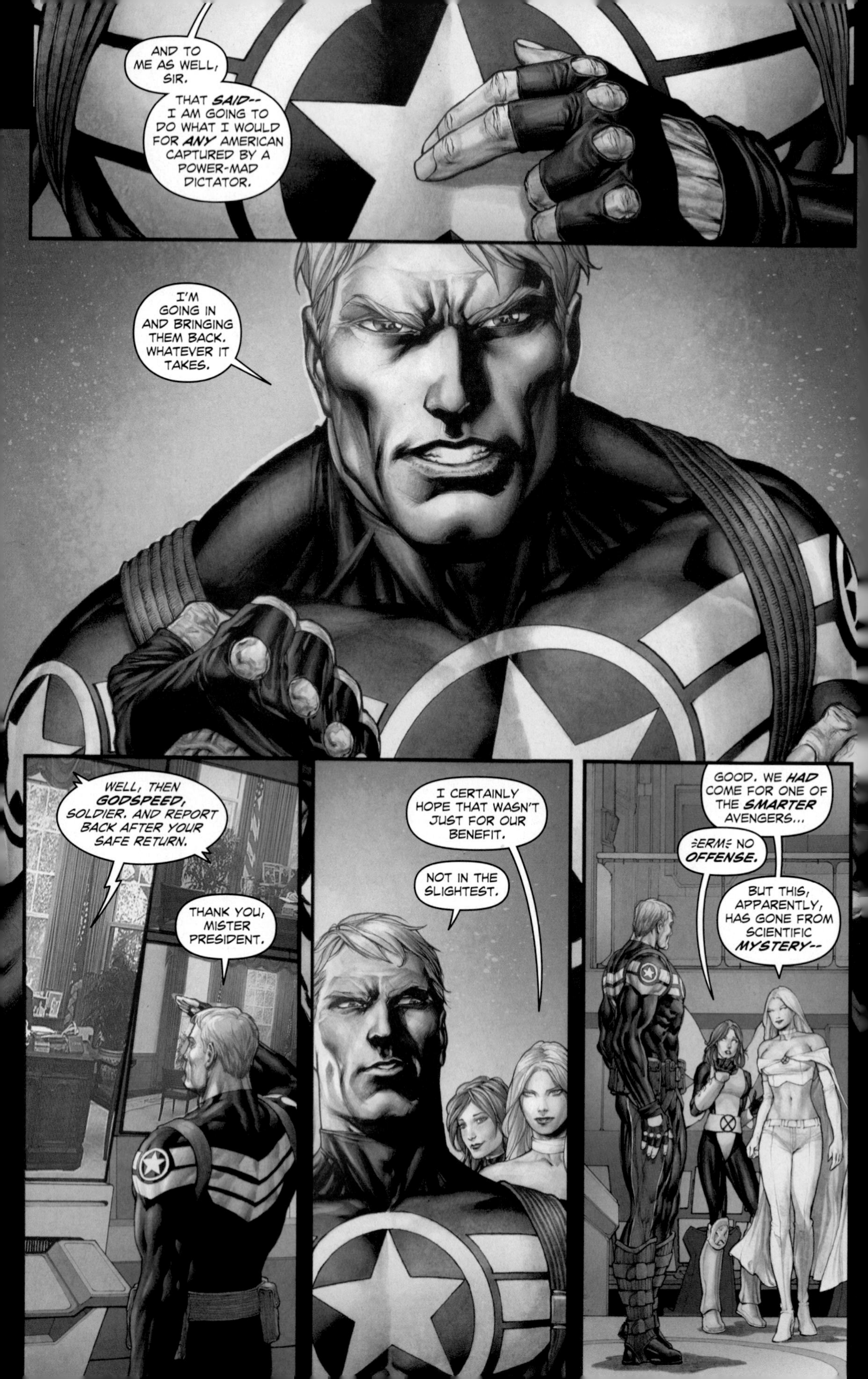
AND TO ME AS WELL, SIR.
THAT SAID-- I AM GOING TO DO WHAT I WOULD FOR ANY AMERICAN CAPTURED BY A POWER-MAD DICTATOR.
I'M GOING IN AND BRINGING THEM BACK. WHATEVER IT TAKES.
WELL, THEN GODSPEED, SOLDIER. AND REPORT BACK AFTER YOUR SAFE RETURN.
THANK YOU, MISTER PRESIDENT.
I CERTAINLY HOPE THAT WASN'T JUST FOR OUR BENEFIT.
NOT IN THE SLIGHTEST.
GOOD. WE HAD COME FOR ONE OF THE SMARTER AVENGERS...
ERM NO OFFENSE.
BUT THIS, APPARENTLY, HAS GONE FROM SCIENTIFIC MYSTERY--

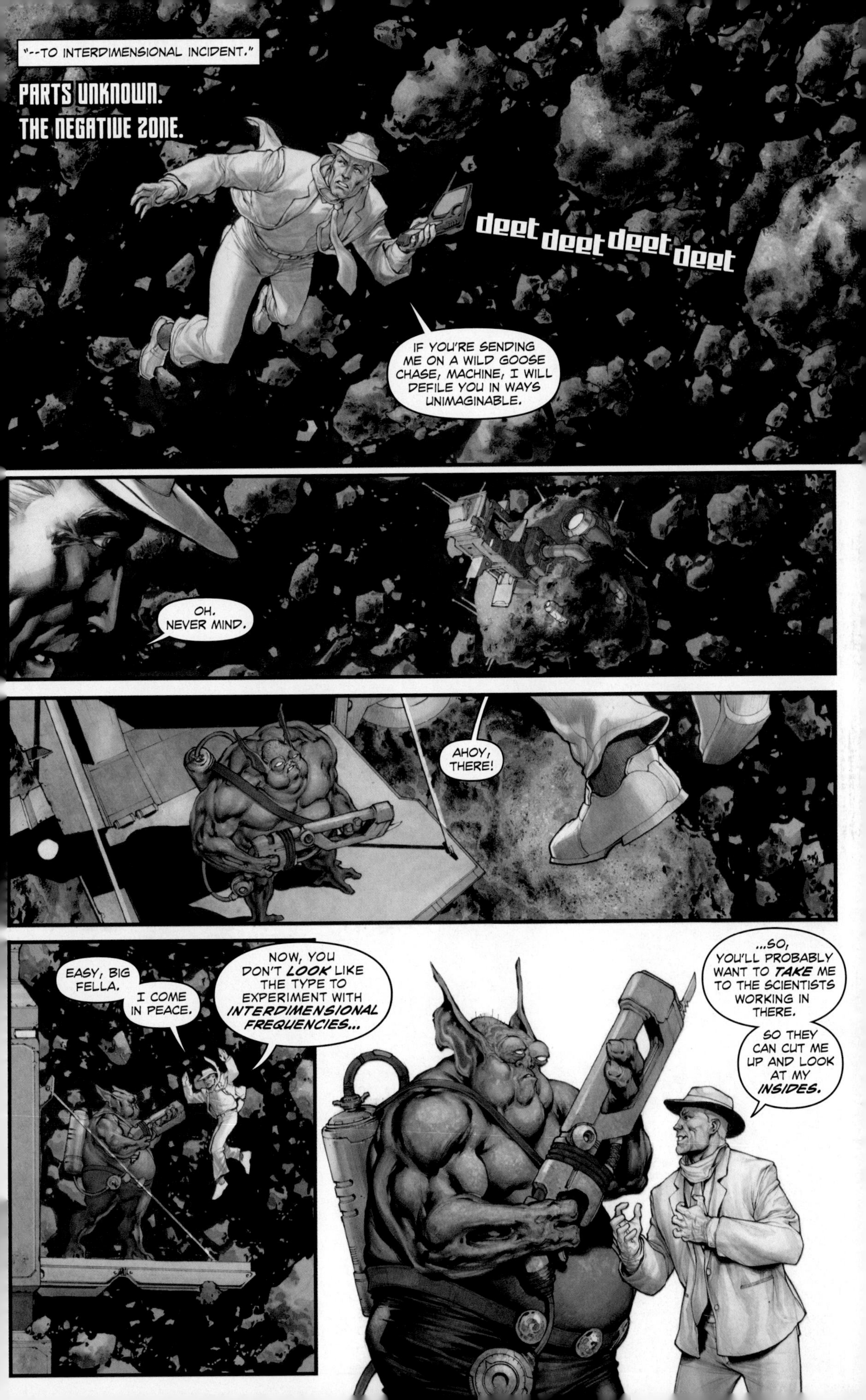
"--TO INTERDIMENSIONAL INCIDENT."
PARTS UNKNOWN.
THE NEGATIVE ZONE.
deet deet deet deet
IF YOU'RE SENDING ME ON A WILD GOOSE CHASE, MACHINE, I WILL DEFILE YOU IN WAYS UNIMAGINABLE.
OH. NEVER MIND.
AHOY, THERE!
EASY, BIG FELLA.
I COME IN PEACE.
NOW, YOU DON'T LOOK LIKE THE TYPE TO EXPERIMENT WITH INTERDIMENSIONAL FREQUENCIES...
...SO, YOU'LL PROBABLY WANT TO TAKE ME TO THE SCIENTISTS WORKING IN THERE.
SO THEY CAN CUT ME UP AND LOOK AT MY INSIDES.

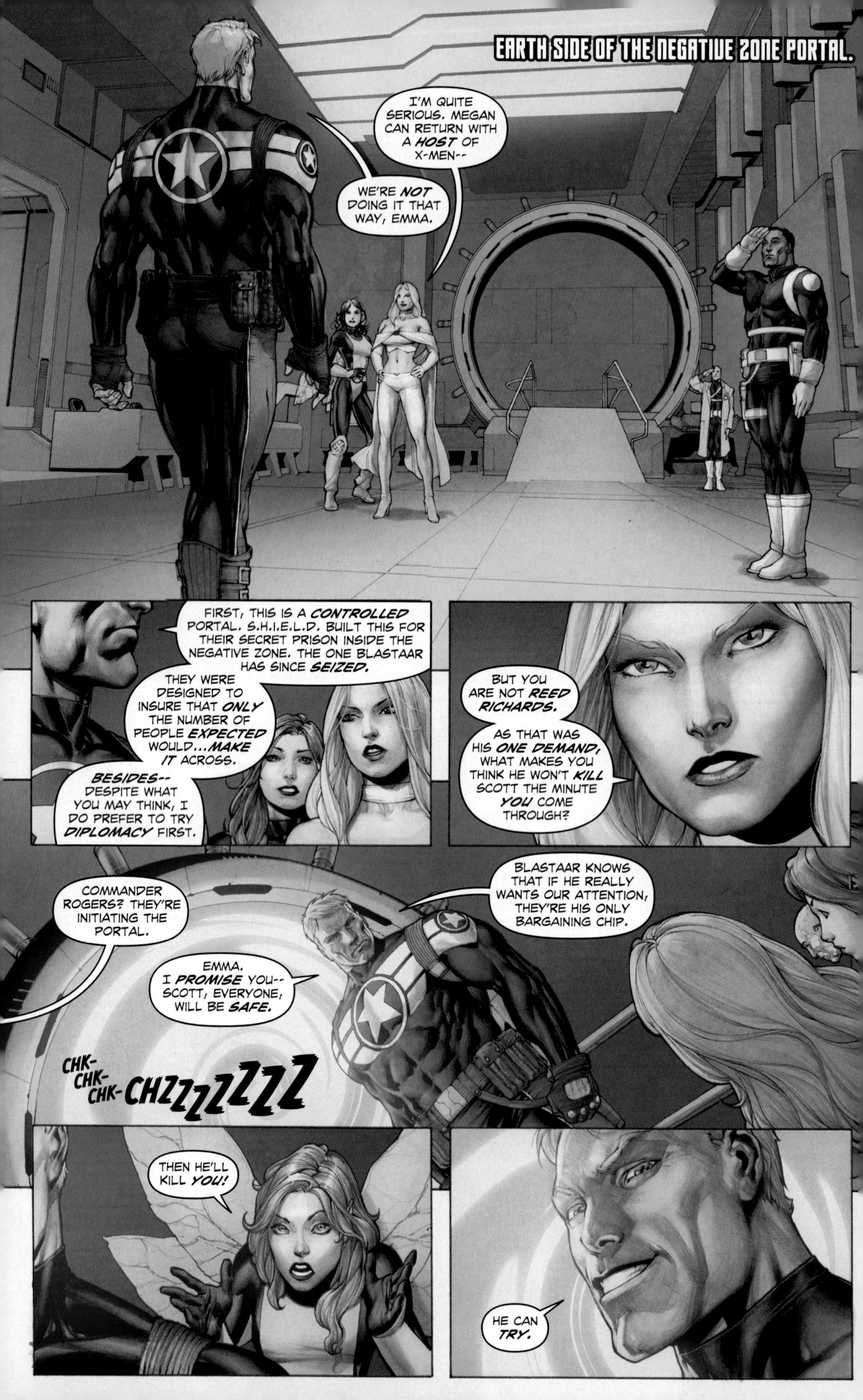
EARTH SIDE OF THE NEGATIVE ZONE PORTAL.
I'M QUITE SERIOUS. MEGAN CAN RETURN WITH A HOST OF X-MEN--
WE'RE NOT DOING IT THAT WAY, EMMA.
FIRST, THIS IS A CONTROLLED PORTAL. S.H.I.E.L.D. BUILT THIS FOR THEIR SECRET PRISON INSIDE THE NEGATIVE ZONE. THE ONE BLASTAAR HAS SINCE SEIZED.
THEY WERE DESIGNED TO INSURE THAT ONLY THE NUMBER OF PEOPLE EXPECTED WOULD...MAKE IT ACROSS.
BESIDES-- DESPITE WHAT YOU MAY THINK, I DO PREFER TO TRY DIPLOMACY FIRST.
BUT YOU ARE NOT REED RICHARDS.
AS THAT WAS HIS ONE DEMAND, WHAT MAKES YOU THINK HE WON'T KILL SCOTT THE MINUTE YOU COME THROUGH?
COMMANDER ROGERS? THEY'RE INITIATING THE PORTAL.
BLASTAAR KNOWS THAT IF HE REALLY WANTS OUR ATTENTION, THEY'RE HIS ONLY BARGAINING CHIP.
EMMA. I PROMISE YOU-- SCOTT, EVERYONE, WILL BE SAFE.
CHK- CHK- CHK- CHZZZZZZZZ
THEN HE'LL KILL YOU!
HE CAN TRY.

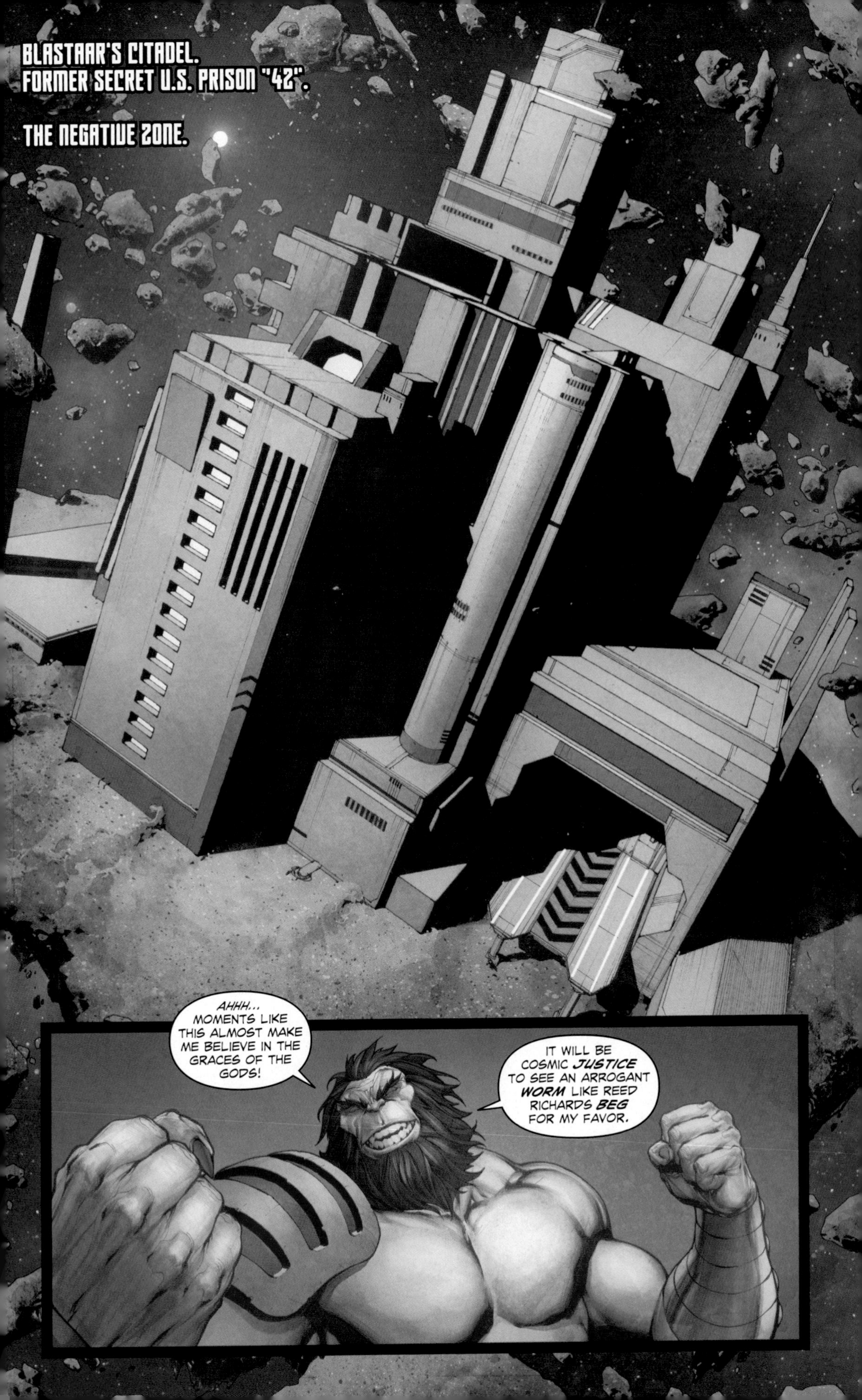
BLASTAAR'S CITADEL.
FORMER SECRET U.S. PRISON "42".
THE NEGATIVE ZONE.
AHHH... MOMENTS LIKE THIS ALMOST MAKE ME BELIEVE IN THE GRACES OF THE GODS!
IT WILL BE COSMIC JUSTICE TO SEE AN ARROGANT WORM LIKE REED RICHARDS BEG FOR MY FAVOR.

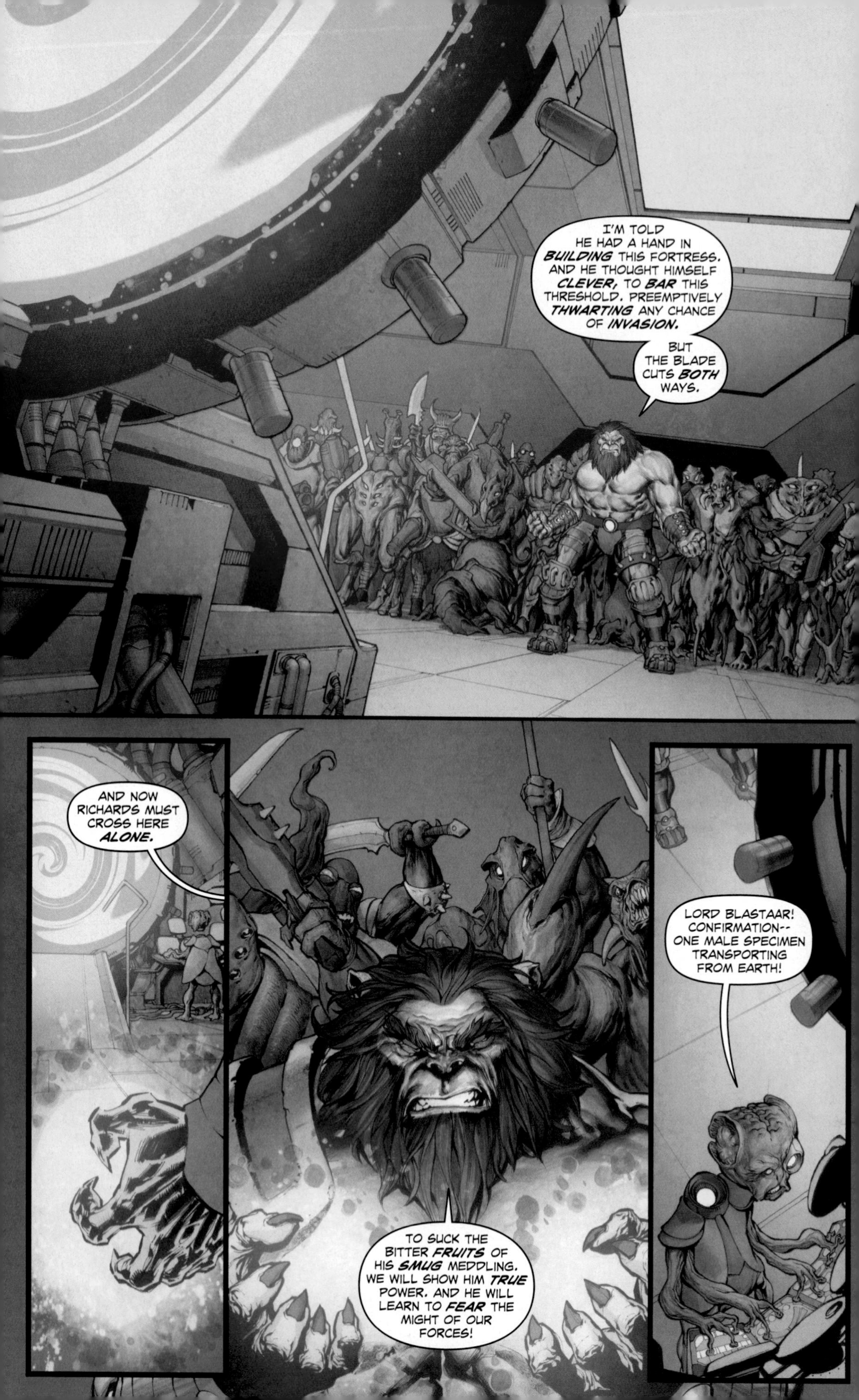
I'M TOLD HE HAD A HAND IN BUILDING THIS FORTRESS. AND HE THOUGHT HIMSELF CLEVER, TO BAR THIS THRESHOLD. PREEMPTIVELY THWARTING ANY CHANCE OF INVASION.
BUT THE BLADE CUTS BOTH WAYS.
AND NOW RICHARDS MUST CROSS HERE ALONE.
TO SUCK THE BITTER FRUITS OF HIS SMUG MEDDLING. WE WILL SHOW HIM TRUE POWER. AND HE WILL LEARN TO FEAR THE MIGHT OF OUR FORCES!
LORD BLASTAAR! CONFIRMATION-- ONE MALE SPECIMEN TRANSPORTING FROM EARTH!

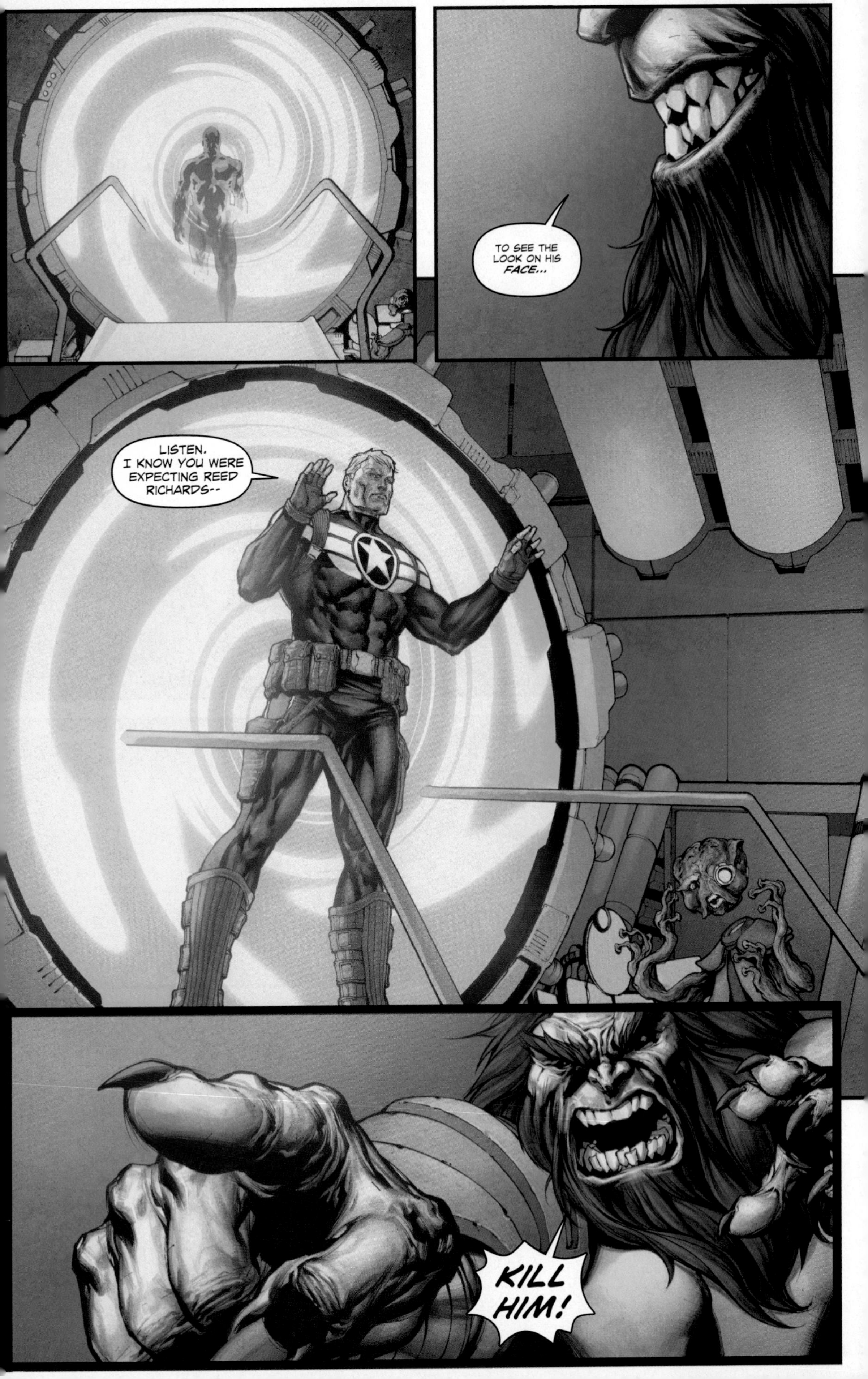

TO SEE THE LOOK ON HIS FACE...
LISTEN. I KNOW YOU WERE EXPECTING REED RICHARDS--
KILL HIM!

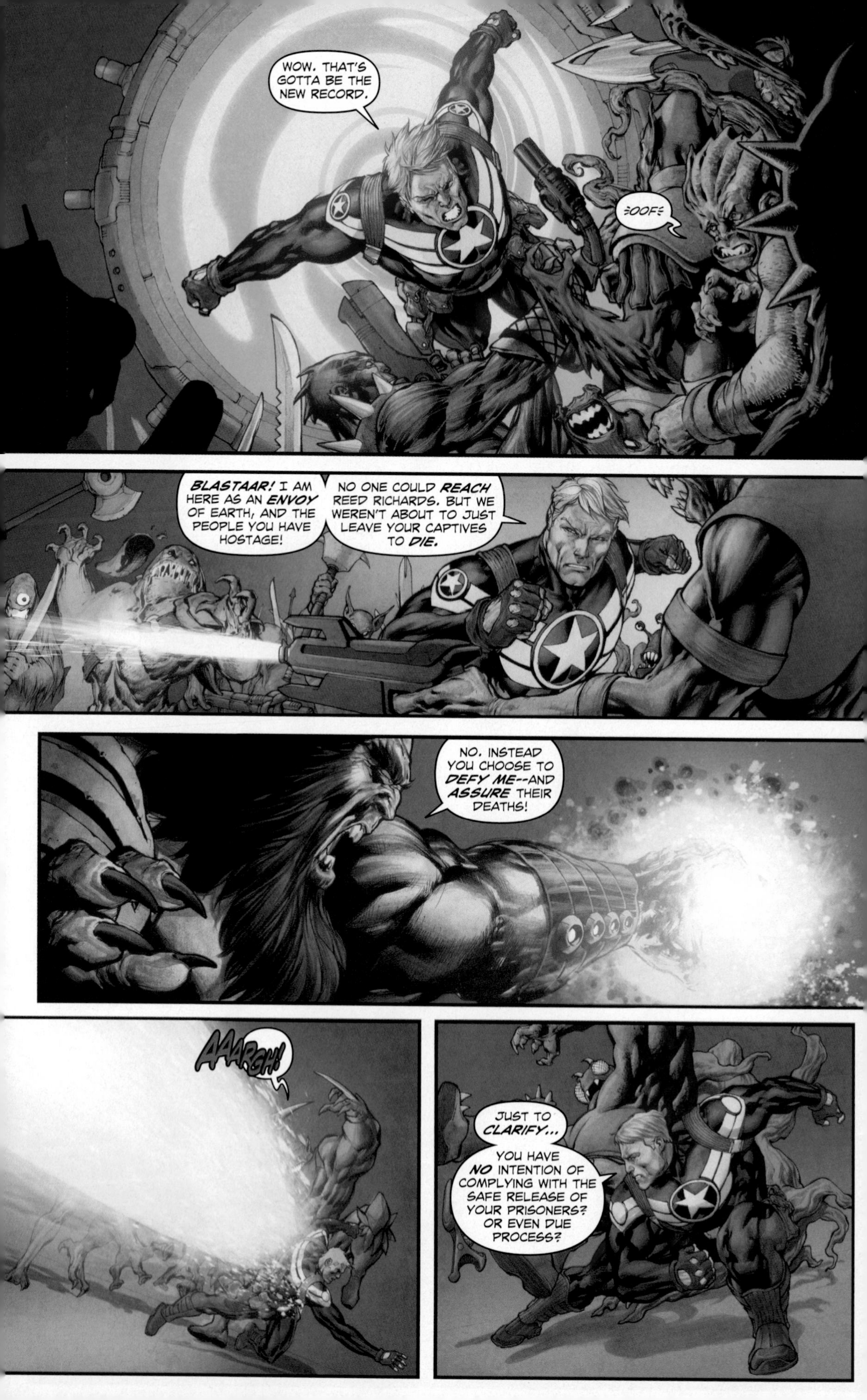
WOW. THAT'S GOTTA BE THE NEW RECORD.
OOF
BLASTAAR! I AM HERE AS AN ENVOY OF EARTH, AND THE PEOPLE YOU HAVE HOSTAGE!
NO ONE COULD REACH REED RICHARDS. BUT WE WEREN'T ABOUT TO JUST LEAVE YOUR CAPTIVES TO DIE.
NO. INSTEAD YOU CHOOSE TO DEFY ME--AND ASSURE THEIR DEATHS!
AAARGH!
JUST TO CLARIFY...
YOU HAVE NO INTENTION OF COMPLYING WITH THE SAFE RELEASE OF YOUR PRISONERS? OR EVEN DUE PROCESS?

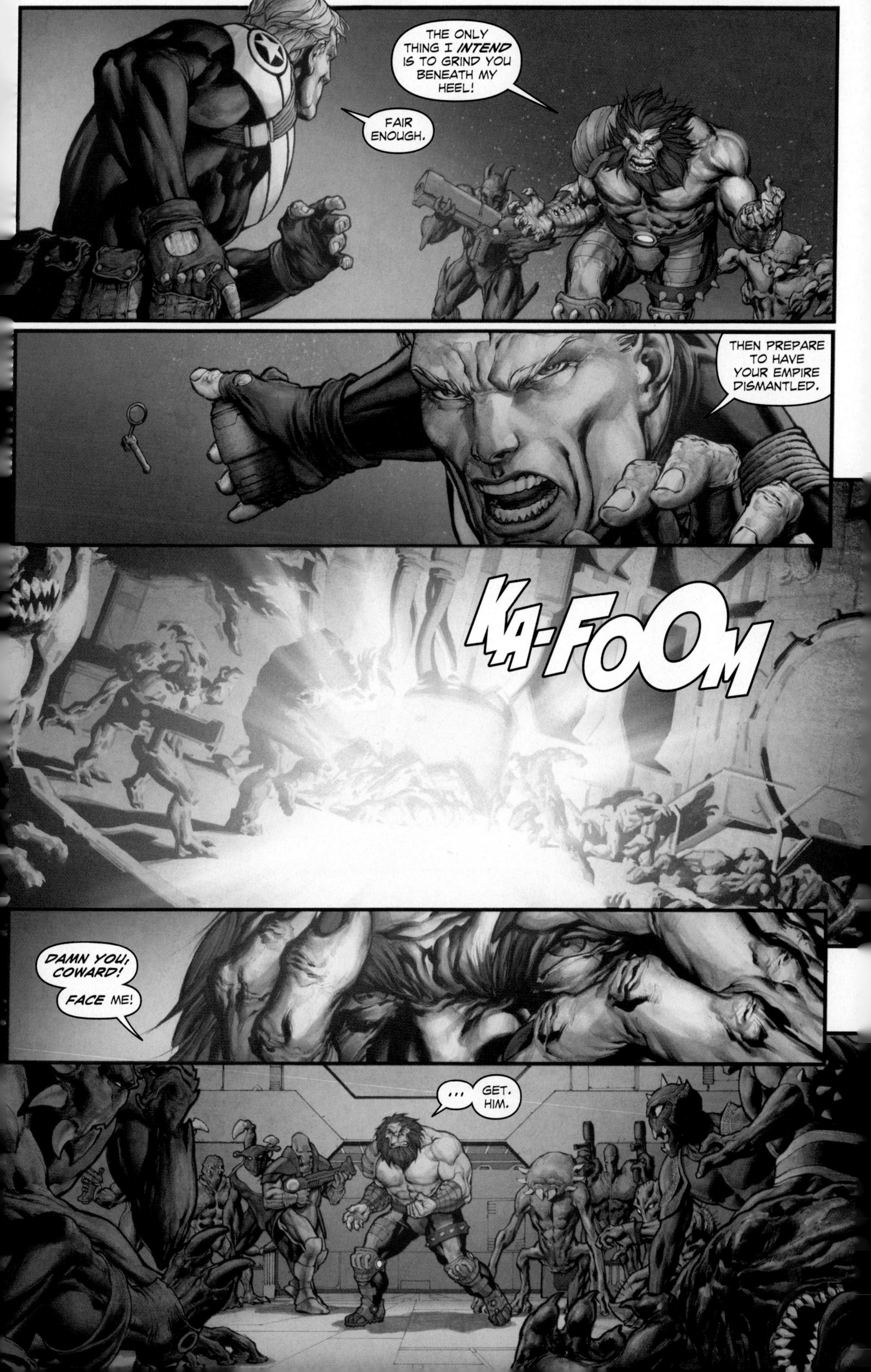
THE ONLY THING I *INTEND* IS TO GRIND YOU BENEATH MY HEEL!
FAIR ENOUGH.
THEN PREPARE TO HAVE YOUR EMPIRE DISMANTLED.
KA-FOOM
DAMN YOU, COWARD!
FACE ME!
... GET. HIM.

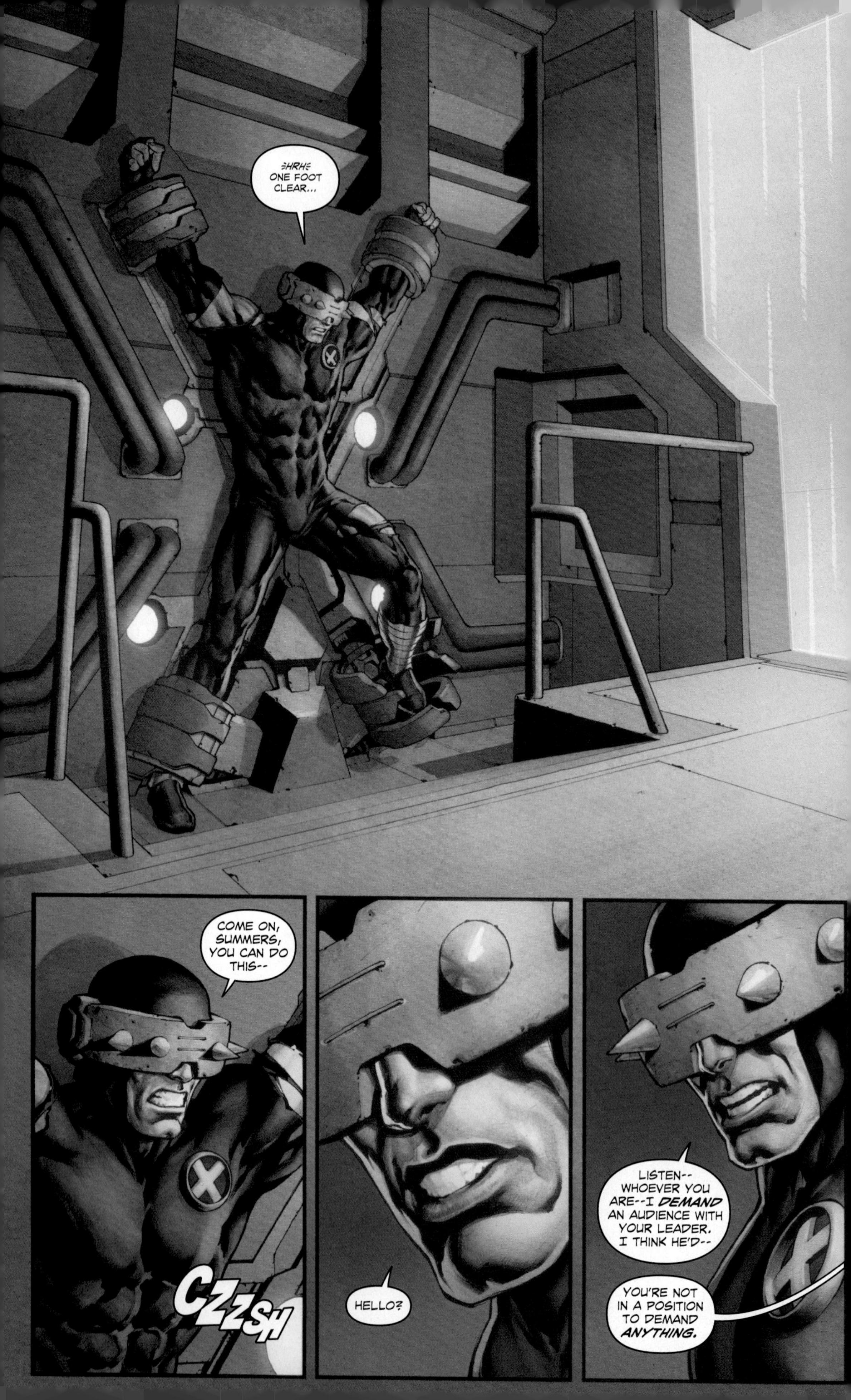

=HRH= ONE FOOT CLEAR...
COME ON, SUMMERS, YOU CAN DO THIS--
CZZSH
HELLO?
LISTEN-- WHOEVER YOU ARE--I *DEMAND* AN AUDIENCE WITH YOUR LEADER. I THINK HE'D--
YOU'RE NOT IN A POSITION TO DEMAND ***ANYTHING.***

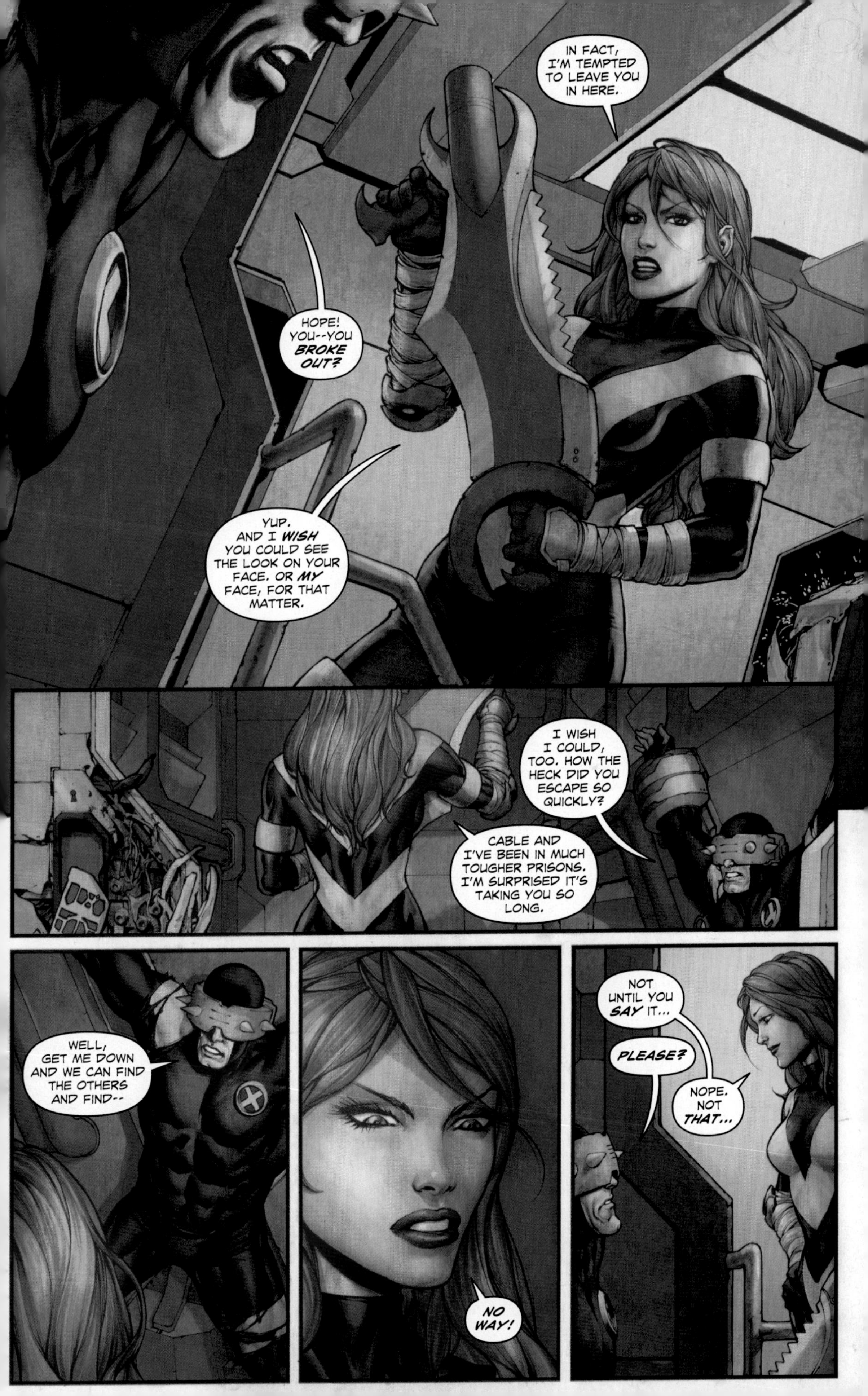

IN FACT, I'M TEMPTED TO LEAVE YOU IN HERE.
HOPE! YOU--YOU *BROKE OUT?*
YUP. AND I *WISH* YOU COULD SEE THE LOOK ON YOUR FACE. OR *MY* FACE, FOR THAT MATTER.
I WISH I COULD, TOO. HOW THE HECK DID YOU ESCAPE SO QUICKLY?
CABLE AND I'VE BEEN IN MUCH TOUGHER PRISONS. I'M SURPRISED IT'S TAKING YOU SO LONG.
WELL, GET ME DOWN AND WE CAN FIND THE OTHERS AND FIND--
NO WAY!
NOT UNTIL YOU *SAY* IT...
PLEASE?
NOPE. NOT *THAT*...

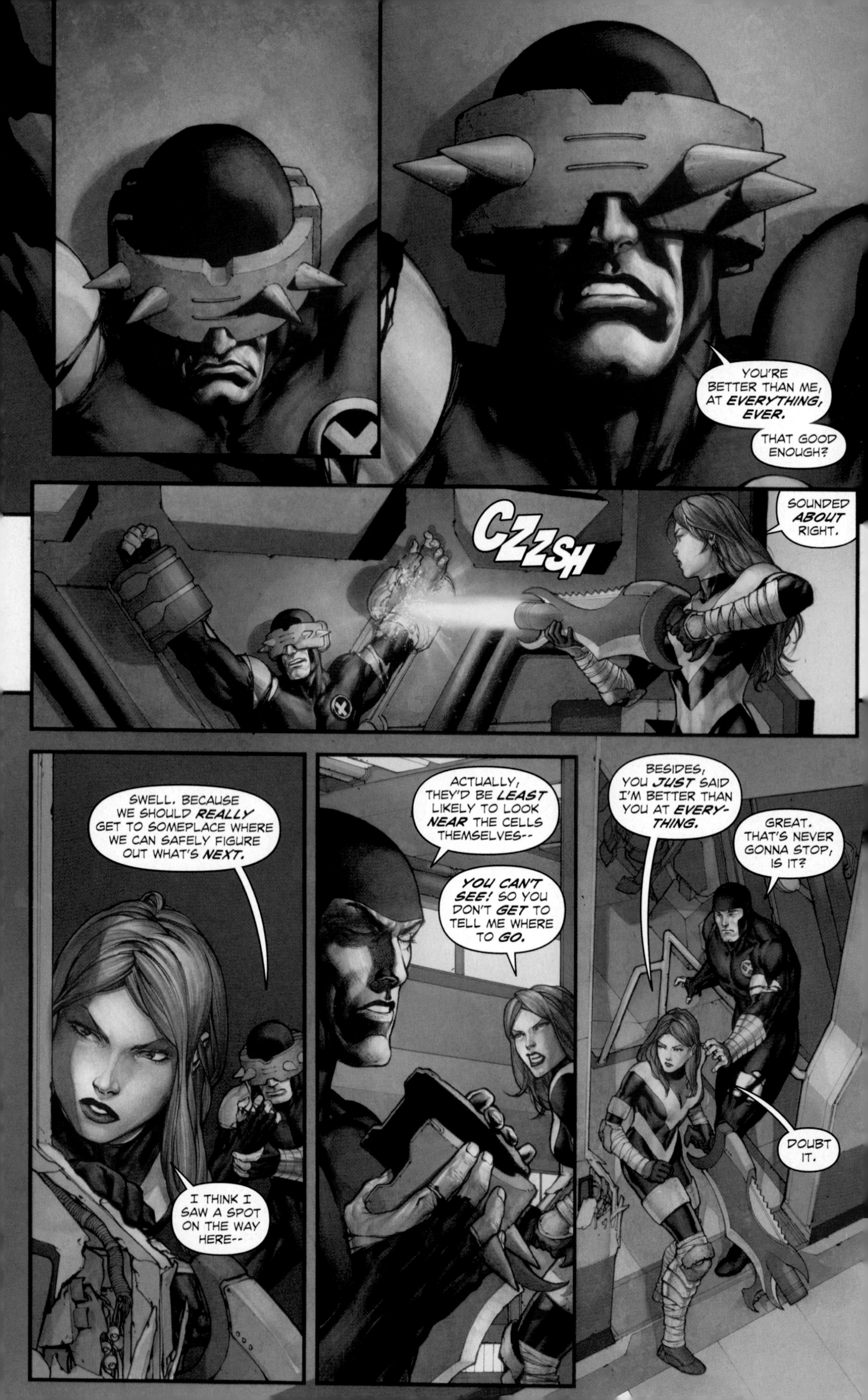
YOU'RE BETTER THAN ME, AT *EVERYTHING, EVER.*
THAT GOOD ENOUGH?
CZZSH
SOUNDED *ABOUT* RIGHT.
SWELL. BECAUSE WE SHOULD *REALLY* GET TO SOMEPLACE WHERE WE CAN SAFELY FIGURE OUT WHAT'S *NEXT.*
I THINK I SAW A SPOT ON THE WAY HERE--
ACTUALLY, THEY'D BE *LEAST* LIKELY TO LOOK *NEAR* THE CELLS THEMSELVES--
YOU CAN'T SEE! SO YOU DON'T *GET* TO TELL ME WHERE TO *GO.*
BESIDES, YOU *JUST* SAID I'M BETTER THAN YOU AT *EVERY-THING.*
GREAT. THAT'S NEVER GONNA STOP, IS IT?
DOUBT IT.

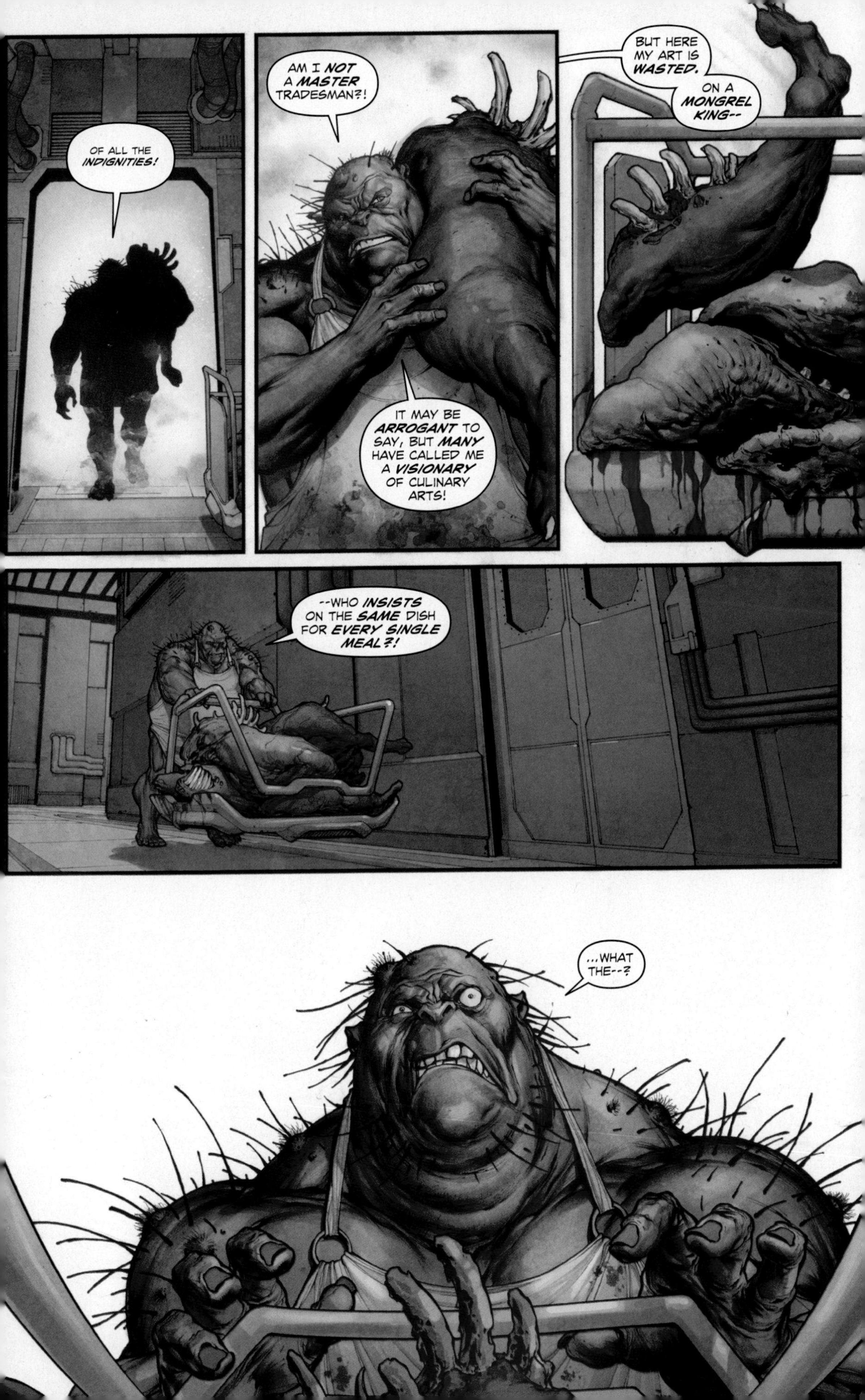

OF ALL THE INDIGNITIES!
AM I NOT A MASTER TRADESMAN?!
IT MAY BE ARROGANT TO SAY, BUT MANY HAVE CALLED ME A VISIONARY OF CULINARY ARTS!
BUT HERE MY ART IS WASTED.
ON A MONGREL KING--
--WHO INSISTS ON THE SAME DISH FOR EVERY SINGLE MEAL?!
...WHAT THE--?

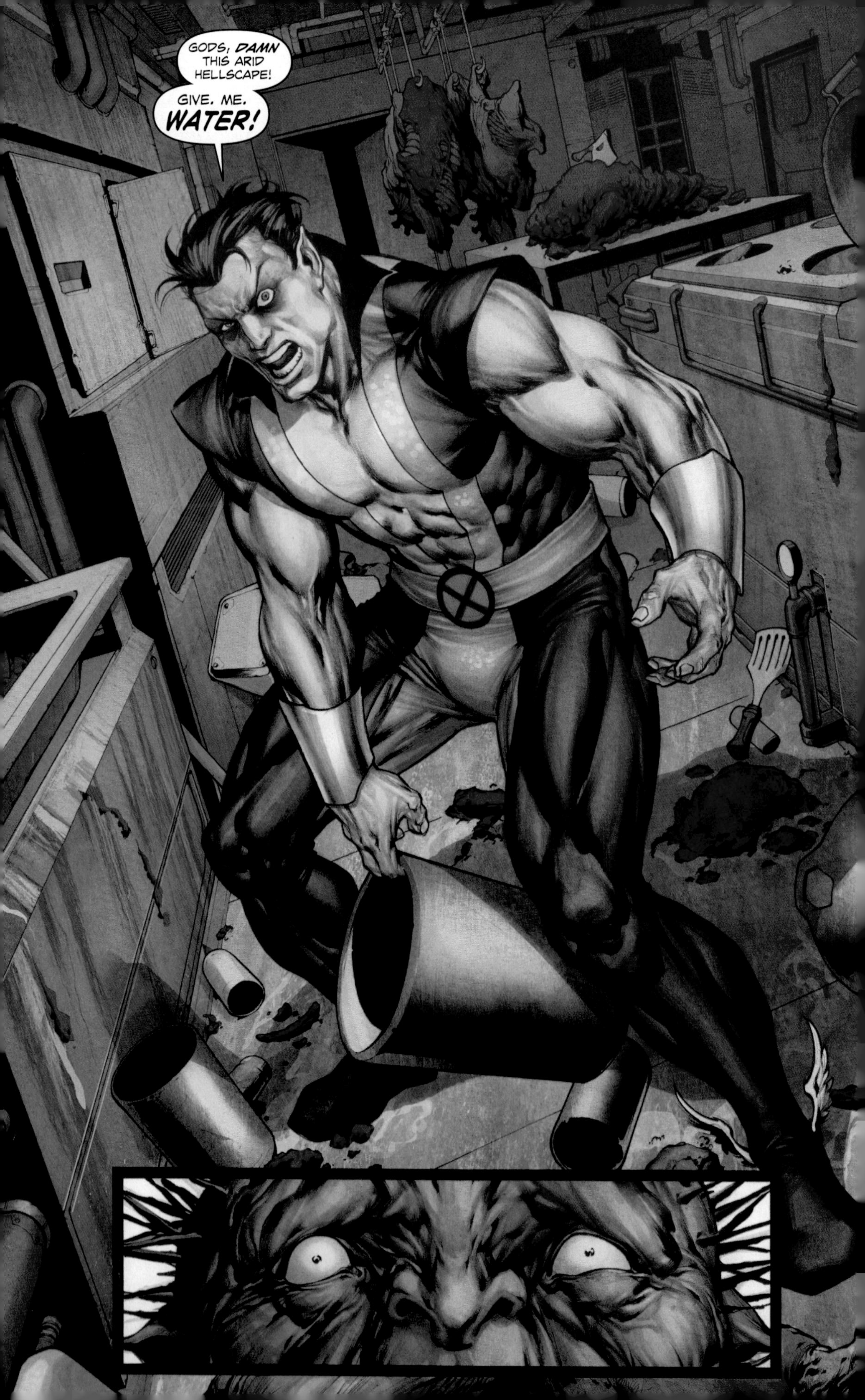
GODS, DAMN THIS ARID HELLSCAPE!
GIVE. ME. WATER!

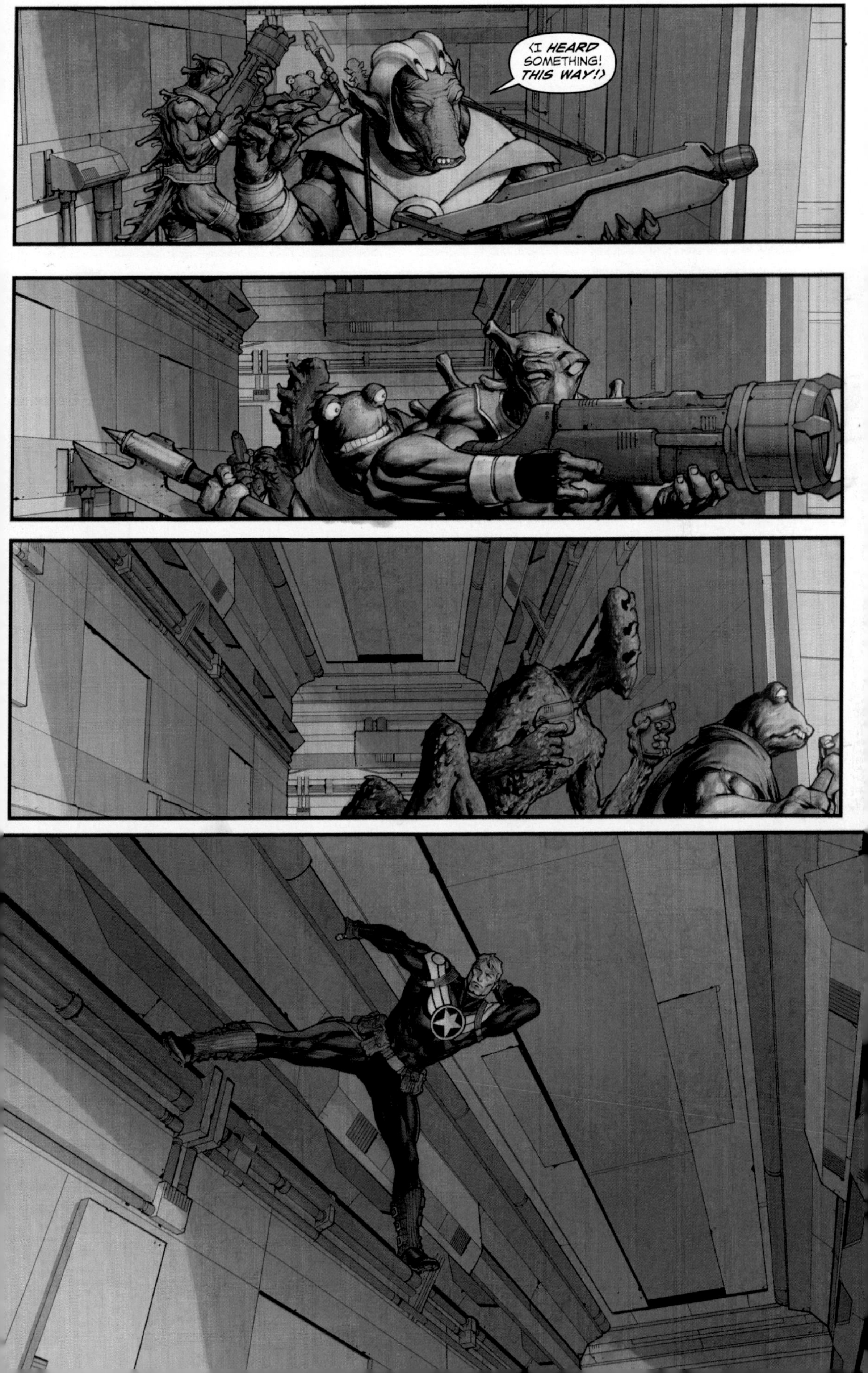
‹I HEARD SOMETHING! THIS WAY!›

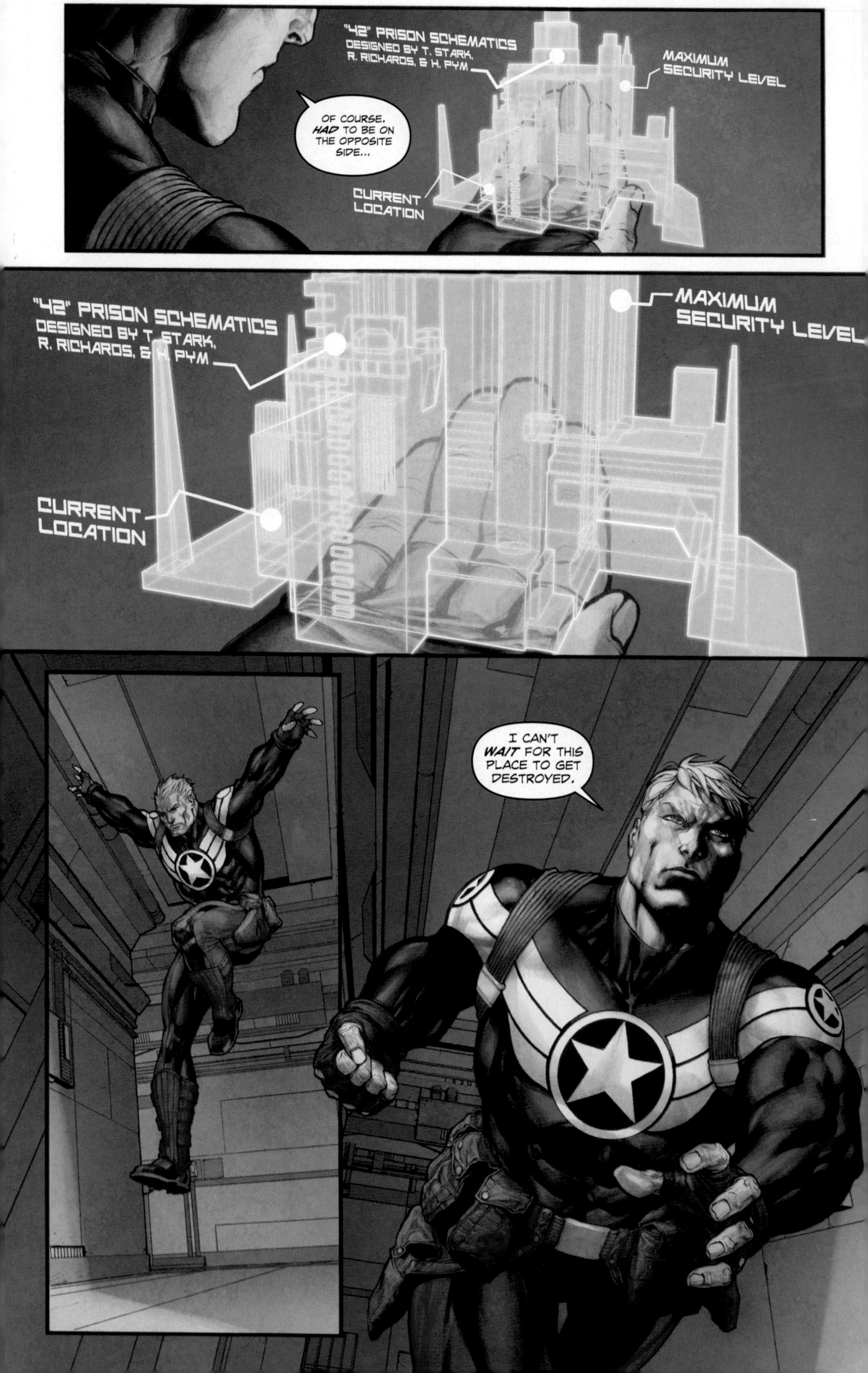
"42" PRISON SCHEMATICS
DESIGNED BY T. STARK, R. RICHARDS, & H. PYM
MAXIMUM SECURITY LEVEL
OF COURSE. HAD TO BE ON THE OPPOSITE SIDE...
CURRENT LOCATION
"42" PRISON SCHEMATICS
DESIGNED BY T. STARK, R. RICHARDS, & H. PYM
MAXIMUM SECURITY LEVEL
CURRENT LOCATION
I CAN'T WAIT FOR THIS PLACE TO GET DESTROYED.

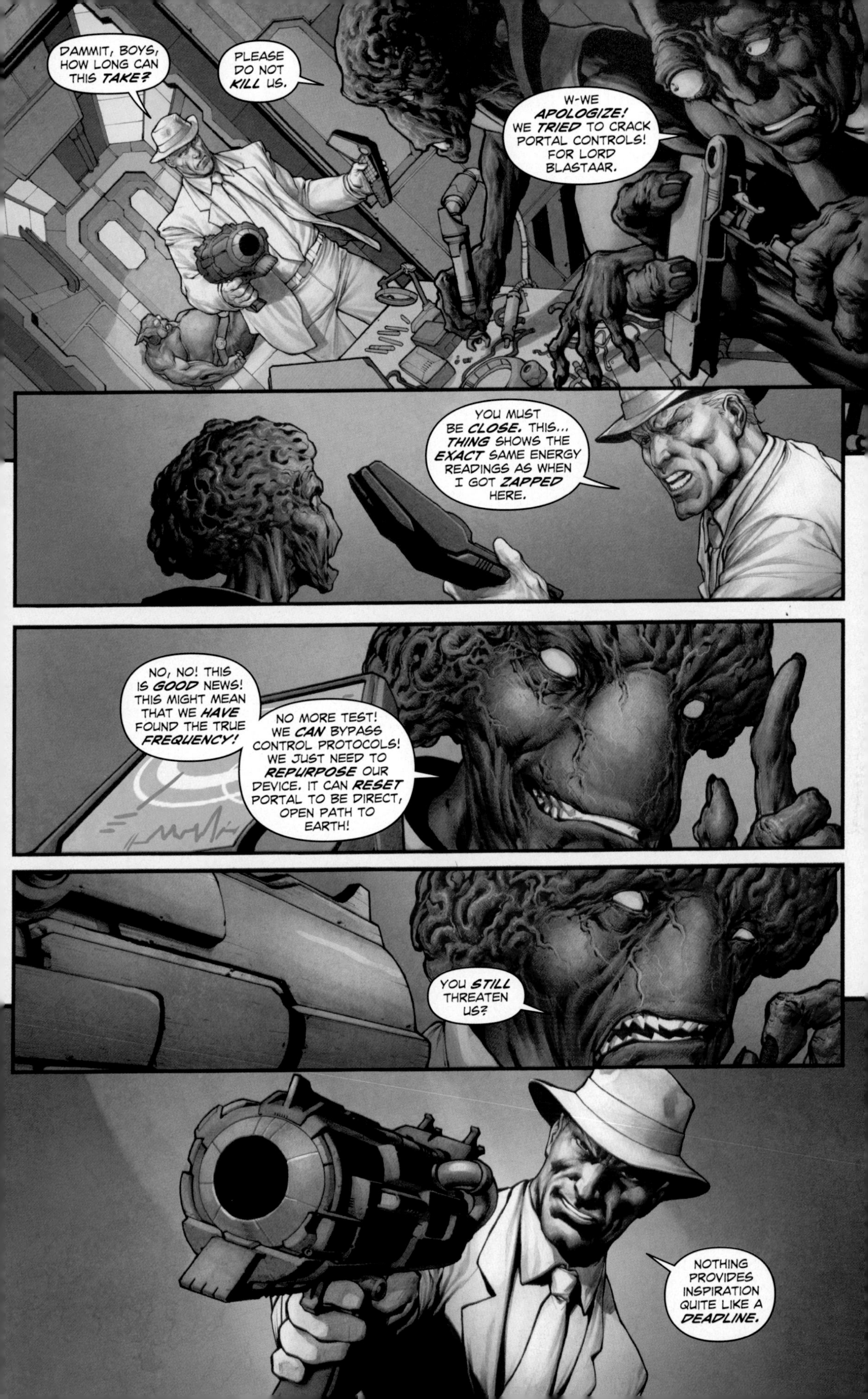
DAMMIT, BOYS, HOW LONG CAN THIS TAKE?
PLEASE DO NOT KILL US.
W-WE APOLOGIZE! WE TRIED TO CRACK PORTAL CONTROLS! FOR LORD BLASTAAR.
YOU MUST BE CLOSE. THIS... THING SHOWS THE EXACT SAME ENERGY READINGS AS WHEN I GOT ZAPPED HERE.
NO, NO! THIS IS GOOD NEWS! THIS MIGHT MEAN THAT WE HAVE FOUND THE TRUE FREQUENCY!
NO MORE TEST! WE CAN BYPASS CONTROL PROTOCOLS! WE JUST NEED TO REPURPOSE OUR DEVICE. IT CAN RESET PORTAL TO BE DIRECT, OPEN PATH TO EARTH!
YOU STILL THREATEN US?
NOTHING PROVIDES INSPIRATION QUITE LIKE A DEADLINE.

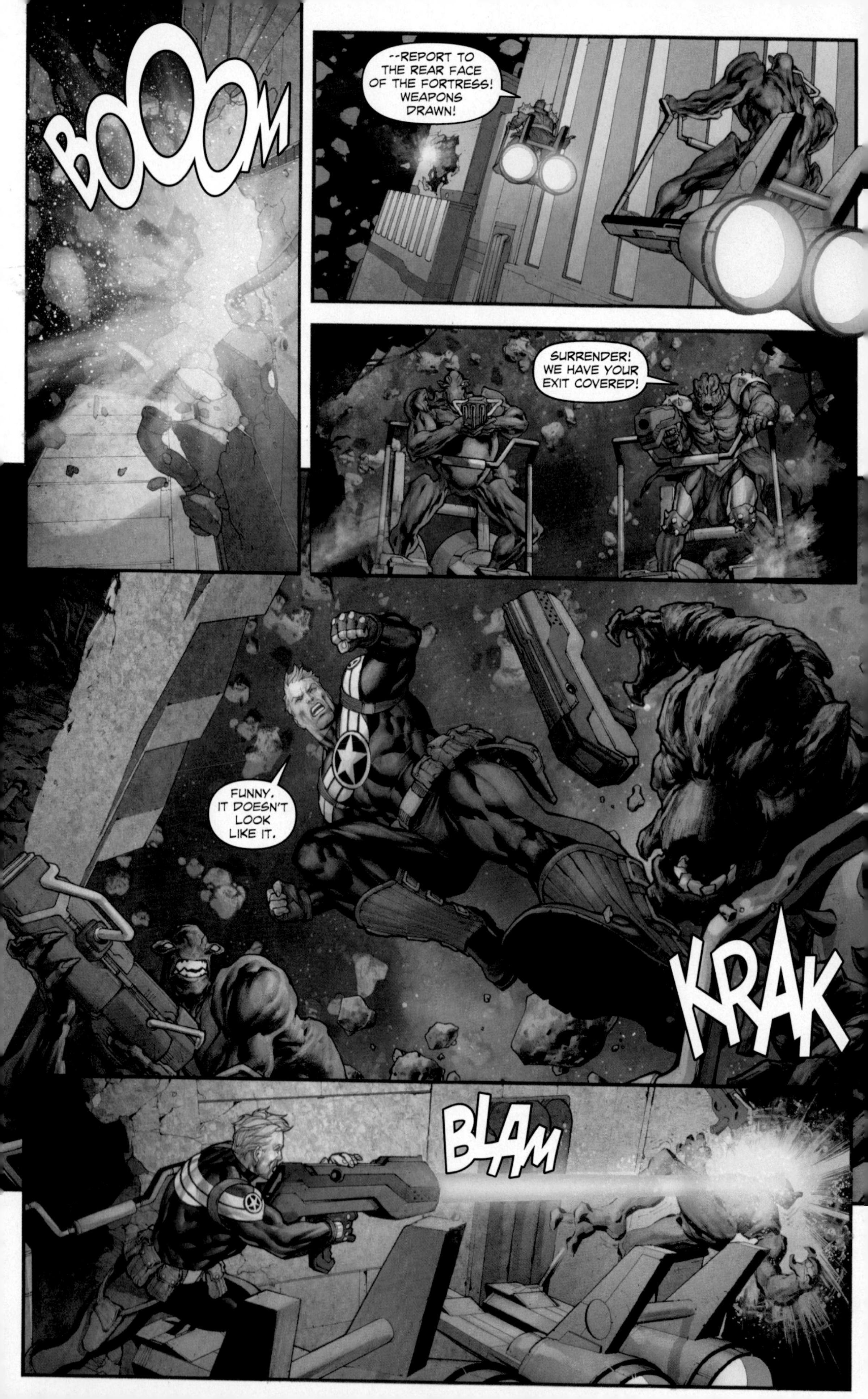
BOOOM
--REPORT TO THE REAR FACE OF THE FORTRESS! WEAPONS DRAWN!
SURRENDER! WE HAVE YOUR EXIT COVERED!
FUNNY. IT DOESN'T LOOK LIKE IT.
KRAK
BLAM

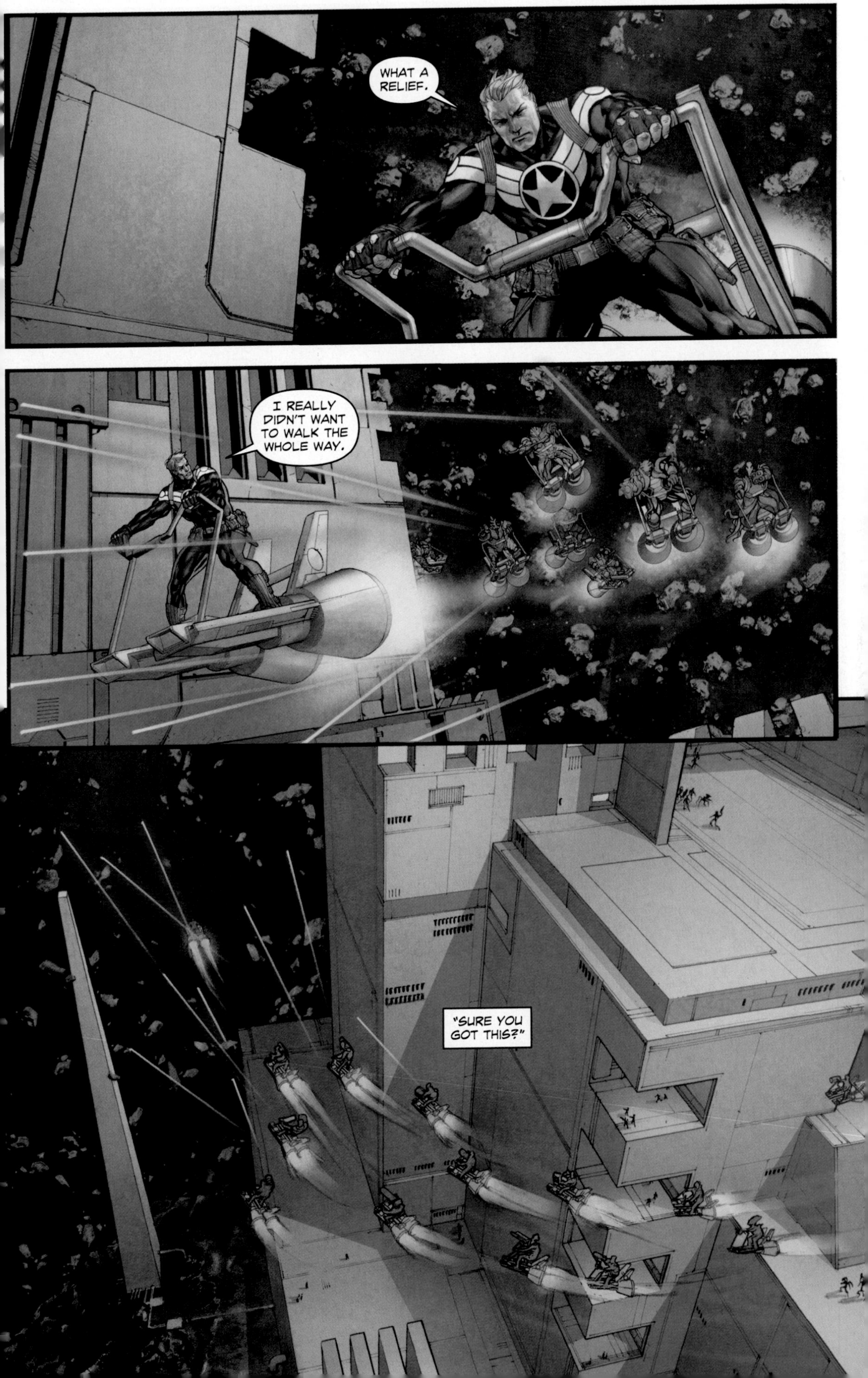
WHAT A RELIEF.
I REALLY DIDN'T WANT TO WALK THE WHOLE WAY.
"SURE YOU GOT THIS?"

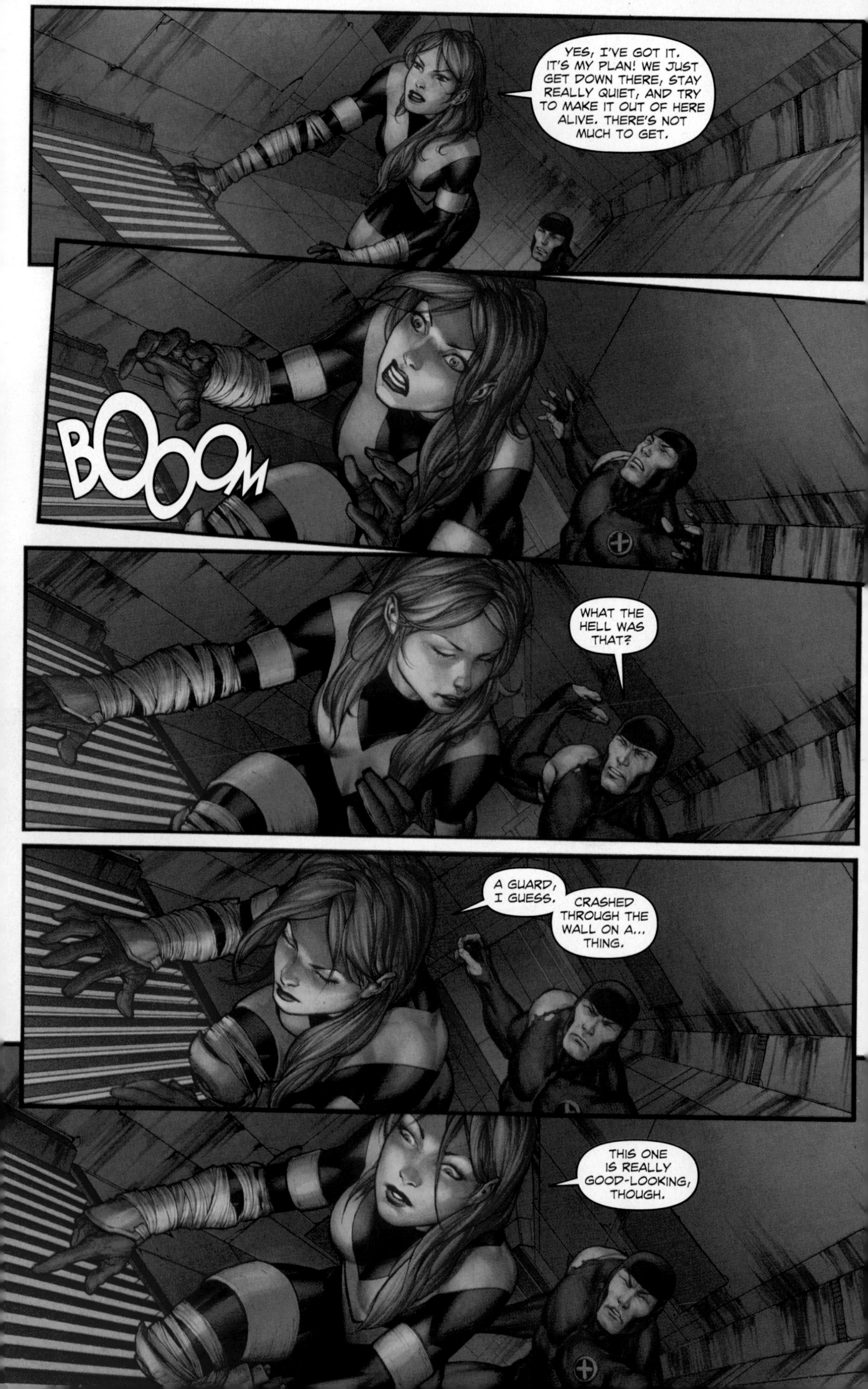
YES, I'VE GOT IT. IT'S MY PLAN! WE JUST GET DOWN THERE, STAY REALLY QUIET, AND TRY TO MAKE IT OUT OF HERE ALIVE. THERE'S NOT MUCH TO GET.
BOOOM
WHAT THE HELL WAS THAT?
A GUARD, I GUESS.
CRASHED THROUGH THE WALL ON A... THING.
THIS ONE IS REALLY GOOD-LOOKING, THOUGH.

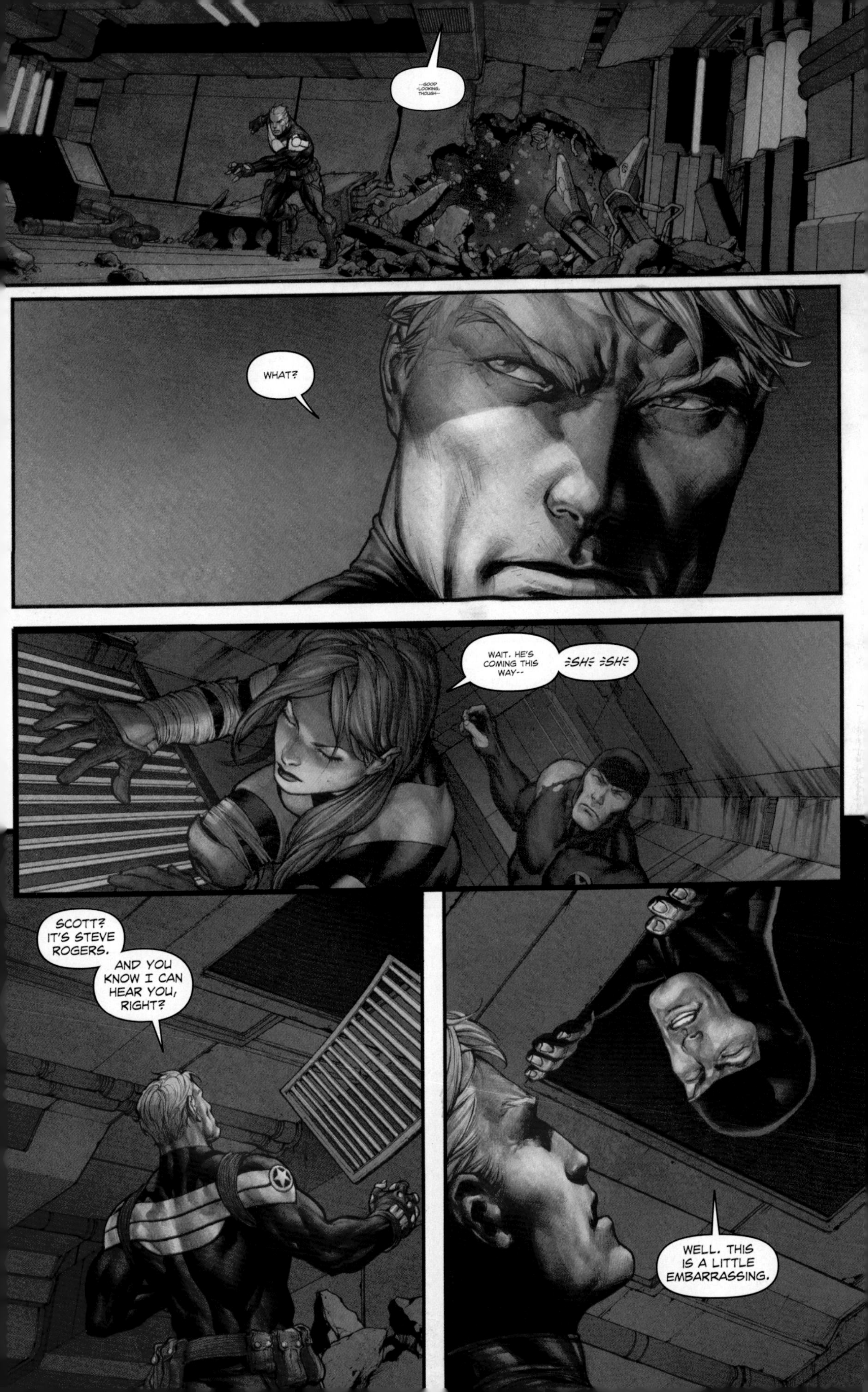
--GOOD -LOOKING, THOUGH--
WHAT?
WAIT. HE'S COMING THIS WAY--
SH SH
SCOTT? IT'S STEVE ROGERS.
AND YOU KNOW I CAN HEAR YOU, RIGHT?
WELL. THIS IS A LITTLE EMBARRASSING.

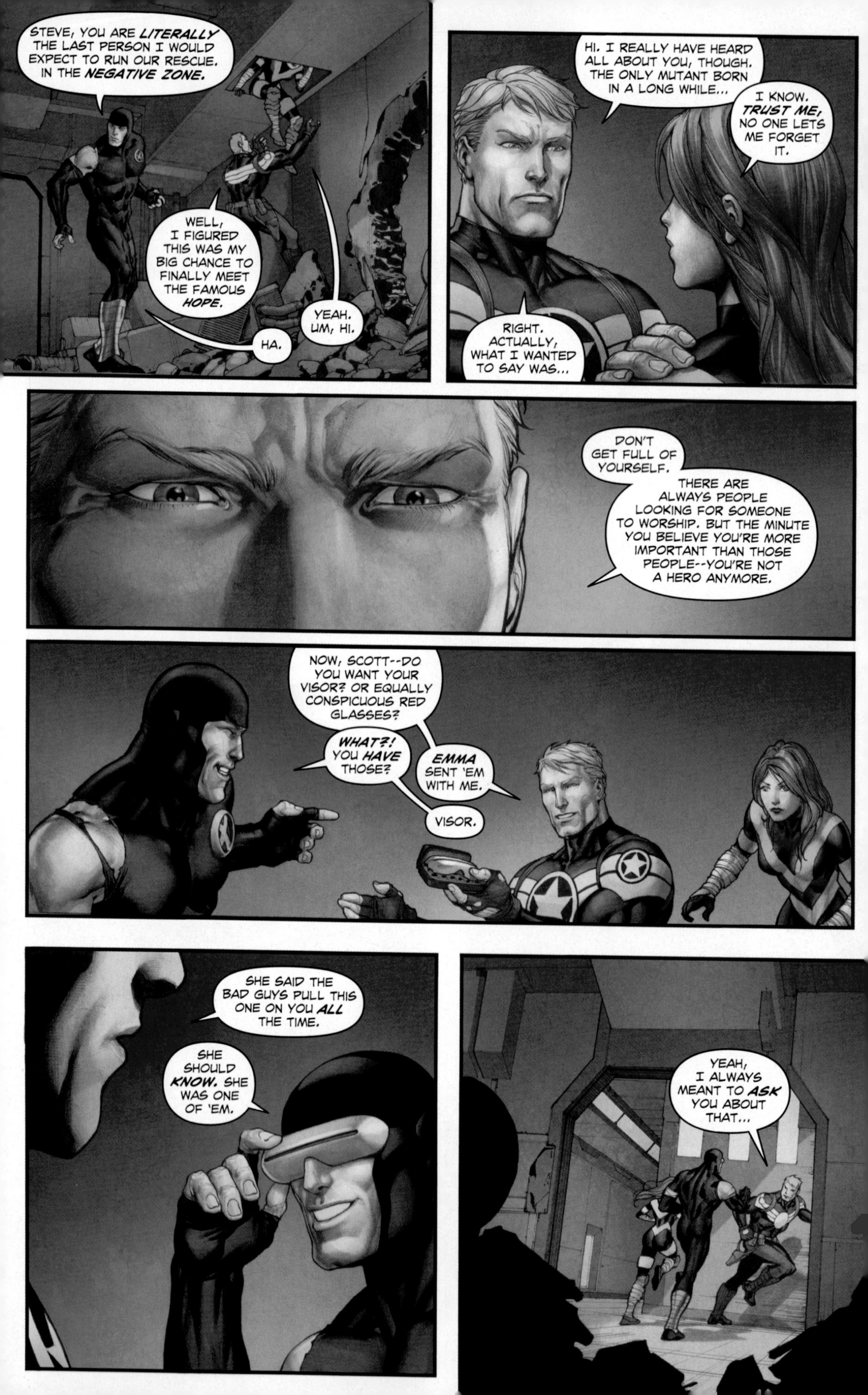
STEVE, YOU ARE LITERALLY THE LAST PERSON I WOULD EXPECT TO RUN OUR RESCUE. IN THE NEGATIVE ZONE.
WELL, I FIGURED THIS WAS MY BIG CHANCE TO FINALLY MEET THE FAMOUS HOPE.
HA.
YEAH. UM, HI.
HI. I REALLY HAVE HEARD ALL ABOUT YOU, THOUGH. THE ONLY MUTANT BORN IN A LONG WHILE...
I KNOW. TRUST ME, NO ONE LETS ME FORGET IT.
RIGHT. ACTUALLY, WHAT I WANTED TO SAY WAS...
DON'T GET FULL OF YOURSELF.
THERE ARE ALWAYS PEOPLE LOOKING FOR SOMEONE TO WORSHIP. BUT THE MINUTE YOU BELIEVE YOU'RE MORE IMPORTANT THAN THOSE PEOPLE--YOU'RE NOT A HERO ANYMORE.
NOW, SCOTT--DO YOU WANT YOUR VISOR? OR EQUALLY CONSPICUOUS RED GLASSES?
WHAT?! YOU HAVE THOSE?
EMMA SENT 'EM WITH ME.
VISOR.
SHE SAID THE BAD GUYS PULL THIS ONE ON YOU ALL THE TIME.
SHE SHOULD KNOW. SHE WAS ONE OF 'EM.
YEAH, I ALWAYS MEANT TO ASK YOU ABOUT THAT...

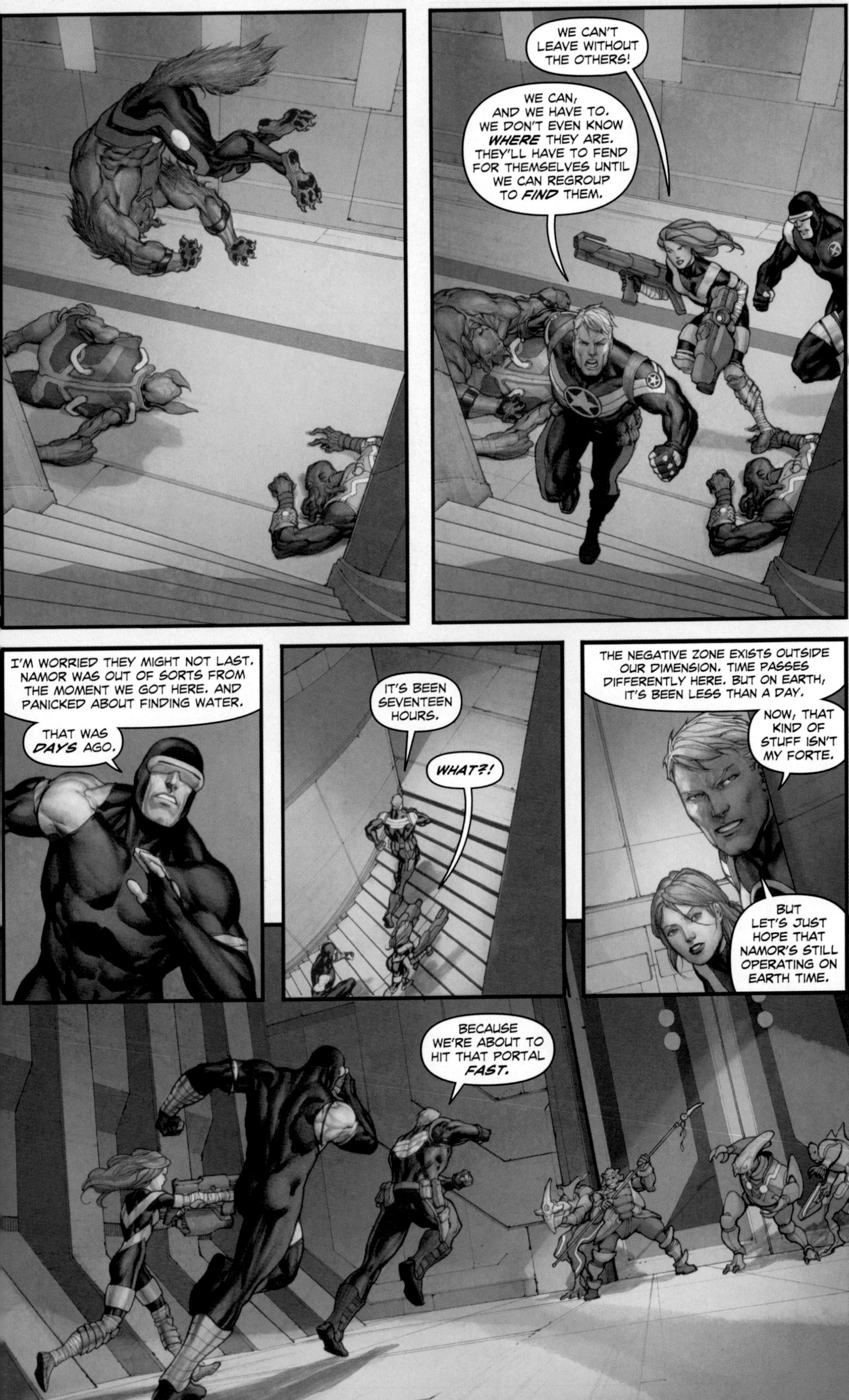
WE CAN'T LEAVE WITHOUT THE OTHERS!
WE CAN, AND WE HAVE TO. WE DON'T EVEN KNOW *WHERE* THEY ARE. THEY'LL HAVE TO FEND FOR THEMSELVES UNTIL WE CAN REGROUP TO *FIND* THEM.
I'M WORRIED THEY MIGHT NOT LAST. NAMOR WAS OUT OF SORTS FROM THE MOMENT WE GOT HERE. AND PANICKED ABOUT FINDING WATER.
THAT WAS *DAYS* AGO.
IT'S BEEN SEVENTEEN HOURS.
WHAT?!
THE NEGATIVE ZONE EXISTS OUTSIDE OUR DIMENSION. TIME PASSES DIFFERENTLY HERE. BUT ON EARTH, IT'S BEEN LESS THAN A DAY.
NOW, THAT KIND OF STUFF ISN'T MY FORTE.
BUT LET'S JUST HOPE THAT NAMOR'S STILL OPERATING ON EARTH TIME.
BECAUSE WE'RE ABOUT TO HIT THAT PORTAL *FAST*.

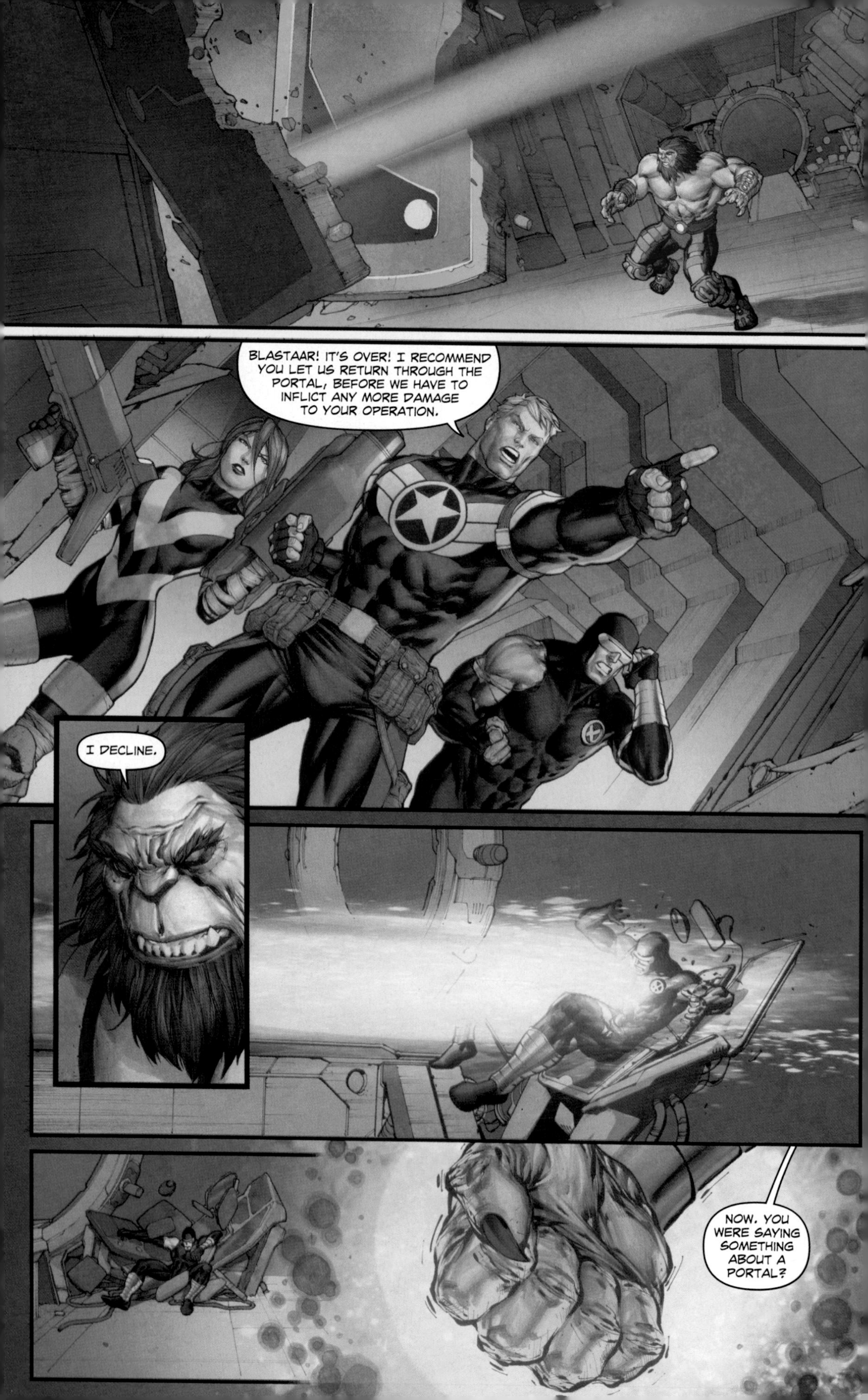
BLASTAAR! IT'S OVER! I RECOMMEND YOU LET US RETURN THROUGH THE PORTAL, BEFORE WE HAVE TO INFLICT ANY MORE DAMAGE TO YOUR OPERATION.
I DECLINE.
NOW. YOU WERE SAYING SOMETHING ABOUT A PORTAL?

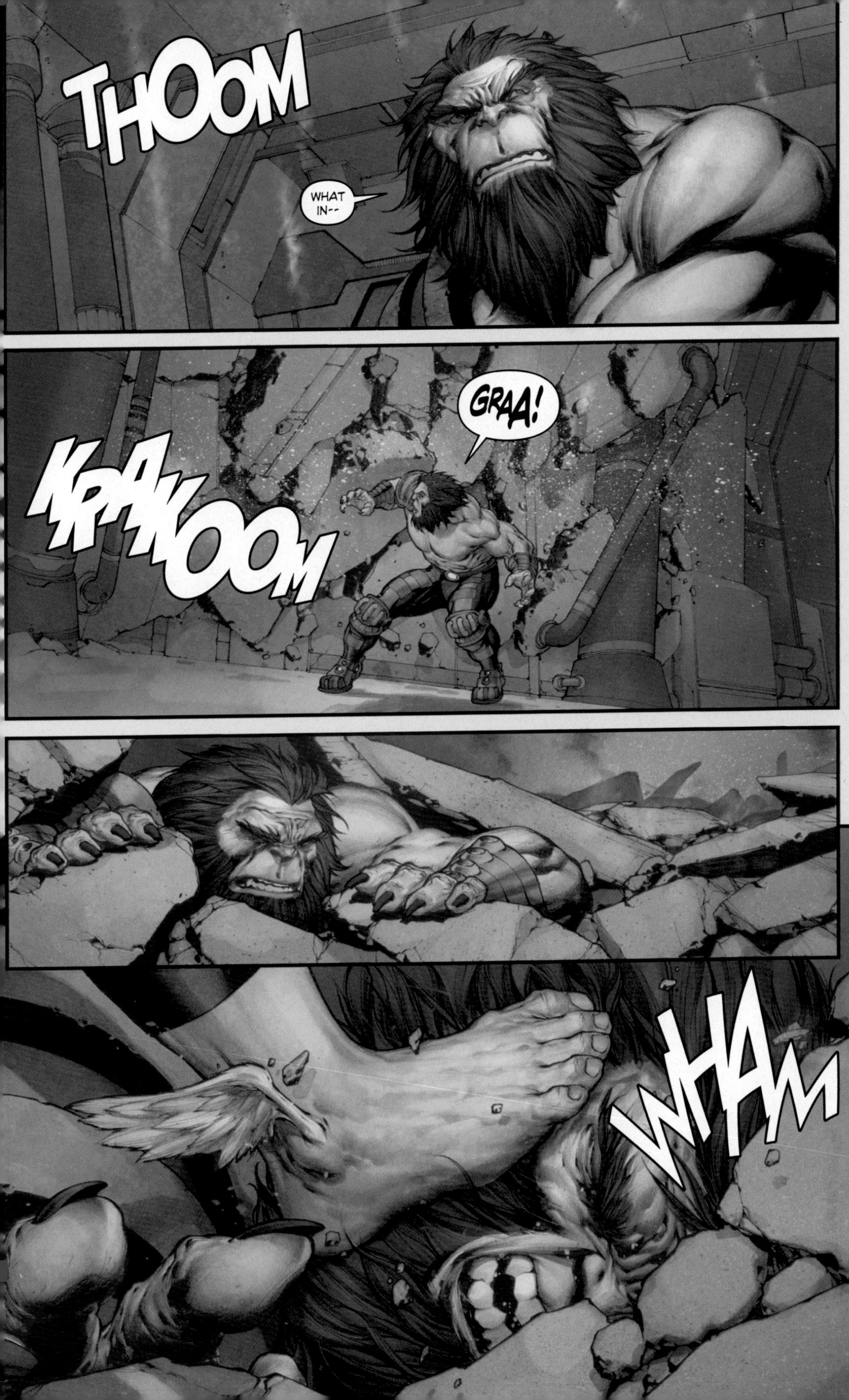
THOOM
WHAT IN--
GRAA!
KRAKOOM
WHAM

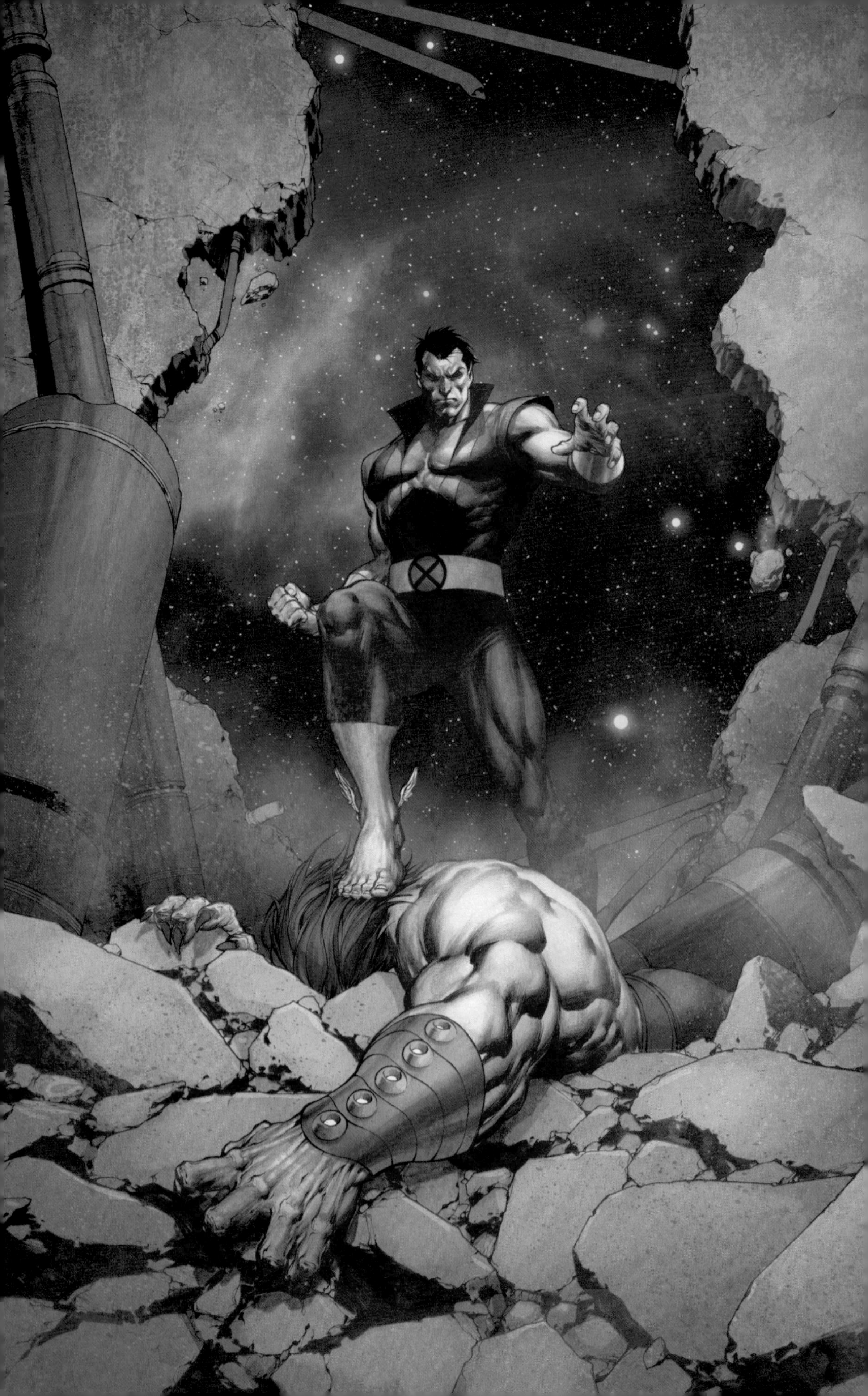

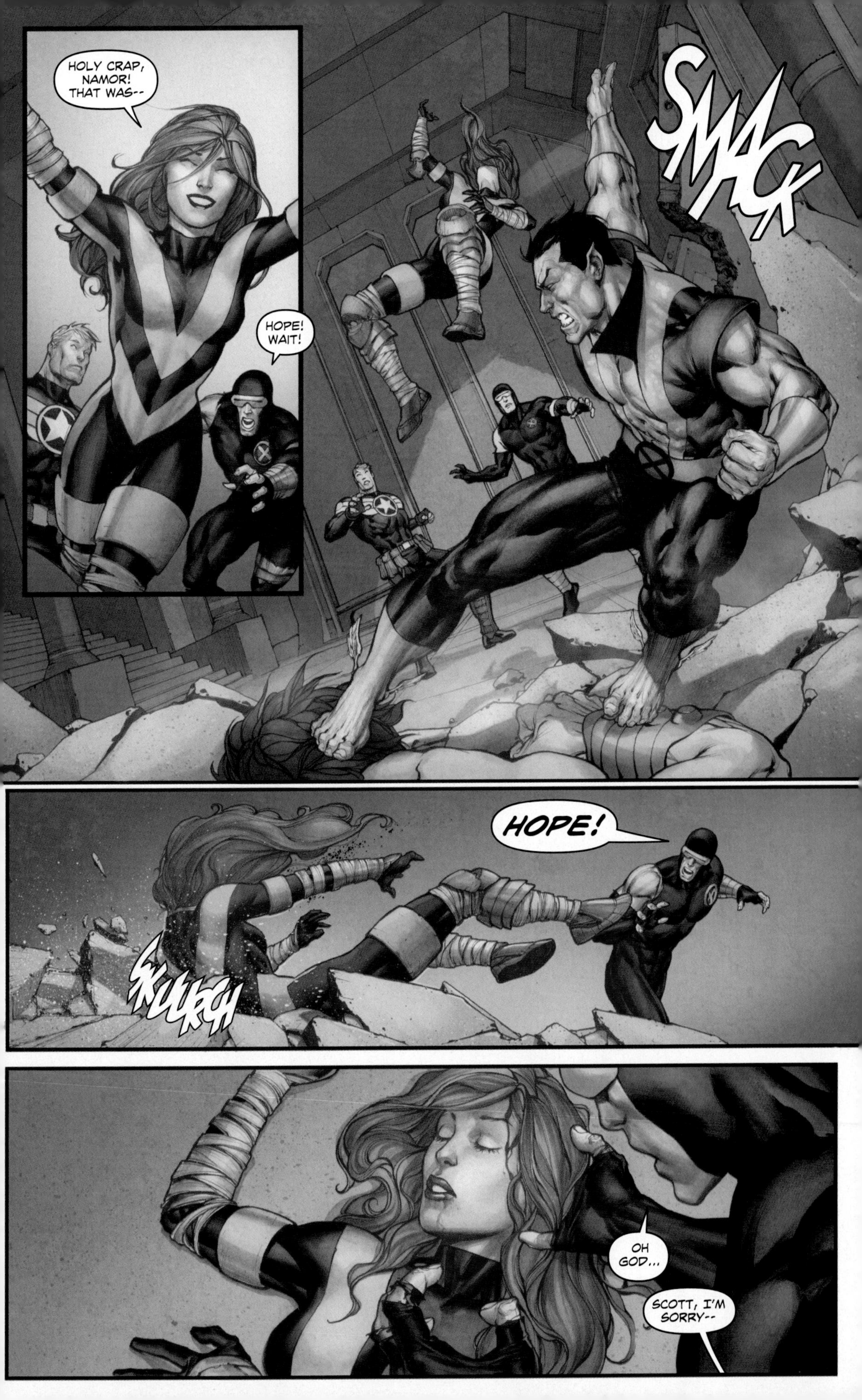
HOLY CRAP, NAMOR! THAT WAS--
SMACK
HOPE! WAIT!
HOPE!
SKUURCH
OH GOD...
SCOTT, I'M SORRY--

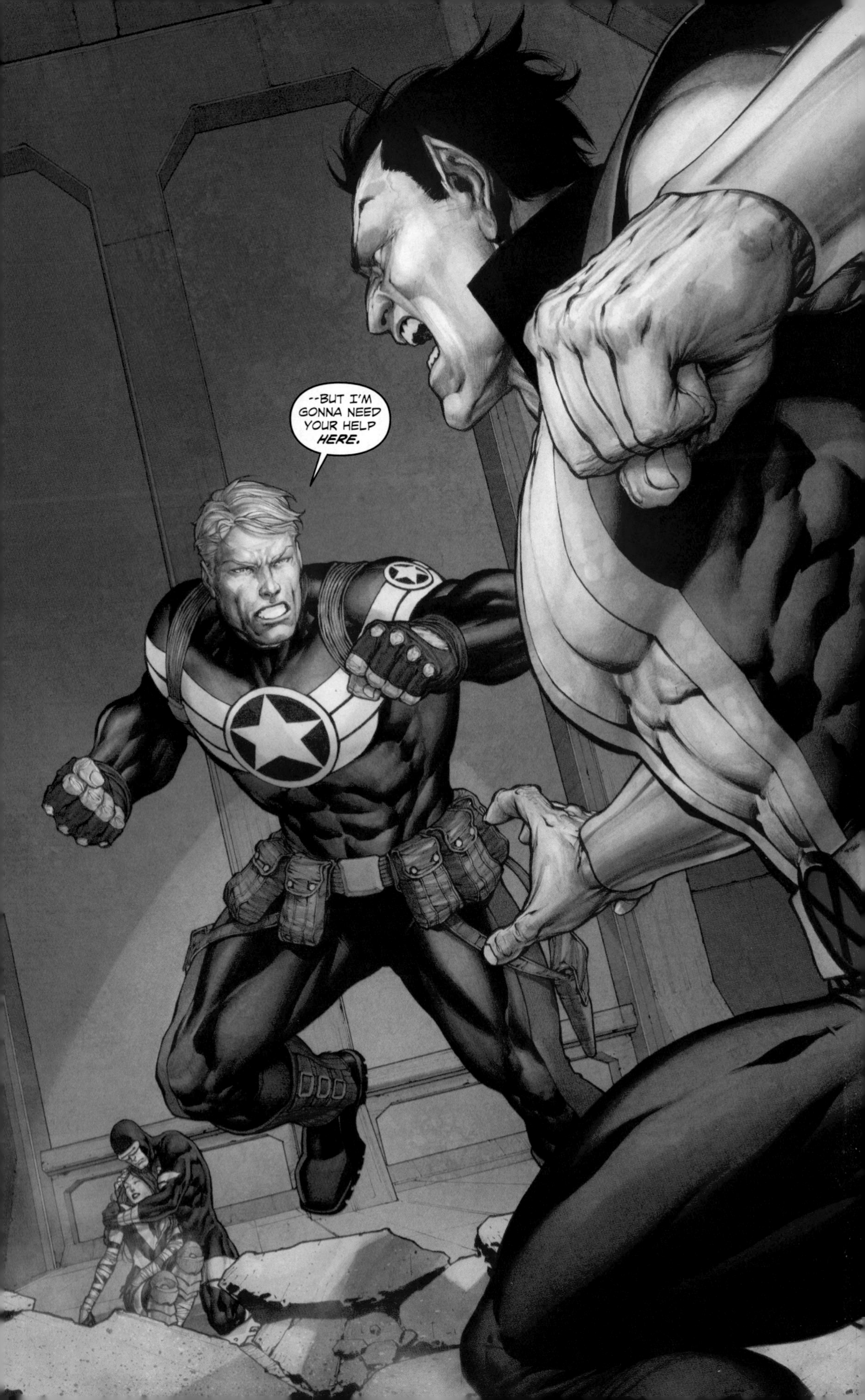
--BUT I'M GONNA NEED YOUR HELP *HERE.*

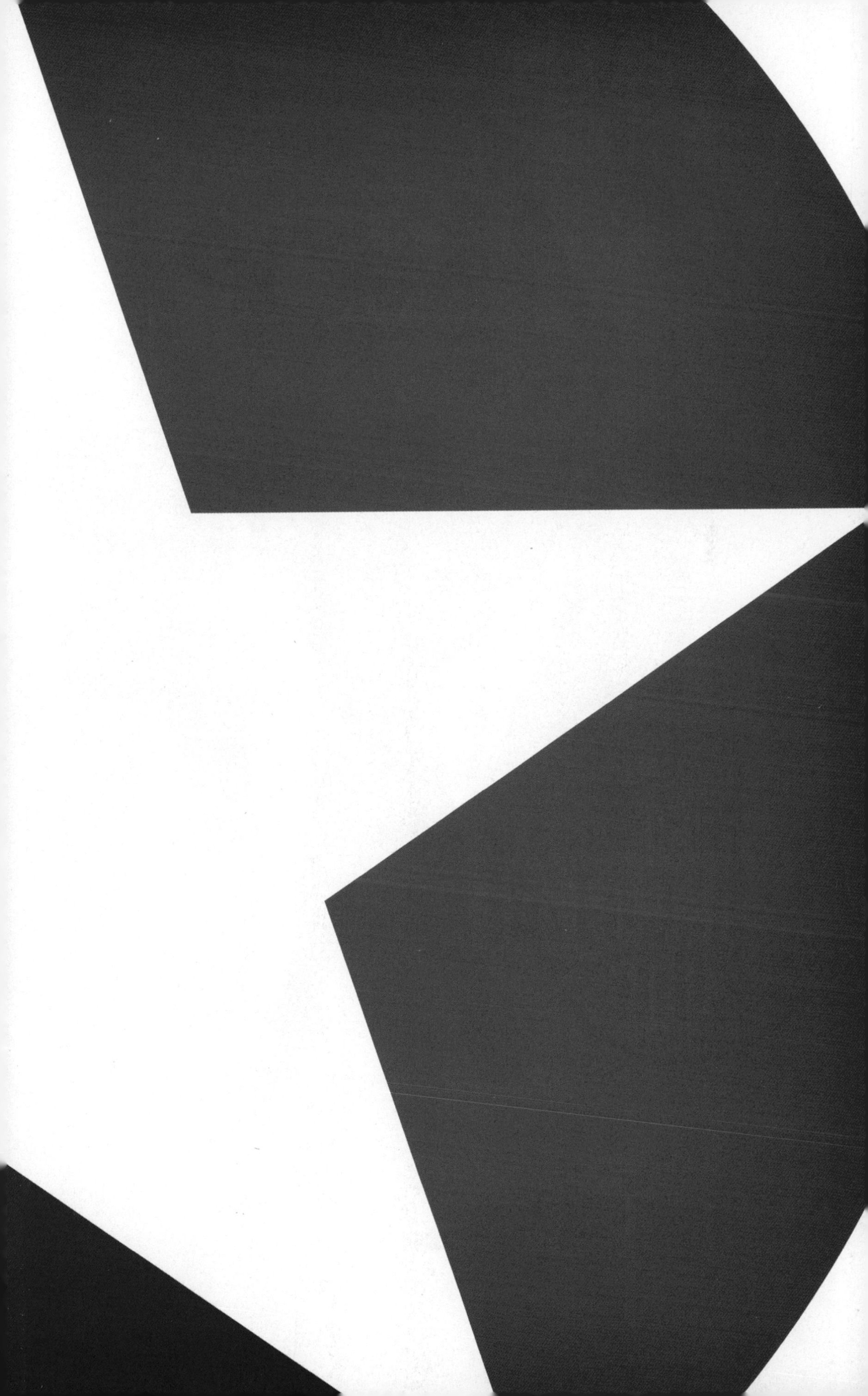

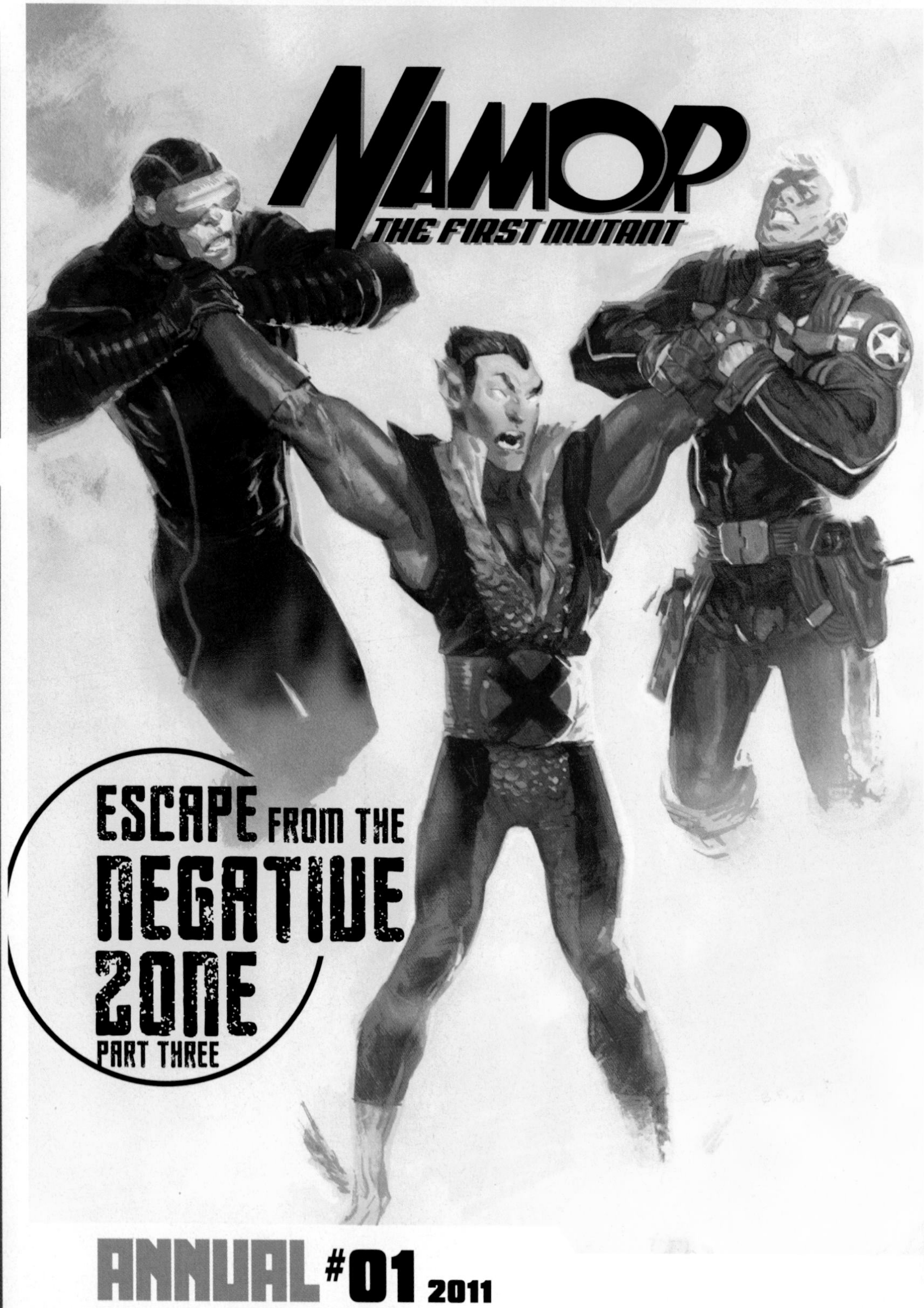
NAMOR
THE FIRST MUTANT
ESCAPE FROM THE NEGATIVE ZONE
PART THREE
ANNUAL #01 2011

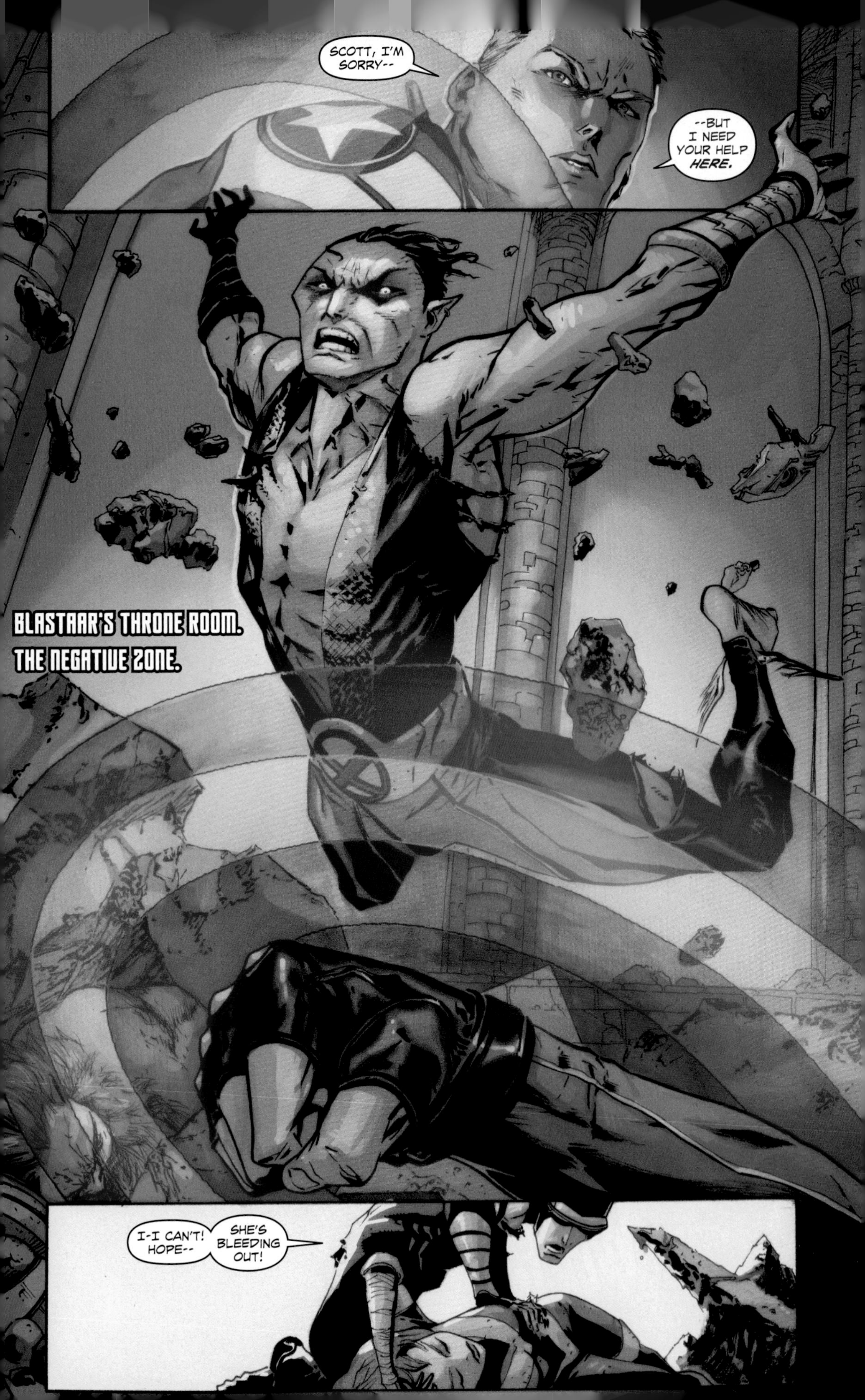
SCOTT, I'M SORRY--
--BUT I NEED YOUR HELP HERE.
BLASTAAR'S THRONE ROOM.
THE NEGATIVE ZONE.
I-I CAN'T! HOPE--
SHE'S BLEEDING OUT!

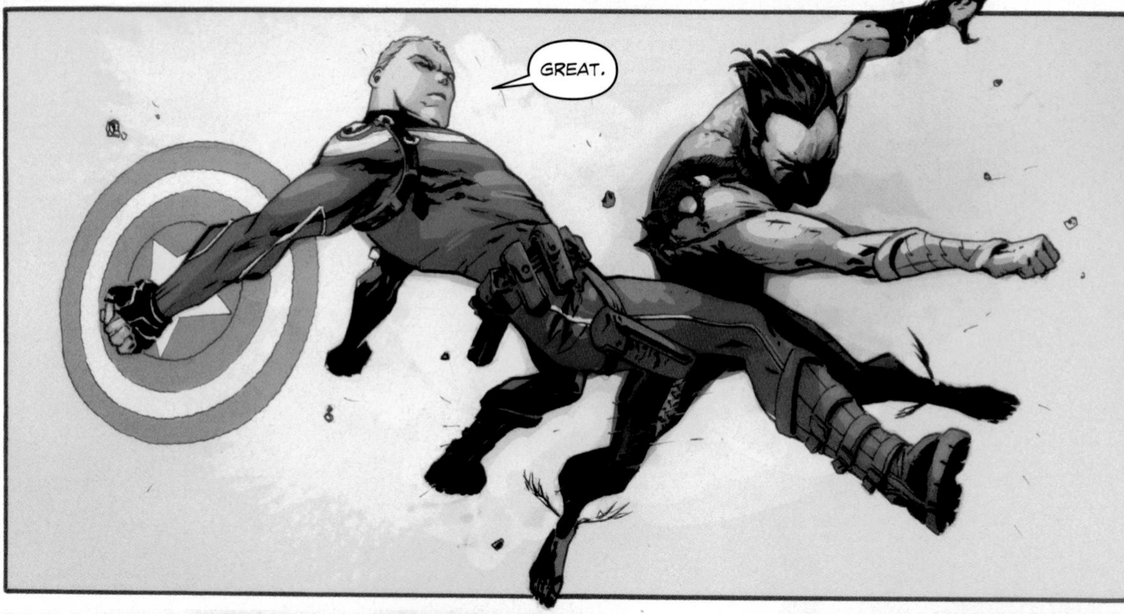
GREAT.

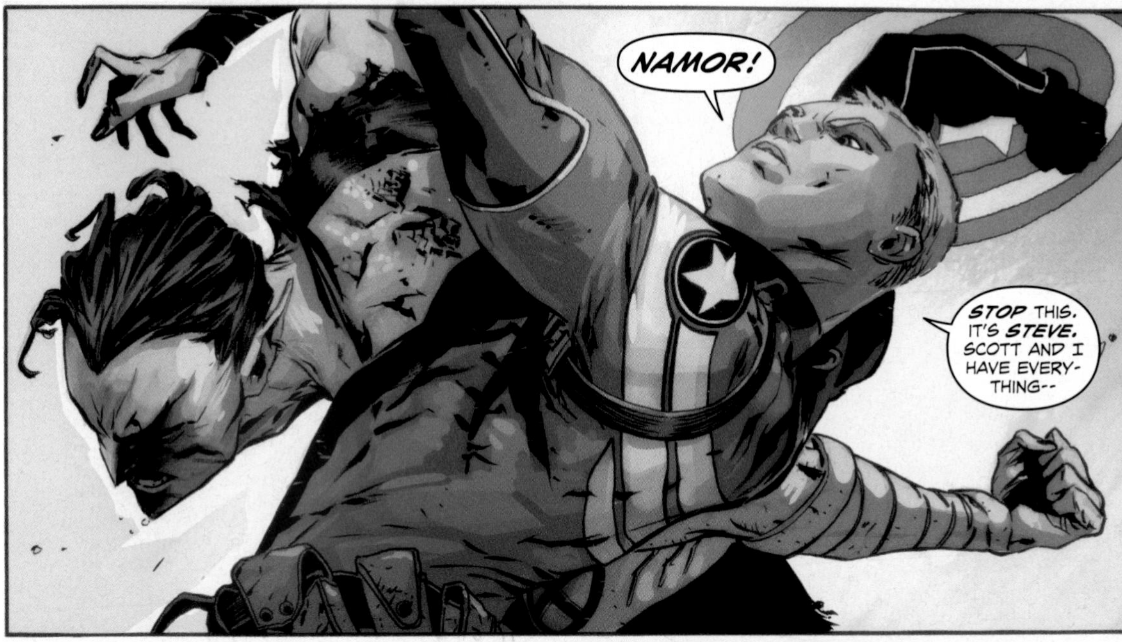
NAMOR!
STOP THIS. IT'S STEVE. SCOTT AND I HAVE EVERY-THING--

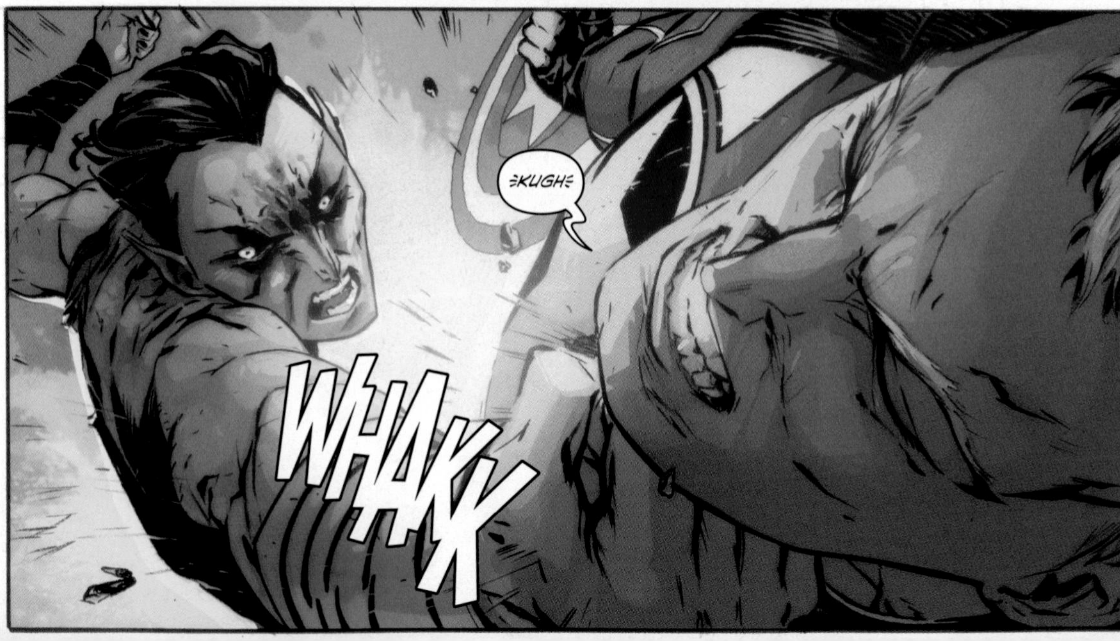
KUGH
WHAKK

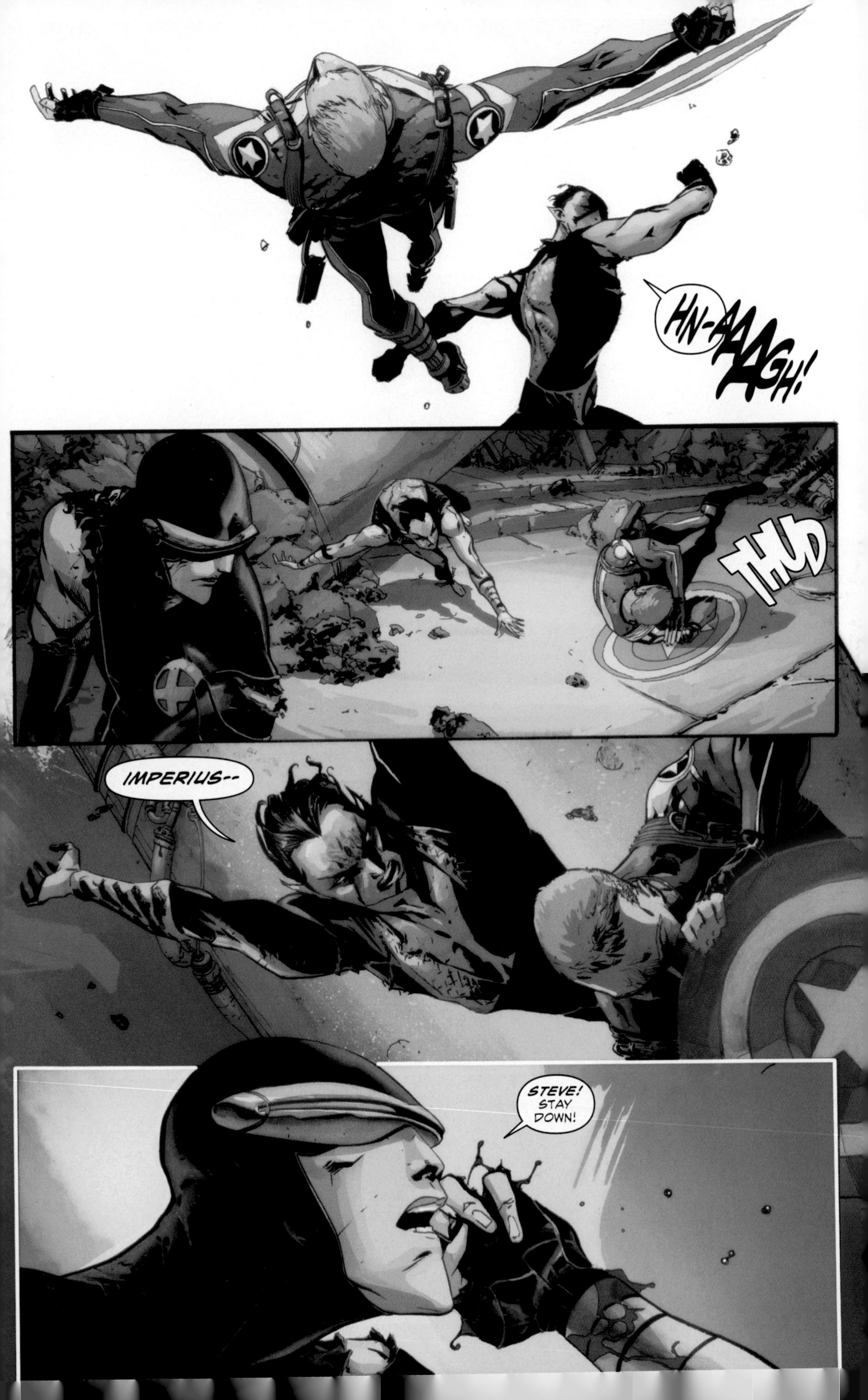
HN-AAAAGH!
THUD
IMPERIUS--
STEVE! STAY DOWN!

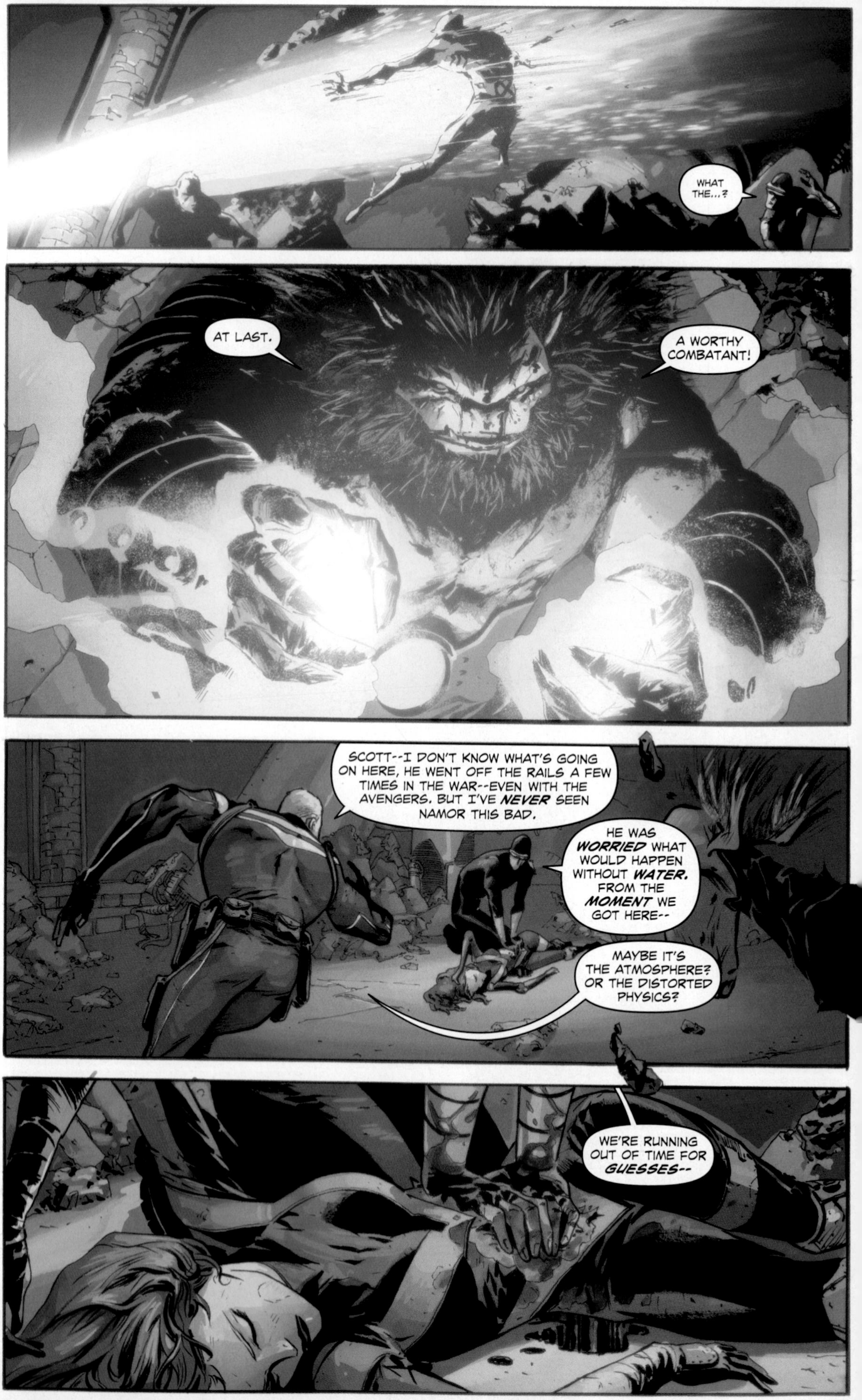
WHAT THE...?
AT LAST.
A WORTHY COMBATANT!
SCOTT--I DON'T KNOW WHAT'S GOING ON HERE, HE WENT OFF THE RAILS A FEW TIMES IN THE WAR--EVEN WITH THE AVENGERS. BUT I'VE NEVER SEEN NAMOR THIS BAD.
HE WAS WORRIED WHAT WOULD HAPPEN WITHOUT WATER. FROM THE MOMENT WE GOT HERE--
MAYBE IT'S THE ATMOSPHERE? OR THE DISTORTED PHYSICS?
WE'RE RUNNING OUT OF TIME FOR GUESSES--

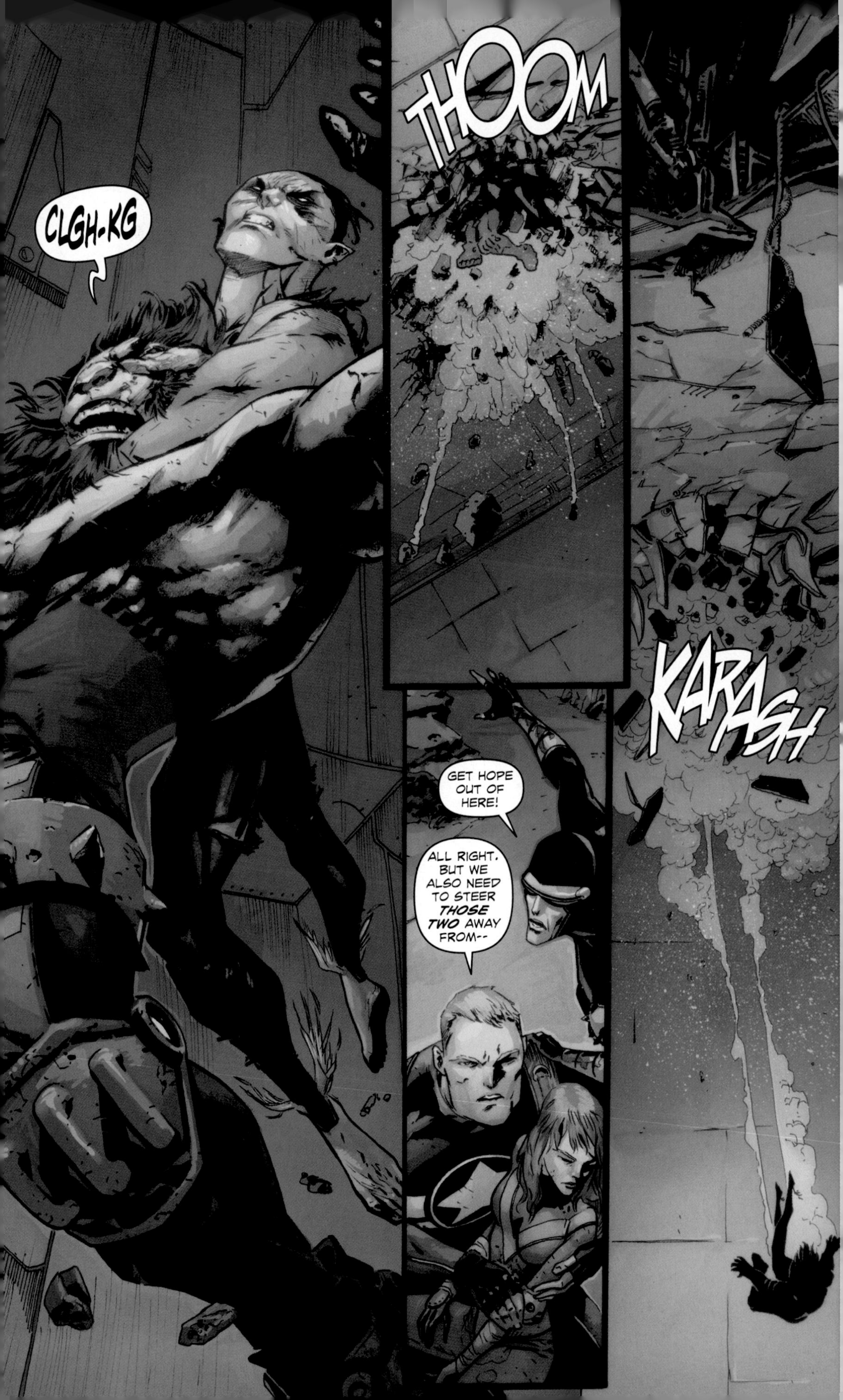
CLGH-KG
THOOM
KARASH
GET HOPE OUT OF HERE!
ALL RIGHT. BUT WE ALSO NEED TO STEER *THOSE TWO* AWAY FROM--

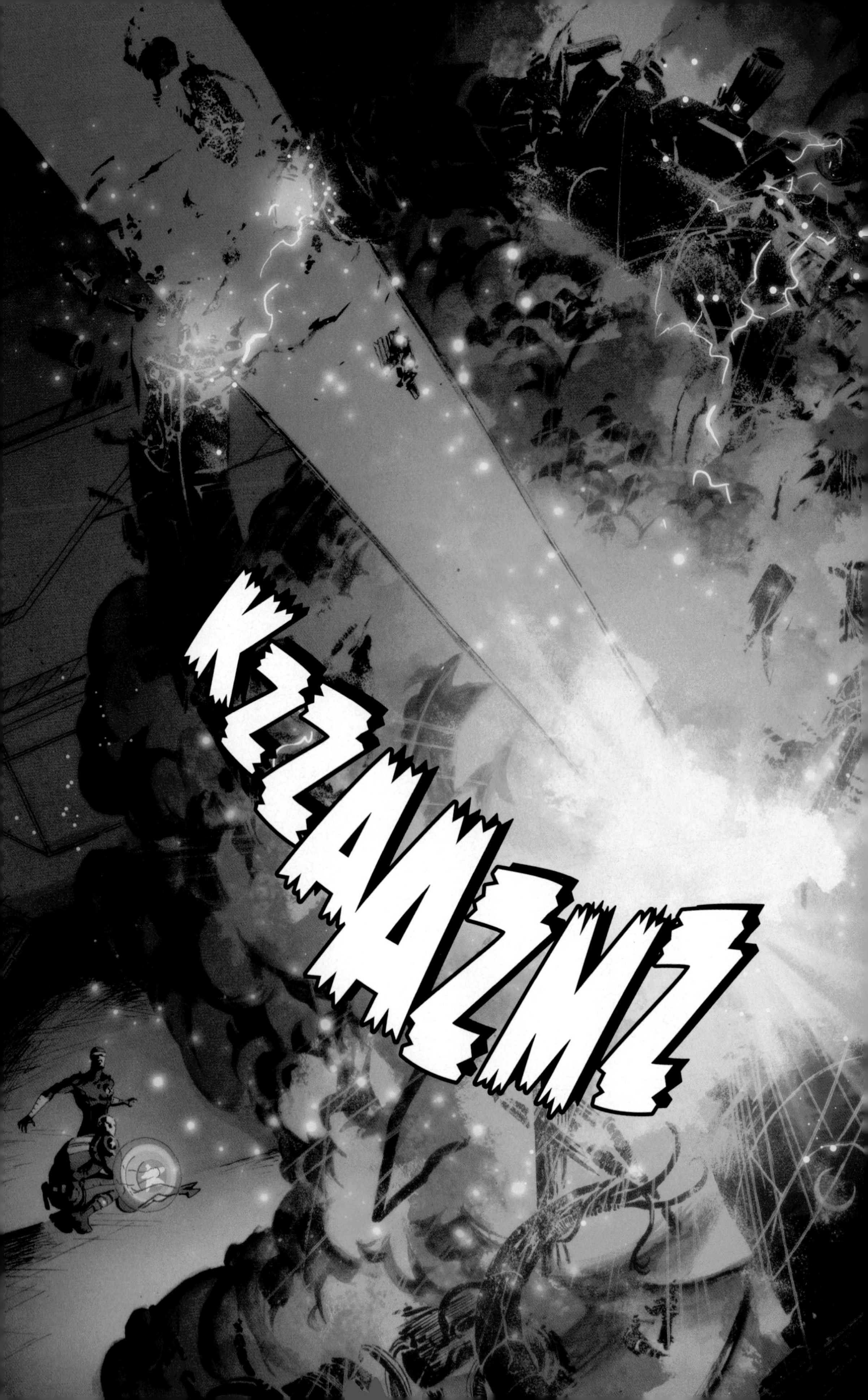
KZZAAZMM

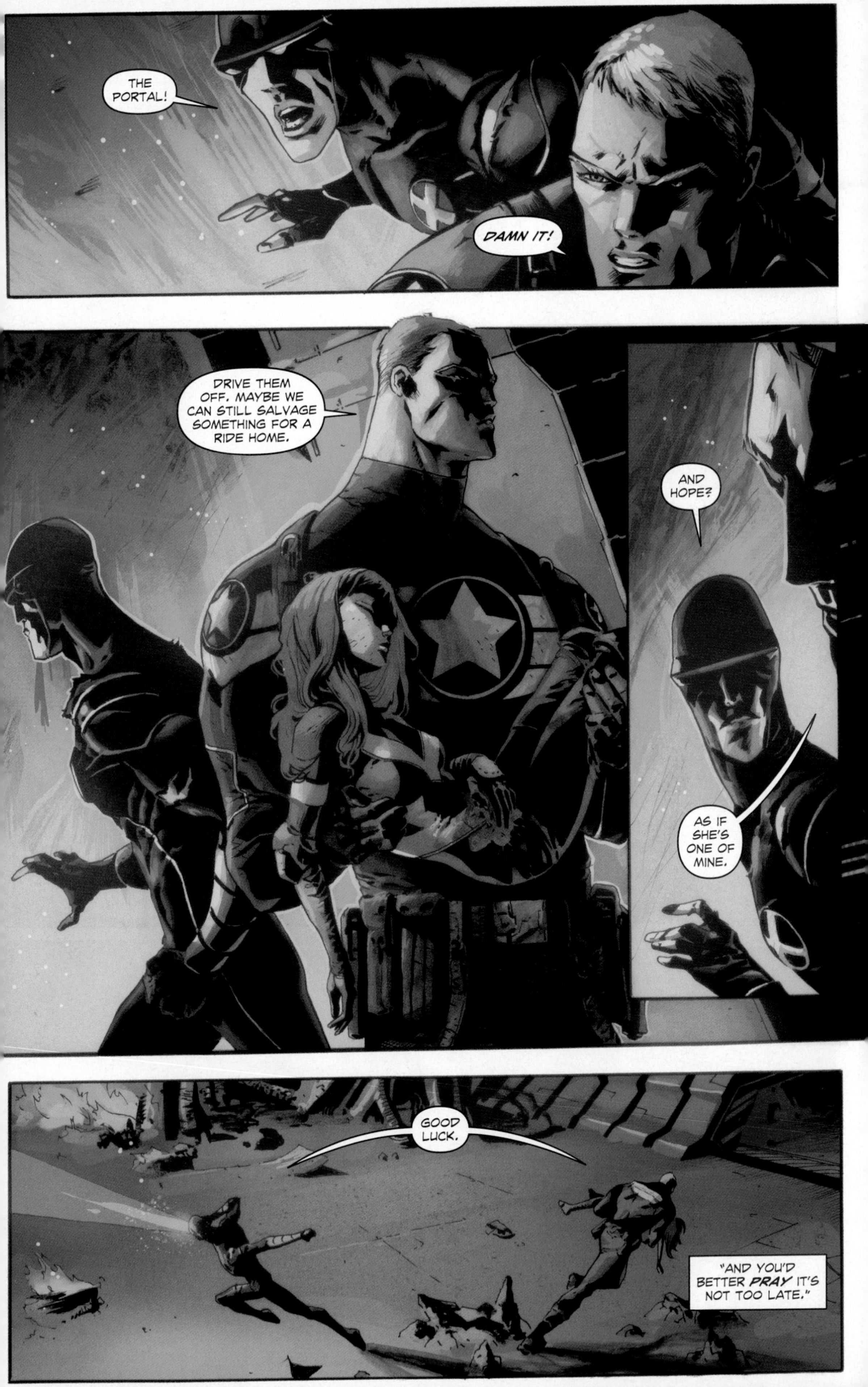
THE PORTAL!
DAMN IT!
DRIVE THEM OFF. MAYBE WE CAN STILL SALVAGE SOMETHING FOR A RIDE HOME.
AND HOPE?
AS IF SHE'S ONE OF MINE.
GOOD LUCK.
"AND YOU'D BETTER PRAY IT'S NOT TOO LATE."

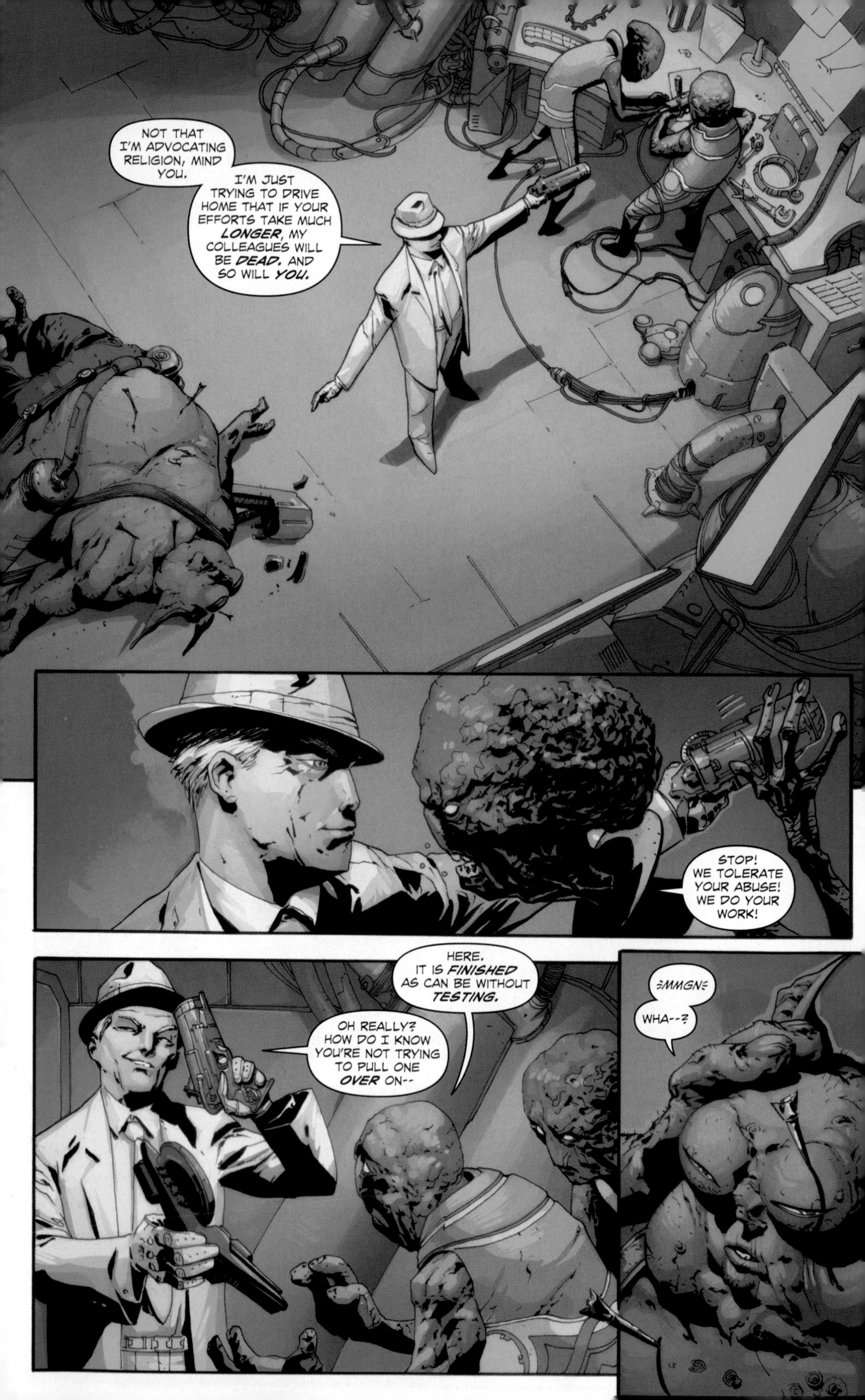
NOT THAT I'M ADVOCATING RELIGION, MIND YOU.
I'M JUST TRYING TO DRIVE HOME THAT IF YOUR EFFORTS TAKE MUCH LONGER, MY COLLEAGUES WILL BE DEAD. AND SO WILL YOU.
STOP! WE TOLERATE YOUR ABUSE! WE DO YOUR WORK!
HERE. IT IS FINISHED AS CAN BE WITHOUT TESTING.
OH REALLY? HOW DO I KNOW YOU'RE NOT TRYING TO PULL ONE OVER ON--
MMGN
WHA--?

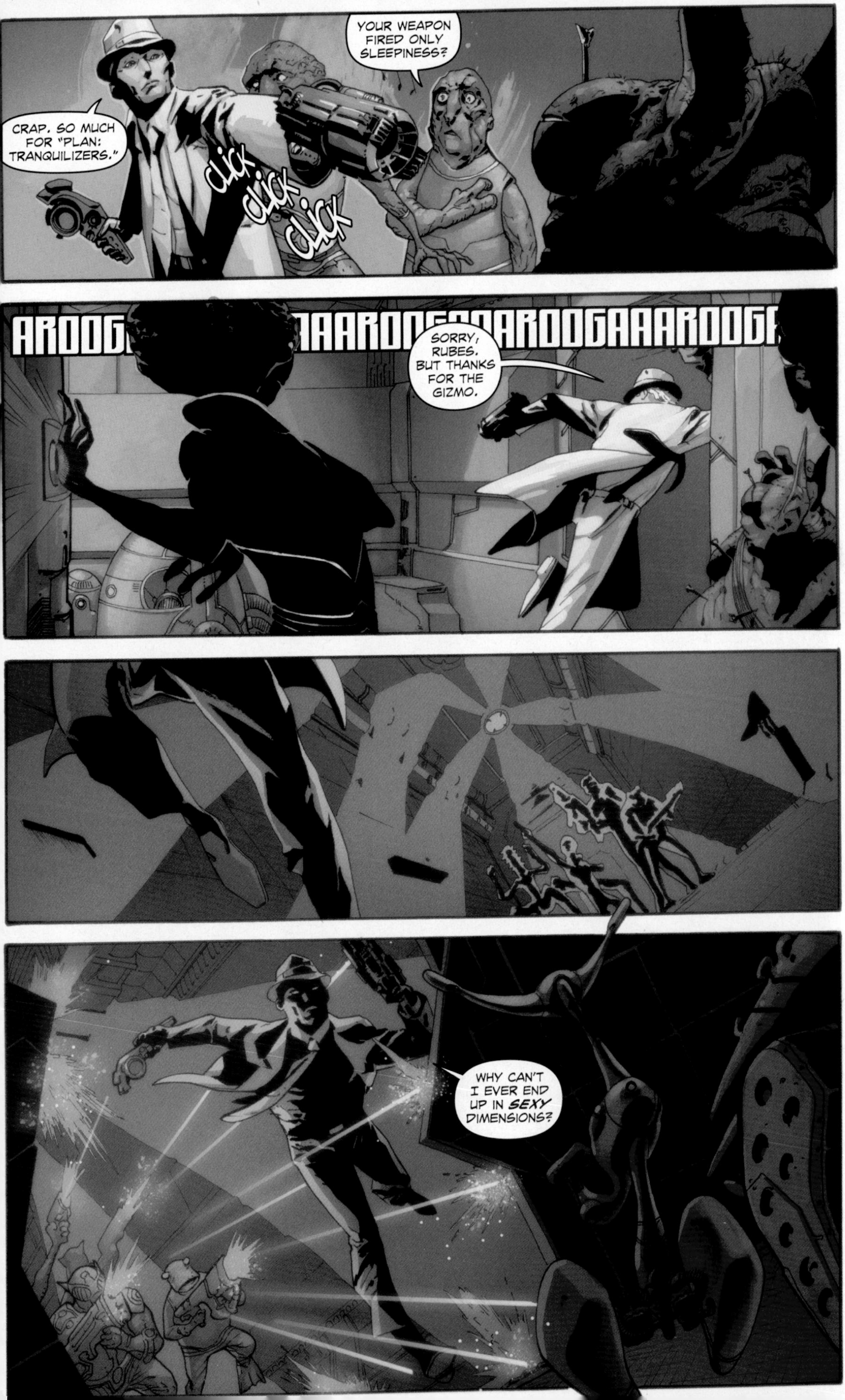
YOUR WEAPON FIRED ONLY SLEEPINESS?
CRAP. SO MUCH FOR "PLAN: TRANQUILIZERS."
CLICK CLICK CLICK
AROOGAAAROOGAAAROOGAAAROOGA
SORRY, RUBES. BUT THANKS FOR THE GIZMO.
WHY CAN'T I EVER END UP IN *SEXY* DIMENSIONS?

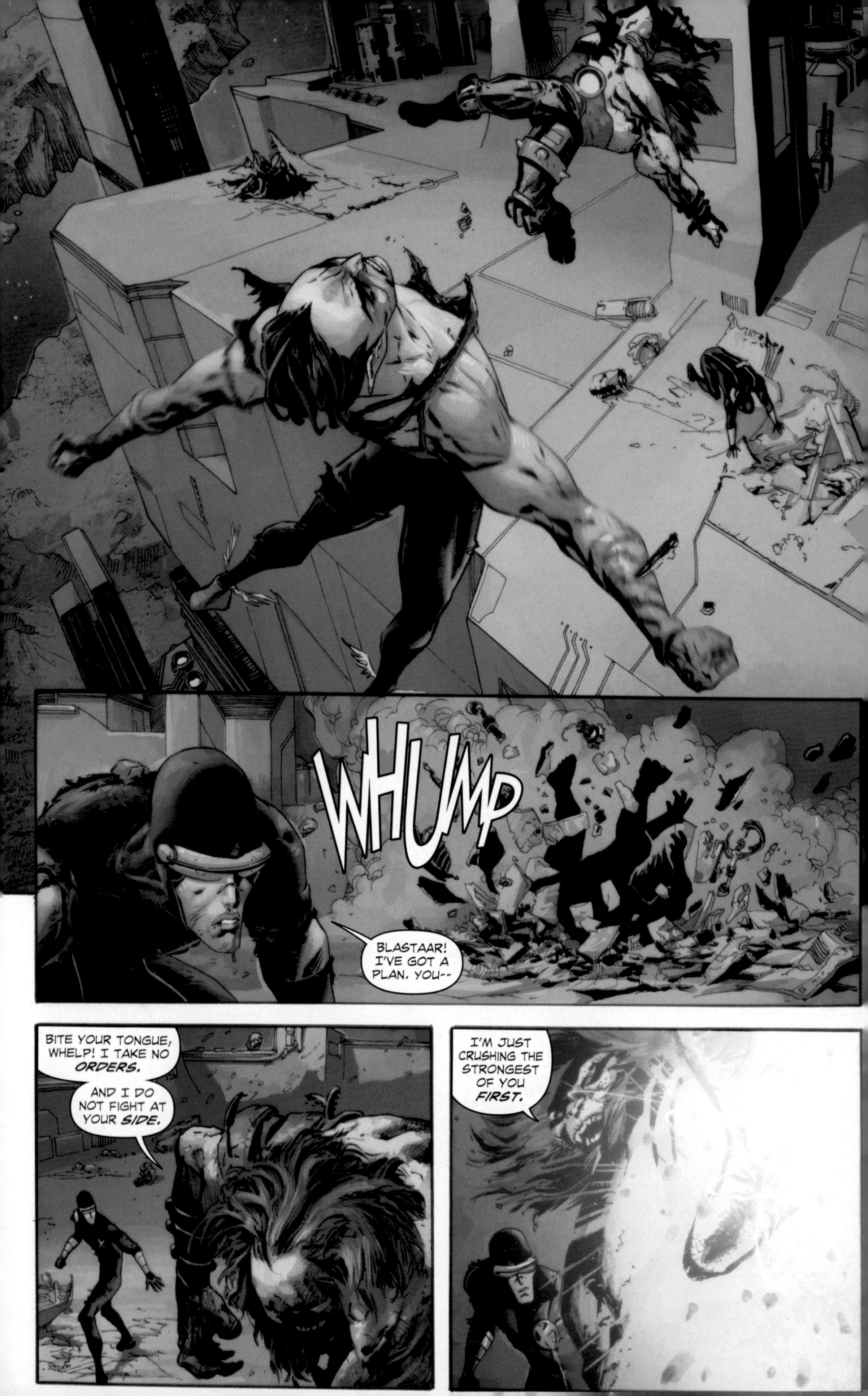
WHUMP
BLASTAAR! I'VE GOT A PLAN. YOU--
BITE YOUR TONGUE, WHELP! I TAKE NO ORDERS.
AND I DO NOT FIGHT AT YOUR SIDE.
I'M JUST CRUSHING THE STRONGEST OF YOU FIRST.

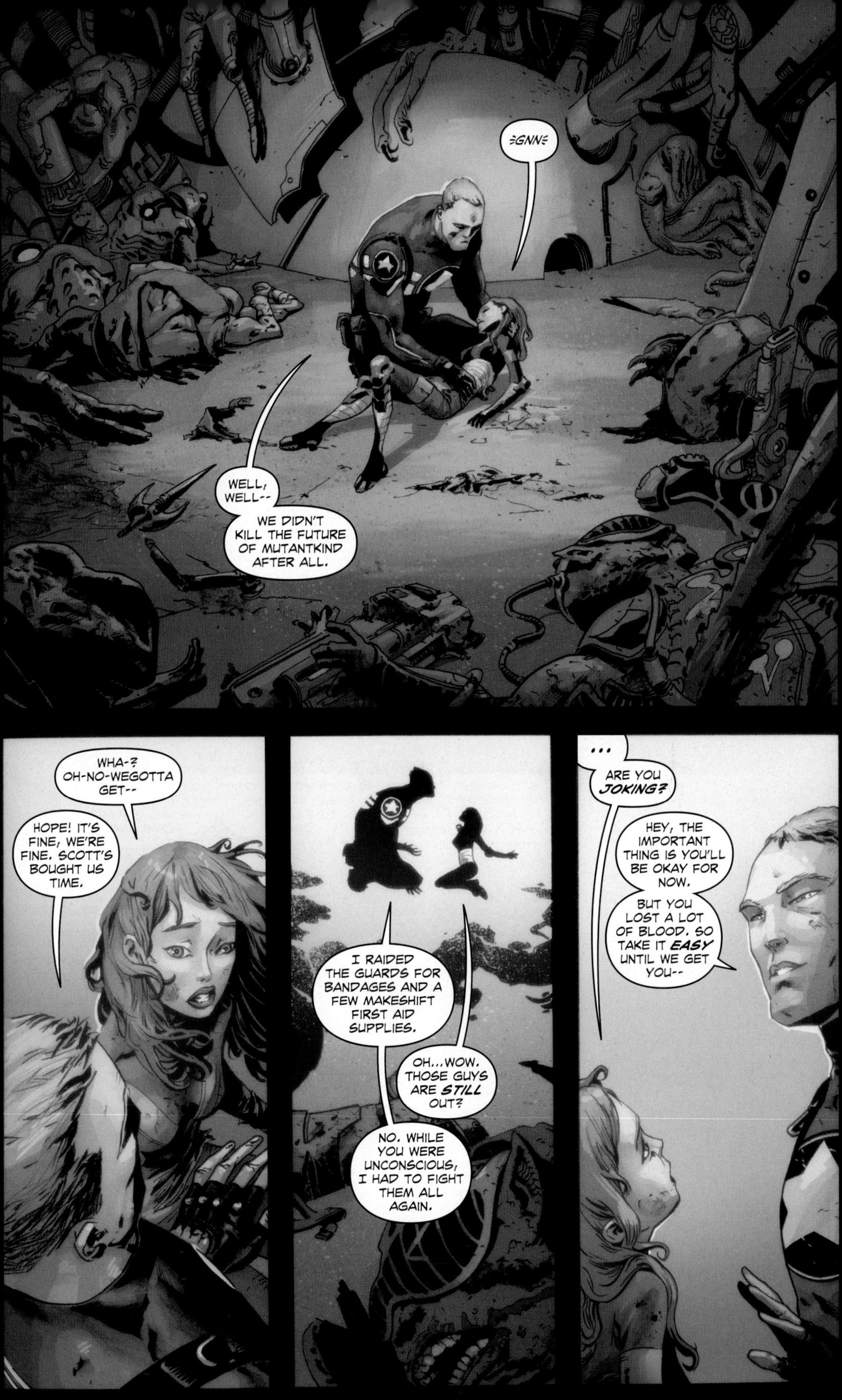
≡GNN≡
WELL, WELL--
WE DIDN'T KILL THE FUTURE OF MUTANTKIND AFTER ALL.
WHA-? OH-NO-WEGOTTA GET--
HOPE! IT'S FINE, WE'RE FINE. SCOTT'S BOUGHT US TIME.
I RAIDED THE GUARDS FOR BANDAGES AND A FEW MAKESHIFT FIRST AID SUPPLIES.
OH...WOW. THOSE GUYS ARE STILL OUT?
NO. WHILE YOU WERE UNCONSCIOUS, I HAD TO FIGHT THEM ALL AGAIN.
...
ARE YOU JOKING?
HEY, THE IMPORTANT THING IS YOU'LL BE OKAY FOR NOW.
BUT YOU LOST A LOT OF BLOOD. SO TAKE IT EASY UNTIL WE GET YOU--

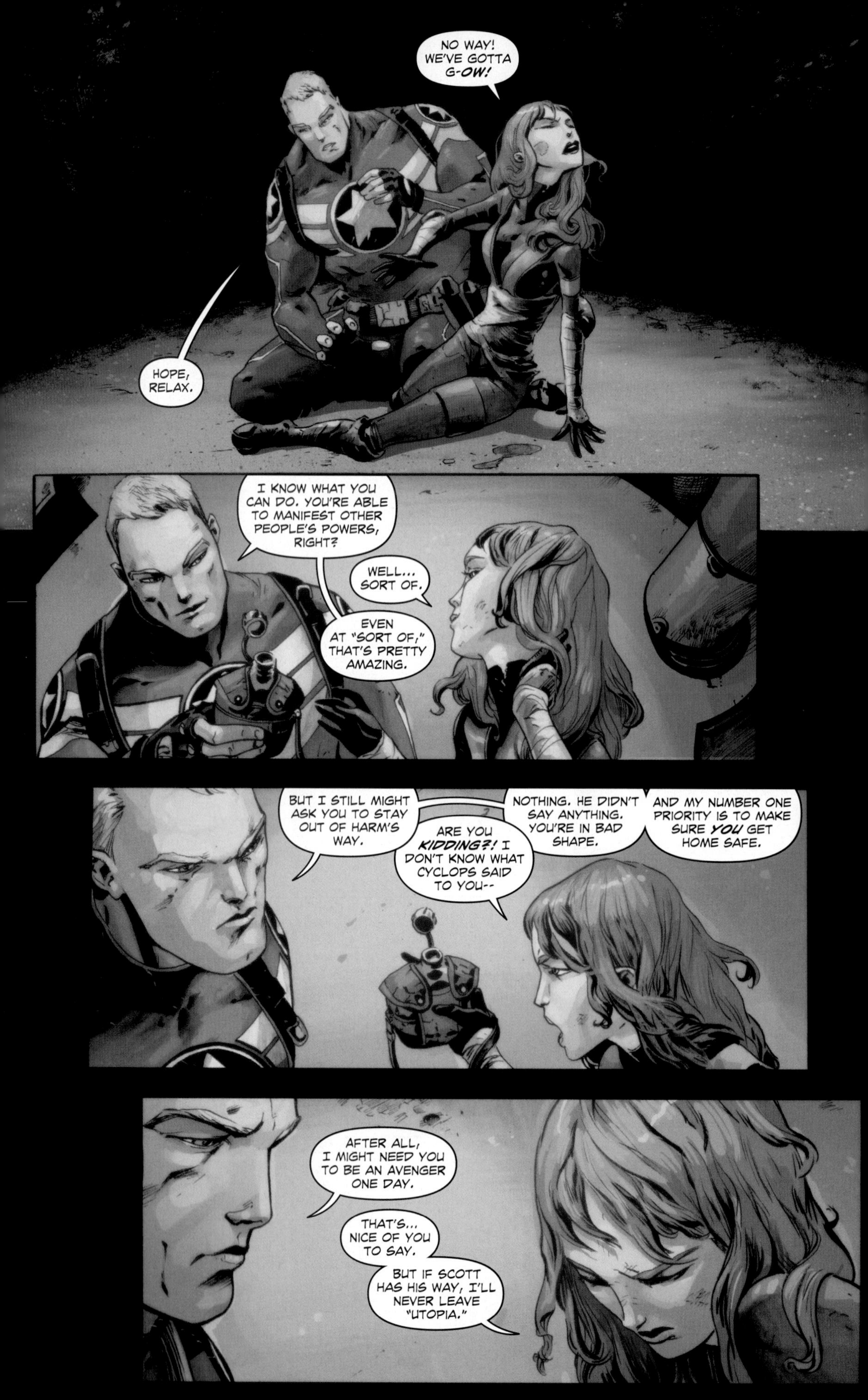
NO WAY! WE'VE GOTTA G-OW!
HOPE, RELAX.
I KNOW WHAT YOU CAN DO. YOU'RE ABLE TO MANIFEST OTHER PEOPLE'S POWERS, RIGHT?
WELL... SORT OF.
EVEN AT "SORT OF," THAT'S PRETTY AMAZING.
BUT I STILL MIGHT ASK YOU TO STAY OUT OF HARM'S WAY.
ARE YOU KIDDING?! I DON'T KNOW WHAT CYCLOPS SAID TO YOU--
NOTHING. HE DIDN'T SAY ANYTHING. YOU'RE IN BAD SHAPE.
AND MY NUMBER ONE PRIORITY IS TO MAKE SURE YOU GET HOME SAFE.
AFTER ALL, I MIGHT NEED YOU TO BE AN AVENGER ONE DAY.
THAT'S... NICE OF YOU TO SAY.
BUT IF SCOTT HAS HIS WAY, I'LL NEVER LEAVE "UTOPIA."

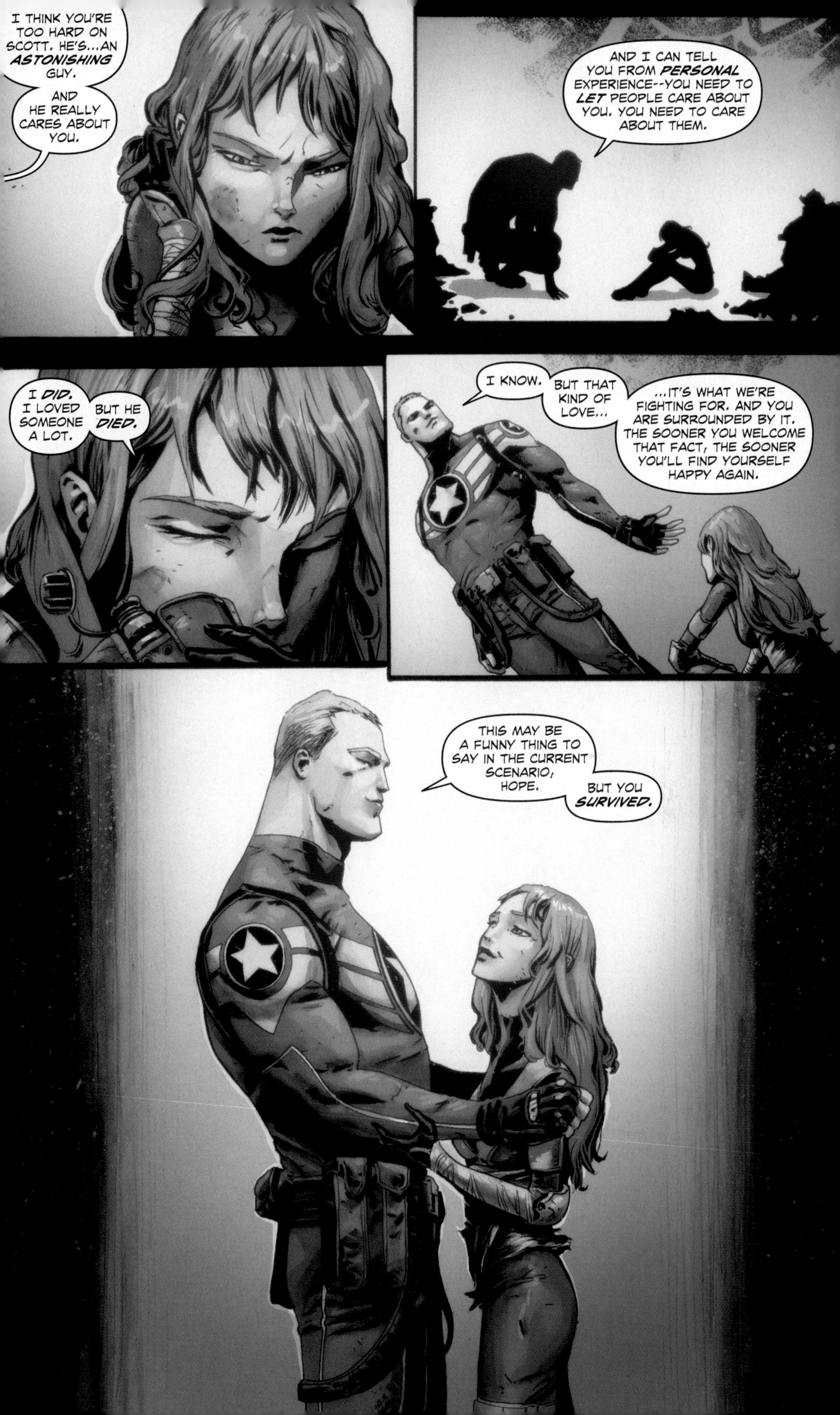
I THINK YOU'RE TOO HARD ON SCOTT. HE'S...AN ASTONISHING GUY.
AND HE REALLY CARES ABOUT YOU.
AND I CAN TELL YOU FROM PERSONAL EXPERIENCE--YOU NEED TO LET PEOPLE CARE ABOUT YOU. YOU NEED TO CARE ABOUT THEM.
I DID. I LOVED SOMEONE A LOT.
BUT HE DIED.
I KNOW.
BUT THAT KIND OF LOVE...
...IT'S WHAT WE'RE FIGHTING FOR. AND YOU ARE SURROUNDED BY IT. THE SOONER YOU WELCOME THAT FACT, THE SOONER YOU'LL FIND YOURSELF HAPPY AGAIN.
THIS MAY BE A FUNNY THING TO SAY IN THE CURRENT SCENARIO, HOPE.
BUT YOU SURVIVED.

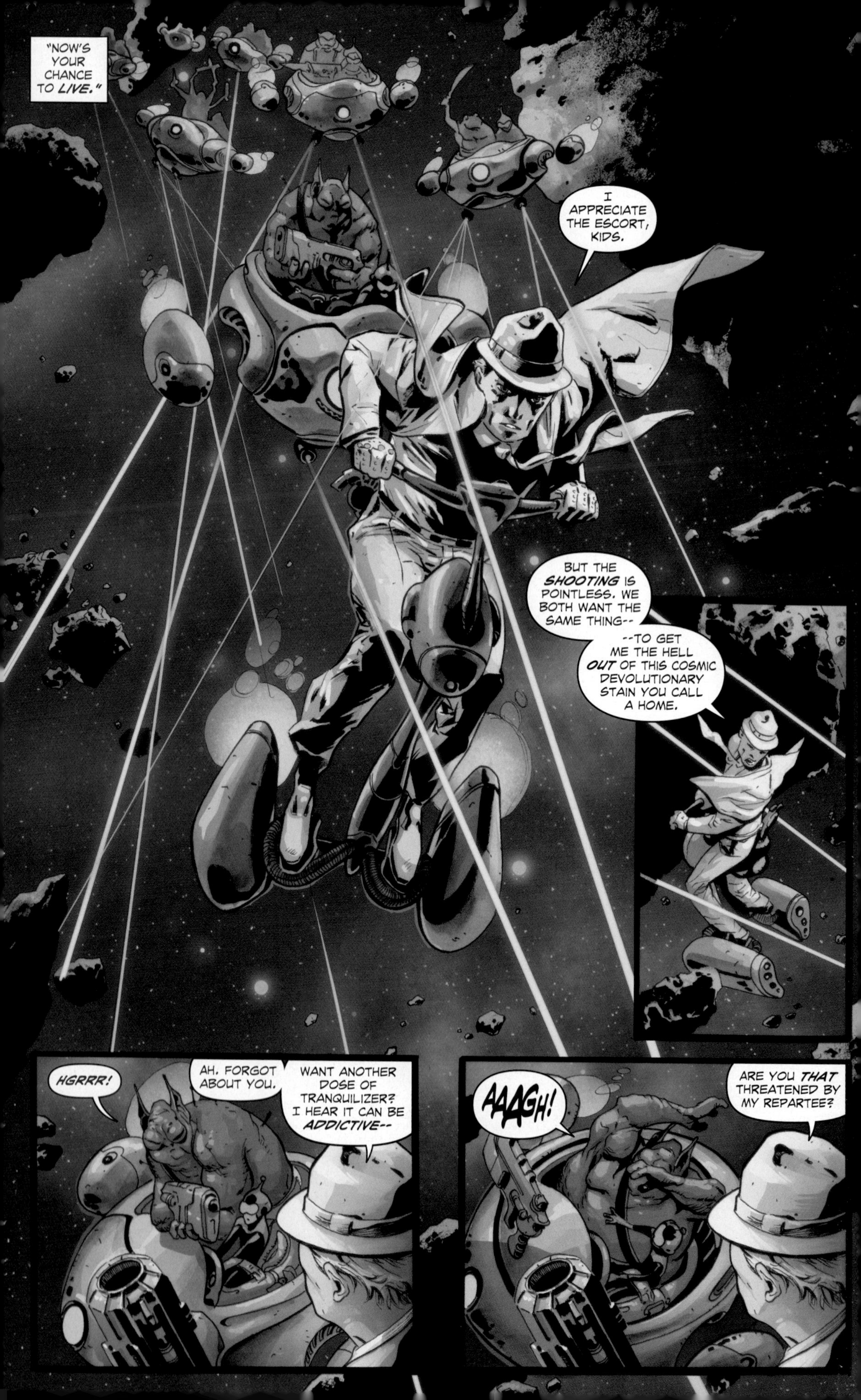
"NOW'S YOUR CHANCE TO *LIVE.*"
I APPRECIATE THE ESCORT, KIDS.
BUT THE *SHOOTING* IS POINTLESS. WE BOTH WANT THE SAME THING--
--TO GET ME THE HELL *OUT* OF THIS COSMIC DEVOLUTIONARY STAIN YOU CALL A HOME.
HGRRR!
AH. FORGOT ABOUT YOU.
WANT ANOTHER DOSE OF TRANQUILIZER? I HEAR IT CAN BE *ADDICTIVE--*
AAAGH!
ARE YOU *THAT* THREATENED BY MY REPARTEE?

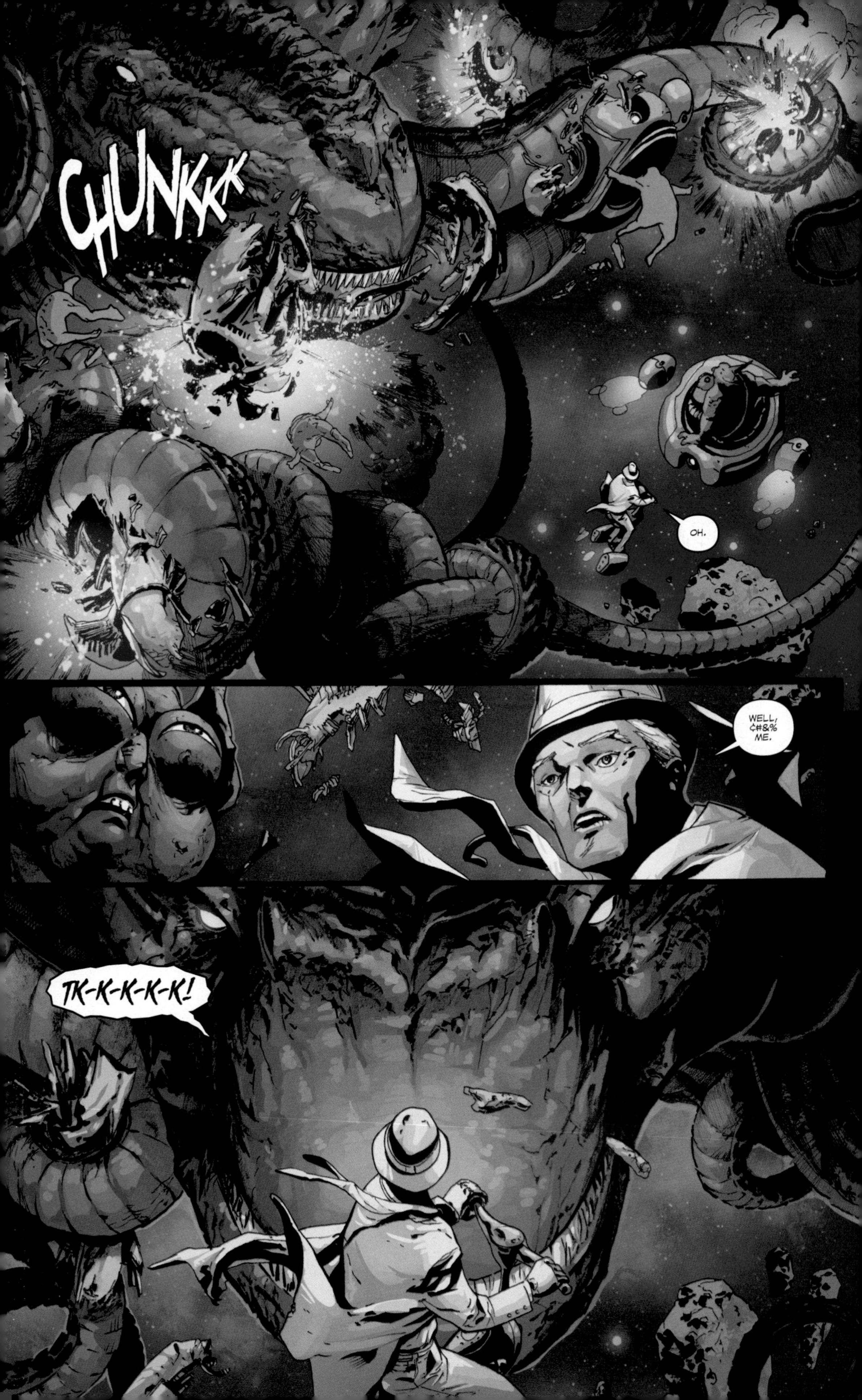
CHUNKKK
OH.
WELL, ¢#&% ME.
TK-K-K-K-K!

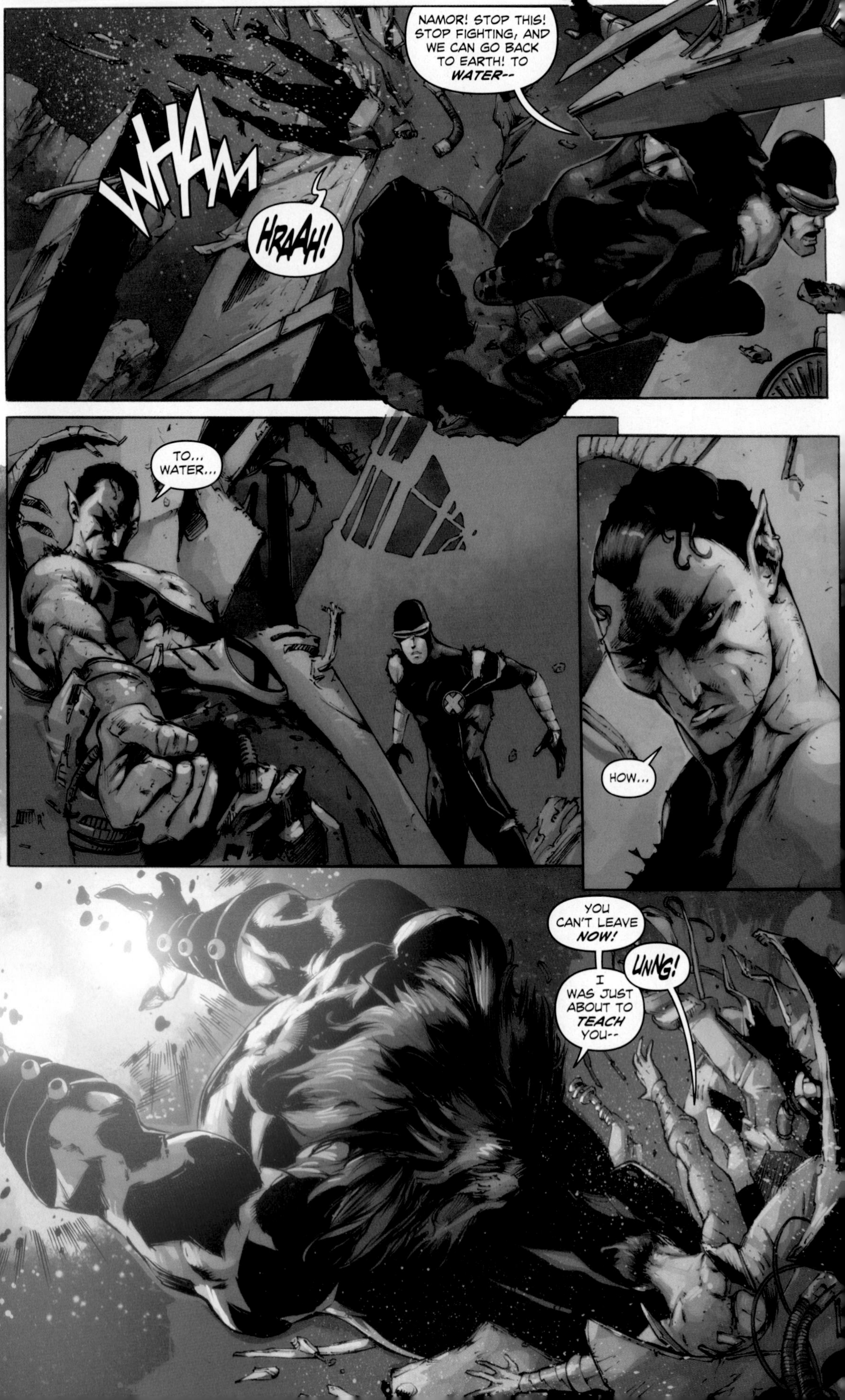
NAMOR! STOP THIS! STOP FIGHTING, AND WE CAN GO BACK TO EARTH! TO WATER--
WHAM
HRAAH!
TO... WATER...
HOW...
YOU CAN'T LEAVE NOW!
I WAS JUST ABOUT TO TEACH YOU--
UNNG!

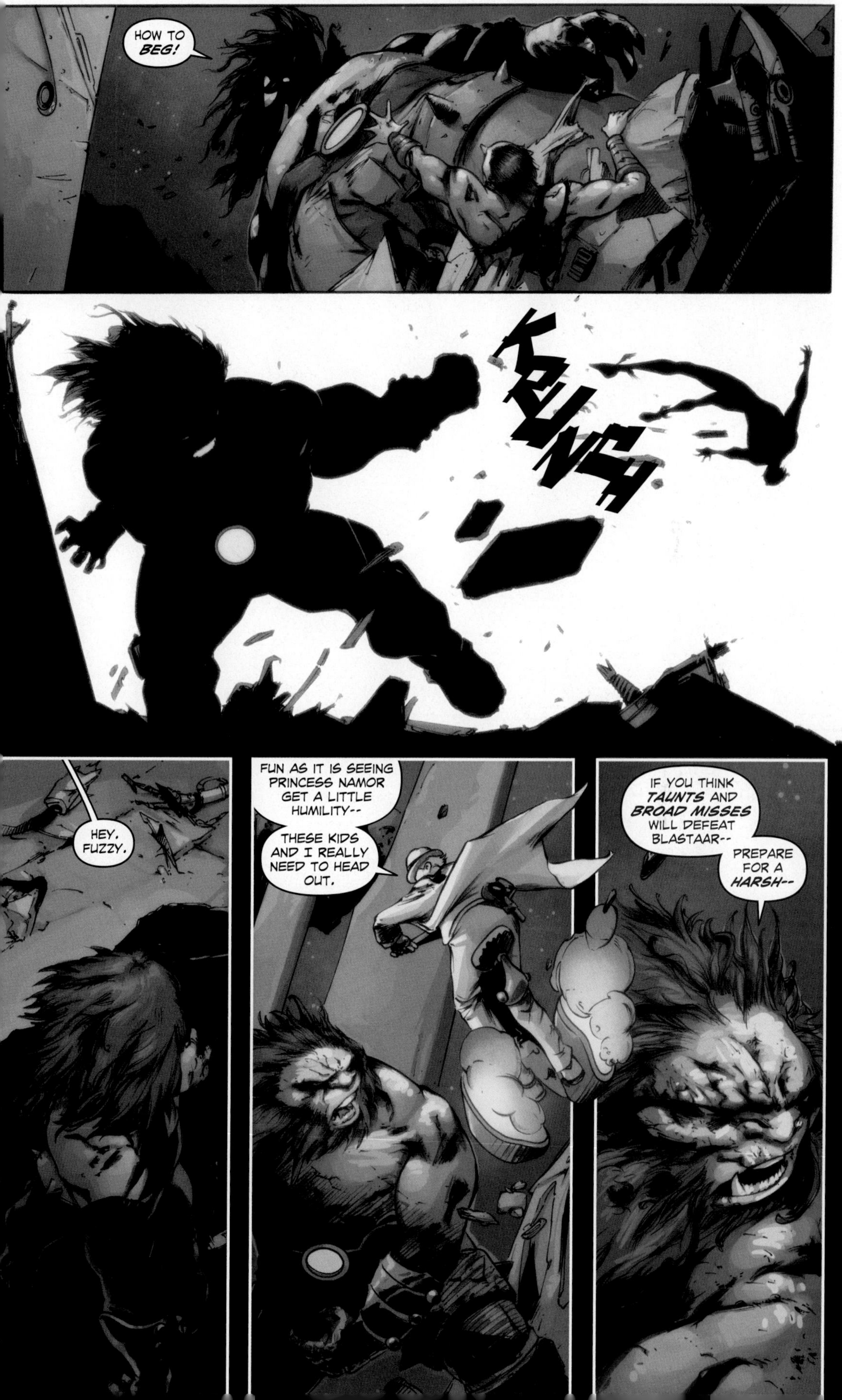
HOW TO BEG!
KRUNCH
HEY. FUZZY.
FUN AS IT IS SEEING PRINCESS NAMOR GET A LITTLE HUMILITY--
THESE KIDS AND I REALLY NEED TO HEAD OUT.
IF YOU THINK TAUNTS AND BROAD MISSES WILL DEFEAT BLASTAAR--
PREPARE FOR A HARSH--

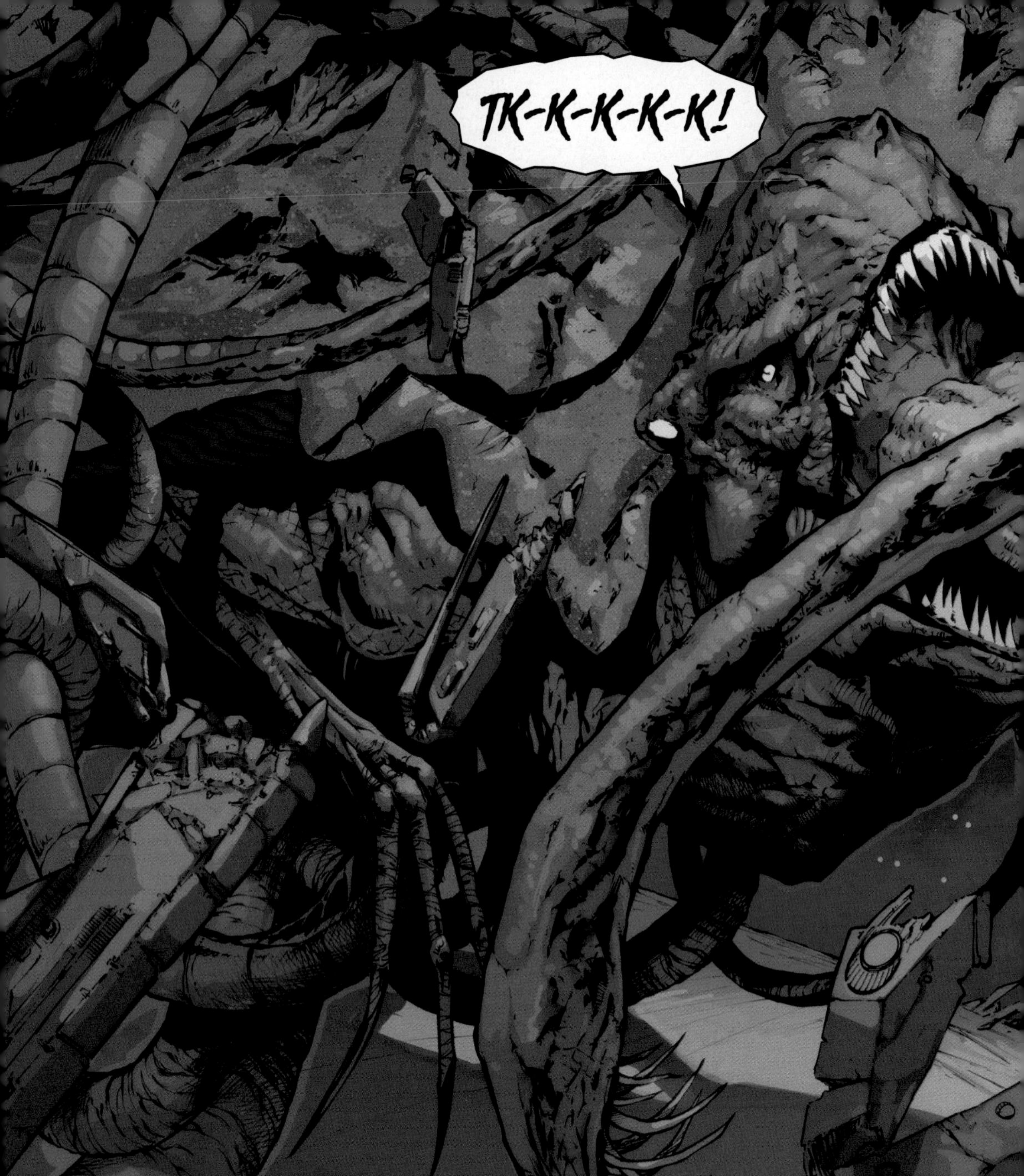
TK-K-K-K-K!

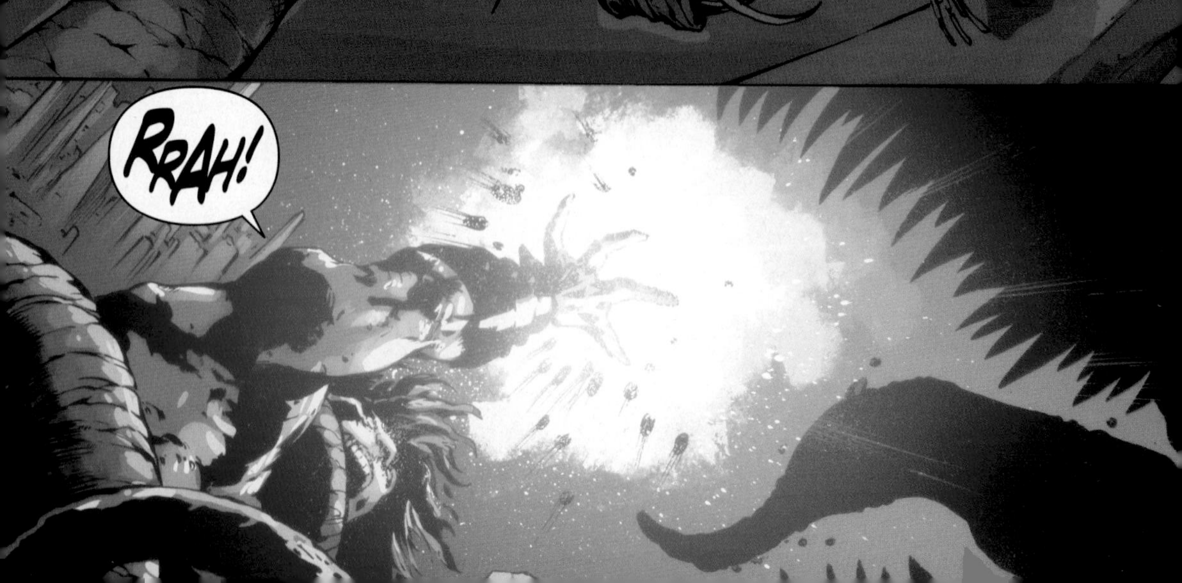
RRAH!

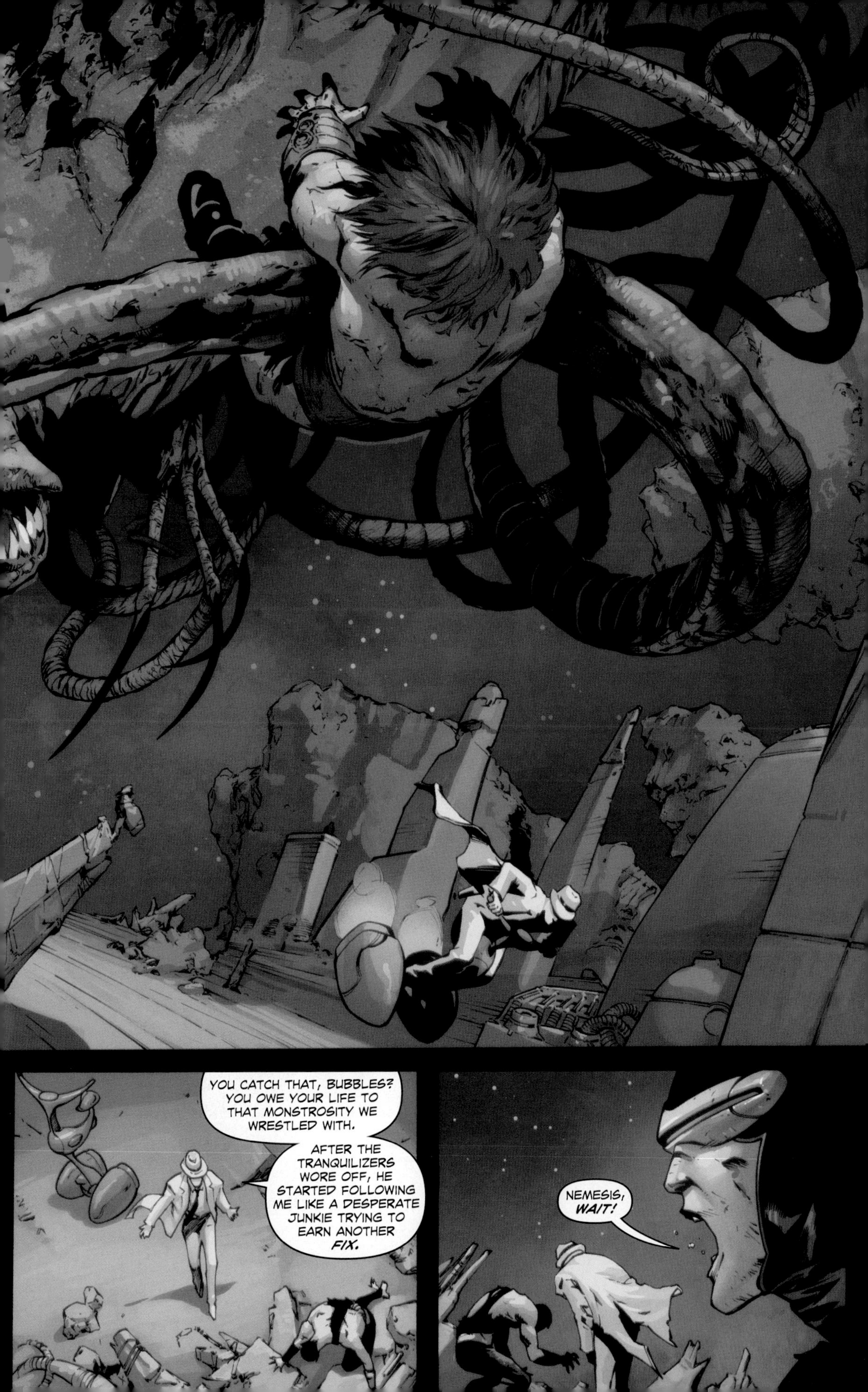
YOU CATCH THAT, BUBBLES? YOU OWE YOUR LIFE TO THAT MONSTROSITY WE WRESTLED WITH.
AFTER THE TRANQUILIZERS WORE OFF, HE STARTED FOLLOWING ME LIKE A DESPERATE JUNKIE TRYING TO EARN ANOTHER *FIX.*
NEMESIS, *WAIT!*

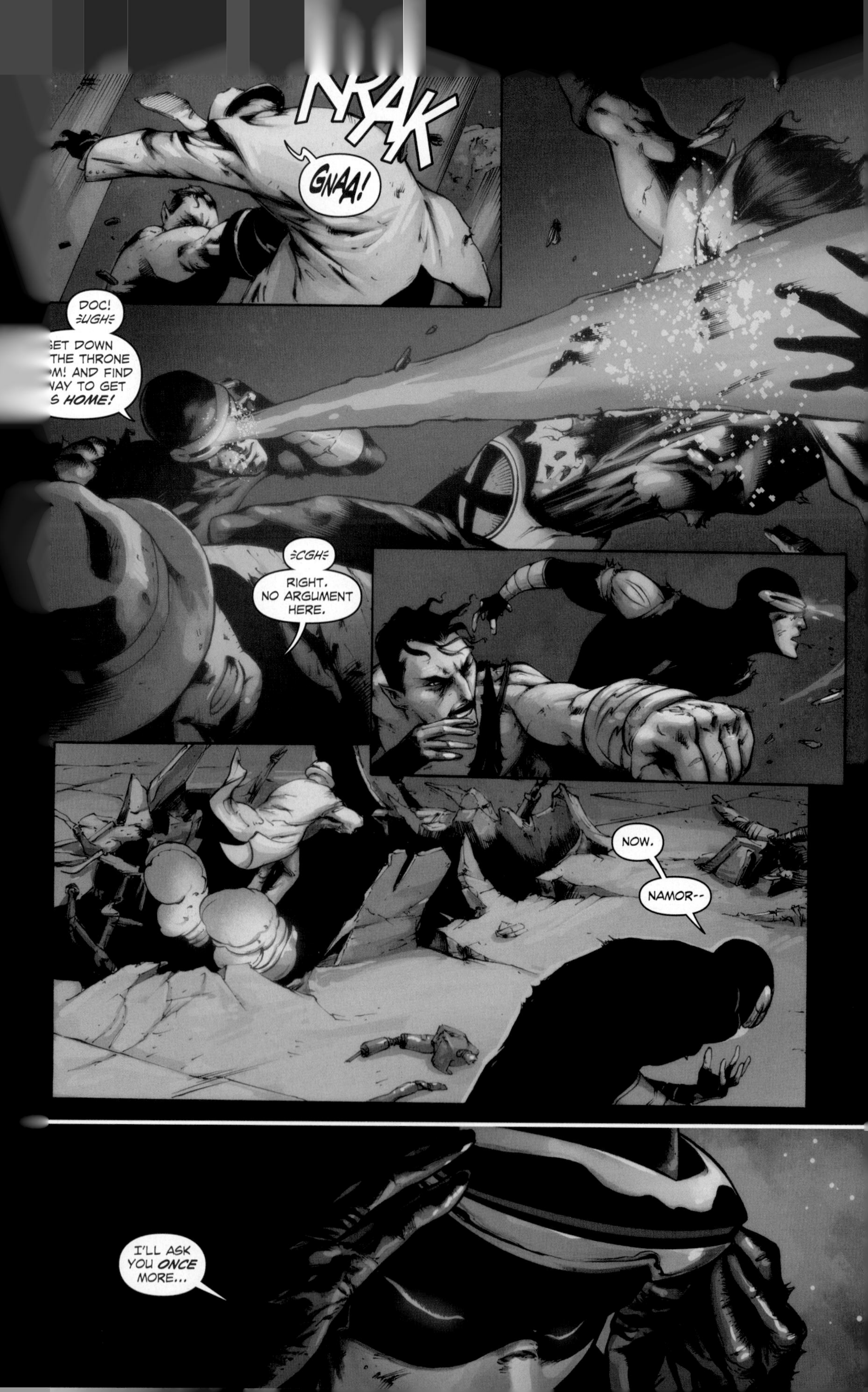

GNAA!
DOC! UGH
GET DOWN THE THRONE OM! AND FIND WAY TO GET S HOME!
CGH RIGHT. NO ARGUMENT HERE.
NOW.
NAMOR--
I'LL ASK YOU ONCE MORE...

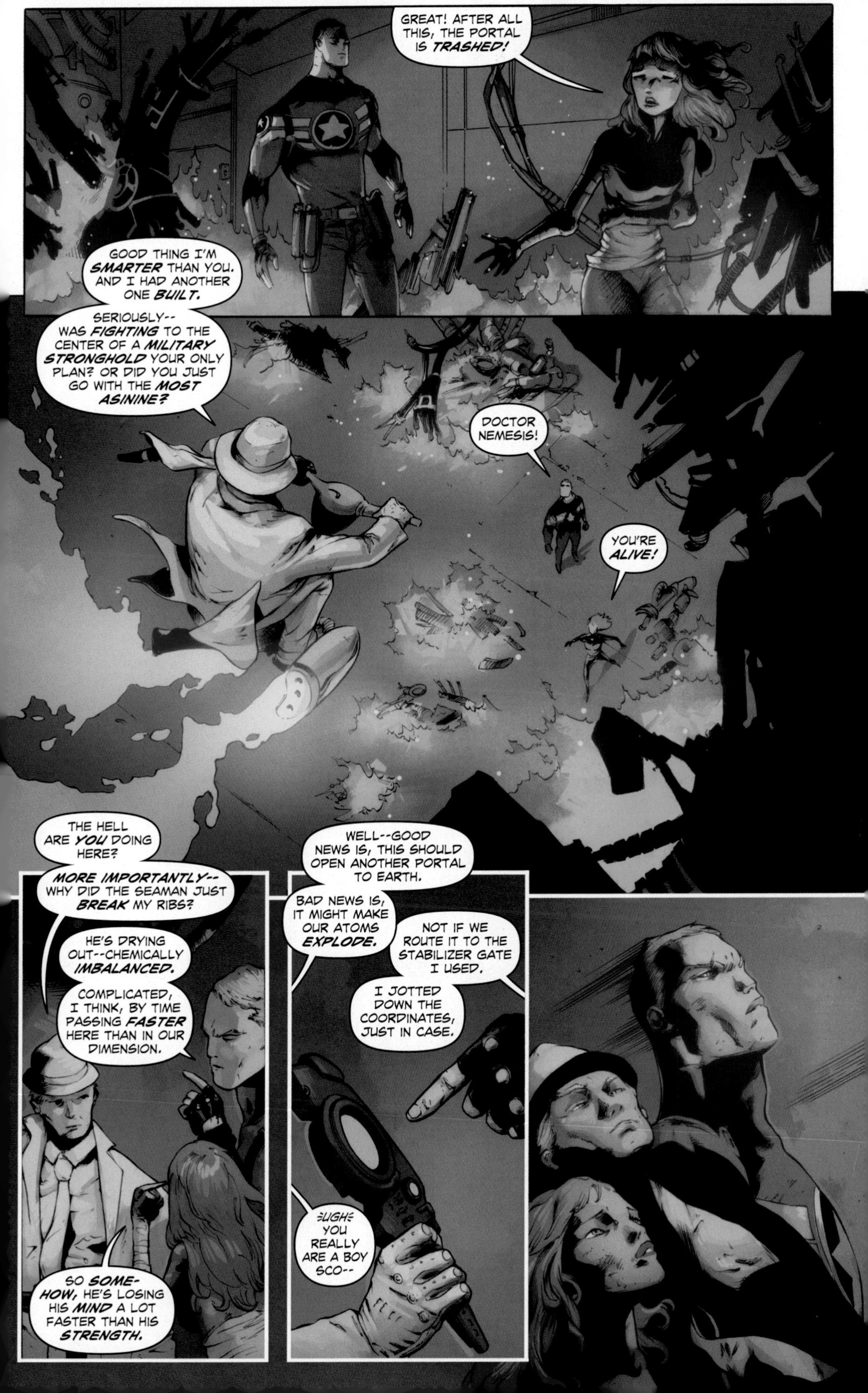
GREAT! AFTER ALL THIS, THE PORTAL IS TRASHED!
GOOD THING I'M SMARTER THAN YOU. AND I HAD ANOTHER ONE BUILT.
SERIOUSLY-- WAS FIGHTING TO THE CENTER OF A MILITARY STRONGHOLD YOUR ONLY PLAN? OR DID YOU JUST GO WITH THE MOST ASININE?
DOCTOR NEMESIS!
YOU'RE ALIVE!
THE HELL ARE YOU DOING HERE?
MORE IMPORTANTLY-- WHY DID THE SEAMAN JUST BREAK MY RIBS?
HE'S DRYING OUT--CHEMICALLY IMBALANCED.
COMPLICATED, I THINK, BY TIME PASSING FASTER HERE THAN IN OUR DIMENSION.
SO SOME-HOW, HE'S LOSING HIS MIND A LOT FASTER THAN HIS STRENGTH.
WELL--GOOD NEWS IS, THIS SHOULD OPEN ANOTHER PORTAL TO EARTH.
BAD NEWS IS, IT MIGHT MAKE OUR ATOMS EXPLODE.
NOT IF WE ROUTE IT TO THE STABILIZER GATE I USED.
I JOTTED DOWN THE COORDINATES, JUST IN CASE.
UGH YOU REALLY ARE A BOY SCO--

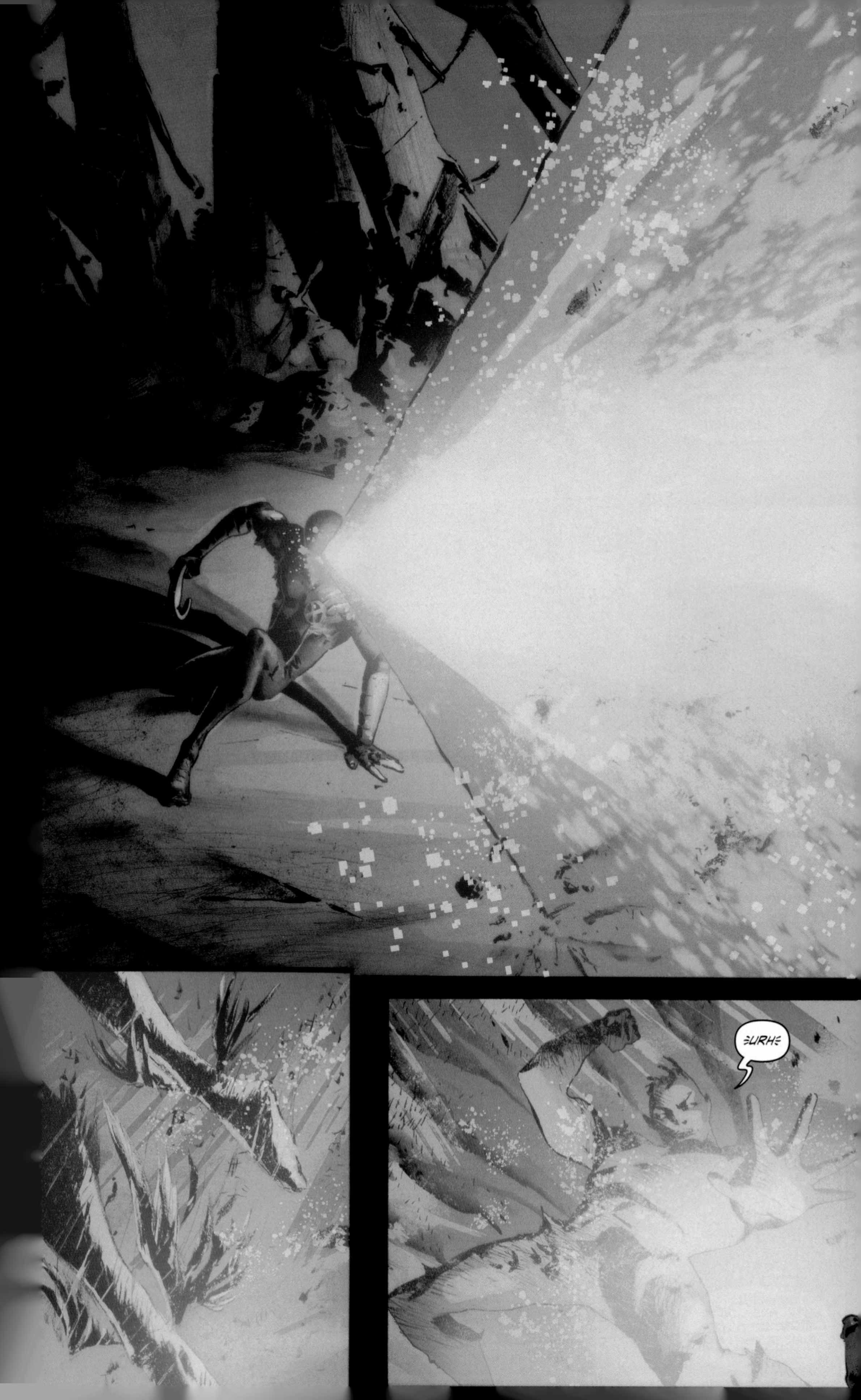
URH

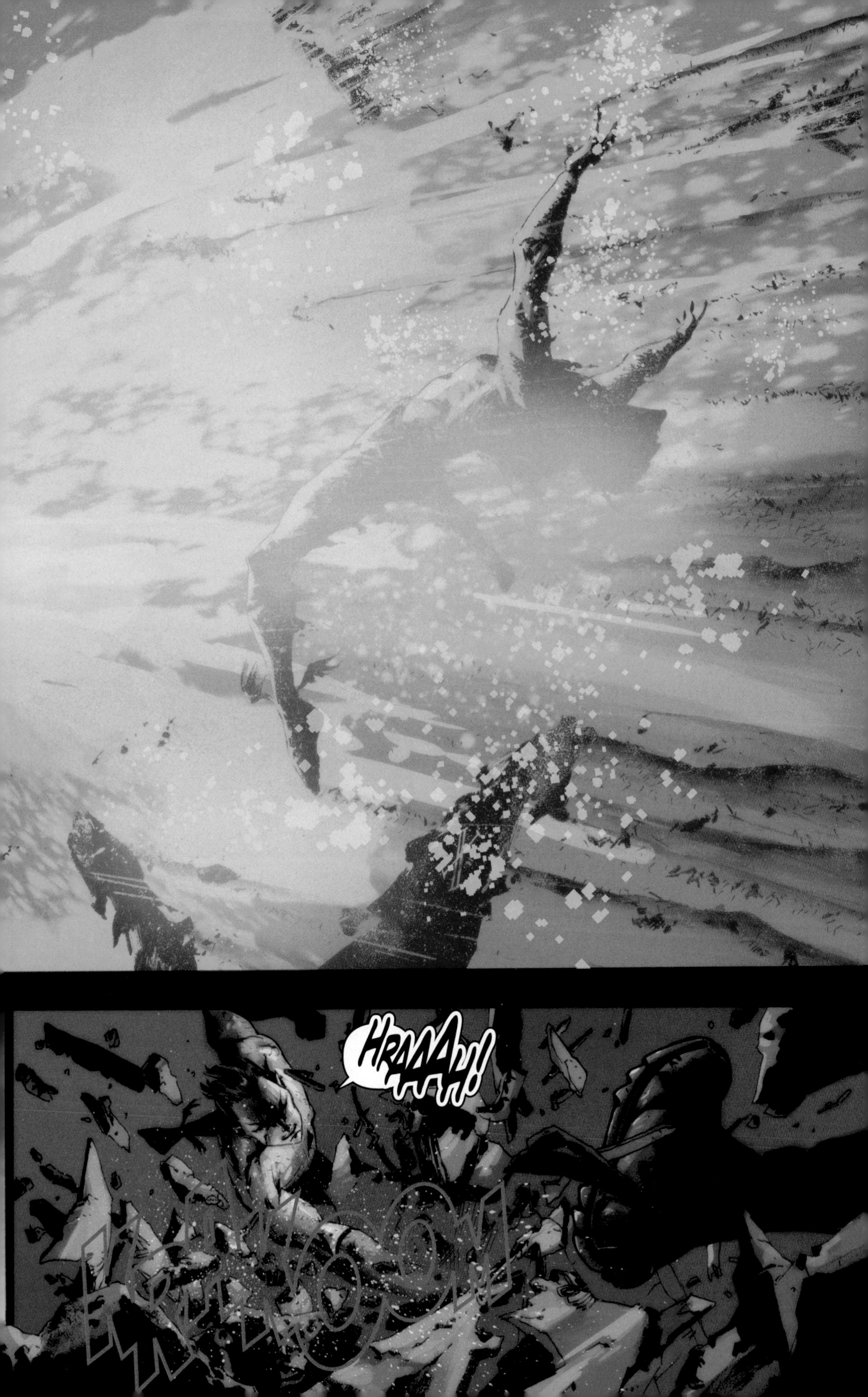
HRAAAH!

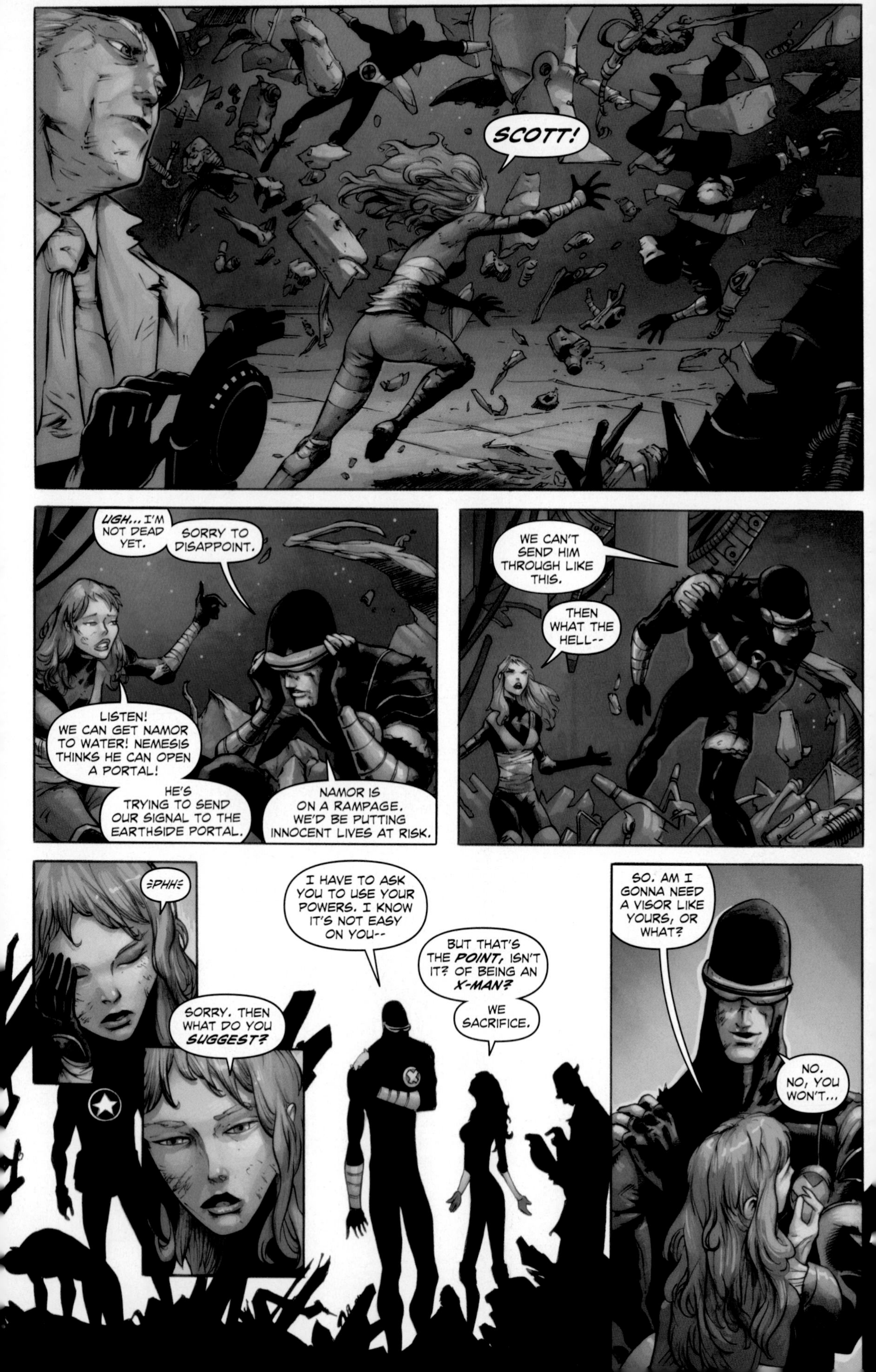
SCOTT!
UGH... I'M NOT DEAD YET.
SORRY TO DISAPPOINT.
LISTEN! WE CAN GET NAMOR TO WATER! NEMESIS THINKS HE CAN OPEN A PORTAL!
HE'S TRYING TO SEND OUR SIGNAL TO THE EARTHSIDE PORTAL.
NAMOR IS ON A RAMPAGE. WE'D BE PUTTING INNOCENT LIVES AT RISK.
WE CAN'T SEND HIM THROUGH LIKE THIS.
THEN WHAT THE HELL--
PHH
I HAVE TO ASK YOU TO USE YOUR POWERS. I KNOW IT'S NOT EASY ON YOU--
SORRY. THEN WHAT DO YOU SUGGEST?
BUT THAT'S THE POINT, ISN'T IT? OF BEING AN X-MAN?
WE SACRIFICE.
SO. AM I GONNA NEED A VISOR LIKE YOURS, OR WHAT?
NO. NO, YOU WON'T...

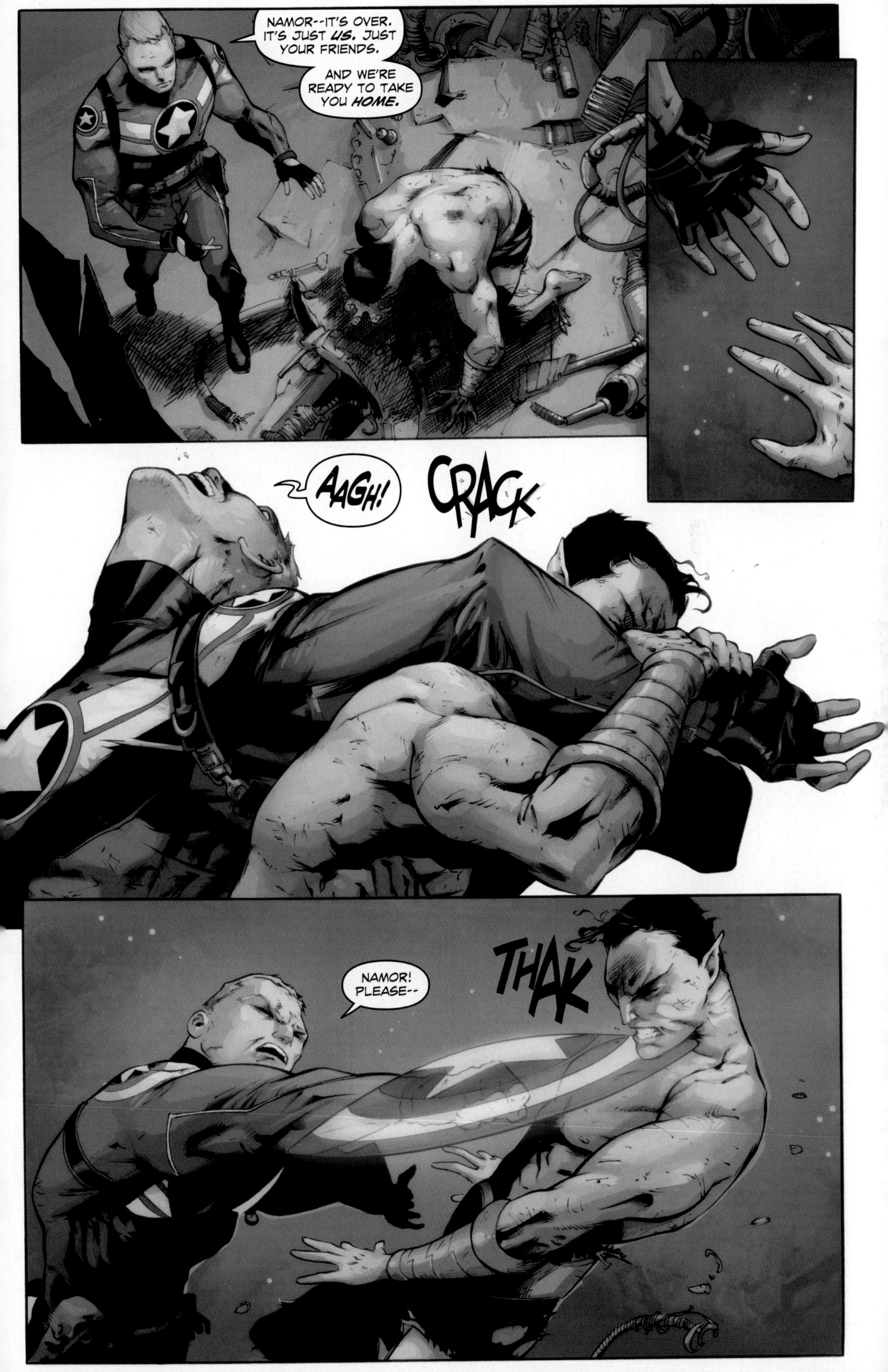
NAMOR--IT'S OVER. IT'S JUST US. JUST YOUR FRIENDS.
AND WE'RE READY TO TAKE YOU HOME.
AAGH!
CRACK
THAK
NAMOR! PLEASE--

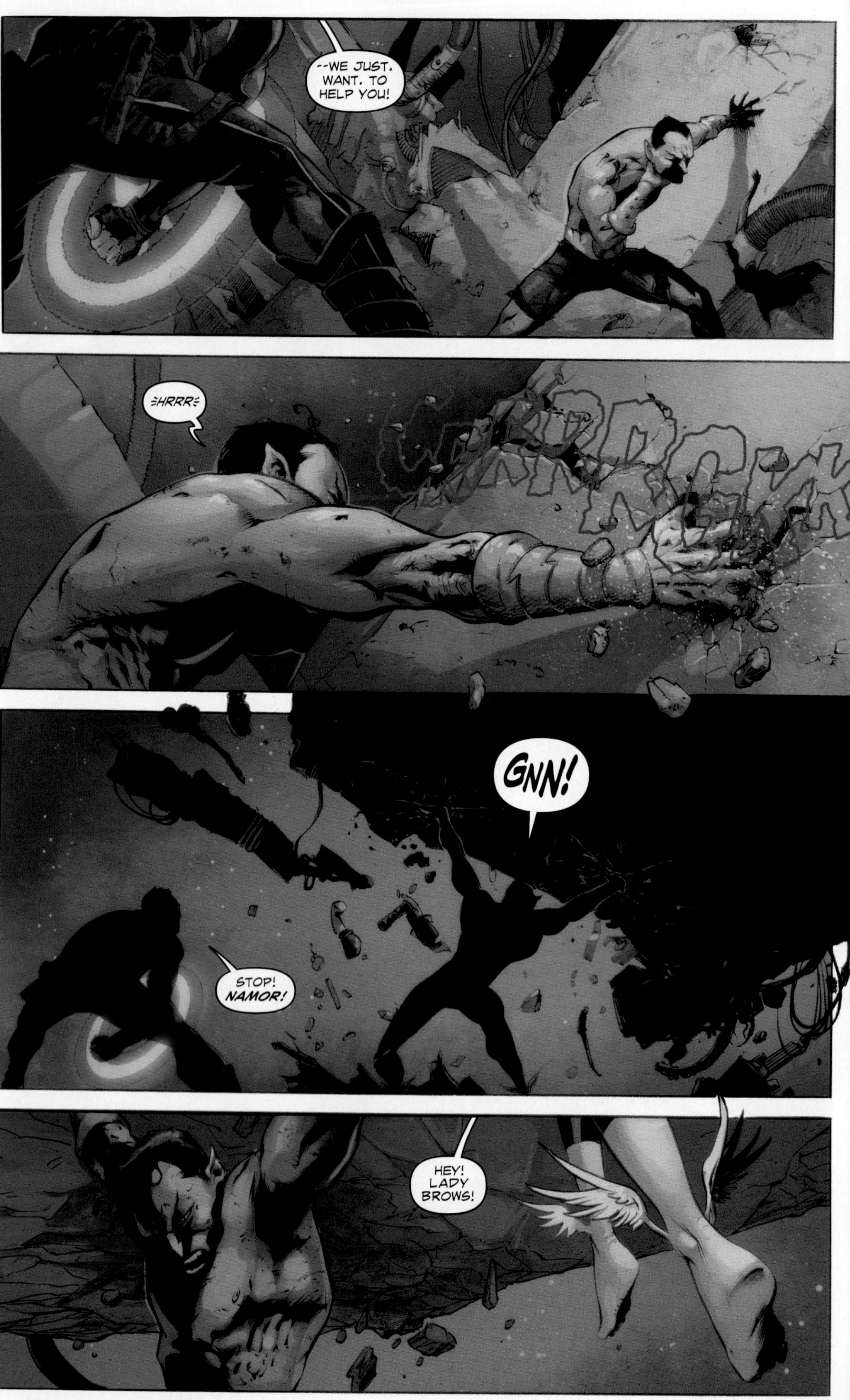
--WE JUST. WANT. TO HELP YOU!
HRRR
GNN!
STOP! NAMOR!
HEY! LADY BROWS!

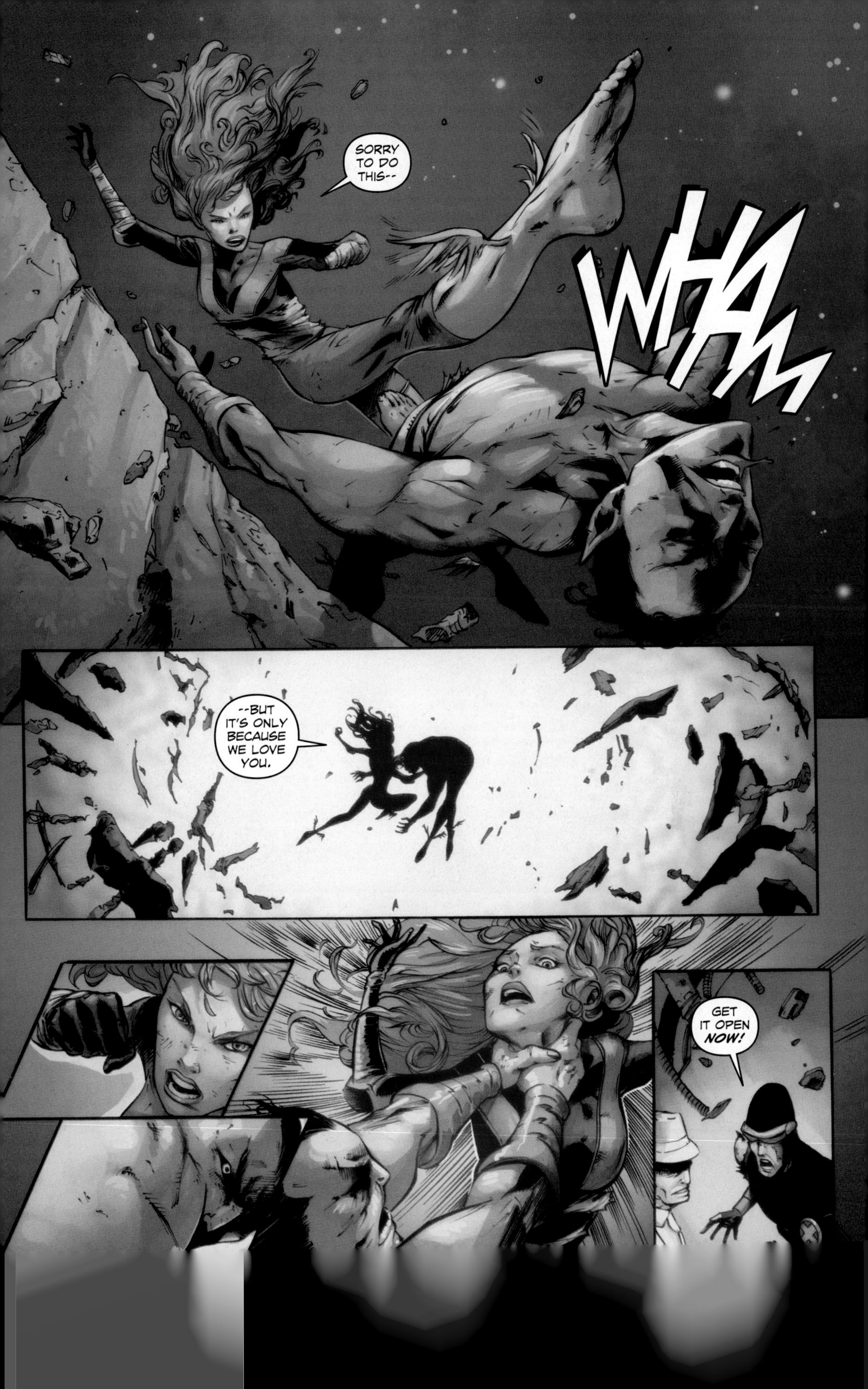
SORRY TO DO THIS--
WHAM
--BUT IT'S ONLY BECAUSE WE LOVE YOU.
GET IT OPEN *NOW!*

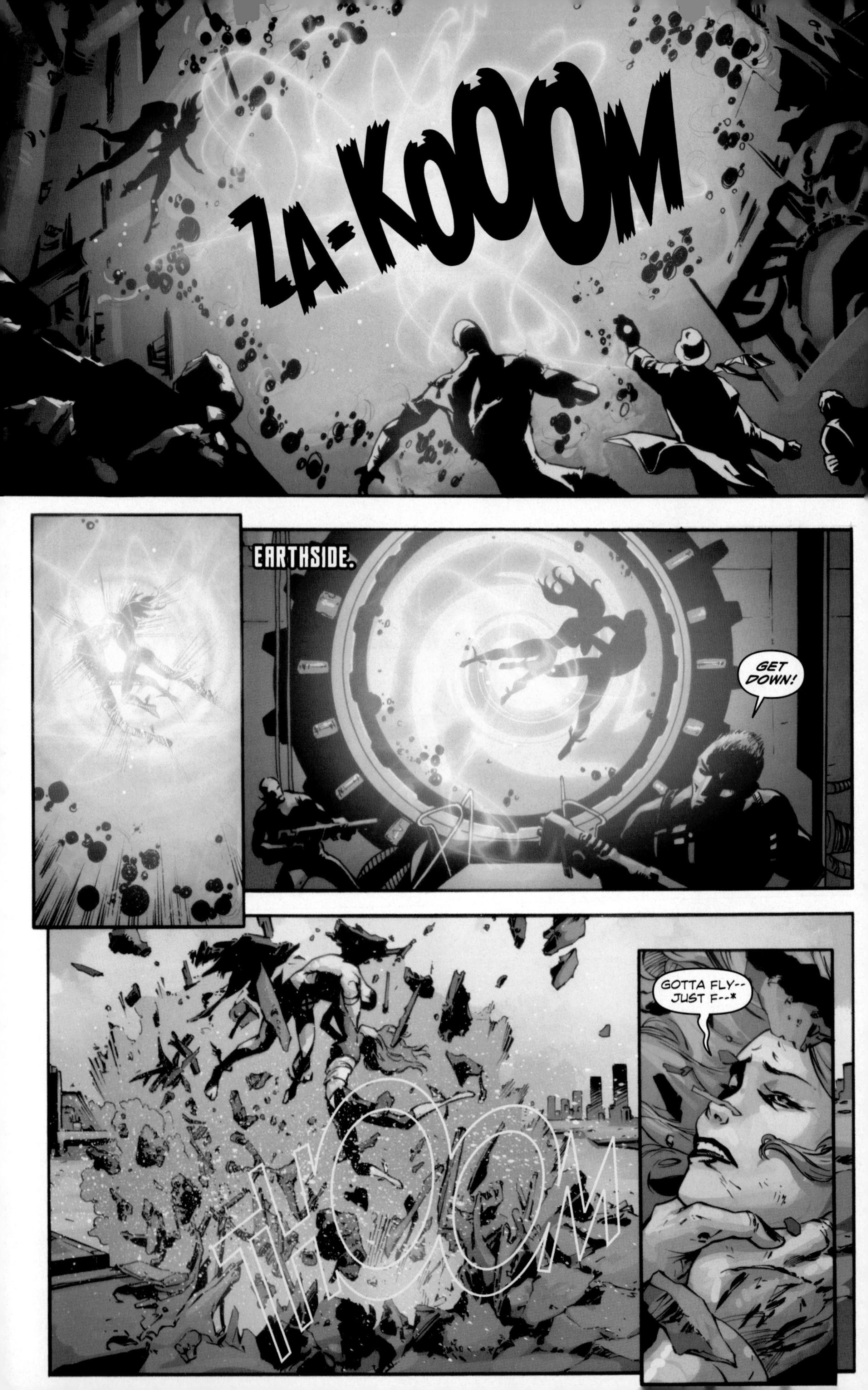
ZA-KOOOM
EARTHSIDE.
GET DOWN!
THOOM
GOTTA FLY--
JUST F--*

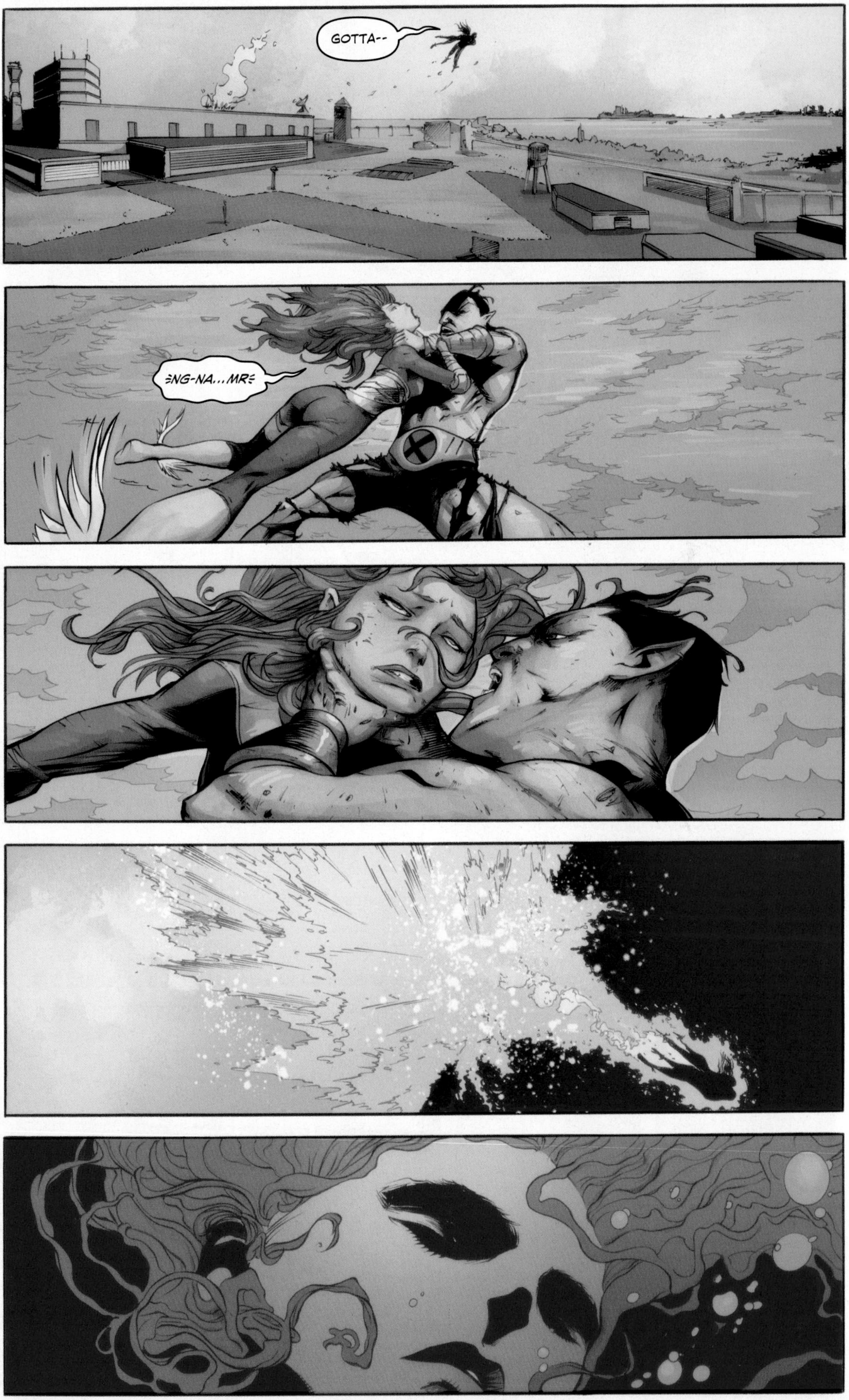
GOTTA--
NG-NA...MR

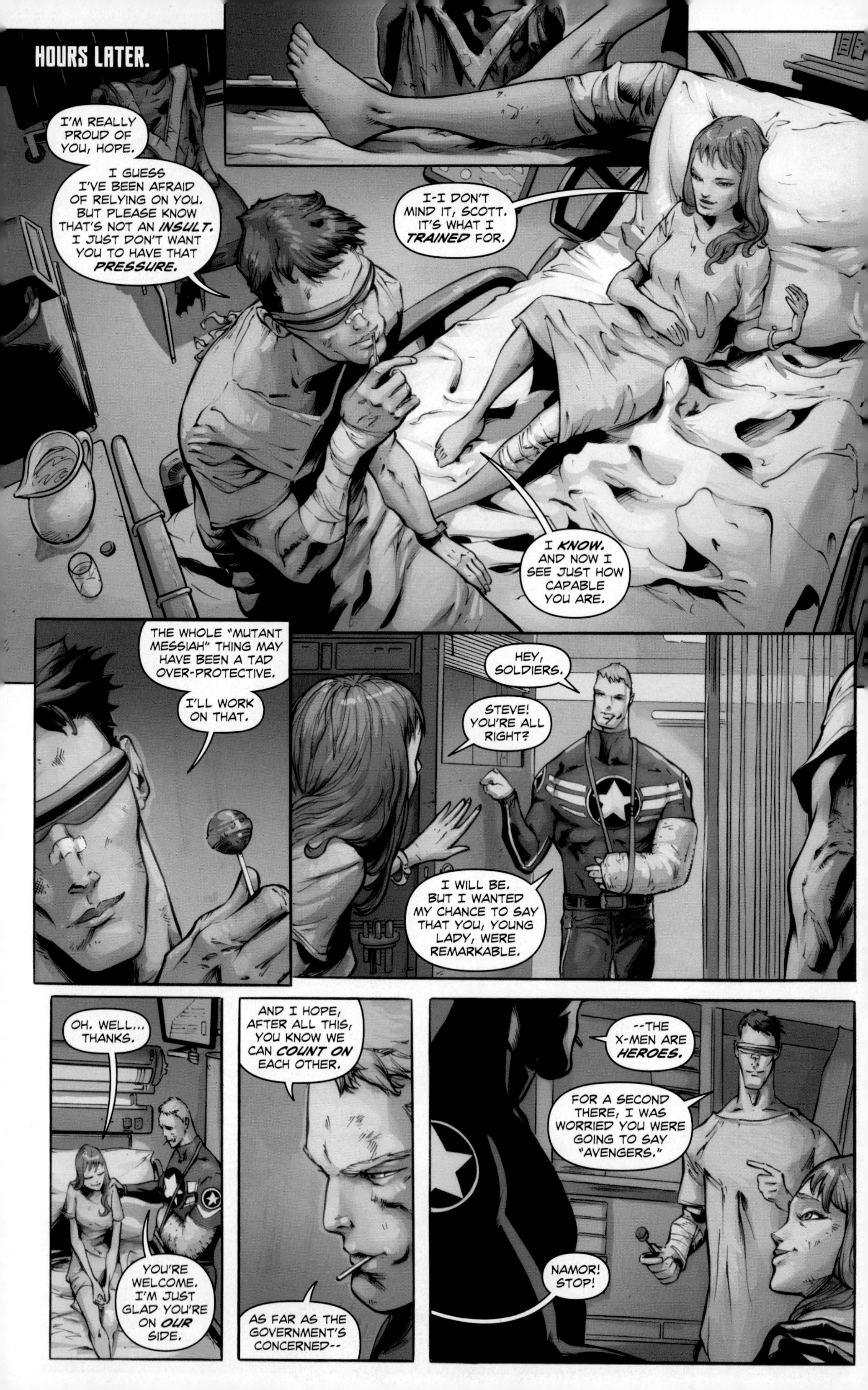
HOURS LATER.
I'M REALLY PROUD OF YOU, HOPE.
I GUESS I'VE BEEN AFRAID OF RELYING ON YOU. BUT PLEASE KNOW THAT'S NOT AN INSULT. I JUST DON'T WANT YOU TO HAVE THAT PRESSURE.
I-I DON'T MIND IT, SCOTT. IT'S WHAT I TRAINED FOR.
I KNOW. AND NOW I SEE JUST HOW CAPABLE YOU ARE.
THE WHOLE "MUTANT MESSIAH" THING MAY HAVE BEEN A TAD OVER-PROTECTIVE.
I'LL WORK ON THAT.
HEY, SOLDIERS.
STEVE! YOU'RE ALL RIGHT?
I WILL BE. BUT I WANTED MY CHANCE TO SAY THAT YOU, YOUNG LADY, WERE REMARKABLE.
OH. WELL... THANKS.
YOU'RE WELCOME. I'M JUST GLAD YOU'RE ON OUR SIDE.
AND I HOPE, AFTER ALL THIS, YOU KNOW WE CAN COUNT ON EACH OTHER.
AS FAR AS THE GOVERNMENT'S CONCERNED--
--THE X-MEN ARE HEROES.
FOR A SECOND THERE, I WAS WORRIED YOU WERE GOING TO SAY "AVENGERS."
NAMOR! STOP!

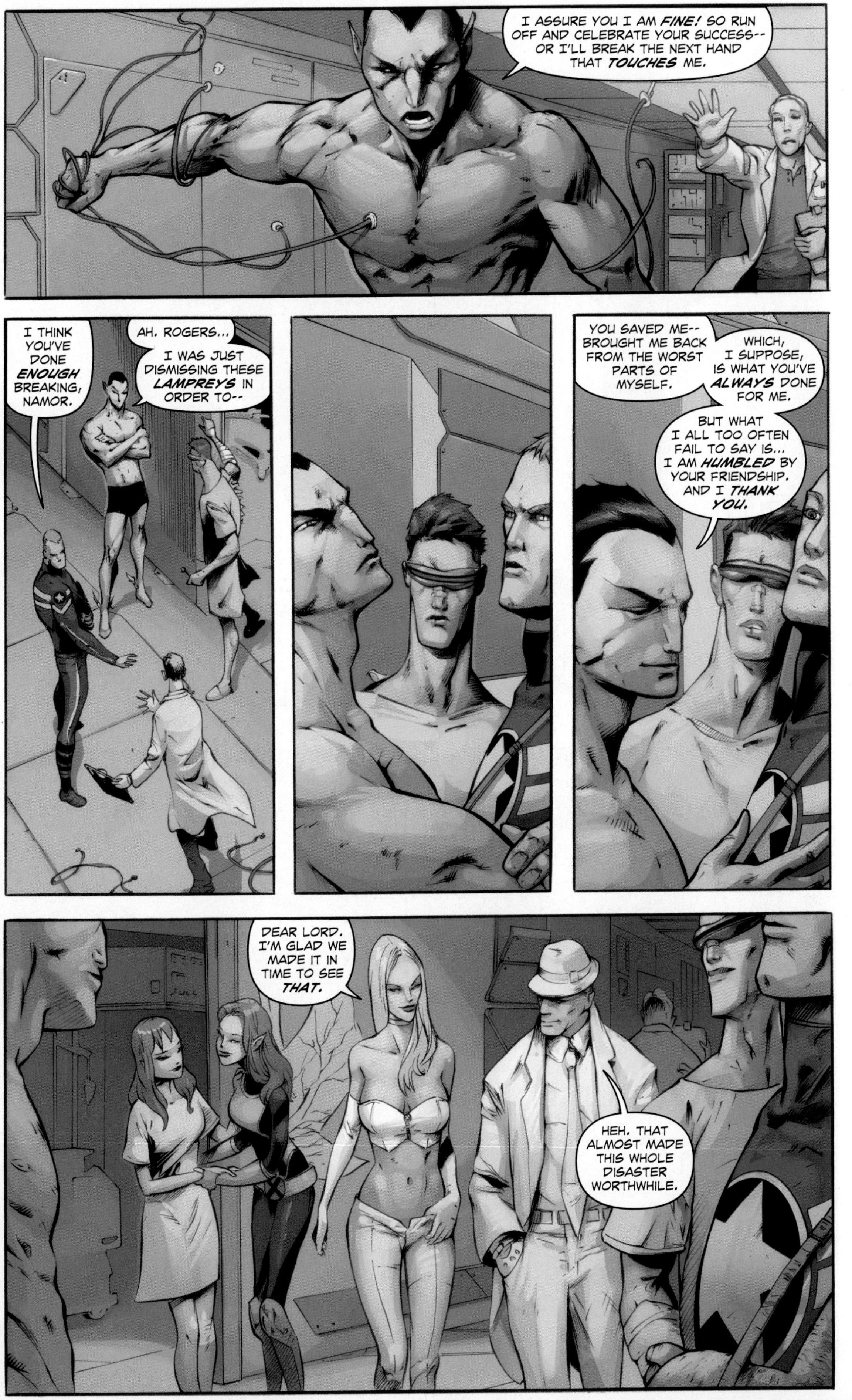
I ASSURE YOU I AM FINE! SO RUN OFF AND CELEBRATE YOUR SUCCESS--OR I'LL BREAK THE NEXT HAND THAT TOUCHES ME.
I THINK YOU'VE DONE ENOUGH BREAKING, NAMOR.
AH. ROGERS... I WAS JUST DISMISSING THESE LAMPREYS IN ORDER TO--
YOU SAVED ME--BROUGHT ME BACK FROM THE WORST PARTS OF MYSELF.
WHICH, I SUPPOSE, IS WHAT YOU'VE ALWAYS DONE FOR ME.
BUT WHAT I ALL TOO OFTEN FAIL TO SAY IS... I AM HUMBLED BY YOUR FRIENDSHIP. AND I THANK YOU.
DEAR LORD. I'M GLAD WE MADE IT IN TIME TO SEE THAT.
HEH. THAT ALMOST MADE THIS WHOLE DISASTER WORTHWHILE.

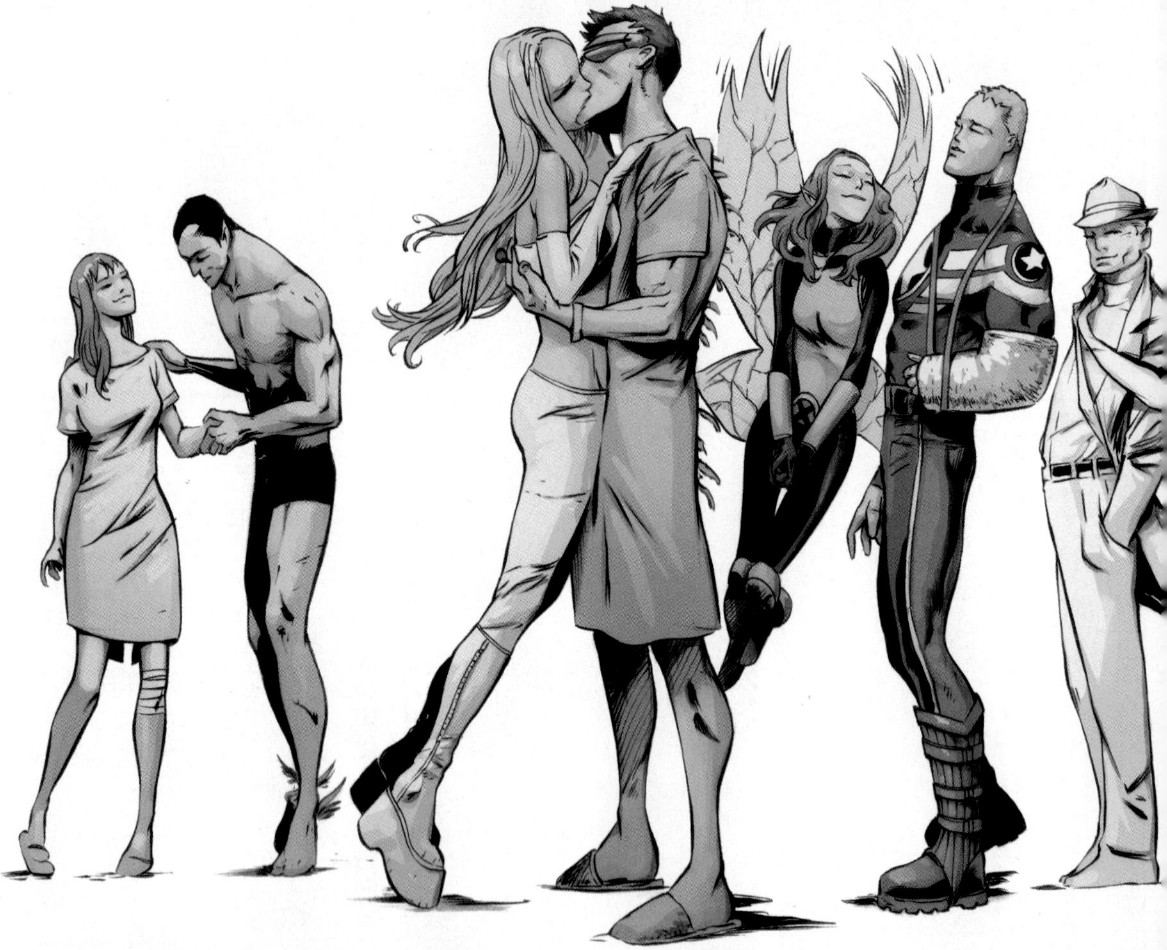

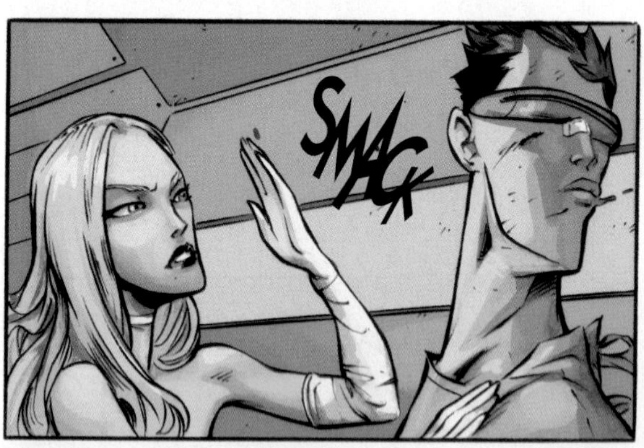
SMACK

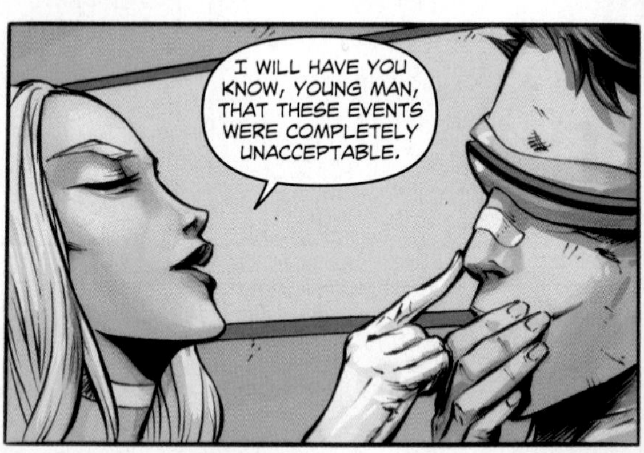
I WILL HAVE YOU KNOW, YOUNG MAN, THAT THESE EVENTS WERE COMPLETELY UNACCEPTABLE.

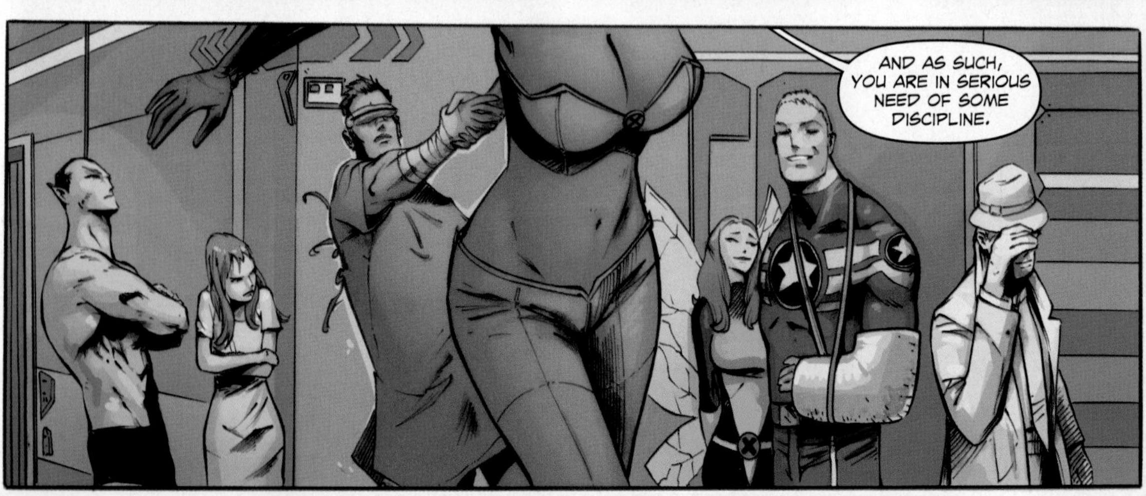
AND AS SUCH, YOU ARE IN SERIOUS NEED OF SOME DISCIPLINE.

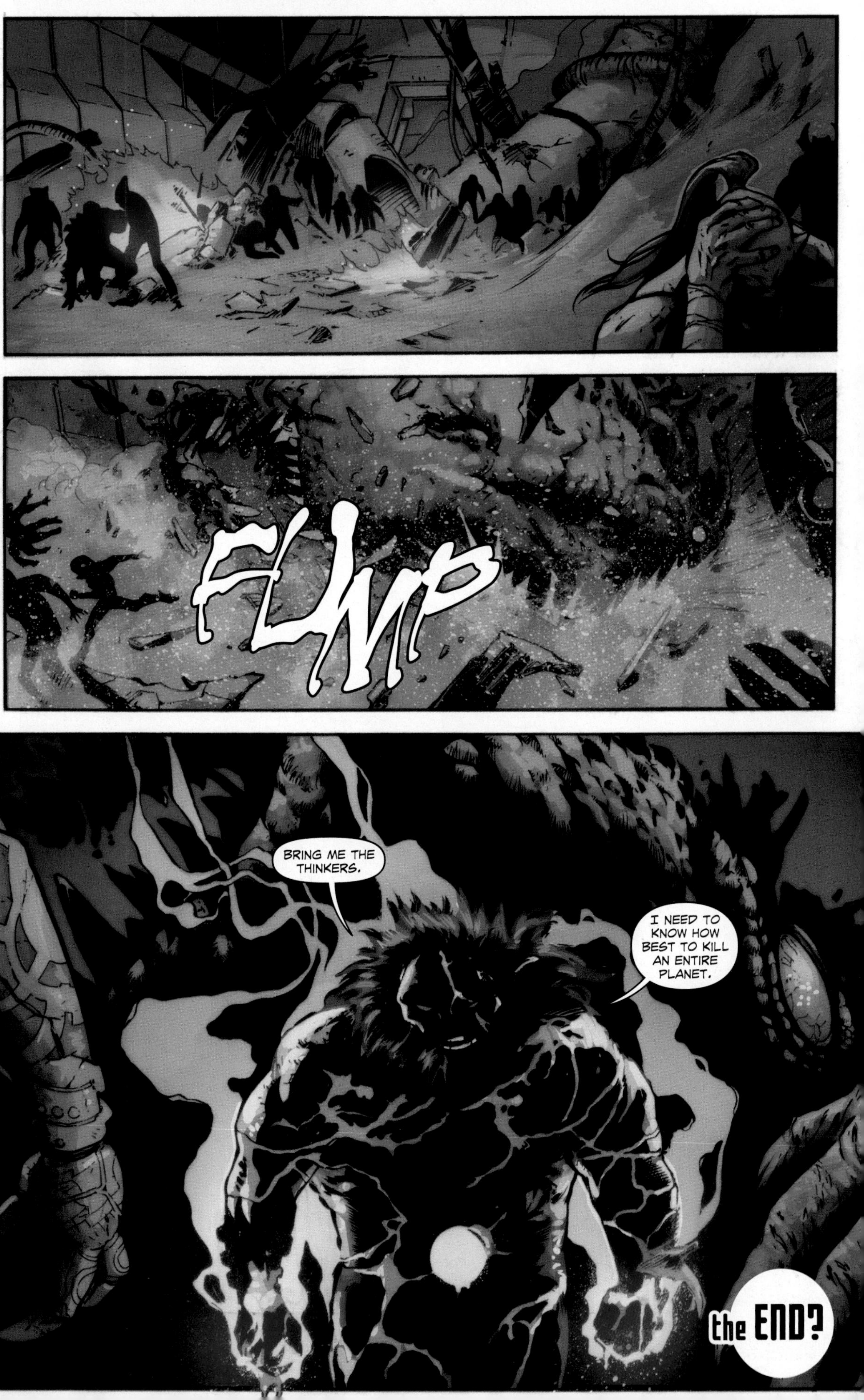
FLMP
BRING ME THE THINKERS.
I NEED TO KNOW HOW BEST TO KILL AN ENTIRE PLANET.
the END?

#1 VARIANT
BY DAVID FINCH, DANNY MIKI & PETER STEIGERWALD

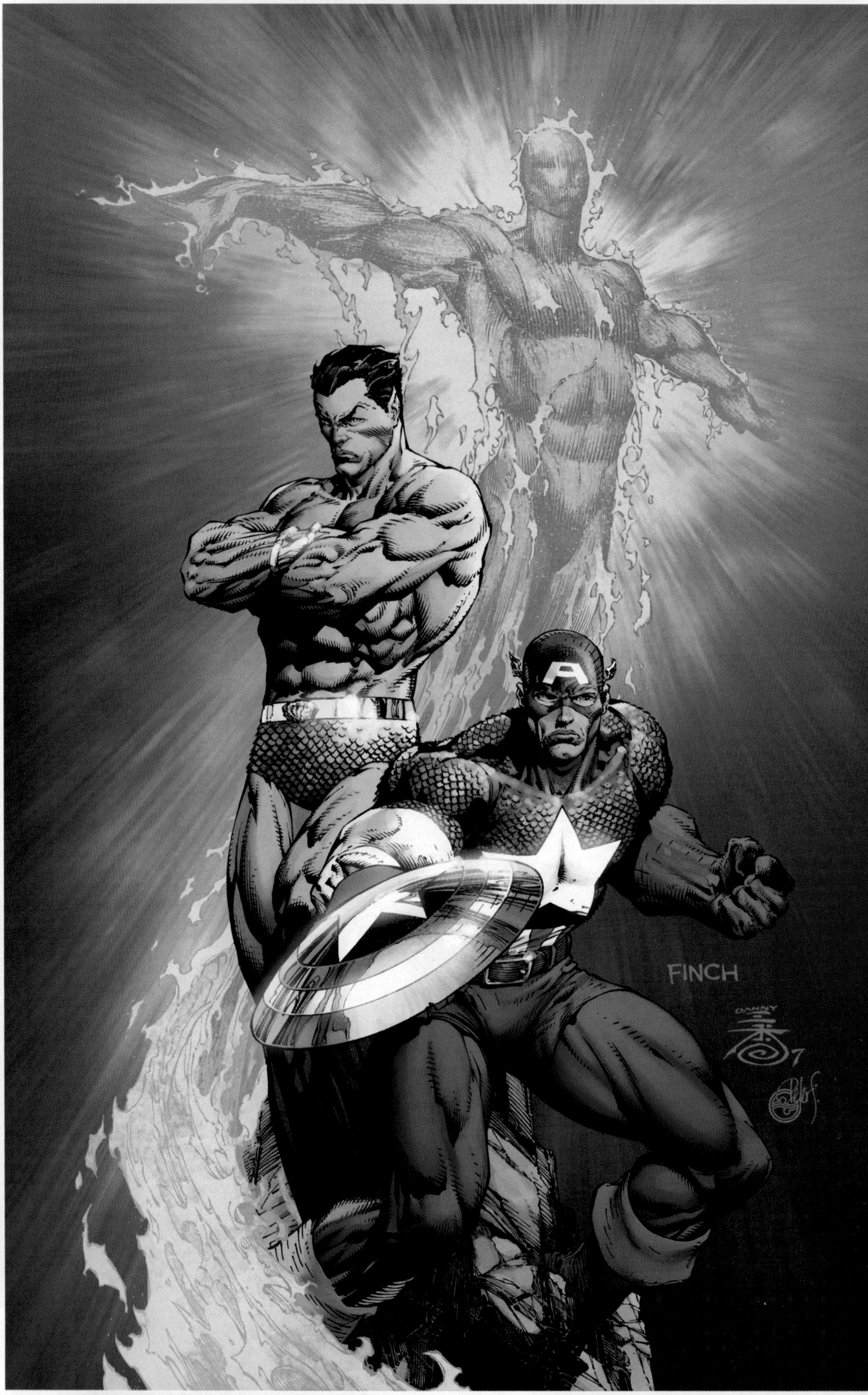
FINCH
DANNY

#1 SKETCH VARIANT
BY DAVID FINCH & DANNY MIKI

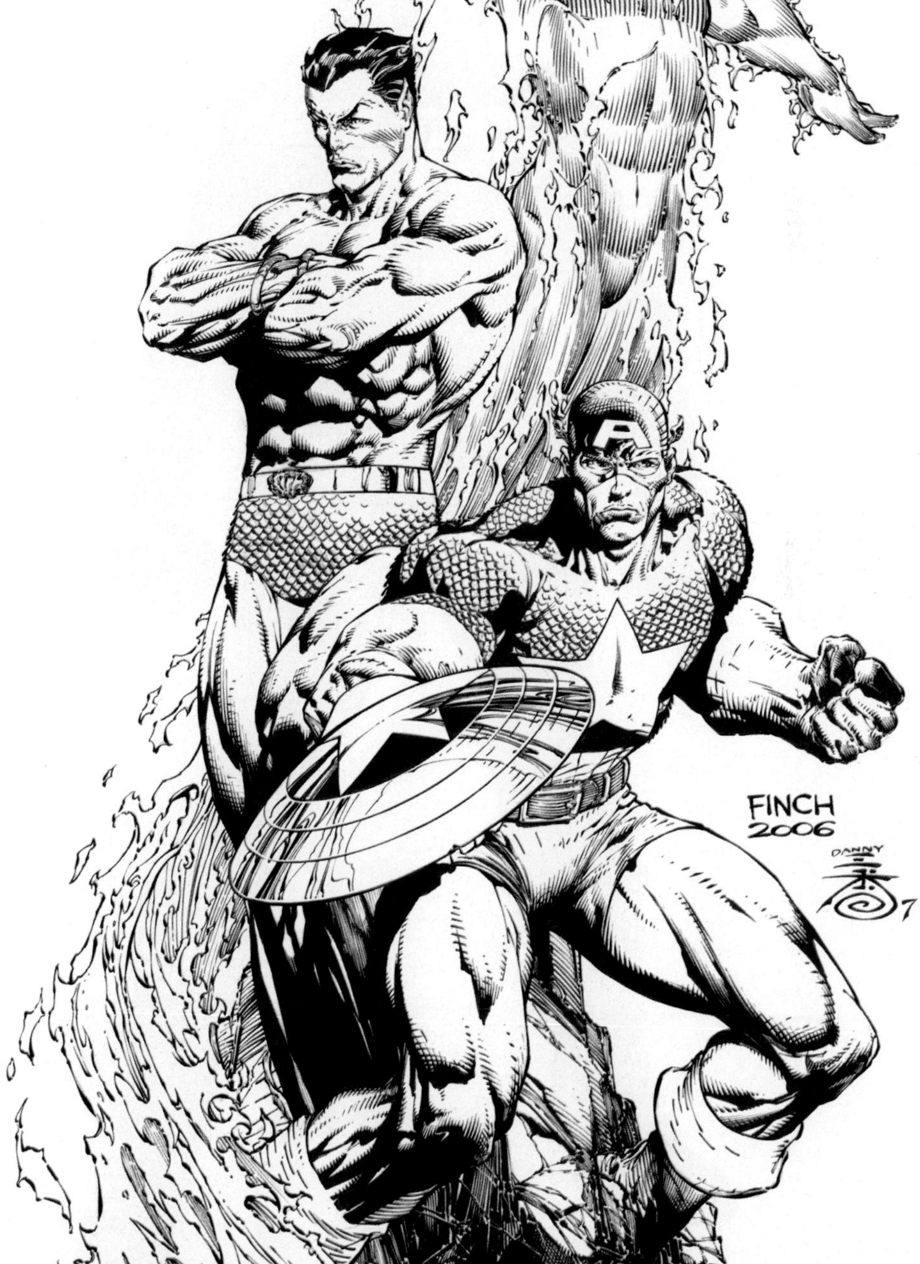
FINCH
2006
DANNY

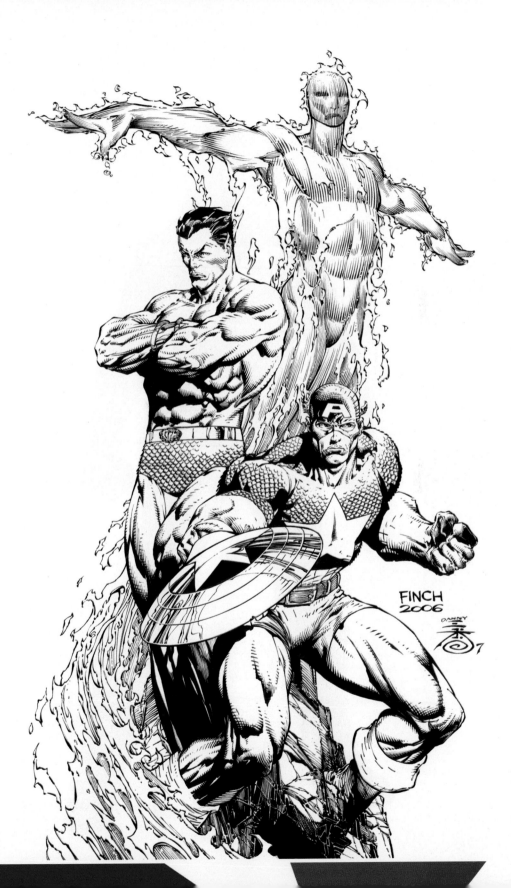

#1 SKETCH VARIANT
BY CARLOS PACHECO & TIM TOWNSEND

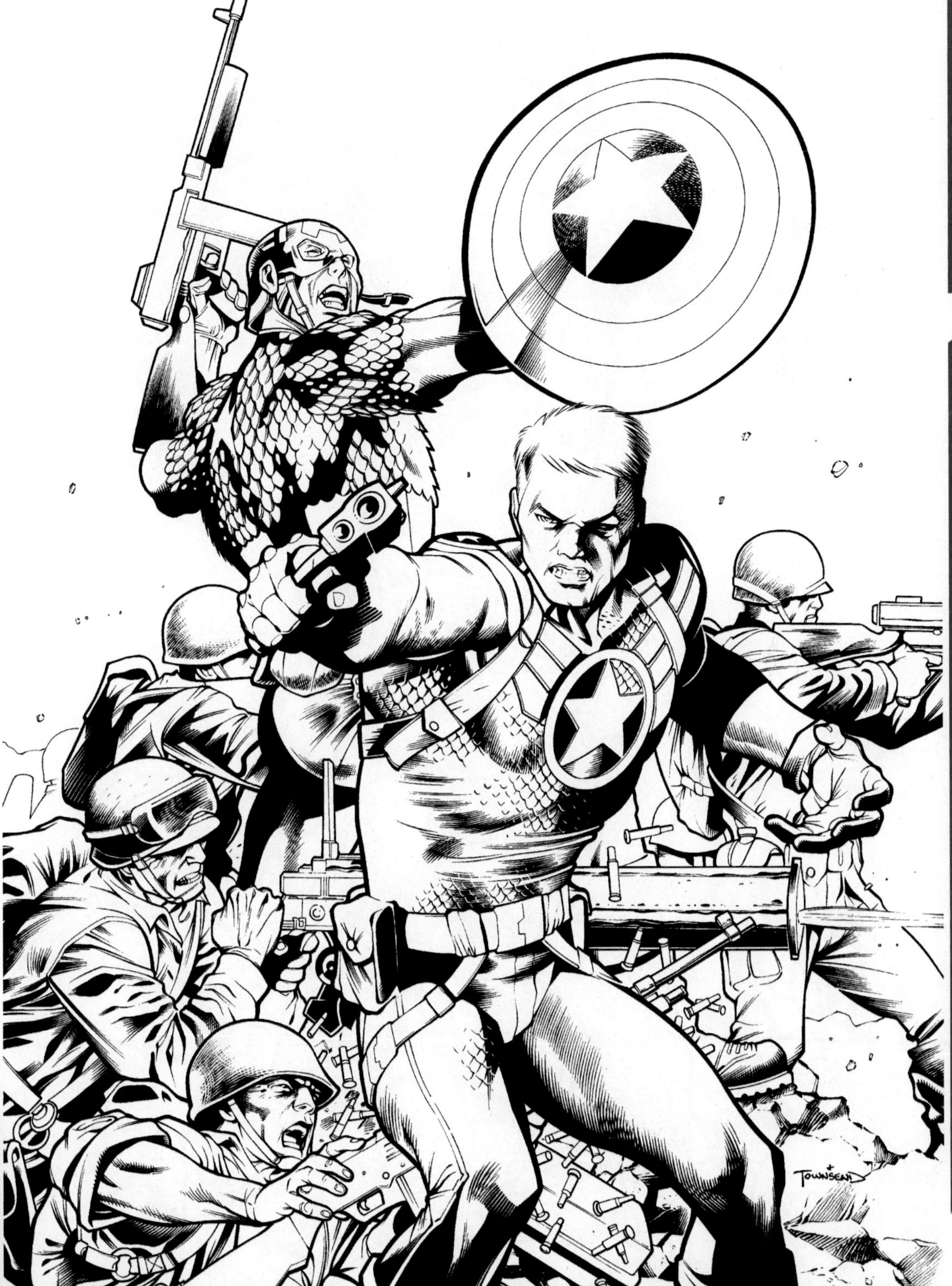
TOWNSEND

#2 2ND PRINTING SKETCH VARIANT

BY CARLOS PACHECO & TIM TOWNSEND

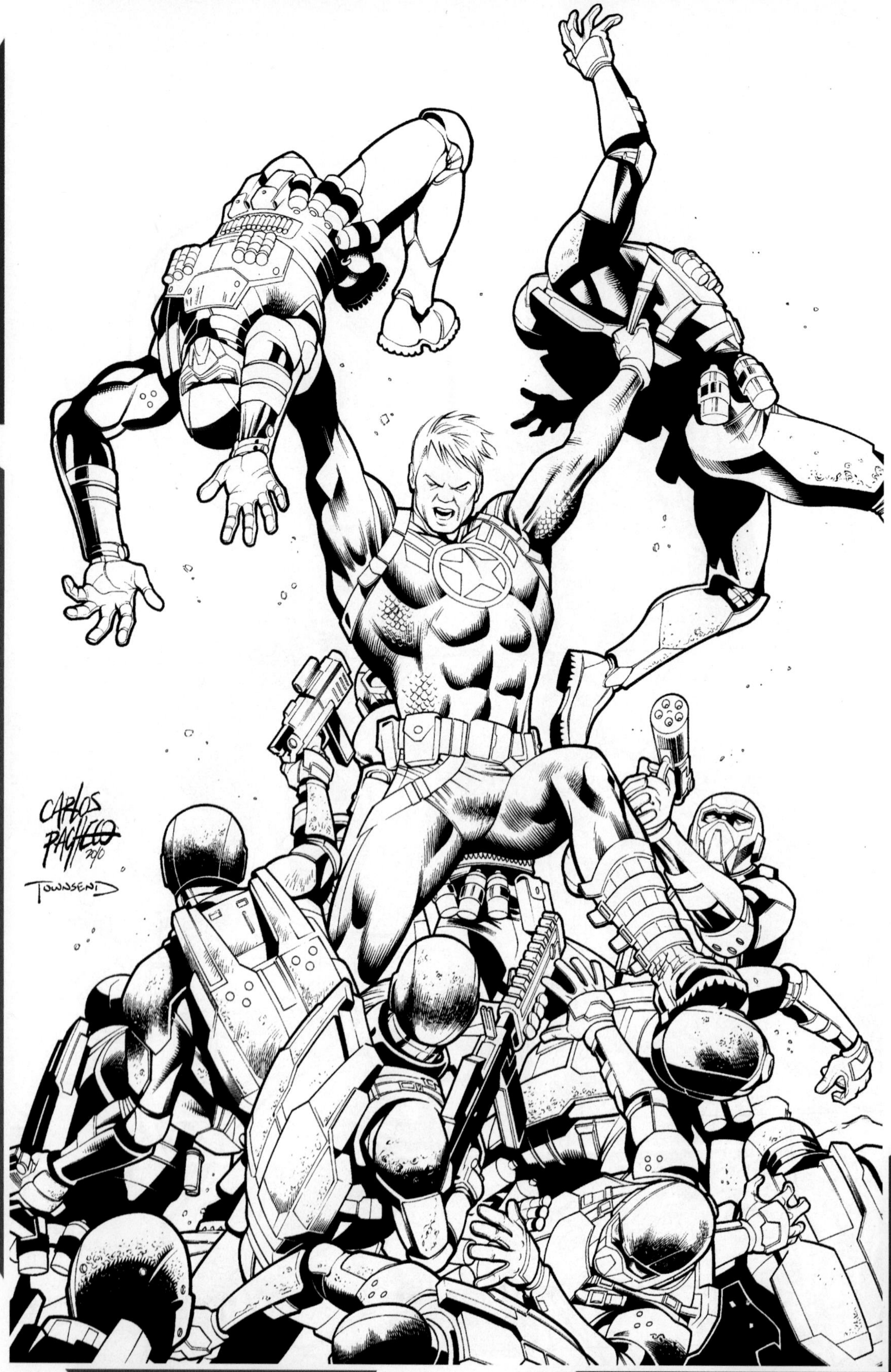
CARLOS PACHECO 2010
TOWNSEND

#3 COVER INKS
BY CARLOS PACHECO & TIM TOWNSEND

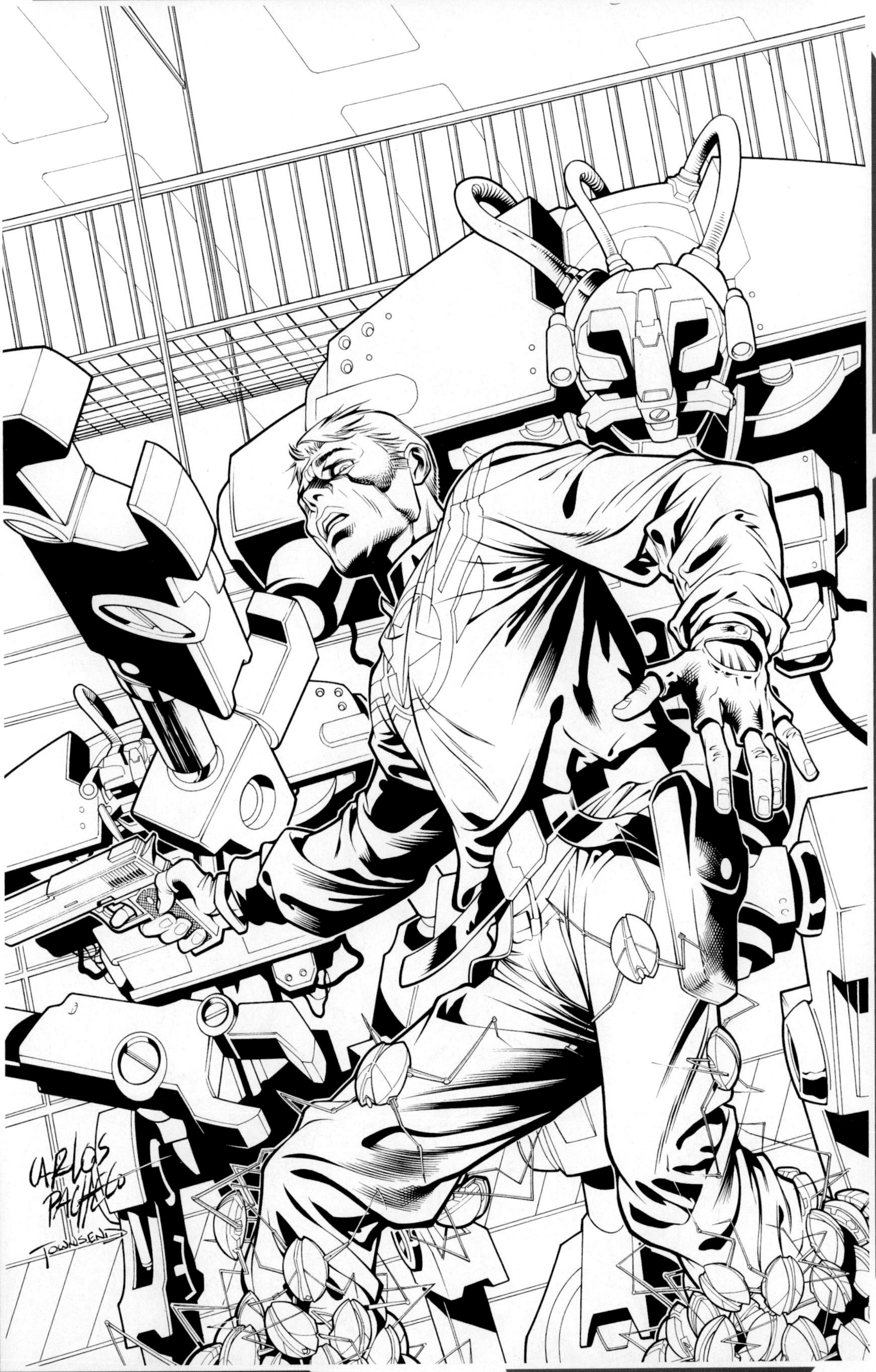

CARLOS PACHECO
TOWNSEND

#4 COVER INKS
BY CARLOS PACHECO & TIM TOWNSEND

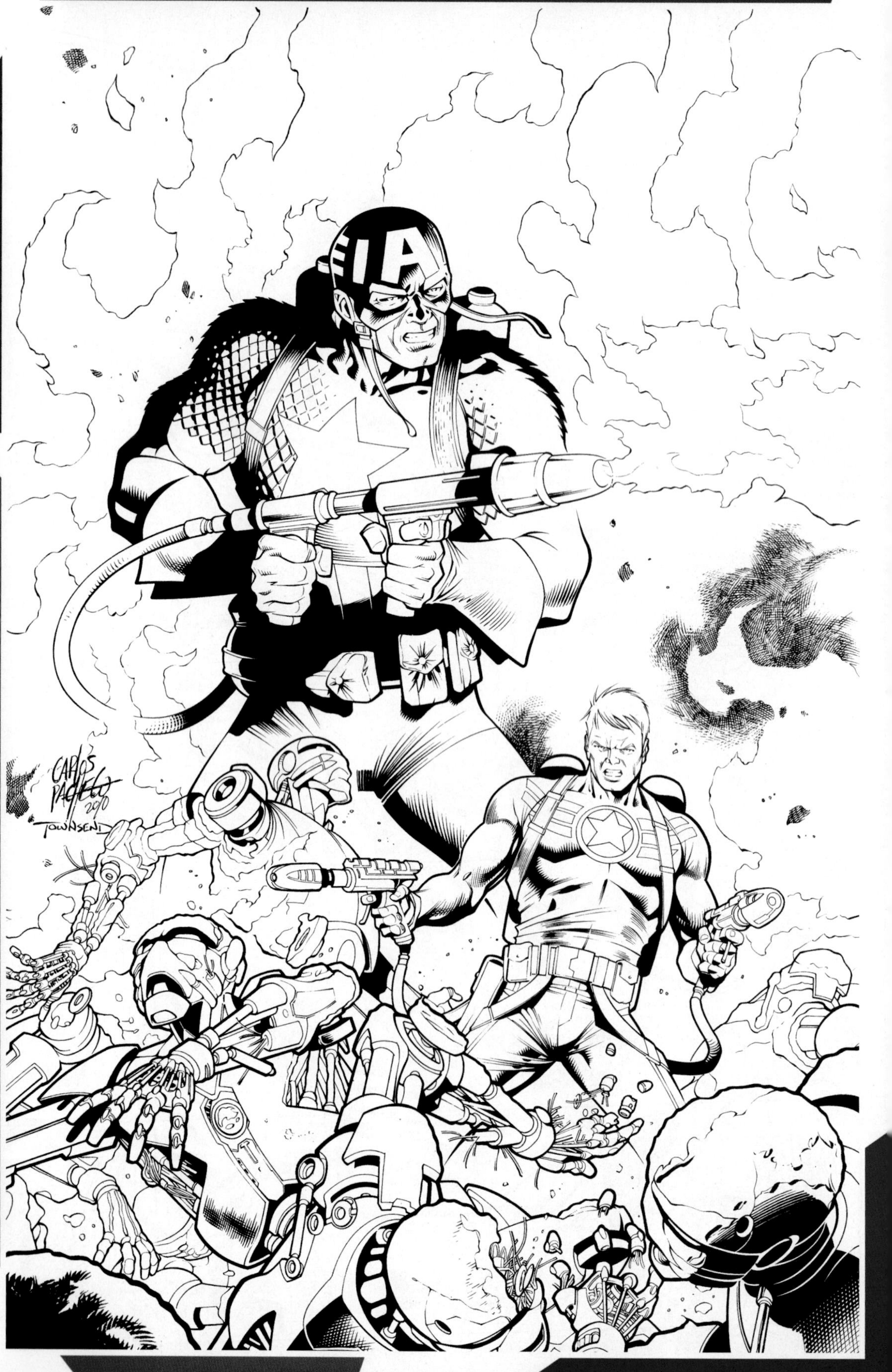

X-MEN/STEVE ROGERS: ESCAPE FROM THE NEGATIVE ZONE TPB COVER ART
BY NICK BRADSHAW & JIM CHARALAMPIDIS

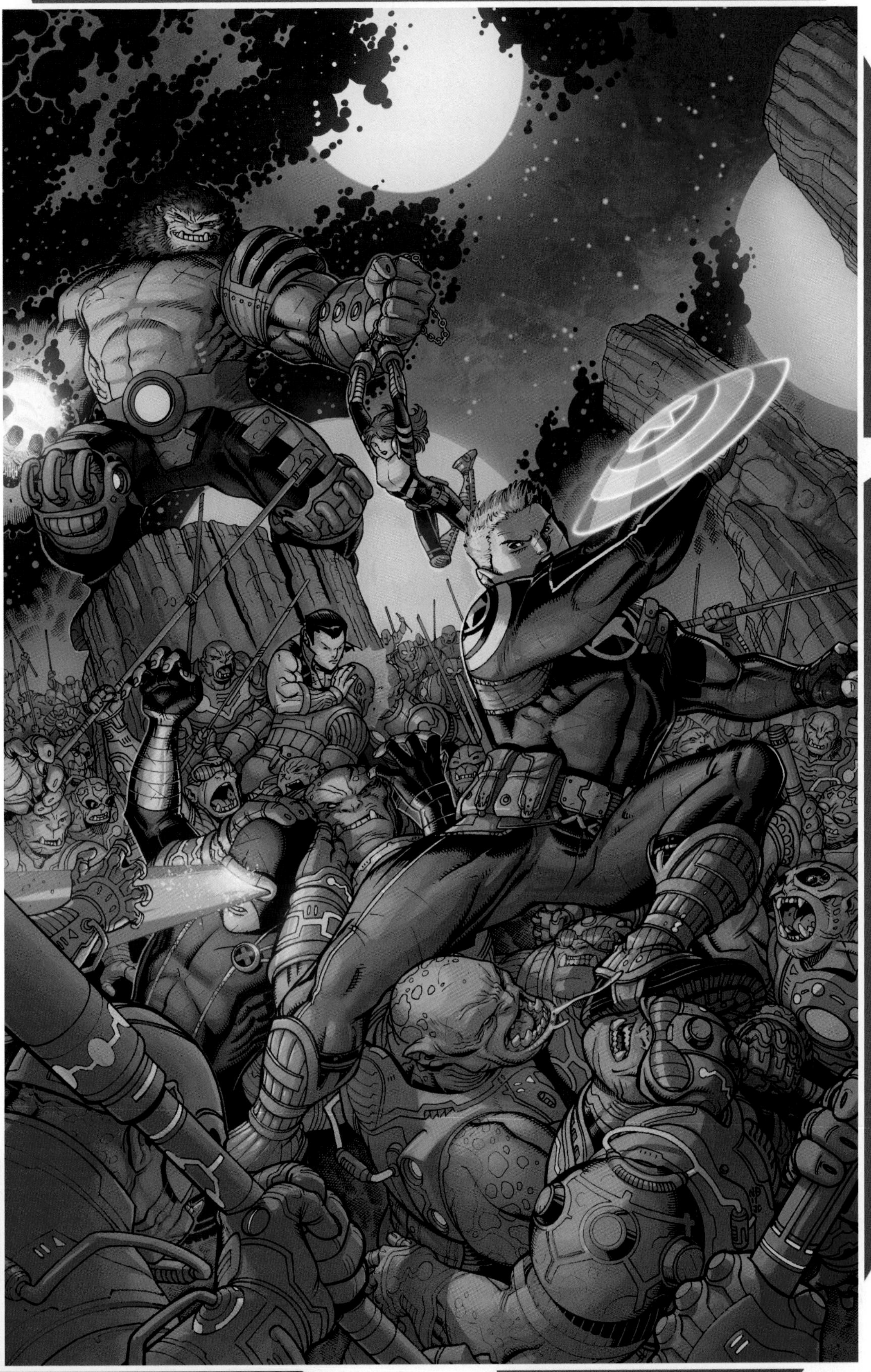

STEVE ROGERS: SUPER-SOLDIER ANNUAL #1 RECAP-PAGE ART
BY IBRAIM ROBERSON & JIM CHARALAMPIDIS

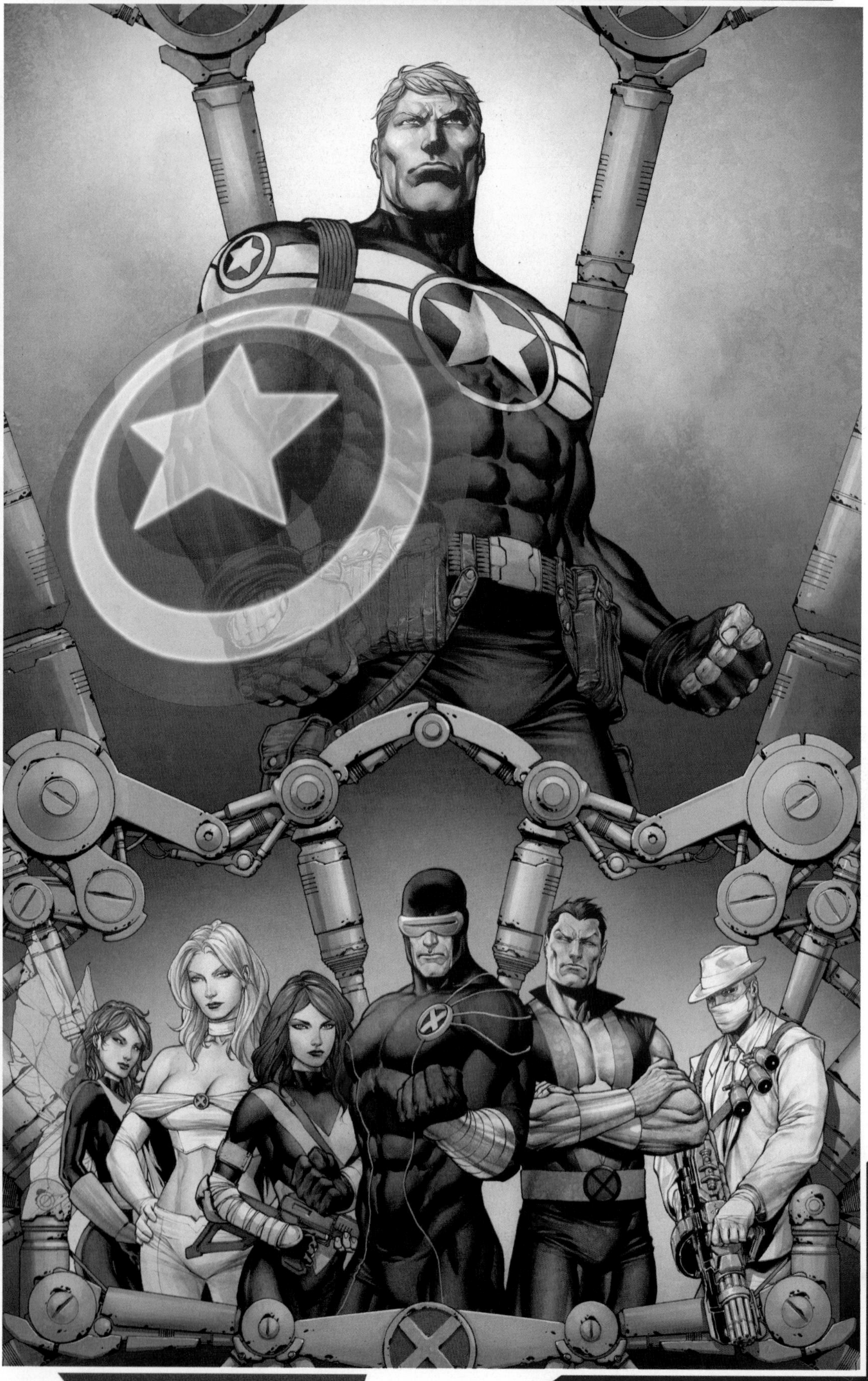

NAMOR: THE FIRST MUTANT ANNUAL #1 RECAP-PAGE ART
BY MAX FIUMARA & JIM CHARALAMPIDIS

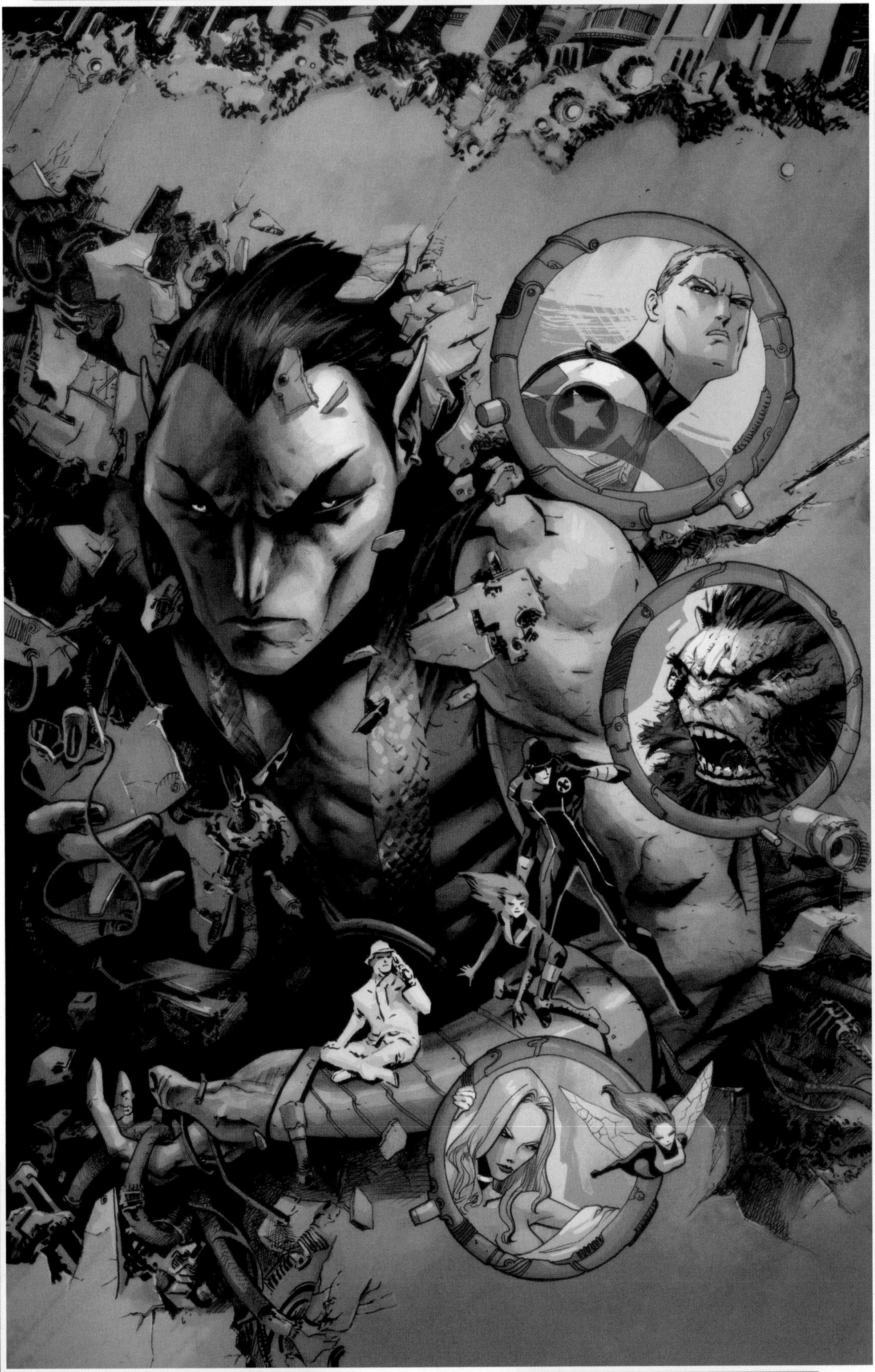

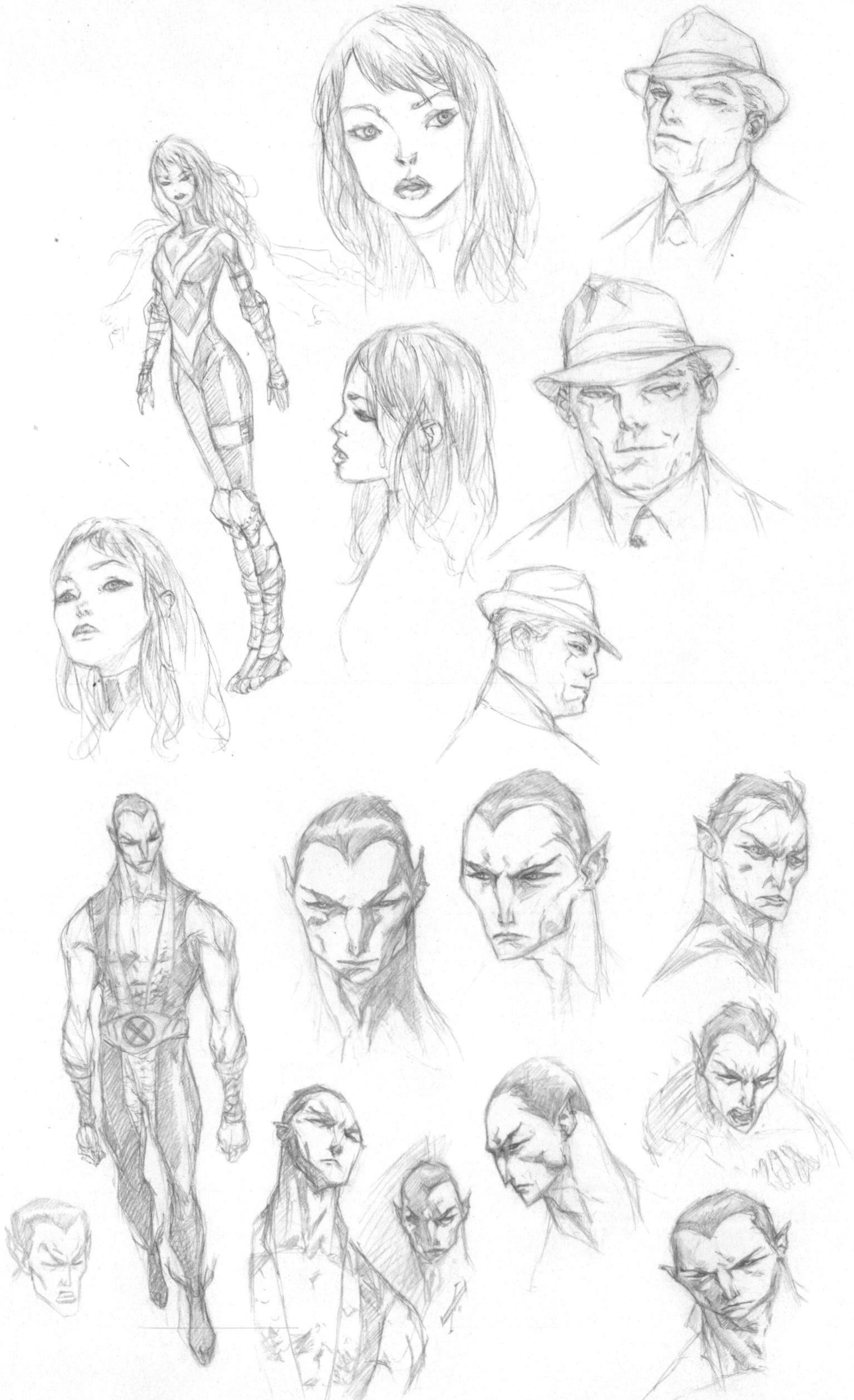

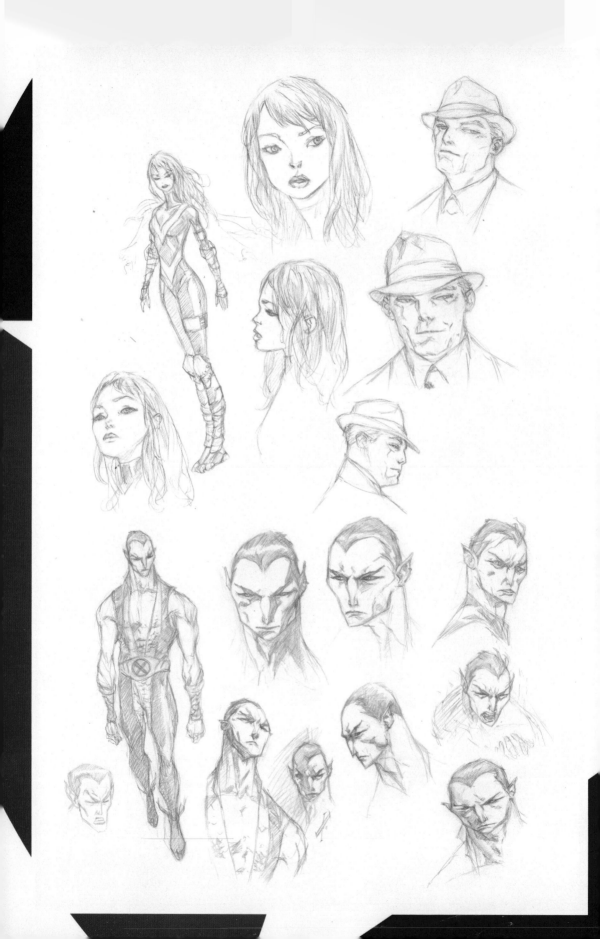